POLITICS AND CULTURAL NATIVISM
IN 1970s TAIWAN

Global Chinese Culture

GLOBAL CHINESE CULTURE
David Der-wei Wang, Editor

Michael Berry, *Speaking in Images: Interviews with Contemporary Chinese Filmmakers*

Sylvia Li-chun Lin, *Representing Atrocity in Taiwan: The 2/28 Incident and White Terror in Fiction and Film*

Michael Berry, *A History of Pain: Literary and Cinematic Mappings of Violence in Modern China*

Alexa Huang, *Chinese Shakespeares: A Century of Cultural Exchange*

Shu-mei Shih, Chien-hsin Tsai, and Brian Bernards, editors, *Sinophone Studies: A Critical Reader*

Andrea Bachner, *Beyond Sinology: Chinese Writing and the Scripts of Culture*

Jie Li, *Shanghai Homes: Palimpsests of Private Life*

Michel Hockx, *Internet Literature in China*

Lily Wong, *Transpacific Attachments: Sex Work, Media Networks, and Affective Histories of Chineseness*

Sebastian Veg, *Minjian: The Rise of China's Grassroots Intellectuals*

Shengqing Wu, *Photo Poetics: Chinese Lyricism and Modern Media*

Calvin Hui, *The Art of Useless: Fashion, Media, and Consumer Culture in Contemporary China*

Politics and Cultural Nativism in 1970s Taiwan

YOUTH, NARRATIVE, NATIONALISM

A-chin Hsiau

Columbia University Press
New York

Columbia University Press
Publishers Since 1893
New York   Chichester, West Sussex
cup.columbia.edu
Copyright © 2021 Columbia University Press
All rights reserved

Columbia University Press wishes to express its appreciation for assistance given
by the Chiang Ching-kuo Foundation for International Scholarly Exchange
and the Council for Cultural Affairs in the publication of this series.

Library of Congress Cataloging-in-Publication Data
Names: Hsiau, A-chin, author.
Title: Politics and cultural nativism in 1970s Taiwan : youth, narrative, nationalism / A-chin Hsiau.
Description: New York : Columbia University Press, [2021] | Series: Global
Chinese culture | Includes bibliographical references and index.
Identifiers: LCCN 2021011492 (print) | LCCN 2021011493 (ebook) |
ISBN 9780231200523 (hardback) | ISBN 9780231200530 (trade paperback) |
ISBN 9780231553667 (ebook)
Subjects: LCSH: Nationalism—Taiwan. | Taiwan—Politics and government—1945– |
Taiwan—Intellectual life—20th century. | Youth—Political activity—Taiwan. |
Chinese literature—Taiwan—History and criticism. | Nationalism in literature.
Classification: LCC DS799.847 .H563 2021 (print) | LCC DS799.847 (ebook) |
DDC 320.545124909/047—dc23
LC record available at https://lccn.loc.gov/2021011492
LC ebook record available at https://lccn.loc.gov/2021011493

Columbia University Press books are printed on permanent and durable acid-free paper.
Printed in the United States of America

Cover image: Opposition leader Huang Xinjie giving a stump speech for Huang Ma
running for Yunlin County magistrate in November 1977. © Chiu Wan-hsing (邱萬興).
Used with permission.

Cover design: Chang Jae Lee

Contents

Acknowledgments   vii
Preface   ix
Notes on Romanization and Translation   xiii

Introduction: Get Real   1

I   Generation and National Narration   13

II   Education, Exile, and Existentialism in the 1960s   26

III   The Rise of the Return-to-Reality Generation
in the Early 1970s   46

IV   The Rediscovery of Taiwan New Literature   61

V   The Reception of Nativist Literature   90

VI   Dangwai Historiography   121

Conclusion: The Renarration of Identity   166

Glossary   175
Notes   189
Bibliography   243
Index   279

Acknowledgments

This book is the result of many years' reading, reflection, and writing. Many individuals contributed in one way or another to its completion. My first debt of thanks is to Professor Darryl Sterk (Shi Dailun), who has helped me by translating and editing. Without his help, I would have had a much more difficult time completing this book. Also, without Chen Lihou (Tulip), my best friend in my university years, I probably would not have started my friendship with Darryl. Lihou will never read this book, but she is remembered with affection.

Professor David Der-wei Wang at Harvard suggested that I share my research on 1970s Taiwan with English readers in book form on his visit to the Academia Sinica long ago. I doubt it would have been possible to embark on the project without his encouragement. I am deeply grateful to him. Professor Richard Madsen has always supported me since I became his student at University of California, San Diego, as far back as 1992. It has been my good fortune to have him as an advisor and part of my academic career. I feel profound gratitude to him.

At the early stage of writing the book, a period of research at the International Consortium for Research in the Humanities (IKGF), University Erlangen-Nuremberg, in 2013 was instrumental in allowing me to reorganize part of the manuscript. I am grateful to Professor Thomas Fröhlich for his friendship and kind invitation to visit the IKGF.

The resources, support, and culture of the Institute of Sociology, Academia Sinica, where I have been affiliated, allowed me to pursue book writing more aggressively. I want to thank my research assistants, Chang Jinwen, Yeh Chunchiao, and Lee Chiahsuan, who also helped in the completion of this book.

My earlier projects on 1970s Taiwan were funded by Taiwan's National Science Council, the former incarnation of the Ministry of Science and Technology (NSC-89-2412-H-001-023, NSC-90-2412-H-001-012, NSC-91-2412-H-001-005, NSC-92-2412-H-001-001, and NSC-96-2412-H-001-015-MY2). This book is based on my Chinese-language book, which carried the English title *Return to Reality: Political and Cultural Change in 1970s Taiwan and the Postwar Generation*, 2nd ed. (Taipei: Institute of Sociology, Academia Sinica, 2010). Part of chapters 2, 3, and 6 of this book were published, respectively, in *The Sixties: A Journal of History, Politics and Culture* 3, no. 1; *Oriens Extremus*, no. 52; and *Studies in Ethnicity and Nationalism* 18, no. 2. I would like to thank the two anonymous reviewers and my editor at Columbia University Press, Christine Dunbar, for their constructive comments and suggestions, which helped me improve the manuscript.

My mother, Li Yen, has always been a model for me of hard work and self-reliance. My wife, Yang Jinshi, has helped me make my dreams come true for most of my life. I owe more to her than I can say, for her quiet strength, congenial company, and enduring love through the vicissitudes of life. Our son, Yunchung, has brought us the sweetest joy of life by being so wonderful. This book is dedicated to my family and is also in memory of my father, Hsiao Yuyi. The longer he is gone, the more I understand a life of suffering and loneliness.

It is said that life is like a candle, and all it needs is a spark to show its blaze of light. I feel blessed that I have met many encouraging and supportive individuals who have sparked my creative passion.

Preface

Writing this book has been a long journey, which started in the 1980s. As a Taiwanese sociologist, I have long viewed myself as a "child of the 1980s" in spirit. It was a decade of radical pursuit of "Taiwan subjectivity" (*Taiwan zhutixing*) based on beliefs in liberty, equality, democracy, and human rights that shaped me during my formative years and drew me into sociology, a discipline dedicated to grasping "history and biography and the relations between the two within society," as C. Wright Mills puts it in *The Sociological Imagination*.[1]

I started my PhD degree in San Diego in the early 1990s, the crest of the "third wave" of democratization, according to Samuel P. Huntington's periodization. Taiwan rode, and continues to ride, this wave. Locally and globally, public opinion and academic research were thick with the discourses of democratization, civil society, and public sphere, along with related issues of ethnicity, nationalism, historical narrative, collective memory, and identity. In dealing with these issues, I reflected on my own political positioning and cultural belonging.

My first book, which was based on my dissertation, was the product of that reflection. *Contemporary Taiwanese Cultural Nationalism* examines how Taiwanese nationalism swept through intellectual and cultural circles in the 1980s and 1990s, the two crucial decades of "indigenization" or "Taiwanization" of politics and culture in the country. It embodies my attempt to make sense of what I had experienced growing up, to grasp the history of Taiwan and my personal biography and the relations between the two. In my mind, I completed the quest: there's a place for me in the collective life story of one of the world's most recent cases of natio-genesis.

When I was putting the finishing touches on the manuscript, I became intrigued by the connection between the politico-cultural change in the 1970s and the rise of Taiwanese consciousness and nationalism in the 1980s and beyond. I became convinced that the 1970s was a pivotal decade in postwar Taiwan. Much research literature, like the abundant studies of *xiangtu wenxue* (Nativist literature) of the 1970s, had indicated the importance of this decade. But whereas this research literature focused on *shengji wenti*—the issue of province of origin (local Taiwanese vs. Mainlanders), I intuited that the Nativist literature was part of a larger generational transition. My intuition has developed into the book you hold in your hands.

This book is another attempt to understand my personal life in historical context. In it I understand myself by comparing myself with the young intellectuals of the return-to-reality generation in 1970s Taiwan. Many members of this generation became Taiwanese nationalists in the 1980s. In documenting that they had been ardent Chinese nationalists just a few years earlier, I may appear to be digging up dirt, muckraking. That is not my intention. Who am I to decide who was right, who am I to pass judgment? I reject an "instrumentalist" explanation of identity change, according to which Taiwanese nationalists were opportunists. I think they were genuinely Chinese nationalists in the 1970s and that they had a sincere change of heart in the 1980s for which their return to reality had prepared them. They were characters in quite a different historical narrative than the one I wrote myself into. They cast themselves in different roles in a different drama, but the casting made sense at the time. As a Welsh proverb says, "The best candle is understanding." I have tried to understand the choices they made in the light of history.

In his *The Old Regime and the French Revolution*, Alexis de Tocqueville wrote:

> I hope and believe that I have written the present book without any *parti pris*, though it would be futile to deny that my own feelings were engaged. What Frenchman can write his country and think about the age in which he lives in a spirit of complete detachment? Thus I confess that when studying our old social system under its infinitely various aspects I have never quite lost sight of present-day France. . . .

My aim has been to supply a picture that while scientifically accurate, may also be instructive. . . . With this in mind I have not shrunk from wounding the feelings of individuals and classes in present-day France, or of affronting certain opinions and ancient loyalties, laudable though these may be. In so doing I have often felt regret but never any qualms of conscience, and I can only hope that those who may be inclined to take offense at anything in this book will realize that its author has aimed at complete honesty and impartiality.[2]

I kept thinking of Tocqueville's confession as I wrote this book. I've tried to follow in his footsteps, to write impartially, without regard for my feelings or anyone else's. But while Tocqueville painted a realistic "picture," I have tried to tell a true "story." This story is my reply to the oracle at Delphi's imperative. We have to know ourselves as historical beings, by casting ourselves in larger stories. No story, no identity; without narrative identity, life is bare. Every society needs to keep telling stories about itself.

In his 2007 study of the public religious revival or renewal of Buddhism and Daoism in Taiwan since the lifting of martial law in 1987 as a contribution to Taiwanese democracy, Richard Madsen observes:

Everyone should be concerned about the fate of Taiwan. Although it is a small island with only 23 million inhabitants, it is worth close attention because it sits on top of a highly unstable political, social, and cultural Asian fault zone. The rise of Asia as the world's most dynamic center of wealth, power, and cultural creativity is perhaps the single greatest challenge for a global order that has for centuries been dominated by Europe and now the United States. A breakdown along some of the fault lines centered on Taiwan could, in the worst-case scenario, become the epicenter for a catastrophe of global proportions.[3]

Human history is contingency. With the rise of a self-assertive China, the future of the island country of Taiwan is, it goes without saying, hard to predict. I would like to end this book in sight of a safe anchorage, but I find myself in stormy seas.

Notes on Romanization and Translation

This book uses the Hanyu Pinyin system to transcribe Mandarin Chinese words. Chinese personal names are transcribed following their conventional order in the original language, with family names before given names (e.g., Jiang Weishui, Ye Shitao). When there is an alternative conventional spelling of a proper name (e.g., Chiang Kai-shek, Taipei, Kaohsiung) I follow the convention. All translations of Chinese sources are mine unless otherwise indicated.

POLITICS AND CULTURAL NATIVISM
IN 1970s TAIWAN

Introduction

Get Real

There have been two major divergences in the history of modern China since the republican revolution in 1911. The first was between the People's Republic of China (PRC) on "mainland China" and the Republic of China (ROC) on Taiwan in 1949. The second was between communist China and democratic Taiwan in the 1990s. This book is an archaeology of the process that led to the second divergence, the democratization of Taiwan. By documenting how a generation of young people turned toward, or as they put it, returned to, the sociopolitical reality of Taiwan in the early 1970s, I will show how they sowed the seeds for a turn away from the Chinese narrative of national humiliation they had been raised on, the very same narrative that has won the hearts and minds of hundreds of millions of young people in the PRC today. Instead of a strong China, they have chosen a democratic Taiwan.

This book is about a generational reorientation in national identity in Taiwan in the 1970s as a result of diplomatic setbacks at the beginning of the decade. The younger generation responded to these setbacks by "getting active." But whereas in a liberal democracy, youth activism can be overtly political, Taiwan was under martial law at the time. At the time, youth activism could not even be overtly Taiwanese, because Taiwan was officially Chinese. Youth activists in Taiwan in the 1970s could not challenge the state directly. But they could do so indirectly; they could be indirectly political. This book will show how young activists poured their

[1]

political passions into historical research and literary creation, and how their creative activities and research results bore unexpected political fruits. It was in the politico-cultural field that national identity was reoriented.

The diplomatic setbacks Taiwan experienced at the beginning of the 1970s have to be understood geopolitically. For the PRC, the 1960s were tumultuous, what with the Sino-Soviet split and the Great Proletarian Cultural Revolution. The 1970s began with the admission of the PRC to the United Nations (UN) in 1971, Richard Nixon's visit to the PRC to normalize the diplomatic relations between the two countries in 1972, and Japan's recognition of the PRC as the sole legal government of China, also in 1972, all of which heralded a new era of rapprochement in world politics. Not everyone benefited, however. The adverse effects of the changed relationship between the two global heavyweights, the United States and the PRC, were felt most keenly in Taiwan, officially the Republic of China. Styling itself "Free China," the authoritarian Chinese Nationalist Party (KMT) regime had ruled in "exile" from the Chinese mainland since 1949 and served as China's international representative for two decades, by virtue of American support. But American support had been wavering or was perceived to be unreliable: the United States had sided with the Japanese in the dispute between Japan and the ROC over the Diaoyutai Islands (called the Senkaku Islands in Japan) in the East China Sea (1969–1972). For several months before the ROC's ouster from the UN there had been a sense of national crisis, particularly among young people. Youth activism had been ignited by the loss of the Diaoyutais. Exile from the UN fanned the flames.

Zooming in from a geopolitical overview to focus on youth activism in Taiwan in the 1970s, it makes sense to interpret the activism in terms of "provincial origin" (*shengji*), in that Taiwan society at the time was divided between Mainlanders (*waishengren*), who had come from China in the late 1940s, and local Taiwanese (*benshengren*), who had lived through Japanese rule (1895–1945). It is tempting to describe activist youths as being inspired by a sense of Taiwanese national identity that they would not be able to publicly voice until a decade later in the 1980s. Indeed, many of the activists I study in this book were local Taiwanese, and I would not deny the importance of their Taiwanese origin to them. But not all activists were Taiwanese; many were Mainlanders, and Taiwanese and Mainlanders alike were motivated by a common sense of Chinese national identity, which they shared with older Mainlanders and which they had absorbed in school. Any notion of a closet Taiwanese national identity is anachronistic in Taiwan for the 1970s. More important than provincial origin to the people involved was generational identity. The people I will be studying in this monograph had grown up too late to remember life under the Japanese or in China. All they knew was democracy and the story of China's humiliation that they had been exposed to in school. Democracy and Chinese nationalism formed them as a generation, as they never tired of saying at the time. They kept talkin' 'bout their generation, to adapt a lyric from a song by The Who. We should, too. What young people knew as a generation was that their parents were wrong to idealize the "good old days" or to view Taiwan as a place of exile. To young people, Taiwan was the only home they had ever known, and the reality to which they should "return." This reorientation toward Taiwan set them apart from, or against, their parents.

The specific thesis I argue for can be summed up as follows: the "Taiwan turn" taken by the "return-to-reality generation" (*huigui xianshi shidai*) is the single most important reorientation in postwar Taiwan, because it formed the matrix of the cultural politics of Taiwanese nationalism and democratization in the following decades.

In arguing this thesis, I hope to make a contribution to Taiwanese political and cultural history. The history of nationalism and national identity in Taiwan since 1980 is extremely well-studied,[1] particularly in terms of political and cultural "indigenization" (*bentuhua*) or "Taiwanization" (*Taiwanhua*), which are generally viewed as beginning in the 1980s and gathering momentum especially after the Democratic Progressive Party (DPP) took power in 2000. Indigenization, one of the main thrusts of which is Taiwanese nationalism, can be traced to the debates on "Taiwanese consciousness" (*Taiwan yishi*) in the early 1980s. What I hope to do is push indigenization and in a sense Taiwanization (though not Taiwanese nationalism) back a decade, to the beginning of the understudied 1970s, to the years following the Defend the Diaoyutais movement (*Baowei diaoyutai yundong*, hereafter *Baodiao*) in the spring of 1971. Mark Harrison's book *Legitimacy, Meaning, and Knowledge in the Making of Taiwanese Identity* dwells on the Baodiao movement and the rise of a new generation of university students and young intellectuals who spoke a particular language of Chinese nationalism.[2] The ensuing youth politico-cultural activism that was crucial to the later development of Taiwanese nationalism and democratization, however, was left unaddressed in his book.

It is in my stress on the youth activism in 1970s as a *generational* phenomenon that involved a reorientation within a national *narrative* that I hope to generalize my thesis beyond Taiwan studies, to make the argument relevant to sociologists, historians, political scientists, and scholars in East Asian studies. Basically, the KMT had viewed Taiwan not as a home but as a temporary base to launch a counterattack against the communists. When that counterattack was successful, the KMT would make China strong again, and China would rise from the ashes of the national shame it had suffered ever since the setbacks of the 1840s, when the Qing dynasty lost the first Opium War. Members of the return-to-reality generation had been told this national narrative over and over again, but there was nothing stopping them from retelling it in their own way, or from casting themselves in new roles within the narrative. The return-to-reality generation did just that. Inspired by the ideals of democracy and personal freedom they had been exposed to in school, they cast themselves as freedom-loving researchers, writers, and in some cases politicians. In doing so, they became a slightly belated current in global youth activism, a current within Chinese nationalism that would swell within a generation into Taiwanese democratization.

Overview

Taiwan was loosely incorporated into the Qing Empire in the late seventeenth century. It was ceded to Japan in 1895. In 1945 General Douglas MacArthur ordered Japanese forces in China and Taiwan to surrender to Generalissimo Chiang Kaishek. The KMT-ROC party-state took over Taiwan and declared it a province of the ROC. Just four years later, in 1949, the KMT government lost the civil war against the communists and retreated or relocated to Taiwan. The island of Taiwan, with a population of about six million inhabitants at that time, composed mostly of local Taiwanese of Han Chinese origin (including Hoklo and Hakka people) as well as a few hundred thousand indigenous people, accommodated more than one million Mainlander refugees (including soldiers) and entered a long period of rule by an alien elite. Before the transition to democracy in the late 1980s, Taiwan endured the so-called White Terror, a period of severe political repression of dissidents, especially local Taiwanese, during what was to become one of the longest periods of martial law in the world (1949–1987).

It was also a period of official exile, and, for many, particularly intellectuals, personal exile. The displacement of mainland Chinese to Taiwan caused by the loss of the civil war is one of most significant cases of exile in the twentieth century. Social existence in post-1949 Taiwan was shaped by the exilic experience of Mainlanders, because the latter controlled the party-state that dominated Taiwan for more than half a century. KMT rule in Taiwan was characterized by the "Sinicization" (*Zhongguohua*) of the island, whose citizens were inculcated with an "exilic mentality." The kernel of this mentality was an unpleasant sense of what Edward W. Said described as "a median state"; that is, of treating one's abode as temporary while keeping faith in the possibility of returning to one's old home.[3] Exile tends to be unpleasant. But it is also productive. For intellectuals, a state of exile may create the conditions for new experiences, new ideas, and even new modes of expression.[4] By the late 1960s, Mainlanders, especially their children, were ready for new experiences, ideas, and modes of expression. Taiwanese children were, too.

But they had to express themselves carefully because Taiwan was ruled as a single-party authoritarian state under the guise of democracy. Taiwan was Free China, in contrast to "communist China," at the time. The KMT-ROC party-state claimed that it was the legitimate guardian of Sun Yat-sen's political vision of Chinese nation-building, laid out in the Three Principles of the People (*Sanmin zhuyi*).[5] The ROC, founded by Sun in 1912, was apparently in good hands. As a displaced regime, it strictly maintained the structure of the government organized according to the constitution adopted in Nanjing in 1936, asserting that the ROC was the sole legitimate government of all China. Fervently anticommunist in the Cold War, the KMT reiterated its determination to retake the mainland and rebuild a rich and powerful China, a desire that was, of course, never satisfied. In fact, by the late 1950s, an increasing number of Mainlander elites no longer believed in the official line that the ROC would recover the mainland.[6] The KMT itself had hinted it would give up on this military objective in diplomatic communications with the guarantor of its security, the United States.[7] But publicly at least, until the end of the Cold War the KMT endlessly reiterated its pledge: to retake the homeland and defeat the communists. For the KMT government and many Mainlanders, Taiwan served merely as a wartime base for counterattacking the communists.

Culturally, exilic nostalgia dominated the public sphere of the island country in the 1950s and 1960s. The KMT government asserted that it was a resolute defender of "orthodox" Chinese cultural tradition, especially Confucianism. The "Chinese Cultural Renaissance movement" (*Zhonghua wenhua fuxing yundong*), initiated by Chiang Kaishek in 1966, was intended as a positive contrast to the radical, iconoclastic Cultural Revolution in the PRC. The KMT's cultural conservatism had profound effects.[8] Mandarin Chinese became the national language, while local languages, including Hoklo (southern Hokkien), Hakka, and aboriginal languages, were suppressed. Orthodoxy in values, symbols, art, music, theater, handicrafts, and the like was defined according to the KMT's idea of Chinese tradition and officially promoted at the expense of merely regional analogues.[9] The landscapes of the Chinese mainland were eulogized, and Taiwan's landscapes mostly went unmentioned. Mainlanders' memories supposedly became everyone's collective memory, and Taiwanese elders were silenced.[10]

The KMT's political and cultural dominance in postwar Taiwan was ideologically justified by a Sinocentric or "grand China" (*da Zhongguo*) historical outlook embodied in a specific interpretation of the island's historical relationship with the Chinese mainland. From 1945 to the 1970s a Sinocentric and Chinese nationalist construction of the collective memory about the historical relationship between Taiwan and the Chinese mainland dominated the public sphere. This construction comprised a set of discursive elements:

1. The ancestral, historical, and cultural connections between local Taiwanese and Mainlanders;
2. The contribution made to the development and cultivation of the frontier island by imperial China before Taiwan was ceded to Japan in 1895;
3. The nationalist sentiment and attachment to the "ancestral land" (*zuguo*), the Chinese mainland, of Taiwanese compatriots during the Japanese colonial period;
4. The inspiration the nationalist revolution led by the KMT's former incarnation in the early twentieth century gave to Taiwanese anti-Japanese activities;
5. The eight-year Anti-Japanese War (1937–1945) fought by the KMT to liberate Taiwan from colonial rule; and
6. The task the Taiwanese should shoulder in retaking the mainland.

TABLE 0.1

The Chinese Nationalist Template of Historical Narrative

Narrator/protagonist	The Chinese people or nation
Theme	The Chinese nation's struggle for sovereignty, involving resistance to political, economic, and cultural invasion or aggression
Time frame	Opium Wars to the present
Plot	**Beginning:** Inveterately weak traditional China endured "national humiliation" (*guochi*), being bullied by foreign powers, which divided it into spheres of influence from the middle of the nineteenth century.
	Middle: China undergoes a Republican revolution, and the growing pains of nation-building at a time when the government could not yet defend the integrity of national territory.
	End: Resistance to foreign oppression, the pursuit of Chinese political, economic, and cultural independence and autonomy in order to make China rich and powerful.

These elements were embedded in a larger nationalist narrative of national suffering and humiliation at the hands of foreigners since the mid-nineteenth century (see table 0.1).[11]

The KMT government promoted Chinese consciousness by encouraging every citizen to "search for roots" (*xungen*). Those roots were supposed to be places in mainland China, not in Taiwan, even for local Taiwanese. This book investigates the emergence of "de-exilic" cultural politics in 1970s Taiwan with the rise of the postwar generation as a countercultural force. It follows the fallout of the call for "a return to reality" (*huigui xianshi*) and "a return to native soil" (*huigui xiangtu*), issued as loudly by Mainlanders as by local Taiwanese. It was a call for attention to the local, and a challenge to the official account of Taiwan's raison-d'être.

It was not until the 1970s that the authoritarian rule of the KMT met significant challenges and major politico-cultural change occurred. The change was widely remarked on at the time and broadly based. Its influence is still felt in contemporary Taiwanese society. This decade can therefore be regarded as the "Axial Age" in the formation of a general sense of identification with Taiwan,[12] which developed into "Taiwanese consciousness" and Taiwanese nationalism in the 1980s. It was not just an axial age because of geopolitical shifts and diplomatic setbacks. Rather, these setbacks came at a particularly delicate time: it was a time of social problems caused by rapid economic growth, such as mass, uncontrolled urbanization, the decline of rural areas, income and wealth disparity, and labor disputes. Facing such problems along with diplomatic setbacks, the KMT government had to develop a new policy: "reforming to preserve Taiwan" (gexin baoTai). The reform partly involved co-optation, recruiting more local Taiwanese elites into the higher echelons of the party and the government. But the government also tried to persuade local elites that it was best able to guide Taiwan's modernization, especially because it was prepared to be flexible. At the time, President Chiang Kaishek was preparing to hand power over to his son Chiang Chingkuo. Authoritarianism, it seemed, was softening, in response to sociopolitical change.

Part of that change was the awakening of the postwar generation. By "awakening" I mean what Molly Andrews describes as a process of "conscientization."[13] By becoming conscious and critical of the failures of their fathers, university students and young intellectuals denounced the KMT-sanctioned "exilic mentality." Their reorientation toward the changing domestic and international political reality and the culture of the "native soil" (xiangtu) was the other side of the same coin. The sociopolitical consequences of their awakening have been so significant that the return-to-reality generation deserves to be termed the "Axial Generation" of postwar Taiwan.

The awakening of the axial generation of postwar Taiwan was also a postcolonial reckoning. Like many postcolonial societies, postwar Taiwan had to deal with the legacy of colonialism. But it was a particularly thorny legacy in Taiwan. On the one hand, for the KMT government and many Mainlanders, Japan was the enemy. It had invaded the mainland and conquered large parts of it. Any sympathy for Japan was a virus that had to be destroyed, so that the local Taiwanese could be cured. Local Taiwanese, it was claimed, had been rendered servile (nuhua) during Japanese colonialism. To emancipate them, or cure them, the KMT prescribed Chinese nationalism. The KMT reminded local Taiwanese, for instance, of their own guerrilla attacks against the Japanese *before* 1920, which were supposed to illustrate their unflagging "ancestral-land consciousness" (*zuguo yishi*).

By contrast, the history of the nonviolent resistance *after* 1920, which took either a liberal, Wilsonian form—the "home rule" movement—or later a leftist form, was overshadowed. The complicated history of Japanese colonial rule was narrated into a simple drama of Japanese oppression and resistance by the "Taiwanese compatriots" (*Taiwan tongbao*), who were members of the great Chinese national family.[14] Any open discussion of the Japanese colonial rule outside these parameters was taboo. Any discussion of the "February 28 Incident" (*Ererba shijian*)—an islandwide revolt in 1947 against the Taiwan Provincial Administration (Taiwansheng xing-zheng zhangguan gongshu) under Chen Yi—and the political purges during the White Terror remained taboo all through the 1970s.

But, if they trod carefully, young activists could revisit the resistance of liberals and leftists in the 1920s. They could rediscover colonial literature about the "native soil." And they could write about the native soil in the 1970s. The members of these three groups within the return-to-reality generation are the heroes of the story I am going to tell: (1) cultural activists who rediscovered the "Taiwan New Literature" (*Taiwan xinwenxue*)—modern literature written by Taiwanese authors in the Japanese colonial era, (2) writers and advocates of a socially conscious "Nativist literature" (*xiangtu wenxue*), and (3) political dissidents who studied the Taiwanese anti-colonial movement that challenged Japanese rule in the 1920s and 1930s.

Whether they were studying the colonial past or representing or even trying to change the present, the members of the generation were emphatically Chinese. They drew on the Chinese national story constructed and inculcated by the KMT to make sense of Taiwan past and present. What changed during the 1970s is that Taiwan's colonial history and contemporary problems became more and more salient in the national narrative. For nearly everyone, however, the "master narrative" according to which they were all Chinese went unchallenged until the 1980s.

The endurance of the master narrative in Taiwan, and its ultimate demise despite the government's best propaganda efforts—in the schools, the media, and the military—are important for us to study today, given the significance of the very same master narrative in the PRC, at the heart of which is the same recovery from national humiliation that once inspired Taiwanese intellectuals to indignant action. Harrison pointed out that by embracing "a far broader understanding of the meaning of the Chinese nation," the youth in the Baodiao movement "used a common language of outrage over the violation of Chinese sovereignty and lamented over China's humiliation by foreign powers."[15] As William A. Callahan indicates, "national humiliation is one of the few discourses that transcended the Communist/nationalist [KMT] ideological divide to describe modern Chinese subjectivity more generally." The "Century of National Humiliation" (*bainian guochi*) is not only "a recurring theme in both pre-1949 Republican writings and post-1949 Taiwanese discourse as well" but also the official view of modern Chinese history in the PRC. Callahan also notes that "while Beijing sees the PRC's joining the United Nations in 1971 as 'cleansing of national humiliation,' Taipei saw it as another horrible humiliation." He points out that Taiwanese discussion of national humiliation reappeared in the 1970s just when Taiwan (as the ROC) faced its most serious crisis of sovereignty and identity.[16]

The world is still feeling the effects of the master narrative in the PRC, but in Taiwan things turned out differently. The following chapters show that while they embraced Chinese nationalism to a significant degree, the return-to-reality generation gradually disengaged from the ideology that called for the construction of a "modern China" (*xiandai Zhongguo*). They became increasingly concerned with the past, present, and future of "native Taiwan" (*xiangtu Taiwan*). Their de-exilic efforts reshaped the national imaginary in Taiwan by laying a basis for the historical narrative and politico-cultural initiatives of Taiwanese nationalism since the 1980s. An examination of their literary activities and historical reconstruction is crucial for understanding not only the de-exilic cultural politics in itself but also the later development of "indigenization" or "Taiwanization" of politics and culture. Taiwan, as Stéphane Corcuff puts it, is "a laboratory of identities."[17] The purpose of this book is to explore when, why, and how a Taiwan identity crystallized in a single generation in this laboratory.

Organization

Noting a dearth of research on generational identity in politics and culture in postwar Taiwan in general and in the 1970s in particular, chapter 1 discusses the approach to generation adopted in this book, which was developed by sociologist Karl Mannheim in the 1920s. In Mannheim's terms, the postwar generation occupied a "generation location." The return-to-reality generation was an "actual generation." Out of this actual generation emerged three "generation units," the core analytical focuses of this book: students of the colonial New Literature, Nativist literary writers and their supporters, and "Dangwai" (literally, "outside the party [i.e., KMT]") dissident-researchers of Taiwanese anticolonial movements. I complement Mannheim with a narrative perspective: activists understood what they were doing according to a Chinese nationalist narrative of history. Most generally, I am studying the interrelatedness of identity, narrative, and action.

Chapter 2 analyzes why and how, compared with the sweeping student and youth movements in the United States, Europe, Latin America, Japan, and other places in the world in the 1960s, the postwar generation in Taiwan remained politically and socially passive. In a word, they felt helpless. Chapter 3 analyzes how a generation "in-itself" became a generation "for-itself" in the early 1970s.

The final three main body chapters treat three "generation units." Chapter 4 discusses how young cultural activists represented Taiwanese literature from the Japanese colonial period as a form of resistance writing. In so doing, they Sinicized Taiwan's colonial literary past, assimilating it to resistance literature from the mainland. The rediscovery of the colonial literary past as a form of anti-Japanese resistance constituted a claim to "Chineseness" and therefore a demand for *benshengren*, or local Taiwanese, to be treated equally.

Chapter 5 examines the rise and reception of Nativist literature in the 1970s in relation to the rediscovery of Taiwan New Literature, focusing on Huang Chunming, Chen Yingzhen, and other Nativist writers and their supporters. Nativism was a generational phenomenon in the 1970s but subsequently was seen in the light of Taiwanese consciousness and nationalism in the 1980s and then disavowed by scholars in the 1990s, who wrote off the "Nativist Literature Debate" (*Xiangtu wenxue lunzhan*) in 1977–1978 as infighting between two rival Chinese nationalist factions.

Chapter 6 analyzes the "new generation" (*xinshengdai*) identity of the Dangwai movement. Dangwai activists made sense of Taiwanese resistance to Japanese colonialism in the 1920s through Chinese nationalism, but their rediscovery of this history contributed greatly to the political mobilization and cultural construction of Taiwanese nationalism that began in the early 1980s.

In conclusion, I reject an instrumentalist understanding of the transition from Chinese nationalism in the 1970s to Taiwanese nationalism in the 1980s, arguing that in the 1970s individuals continued to narrate their lives in a public and collective story of China's fall and rise, a story that situated the individual in time and structured his or her agency, until the time came for agency to decisively restructure structure.

CHAPTER I

Generation and National Narration

T his chapter reviews the literature on the role of generation in politico-cultural change in postwar Taiwan and constructs the theoretical apparatus out of three concepts: generation, narrative, and conscientization. I end with my materials and method: discourse analysis.

The Literature on Postwar Politico-cultural Change in Taiwan

Sociological and political studies of the 1970s are almost exclusively concerned with social cleavage based on provincial background.[1] Provincial background undoubtedly had a significant effect on the postwar generation's challenges to the political system and their cultural reconstructions in the 1970s. Local Taiwanese interest in the colonial period and the native soil as represented in literature can be explained by their provincial background. The same goes for protests by young Mainlanders against KMT rule in the early 1970s.

But provincial background is not the whole story and was less important in the 1970s than it would be in the 1980s. For most of the 1970s, the critique of KMT rule arising as a result of Taiwan's diplomatic failures went across provincial boundaries. Differences of provincial background were less salient to members of the return-to-reality generation than their generational identity.[2] Generational identity, particularly in the 1970s, has been almost completely neglected (except for scattered references in works by Teresa Wright and Shelley Rigger).[3] There is some research on university students and young intellectuals in the political protests at the beginning of the 1970s,[4] but nothing on generation per se.

There is some quantitative research in which political orientation and voting behavior are studied by age bracket.[5] In these studies, age is treated objectively as a factor in the social background of the respondents, rather than as constitutive of subjective identity. Quantitative survey research can track trends, which can be extrapolated. But sudden major events and dramatic or violent social upheavals are by nature unexpected. They buck the trend and confound prediction. It is only in retrospect that we can reconstruct such upheavals and sort out the outsized roles played by small groups of individuals. As June Edmunds and Bryan S. Turner put it, it is simply "easier to unravel the formation and impact of a past generation than to point to one in its formation. It is with hindsight that historians or sociologists can see the full force of a generation such as the 1960s generation."[6] It is with hindsight that I will unravel the formation and impact of the return-to-reality generation.

A few studies have provided a detailed record of the demands for sociopolitical reform and related actions of the postwar generation in the 1970s. For instance, focusing on the Baodiao movement and the loss of the seat in the UN, Mab Huang's (Huang Mo) book is based on observations of and interviews with activists from National Taiwan University (NTU) and *The Intellectual* (*Daxue zazhi*) (see chapter 3). Huang discussed these activists as "young intellectuals" (*nianqing zhishi fenzi*), not as members of a generation.[7] One of the activists, Chen Guying, went on to describe Dangwai dissidents as "a new generation."[8] His discussions of social status in relation to generational transition, intergenerational conflict, and generation gap are foundational for further research. Chen is more analytical than Huang, but he uses the term "generation" (*shidai*) descriptively. A decade later, another activist, Hong Sanxiong, documented the same period but made no analytical advance.[9]

What, exactly, is a "generation?" We use the term all the time. The "Me generation," "E-generation," "Generations X and Y," the "consumer generation." These examples all make the concept of generation seem intuitive: a generation would seem to be a group born in a certain period or at the same time whose members have similar social features and common experiences owing to their participating in a certain historical process. This is a workable definition. With a view to its refinement, I review generation theory, especially in the sociological tradition.

Two Approaches to "Generation" and Mannheim's Theory

There are two main approaches. The first understands the term as a demographic slice called an "age cohort" or "birth cohort."[10] This approach is, not surprisingly, often employed in demography, but also in the sociology of education and aging.[11] Cohorts progress through their "life course,"[12] trying to adapt to a changing social environment. There is a place for human agency in the approach, but the emphasis is on social structure.[13]

The other approach focuses on the space for collective age-defined agency in particular historical periods. The collectivity in question is age-defined, but not as strictly defined. Generation is instead defined by major historical events that have political and cultural effects on a particular group of people who, typically by virtue of youth, are responsive to the events and agents of important effects.[14] The receptive young people are the focus of analysis, particularly ideological groups thereof. Scholars who study generation in this way generally adopt the conflict perspective on social change, especially Karl Mannheim's.[15] Conflict seems to open a space for human agency, so that this approach is characterized less by inexorability than by opportunity. The latter approach is taken more often by historians than by sociologists.[16] It is the one adopted in this book.

In sociology, Mannheim refined the second approach as part of his theory of sociology of knowledge, particularly in a long article in the late 1920s entitled "The Problem of Generations."[17] Though Mannheim saw generation as born out of social conflict, his was a non-Marxist theory of conflict; class was not the primary determinant. He understood the foundations of knowledge and the causes of social change in other terms. Mannheim's theory has become foundational in sociology. It is a point of departure for contemporary sociological discussions of how age-defined collectives become agents of social change.[18]

Age-defined collectives become agents when they "come together," as the saying goes. Proximity in space and time is not enough for a generation to come together. As Melissa Hardy and Linda Waite put it, "For a generation to trigger social change . . . they must forge an additional bond that allows a shared consciousness that motivates them to 'participate in a common destiny.'"[19] Mannheim points out that people have to reach a certain age to share such a consciousness. To him, early adulthood is pivotal, because only then, for the first time, do people live "in the present." He writes that "the 'up-to-dateness' of youth . . . consists in their being closer to the 'present' problems" as a result of their "potentially fresh contact" with the social and cultural heritage.[20]

Mannheim analyzed generation into three notions: "generation location," "actual generation," and "generation unit" (see figure 1.1). Just as age is not strictly defined in Mannheim's theory, neither is location. The location in question is not necessarily a physical location. Though members of a generation might come together in a mass gathering, a generation is not a face-to-face group. Its membership is *not* a function of social bonding of the kind that results in the formation of families, tribes, sects, and organizations for specific purposes. The location in question is, like "class," a special type of social location.[21] To have the same generation location, however, people have to grow up in the same historical and cultural area.

Mannheim's second term is a "generation as an actuality" or an "actual generation." The term refers to a group of individuals of roughly similar age who respond to the special social and intellectual currents of their epochs and societies. Experiencing the interplay of forces that have come together to create the new environment, they contribute to its creation.

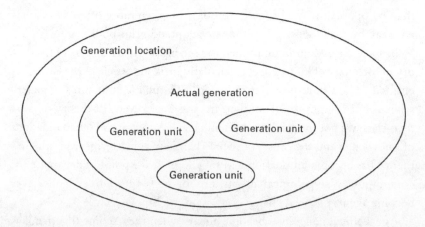

Figure 1.1 Karl Mannheim's theory of generation.

People who confront the same historical problems, however, may respond to them in different ways. For instance, during the anti-Napoleonic wars in early nineteenth-century Europe, German youth separated into two camps, the "romantic-conservatives" and the "liberal-rationalists." This brings us to Mannheim's third term. Within any "actual generation," there are distinct "generation units."[22]

Trauma, Conscientization, and Narrative

Many sociologists, however, have attempted to refine Mannheim's theory because it does not provide "an empirical model or any guidelines as to how the investigation of generational phenomena is to proceed."[23] A central problem is how a generation comes to develop a social solidarity or an active consciousness of agency due to shared experience or a common worldview.[24] Mannheim says that the transformation of the occupants of a generation location into a generation as an actuality or even a generation unit often occurs in times of rapid sociopolitical change for members of the younger generation, but he does not specify the mechanism.[25] That is what Molly Andrews tries to do. Drawing from Paulo Freire's pedagogy of the oppressed, she argues that the members of a generation location must experience a process of "conscientization." People overcome their fatalistic belief that they cannot change the conditions of their lives. They adopt a critical consciousness. They begin to feel that they can actively reflect on the status quo. The status quo is now understood in the broader context of power relations and the social structure. Individuals intuit that others understand the status quo in the same way, and that together "we" might take action to change the status quo. That is conscientization.[26]

Other scholars have tried to characterize more precisely the kind of event Mannheim had in mind. The drastic social change that precipitates conscientization usually occurs in times of war, civil disorder, exile, and other such traumatic events. Such events give people "the sense of a rupture in time and gather those who confront it into a shared sense of ordeal."[27] Typically, it is only when individuals in a specific generation location experience great trauma that they change from being part of a passive "generation in-itself" into an active "generation for-itself."[28] A self-conscious generation as an actuality—what Richard G. Braungart calls a "historical generation" and Edmunds and Turner call a "strategic generation"—does not passively accept the dominant culture. Rather, its members often succeed in creating a powerful generational consciousness or political ideal that empowers them to effect major social change. The politico-cultural ideals and practices of the generation in question establish the reference framework or limiting conditions for thought or action for succeeding generations.[29]

Another problem with Mannheim's theory is that although he stresses the generational consciousness that is necessary for the formation of an actual generation, he does not explain what generational consciousness means for empirical analysis.[30] How do members of a generation position themselves after they awaken? Scholars have suggested they position themselves in a larger historical process grasped as a kind of story. For instance, in researching the generational consciousness that inspired the leaders of the opposition movement in the former East Germany during the drastic political change in 1989, Andrews points out that an individual's sense of generational position and his or her resulting social and political opinions and actions were expressed in narrative form.[31]

Narrative includes "forms of discourse that place events in a sequential order with a clear beginning, middle, and end."[32] Seeing an event or a series of events as having an order—a beginning, middle, and end—gives it a "plot." "Emplotment" turns an event into an episode in a larger story. It gives seemingly independent events meaning by linking them as different parts of a narrative into a larger whole. As a means of making sense of reality, narrativization is not simply the reflection of reality. Narratives or stories give events a clear beginning, middle, and end via selection, rearrangement, and simplification.[33]

Roland Barthes claimed narrative is a human universal: "narrative is present in every age, in every place, in every society; it begins with the very history of mankind and there nowhere is nor has been a people without narrative . . . narrative is international, transhistorical, transcultural: it is simply there, like life itself."[34] Narrative may be universal, but only with the "narrative turn" in the 1980s did it become so important in the social sciences.

Many scholars have investigated the interrelationships of narrative, identity, and action through a motivational "narrative identity." A narrative succeeds when people identify with the characters and their situations. They identify because they share something with the characters, perhaps a quality, perhaps a problem that needs solving. As Erik Ringmar puts it, a good plot has a kind of *problématique*, which is to say a conflict in need of resolution. It is the character in the story who has to take the action required for resolution.[35] A person who identifies with a character experiences a vicarious resolution that might spill over into real life. Erik Ringmar sums up:

> From the perspective of the story's participants, the directedness of narrative can be understood in terms of the *intentional* aspect of action. To be a conscious human being is to have intentions and plans—to be trying to bring about certain effects—and the link between intention and execution is always rendered in narrative form. In this way story-telling becomes a prerequisite of action. . . . We tell ourselves what kind of a person we were/are/will be; what kind of a situation we were/are/will be in; and what such people as ourselves are likely to do under these particular circumstances.[36]

In telling stories, we are asserting various things about ourselves. We are always within the stories we tell.[37] Narrative is a basic mode of our existence and a fundamental way we construct ourselves.[38] As Anthony Giddens argues, to develop and maintain a coherent sense of self-identity—or, in Chris Barker's phrase, "a mode of thinking about ourselves"[39]—a narrative of the self is necessary.[40] Identity and narrative are mutually constitutive and constructive. The stories we tell about ourselves answer questions concerning personal existence and self-realization.[41]

Individual life stories are nested within public narratives that are concerned with a certain collective and serve as a reference framework for meaning making. Generational stories are such public, collective narratives. Molly Andrews describes the formative influence of narrativity on generational identity as follows:

> For a generation to realize its potential, for it to become a self-conscious group which acts to transform the world and is itself transformed in the process, requires a consciousness of generations which have come before and which will follow; in other words, historical consciousness is a necessary but insufficient condition for generational consciousness. . . .
>
> We come to know ourselves, and others, as members of a generation through acts of narration. Temporally, these narratives are both horizontal and vertical. All beings living at a particular moment

construct and are constructed by stories. At the same time, stories pass between generations; they are the stuff of cultural identity, and it is this which we inherit from preceding generations and bequeath to the next. It is through these stories that individuals, as members of a generation, locate themselves in the historical process, and in so doing, create a framework which optimizes the possibility of realizing their own ability to effect real change.[42]

In short, the historical consciousness that informs people's generational identity is structured by a public historical narrative. Such narratives are important interfaces that link the individual and society, the present moment and history, the micro and the macro, and agency and structure. Individuals who experience awakening (conscientization) because of major traumatic events and go on to participate in social and political affairs rely on public historical narratives in order to position themselves or their generations and to construct the meanings of their actions. These narratives are important mechanisms linking people's little lives to wider spheres of time and space.

Nationalism, Narrative, and the Return-to-Reality Generation

The nation has become one of the main providers of collective public narratives in modern society. National narratives are "about" *ethnies* or nations: the main character of an individual narrative will represent an *ethnie* or nation, and the narrative will in some way emplot or unfold ethnic or national identity. It will situate people in the world, and orient them. It will frame people's judgments of truth, goodness, and beauty, because a narrative of national identity can have a moral or ethical function.[43]

While classic works such as Elie Kedourie's *Nationalism* investigated the importance of youth in the development of nationalism in Europe, researchers working on nationalism, the nation-state, and national identity still need to focus more on the role of generation.[44] From the beginning of the nineteenth century, most "actual" generations were inspired by some form of nationalism, which they then reshaped. They emerged at pivotal moments to lay or relay the foundation for a national consciousness and conceptions of national character.[45]

Some early research shows that in Taiwan at the beginning of the 1970s, most college students (including high school students) tended to limit their social interactions to people of the same provincial background. It was also noted, however, that in their responses to many political issues, local Taiwanese and Mainlanders of the younger generation revealed only small differences.[46] This similarity speaks to their shared experiences of Chinese nationalist education under the KMT. This educational experience differentiated local Taiwanese of the postwar generation from their parents' and grandparents' generations, who had grown up under the Japanese. Similarly, for Mainlanders, this educational experience distinguished them from their parents, who had been refugees. In short, whether local Taiwanese or Mainlander, members of the younger generation were assimilated into a collective distinct from previous generations. They absorbed the Chinese nationalist narrative of history. In response to perceived national shame at the beginning of the 1970s, they relived the trauma of China's modern mistreatment, and they responded by going back to reality. The return-to-reality generation regarded Taiwan's situation as a national crisis. They believed that modernization was a potential solution and longed for a modern and democratic society.

In Mannheim's terms, the postwar generation in 1970s Taiwan occupied a common "generation location." College students and young intellectuals living in urban areas, especially in the North, bore the brunt of sociopolitical change. Their response to change in the 1970s made them an "actual generation." Those who participated in a movement that demanded sociopolitical reform and a return to "native soil" and Taiwan's social reality can be regarded as important "generation units." The critical period for the formation of these units was from 1971 to 1973. Among them, cultural figures who rediscovered the Taiwan New Literature of the Japanese colonial period, writers of Nativist literature and their proponents, and dissidents of the Dangwai new generation who studied the Taiwanese anticolonial movement in the 1920s form the principal analytical focuses of this book (see figure 1.2). Combining Mannheim's theory of generation and the theory of narrative identity, this book aims to examine how the return–to–reality generation became socially engaged by casting themselves in new roles in a nationalist historical narrative, thereby initiating a "de-exilic" cultural politics.

In fact, youth activism contributing to the de-exilic cultural politics was not limited to the three generation units on which I focus. In the cultural

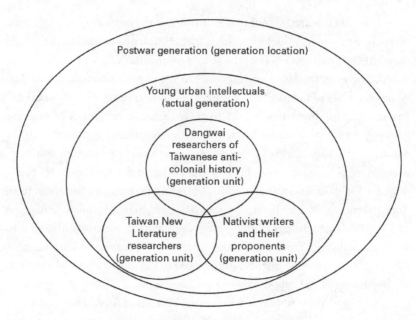

Figure 1.2 Karl Mannheim's theory applied to 1970s Taiwan.

arena, for example, the return-to-reality and return-to-native-soil pulse also beat distinctly throughout Lin Huaimin's Cloud Gate Dance Theater (Yunmen wuji)—a modern dance group devoted to the advocacy of "Chinese modern dance" (*Zhongguo xiandaiwu*)[47]—and throughout the "Chinese Modern Folk Song movement" (*Zhongguo xiandai minge yundong*) launched by Yang Xian and Li Shuangze (see also chapter 2, note 50).[48] They played a quite marginal role, however, in renarrating the national identity and reshaping the national imaginary in Taiwan, much less important in this regard than the three generation units.[49]

It has to be noted that many intellectuals who were part of the return-to-reality generation were more than thirty years old, not all that young, in the 1970s. Generally speaking, the political or cultural activists discussed in chapters 4, 5, and 6 were about ten years older than the university students and younger intellectuals dealt with in chapter 3 who initiated political and social activism with the Baodiao movement at the beginning of the 1970s. As explained earlier, the approach to the study of "generation" that I adopt focuses on the space for collective age-defined agency in particular historical periods. The collectivity in question is age-defined but not as strictly defined. Members of a particular generation in this sense tend to define themselves by their difference from or confrontation with the older generation, even when the latter is not all that much older in numerical terms. This is precisely the case for the return-to-reality generation— young and not-so-young reform-minded people all regarded themselves as "the younger generation," "the new generation," "young intellectuals," and so on.[50]

The 1970s were a "golden age" for intellectuals in postwar Taiwan, especially for those of the younger generation, in that the challenging historical conjuncture gave them a chance to make the most of their cultural capital.[51] Over the decade, "intellectuals, with expanding popular support, began to challenge the KMT's political, social and cultural hegemony in civil society."[52] The three generation units I examine were typical of the intellectuals in their golden age.

I focus on how members of the return-to-reality generation linked self to society and nation through historical narrative and thereby constructed the meaning of individual existence, collective (generational) identity, and politico-cultural activism. I show that the return-to-reality generation's stress on the land, history, and culture of Taiwan paved the way for the Dangwai's political mobilization and cultural construction in terms of "Taiwanese consciousness," which emerged after the Kaohsiung Incident (*Gaoxiong shijian*) of 1979 (see chapter 6). While this book mainly focuses on the 1970s, it links the history of the 1970s to the rise of Taiwanese cultural nationalism in the 1980s and beyond.[53]

As Wu Naiteh argues, it was during the 1970s that "a national oppositional force ideologically opposed to the established order" emerged.[54] The leaders of this collective politico-cultural dissidence and their followers were members of the postwar generation who embraced the ideal of returning to reality. In the 1970s and 1980s the significant development of the opposition movement and the solidification of their personal political ideology were mutually reinforcing. Beginning in the 1990s they entered what Wu describes as "middle age" or "elderly age" strata and became important exponents of party (or political) identification. Closely examining the words and deeds of this key generation in the 1970s is essential to understanding the subsequent indigenization or Taiwanization and democratization.

It is also critical to understanding the opposition between competing national narratives in Taiwan since the 1980s. A national historical narrative can be disseminated through formal education during the formative years to win young hearts and minds, but the state is not the only agency in society that can tell stories about the nation, and disseminators of other stories might end up taking power, as happened in Taiwan in 2000, when the DPP replaced the KMT as the ruling party in the presidential election for the first time. Hence the sometimes apparently intractable ethnic politics of the past three decades, which we can understand in terms of narrative identity theory. Different storytellers begin from different subject positions. They give the same historical experiences or events different meanings by emplotting them differently. Since a plot constitutes a whole, and since the meaning of an experience or event comes from the whole structure and from the position of the individual experience or incident within that whole (rather than inductively from the accumulation of experiences and events, out of which the entire meaningful framework is generated), conflicts in historical outlook or historical interpretation constitute conflicts over the whole of the reference framework—or one could say the paradigm or worldview.[55] As a result, people on both sides of such a conflict often have a sense of strong and full-scale moral antagonism that leaves them so inflexible that they cannot easily respect or even recognize each other.[56]

I could not claim that my research will be the basis for an "aha" moment of mutual recognition and respect, but at least it clarifies the problem.

Materials and Method

My materials are textual, including newspapers, magazines, compilations, tracts, and student publications containing statements and descriptions of actions by the return-to-reality generation. I also use literary texts, especially in chapter 2, to capture the condition and mentality of the politically and socially passive younger generation in the 1960s. I use these texts to document their generational challenge to the political and cultural establishment.[57] My method is discourse analysis. There are different definitions of discourse. One commonality is that our language does not neutrally reflect our worlds, identities, and social relations. Rather, our language plays an active role in creating and changing them.[58] Analysis of discourse isolates discursive elements and studies how they combine.[59] These elements are regularized ways of talking about, understanding, and functioning in the world.[60] They are to be understood in terms of historical, cultural, and political forces and in relation to social action.[61]

This book analyzes the discourse of the return-to-reality generation in the 1970s, the forces that shaped this discourse, and the discourse's implication for their social action. My emphasis is especially on the interaction between a generational discourse and a national historical narrative—a mode of discourse in which time is "nationalized" and sequenced in order to construct the meaning of epochal events, such as those catalyzing the formation of the return-to-reality generation at the beginning of the 1970s in Taiwan, the period to which I turn in chapter 3. But before getting to the 1970s, I have to set the stage with an account of the younger generation when it was still for the most part a generational in-itself in the 1960s.

CHAPTER II

Education, Exile, and Existentialism in the 1960s

lobally, but especially in the West, the 1960s are usually defined by political, social, and cultural change driven largely by the baby boom generation. Young boomers put their stamp on the decade. To be young meant to be free, idealistic, enthusiastic, and full of optimism. The spirit of liberation the young felt "went hand in hand with a critique of what existed: old forms were to be superseded and even destroyed in order to inaugurate the new."[1]

When we turn to Taiwanese youth in the 1960s, we find a very different profile. They were passive and demoralized, outside of the supposedly global circuits of political action and emancipatory longing. In Taiwan, we see the limits of global youth rebellion. The purpose of this chapter is to analyze why and how, in sharp contrast to their counterparts in North America, Europe, Latin America, Japan, and other parts of the world, young intellectuals of the postwar generation in Taiwan—even the reform-minded ones—remained politically and socially inert in the 1960s, even though some of them had a sense of generational consciousness.

The postwar growth in Taiwan's youthful population and the rapid development of higher education created a stratum of young intellectuals in the 1960s. The nation's intellectual youth were kept in line through thought policing and kept patriotic through propaganda. But the peculiar secondhand sense of exile they absorbed at school and through the media left them feeling powerless, particularly given the impossibility of overcoming this exile: there was no way the ROC was going to reconquer the mainland and unify China, the official national goal. As a result, Taiwan's youth constituted a passive "generation in-itself" in the 1960s instead of an active "generation for-itself" that could create a potent generational consciousness and bring about significant political and social change. While the rest of the world was in rebellion, they sat on the sidelines. There they would stay until they came out of exile at the beginning of the 1970s according to their own definition and set themselves a more manageable task.

Political Control, Education, and a Silent Generation

Student rebellions that emerged around the globe in the 1960s were partly an effect of the growth in the young population and the expansion of higher education. When the baby boomers came of age, more of them than in any previous generation went off to college. For example, in the United States, the 1960s became "the most explosive decade in the entire history of educational expansion," especially "higher education."[2] The dramatic expansion of higher education occurred as well in Western Europe, much of Latin America, Eastern Europe and the Soviet Union, China, and other parts of Asia. All these regions had student and youth movements that challenged the status quo. The members of these movements spoke a common, unprecedented, international "language of dissent."[3]

In respect to the expansion of higher education, Taiwan was no exception. Unlike in other countries, however, students in Taiwan did not challenge the status quo. A politically and socially passive generation formed, attesting to the success of the KMT's approach to indoctrination. The postwar generation was the first the KMT had educated under peacetime conditions with its particular version of Chinese nationalism. KMT-style Chinese nationalism homogenized young people's political attitudes, thereby differentiating them from their parents, who had been educated on the mainland or in Taiwan under Japanese colonial rule before 1945.

The KMT also channeled young people's political passions through particular activities. If these activities can be described as political activism, it was very much state-directed, especially through the China Youth Anti-Communist National Salvation Corps (Zhongguo qingnian fangong jiuguotuan, hereafter CYC), established in 1952. Its main task was to mobilize youth, especially students, under party leadership. CYC youth were educated to be patriotic and loyal to Chiang Kaishek.[4] Chiang's son Chiang Chingkuo was in charge. The CYC penetrated into every high school, college, and university. From the early 1950s to the late 1960s, it initiated patriotic and anticommunist movements, such as the Battleship Building for Revenge movement (*Jianjian fuchou yudong,* 1954–1955), the Support Wuhan Student Anti-Communism movement (*Zhiyuan Wuhan qingnian xuesheng fangong kangbao yundong,* 1956), the Chinese Youth Self-Fortification movement (*Zhongguo qingnian ziqiang yundong,* 1961), and the Never Forget the Recovery of the Chinese Mainland movement (*Wuwang zaiju yundong,* 1965).[5] But these were obviously not autonomous activities. They were, indeed, attempts to preempt any independent youth activism.[6]

Another means of preemption was to smear overseas student movements in newspaper and magazine reports. Most of the coverage emphasized the destructive qualities of these putatively left-leaning movements and their capacity to corrupt young minds.[7] An analytic view of student activism in other countries was the exception.[8] A positive response to these movements would not be expressed until the early 1970s.[9]

Members of the postwar generation did occasionally engage in self-directed sociopolitical criticism in the 1960s, but for the most part their criticisms toed the party line. Most of the critics were Mainlanders, and they had a strong generational consciousness.[10] In the spring of 1961 Wang Hongjun, at the time chair of the Department of Journalism at National Chengchi University, published an essay entitled "How to Get Young People to Take the Baton?" (Ruhe shi qingnian jieshang zheyibang) in *Free Youth* (*Ziyou qingnian*).[11] Wang was invited to submit a contribution addressing the problems of youth for the magazine's Youth Day special issue. At thirty-nine years old, he must have been the oldest youth in the country, but that is how he saw himself, as a young person. At any rate, the baton in question was a national mission: making the ROC strong enough to retake the mainland. He wrote: "To be honest, if we cannot count on the youth to take on the mission of fighting against the communists and reuniting our country, who else can we count on? If we cannot educate this generation of young people to have high aspirations and great capabilities and make them willing to shoulder the responsibility of reviving our nation, who can we count on, and do we still have any future?"[12]

Wang worried that the nation's youth would not be ready or willing to take the baton. His article provoked much public discussion on the "take-the-baton" problem (*"jiebang" wenti*), including Li Ao's essay "The Old Man and the Baton" (Laonianren han bangzi) published in *Apollo* (*Wenxing*, 1957–1965), at the end of 1961. Li Ao, a young Mainlander with a degree in history from NTU, had just been discharged from his military reserve service.[13] Nobody could gainsay his claim to youth. He would become the most popular young antitraditionalist when he started the "debate on Chinese and Western culture" (*Zhongxi wenhua lunzhan*) in a series of articles in *Apollo* in 1962 that harshly attacked older Mainlander intellectuals like Qian Mu (1895–1990), Liang Shuming (1893–1988), Xu Fuguan (1903–1982), and Hu Qiuyuan (1910–2004). In his first contribution to *Apollo*, "The Old Man and the Baton," Li put a different spin on the problem. While Wang had exhorted young people to take the baton, Li implied that the older generation was holding on to the baton instead of passing it on and letting young people run with it.[14]

Li Ao was about as critical of the authorities as young people got, and the government took notice. In a book written three and a half decades later, Li claims that after submitting his baton article, he was given the following warning by an ex-convict released from the political prison on Green Island (Lüdao): "If you keep writing this way, sooner or later you'll be headed there [to Green Island] too!"[15] But ultimately, Li Ao toed the party line, probably because he fervently believed in it. If and when the baton was finally passed, he would be ready to take it and run with it, across the Taiwan Strait. When that longed-for day finally came, "the field of vision [of the younger generation] will not be limited to this tiny island, but will extend to the days when the lost mainland is recovered".[16]

In May 1963 a young American student named Don Baron (writing under the pen name Di Renhua) and a Mainlander scholar named Yu Shuping each submitted editorials to the KMT's official newspaper, *Central Daily News* (*Zhongyang ribao*). They accused people in "Chinese" society, that is, Taiwan, of lacking civic-mindedness and of admiring all things Western, evident in young people's desire to purchase American products and go to America. Students at NTU started a "Self-Awakening movement" (*Zijue yundong*) in response. They called on young people to be less selfish and more patriotic.[17] They constantly referred to their generational identity, with slogans such as "Don't Let History Judge Us to Be a Decadent and Selfish Generation!"; "We Are Not a Resentful Generation! We Are Not a Lost Generation! We Are Not a Decadent Generation!"; "We Are an Honest and Dedicated Generation!"; and "We Are an Awakened Generation!" The reason they were supposed to wake up as a generation is that the future of the nation was at stake: "If we still cannot awaken to the need for self-renewal, then the Chinese nation that has existed nearly for five thousand years has no future."[18] In the end, the KMT endorsed the movement by publishing a supportive editorial in *Central Daily News*. The editorials were music to KMT ears, and the movement had not gotten out of hand.

Young people might have shied away from criticism of the government in light of the fate of Lei Zhen. In September 1960, less than six months before Wang Hongjun published his article on the take-the-baton problem, Lei, once a follower of Chiang Kaishek, was arrested and charged with sedition. The magazine *Free China*, established by Lei and other liberal Mainlanders, was shut down, as was a related publication, *Public Comment* (*Gonglunbao*). Lei's attempts, in cooperation with local Taiwanese politicians, to found a new party came to an end.[19]

While it was not publicized like Lei Zhen's arrest and sentencing, Peng Mingmin's demise must have given any potential critic who had access to the grapevine pause. Peng was a Taiwanese political science professor at NTU. In 1964 he and two of his students prepared a manifesto calling for a new democratic constitution and Taiwan's independence (*Taiwan duli*). They declared that "retaking the mainland" was impossible and that the people of Taiwan must overthrow Chiang Kaishek's regime.[20] Before this manifesto could be issued, the three were caught and imprisoned.[21] Another case of a radical underground challenge to KMT rule occurred two years later. In 1966 Lü Guomin (1937–1991), Xu Caode (1937–2018), Yan Yimo (b. 1940), and Huang Hua (b. 1939), all young local Taiwanese intellectuals, secretly organized the Association for Promoting Nationwide Youth Solidarity (Quanguo qingnian tuanjie cujinhui) in order to form a party, reestablish multiparty democracy, and pursue Taiwan's independence. Shortly after the association formed it was broken up by the national intelligence bureau, and its founders were arrested.[22]

If these examples did not deter them, personalized messages from the resident "military instructor" (*junxun jiaoguan*) might have. Many young people got a taste of the "White Terror" starting in secondary school.[23] As a magazine writer recalled at the beginning of the 1970s:

In high school, I once wrote an essay criticizing the police in my neighborhood for taking vegetables without paying and generally throwing their weight around. I felt it was official corruption. As a result, my National Language [*Guowen*, Mandarin Chinese] teacher turned the essay over to the school Office of Student Affairs (Xundaochu). I was called down to the office, where I was met by the director, the military instructor, the tutor of my class, and the National Language teacher. They asked me what my father did, whether we had a subscription to *Public Comment*, whether we often read *Free China* . . . and they wanted me to write a confession and a letter of contrition and declared in class that I had an "ideological problem." They even had a classmate report on the sly on what I said and did. Subsequently . . . I was so scared that I filled out the form to join the KMT.

. . . Eight years ago, when the Self-Awakening Movement was launched . . . there were immediately people who said that as individuals they were unwilling to make any public criticism of social evils. Their reason was fear of getting on the blacklist, which would leave them unable to leave the country or would affect their futures.[24]

Chen Zhangsheng was only able to publish the account in the relatively liberal atmosphere at the beginning of the 1970s.

A Stifling Atmosphere, Intergenerational Apathy, and the Vogue for Overseas Study

At the beginning of the 1960s the London-based journal *China Quarterly* had published a special issue on Taiwan. A feature article described older Mainlander intellectuals in the following terms:

With the collapse of the Nationalists [KMT] most of the intellectuals who fled the mainland had lost confidence in themselves and could find no meaning in the life for which they were trained. They can do little more than cherish the myth of the return to the mainland. When the intellectuals arrived on Formosa [Taiwan] they were not prepared for permanent exile. Many cherished the Chinese tradition of returning to die in one's hometown. "Even if a tree is as tall as 1,000 feet, its leaves fall back to the very spot where it is rooted." Quite a few see many more opportunities on the "conquered" mainland than on Formosa. Some rationalize the present unsatisfactory conditions on the island. Once back on the mainland, democracy will be realized, taxes reduced, and all will be well with the world. The Nationalists have fostered this myth, which in so many ways is its *raison d'être*. To Chiang Kaishek it must seem that to rethink the ideology of his régime could only lead into dangerous ways. Dogma is the order of the day.[25]

Older Mainlander intellectuals, as this passage attests, were in an uneasy, "median" exilic state. They were torn between adjusting to their new home in Taiwan and keeping the faith that they would return to the mainland.

This exilic mentality was found not only in intellectual circles. In fact, it deeply penetrated nearly every aspect of life of Mainlanders of whatever social status. In November 1957, several years before his "baton" article, Wang Hongjun published a short piece in the founding issue of *Apollo*. In it, he said he was fed up with the "spiritual low-pressure zone" in Taiwan. The causes of the spiritual squalor were "the despondency, numbness, and escapism in people's hearts and minds."[26] Two years later, Wang described the general mentality of exiled Mainlanders:

People from the mainland have already spent ten years on Taiwan. A couple of months ago, a magazine asked a few prominent figures to express their feelings in writing on this topic. . . . The general sense was that after ten years the youth of yesterday is middle-aged today, and the middle-aged man is already graying. In only a few words, one felt the inexorable chill of the autumn wind. . . .

The feelings [these prominent figures expressed] were all authentic. They all had a deep sense of humanity. No one could deny them or reproach them. In fact that's the way it feels. Ten years of confinement is enough to erode anyone's will. The international situation seemed dark and uncertain. Although the fires of revolt are always lit on the mainland, we need to wait for the right opportunity for the epic act of reconquest. Many people have gradually gone from expectation to anxiety, from anxiety to disappointment, and from disappointment to passivity. . . . What's their time frame? Today. How far out are they looking? Taiwan. If you ask them where they came from, why they came, where they're going, they have nothing to say.[27]

That was how a man on the cusp of middle age saw his fellow Mainlanders, especially the older generation.

The stifling atmosphere of exile was well captured in *Taipei People (Taibeiren)* by Bai Xianyong (Pai Hsienyung, 1937–), a Mainlander writer of the postwar generation whose father was a prominent KMT general.[28] This collection of Bai's short stories vividly depicts a variety of Mainlanders whose paradise, once lost, could never be regained except in memory, and who were haunted with a sense of marked contrast between the diminishing present and their glorious or heroic past: taxi dancers, sing-song girls, high-tone ladies, venerable generals, elder statesmen, depressed scholars, old soldiers, air force widows, aging domestic servants, a proud food-shop proprietress, and an aging homosexual movie director.[29]

Some short stories written in the 1960s by Chen Yingzhen (1936–2016), who was later hailed as one of the leading writers of Nativist literature in the 1970s (see chapters 4 and 5), shared similar themes and concerns about Mainlanders in exile with Bai Xianyong's *Taipei People*. In his "My First Case" (Diyijian chaishi), a twenty-five-year-old policeman of local Taiwanese origin was investigating a thirty-four-year-old middle-class Mainlander urbanite with a good job and a happy marriage who committed suicide in a cheap hotel in a small town. A forty-two-year-old Mainlander primary school teacher of physical education happened to meet this younger Mainlander before his death. Proud of his past fight against the communists as a member of KMT secret service, the teacher told the policeman about the difference between the exiled and the native: "In other words, you grew up here safely and peacefully for twenty-five years. Your relatives and friends are all around . . . you can take things for granted, like a tree: it grows naturally." He continued by quoting the dead: "But as for us . . . we're like branches cut off, lying on the ground. Either because of the dew, or because there is still water in them, they can live for a while. Yet when the north wind blows on them, and the sun shines on them, they are bound to wither."[30]

Indicating the similarity in characters found in Bai's and Chen's stories, Yu Tiancong (1935–2019), a Mainlander literary critic, considered how Mainlanders of the older generation, especially those of higher social status, shaped their children: "It was precisely because those characters carried the burden of such a 'past' that the minds of their children have always been dominated by irresistible nightmares. These nightmares were like ghosts, constantly eroding the lives of their children."[31] As the self-criticisms voiced during the Self-Awakening movement attested, the younger generation saw itself in similar terms. In fact, over the 1960s the postwar generation was commonly described as "depressed," "passive," "selfish," "silent," "apathetic," "having no dream," "self-seeking and indifferent to any public issue," and the like. A story by local Taiwanese young writer Lin Huaimin (1947–), "Cicada" (Chan, 1969), poignantly described this particular generational atmosphere by presenting a group of frustrated, bored, and slightly cynical university students hanging around in a café in Taipei:

As the lamp went out, Chuang Shihhuan caught the thread of a song. Wu Che had the record—it was Bob Dylan, moaning as though half awake and talking in his sleep, singing. . . .

As he sat in darkness, the lights and the shadows of people around him suddenly came alive. That long hair, those shaggy haircuts, those bright and dazzling clothes kept swinging back and forth before his eyes. Light and shadow, flowing and ebbing, came and went upon their faces. Moving, gesturing with their hands, shaking their legs, crossing and uncrossing them. Kicking off their shoes and resting their feet on the chairs. Shaking their heads and nodding. Opening and closing their mouths like fish in the water. Mandarin blending into Taiwanese [Hoklo language], into English. The Kuang-hua Express rushed by, one car after another. Conversational partners changed as fast as the topic of conversation. The drone of conversation gave way to laughter. Between the talking and the laughter, a temporary pause sewed their lips shut; they smoked, drank, ate.[32]

One option for a young person that might indicate indifference to any domestic issue was to go abroad. The vogue for overseas studies, especially in America, had come to the attention of scholars early in the 1960s.[33] This vogue and its repercussions, particularly among Mainlanders, was nowhere better depicted than in the novel *Palms Again* (*Youjian zonglü, youjian zonglü*, 1967) by Yu Lihua (1931–2020), a young Mainlander writer. The protagonist of this pioneering, classic work of "overseas student literature" (*liuxuesheng wenxue*), a distinctive genre that emerged in the 1960s as a result of the vogue, was Mou Tianlei, who earned his Ph.D. degree in journalism in the United States but could not find a better job than teaching Chinese in a college. He went home for a visit ten years later but was unable to decide whether to stay in Taiwan or return to America. He complained:

From university students to cooks, everyone wants to go to America, to study for a doctoral degree, to make money, and to have a Western wife. Everyone wants to leave this place, anyway. I really don't understand. Here people still want to get out of this place, even if they haven't endured any hardship; they don't want to come back, even if they suffer great hardship there. This is really the strangest phenomenon in the twentieth century.[34]

The heroine, Chen Yishan, also a Mainlander, went on a blind date with Mou because he was a ticket to America. She frankly told him: "If you want to marry me, you have to take me to America right now. For so many years, what I want most is to go abroad. I can't stand staying here anymore, such a small place. . . . I'm stifled and about to explode. . . . Almost all of my classmates have gone."[35] In a nutshell, "in innumerable hearts the greatest wish was to 'Come come come, come to NTU' [widely regarded as the most prestigious university in Taiwan] and then 'Go go go, go to the USA' (*Lai lai lai, lai Taida, qu qu qu, qu Meiguo*)."[36]

Later in the 1960s the vogue became the epitome of the failure of the younger generation to take an interest in the fate of the nation, and the failure of the older generation to cultivate national sentiment in their children. Xu Fuguan, a prominent New Confucian in his sixties who taught at Tunghai University, blasted Mainlanders for the vogue for overseas study. Most parents, he alleged, were in fact proud of having emigrant children.[37] This was precisely what Mou Tianlei wanted to point out when Chen Yishan kept talking about America. He said, "Having a son or daughter in America symbolizes a lot: the family has a way with things and their children are promising, having the world before them."[38] Truth be told, there was a vogue for criticizing the younger generation, especially the vogue for overseas study among them.[39] What changed in the early 1970s (see chapter 3) was the stridency of the attacks by the younger generation. The following critique by a young intellectual is representative:

The parents who came from the mainland to Taiwan had experience fighting the CCP, but these were experiences of pain and failure. *Although they've been singing the tune of the great task of restoring China, they're the ones who most lack the confidence to do so.* They basically are unwilling for their sons and daughters to get caught up in the maelstrom of political struggle. They even hope that their children may escape this contentious island of Taiwan. *They started the overseas study current, which has been flowing for twenty years. They're defeatists, and they have passed on their defeatism to the next generation.* (Emphasis original)[40]

The aspiration toward Western learning and the powerful influence of American culture on expatriate students supposedly exacerbated a sense of separation from their own national history and fate.[41] A well-known writer, the Mainlander Zhang Xiguo (1944–), commented:

I think the education we received in Taiwan . . . left modern "intellectuals" with an extraordinary lack of knowledge about China. The cohort who grew up on Taiwan is spiritually Americanized. Before leaving the country, they never had any chance to understand China, much less Taiwan. They have no relations, except family relations, chaining them to Taiwan. They have no feeling for or insight into Taiwan. They don't feel Taiwan is their home. Spiritually speaking, they're disjointed from either Taiwan or the Chinese mainland.[42]

Again, Mou Tianlei epitomizes this alienation. Feeling that the ancestral mainland had become "a dreamland without substance" and lamenting his failure to put down "roots" in Taiwan, he dubbed his generation "the rootless generation" (*meiyougen de yidai*).[43]

In this regard, there was little difference between young Mainlanders and their local Taiwanese counterparts. Take literary circles, for example. A seasoned Mainlander poet, Ji Xian (1913–2013), tried to resurrect a minor tradition of modernist poetry he helped build in China in the 1930s by founding a new journal, *Modern Poetry* (*Xiandaishi*), in 1953. Then he established the Modern Poetry Society (Xiandai shishe) in 1956, which leaned toward total Westernization in poetry. Modern poetry began to prosper, as two other influential bodies were formed in 1954: the Epoch Poetry Society (Chuangshiji shishe) and the Blue Star Poetry Society (Lanxing shishe). Following poetry, the modernist movement in fiction was started by a group of students in the Department of Foreign Languages and Literatures at NTU who established the journal *Modern Literature* (*Xiandai wenxue*) in 1960—Bai Xianyong, Wang Wenxing (1939–), Li Oufan (Leo Oufan Lee, 1939–), Chen Ruoxi (Lucy Chen, 1938–), Ouyang Zi (1939–), and so on.[44] As the Japanese scholar Matsunaga Masayoshi notes, for this group of young writers, generational status trumped provincial background:

"They did not distinguish between Mainlanders (Bai, Wang and Li) and local Taiwanese (Chen and Ouyang). They shared in a common literary atmosphere. To start with they had almost no experience of the Japanese occupation or of the mainland. They all belonged to the generation that grew up on Taiwan after the Retrocession (*guangfu*) [of Taiwan to ROC rule]." He argues that for local Taiwanese, they belonged to the first generation that received a Chinese education right from elementary school and that "rather than distinguish them in terms of Taiwanese and Mainlander," it is better to say that they were all members of the new generation.[45] Similarly, this was Lin Huaimin's author's profile in the collection of his stories, *Cicada (Chan)*:

Lin Huaimin, a "local Taiwanese." The point of putting it in this way is not to emphasize his provincial background, but to indicate the milieu in which he lives. Like hundreds of thousands of children who were born in the postwar period and live here, he has grown up in the society that has become stable and prosperous over the past two decades. The "chaos" of "war"—these are just words to young people like him. They are familiar with everything [they were told about] the Chinese mainland but have no memory of it themselves. What they have is only "the present." They crammed and went to high school, squeezed through the narrow gate of the entrance exam and went to university, read some things that Confucius and Sun Yatsen said, learned something about the ABCs, and watched a lot of movies and TV.[46]

The younger generation was alienated not only from the China's past, but also from Taiwan's history. As far as local Taiwanese members of this generation were concerned, this was especially ironic. A telling example is Ye Rongzhong's (1900–1978) daughter, Ye Yunyun (1945–). Ye Rongzhong was secretary to Lin Xiantang (1877–1956), one of the most important leaders in the Taiwanese anticolonial movement in the 1920s under the Japanese. He wrote a series of important historical works in the 1960s that apparently did not even make an impression on his own daughter. In retrospect, Ye Yunyun confessed:

During the 1960s, I usually helped my father copy his manuscripts, becoming the first reader of his works. However, I was not different from a great many young people of my generation. In those days, I was oriented towards the West and felt little interest in the history of which I myself was a part. Upon reflection, it was not until I left my island homeland that I began to take a serious interest in learning Taiwanese history.[47]

If this was the experience of a child whose parent was a member of the Taiwanese anticolonial elite, it is not surprising that ordinary young intellectuals of local Taiwanese origin—let alone those of Mainlander origin—knew next to nothing about the island's past. In a word, the younger generation felt "uprooted" or "lost."[48]

Quasi-exile and Postmemory

I would like to diagnose the problem in terms of "exile" and "memory." The Mainlander Zhu Yunhan (1956–) reflected on the ironic contrast between the small island on which the postwar generation lived and the big country they felt themselves a part of:

> If, having been born and grown up here, the spatial sense of this young generation of intellectuals was limited to [Taiwan], that would indeed be a pity. We would feel just about as inferior as young people in [small countries such as] Ceylon, Madagascar, and the Philippines once they begin to transcend the petty chauvinism of nationalist school textbooks and confront the wider world. But, fortunately, we've inherited a historical tradition that has compensated for the deficiency of our current spatial sense. We find in the past a support for the future. We can hold our heads high as we face the world. We only temporarily lack a link [to the mainland]. . . .
> Nevertheless we happen to grow up within the space of this "temporarily." Thus, the stark contrast between our historical tragedy and our contemporary complacency, combined with the distinctive feeling of living "temporarily," have constituted the spatio-temporal coordinates for this generation of young intellectuals.
> Perhaps, today's university students cannot help sighing: being a Chinese is a blessing, but it's sad to be Chinese in the present world,

and hard to express the experience of growing up in Taiwan as a Chinese.[49]

Zhu's description matches Edward Said's characterization of the exilic feeling of existing in a median state, one that they could never exit: there was no going back to the Chinese mainland; they were stuck on Taiwan, and the only out was escaping from it to America. But the younger generation was different from the older generation. Many young Mainlander intellectuals were too young when they arrived in Taiwan to remember fleeing the mainland or being refugees. Others were born in Taiwan. These young intellectuals had a "quasi-exilic mentality," in the sense that their feelings were not based on their personal experiences. Reflecting on the influence her parents' nostalgia had on her, a college student commented in an essay published in a school bulletin in the 1970s that although the Mainlanders of her generation had never been to the mainland, they usually felt homesick for their parents' hometowns. She wrote:

Sometimes I wasn't really sure where I was from. It stood to reason that since I was born in Taiwan I was Taiwanese, but when people asked me where I was from, I would without thinking reply: "Hunan." My elders would often go on to reply: "Hunan's a nice place!" I couldn't help feel a little proud of myself. As a child, whatever I read about Hunan in geography class I would swallow whole, hungry for knowledge. Since it was my homeland I should understand it and love it, right? But I'd never seen this homeland. It was distant and vague. . . .

Those of us who'd never been to the "homeland" could still sing "Four Stanzas on Homesickness" (Xiangchou siyun) to tempo or even poignantly. . . . Weren't we waiting for the bugle to start playing, for the time we'd leave this temporary resting place and reconquer the mainland?

I don't know how many in our generation "sighed with homesickness looking at the province of origin on their ID cards." At least that's how I grew up, and that's what my elders taught me.[50]

Similarly, Wang Fusu (1952–), a medical student at NTU, displayed the quasi-exilic mentality in an article published in a school magazine. "Those who have never touched the land, gazed at the blue sky, or eaten the rice of home can only be homesick for a place they've seen on a map or in a photograph. Ah! This is the tragedy of our times!"[51] A Mainlander writer popular with young people in the late 1960s, Zhang Xiaofeng (1941–), published a volume of essays entitled *Homesick Stone* (*Chouxiang shi*). Her preface to it epitomized the quasi-exilic mentality:

> I write about my kid and about nature, but half of this book is about my nostalgia for my homeland. Now that I think about it, I am hardly qualified to feel homesickness. I was just eight years old when I came ashore in Keelung and then lived happily in a Japanese-style house [left by a repatriated Japanese family]. In an instant, I grew up and then became a wife, and then a mother. My memory of the homeland became dim and it seemed like a lifetime away from me. But I don't know why this homesickness turned out to be latent—persisting well beyond my childhood and girlhood, an outbreak of it occurred one day in autumn, which would have been a good day to go back the homeland. And it reoccurred again and again. It is a chronic disease which cannot be cured and which I can't be bothered to have cured.[52]

Examining the collective memory of the Holocaust, Marianne Hirsch describes how generational factors condition how Jewish survivors and their children related to the trauma. For Hirsch, these children are "exiled from a world that has ceased to exist, that has been violently erased." They "live at a further temporal and spatial remove from that decimated world" than their parents. She argues that the distance separating Holocaust survivors from their children is unbridgeable. Survivors' children can only have what Hirsch calls "postmemory":

> Postmemory is a powerful form of memory precisely because its connection to its object or source is mediated not through recollection but through an imaginative investment and creation. That is not to say that memory itself is unmediated, but that it is more directly connected to the past. Postmemory characterizes the experience of those who grew up dominated by narrative that preceded their birth, whose own belated stories are displaced by the stories of the previous generation, shaped by traumatic events that can be neither fully understood nor re-created.[53]

Postmemory is applicable to second-generation memory of other cultural or collective traumatic events and experiences. Young Mainlander intellectuals' "quasi-exilic mentality," born of events unquestionably less extreme, nonetheless shares striking similarities with Holocaust postmemory. When they sighed with homesickness, young Mainlander intellectuals' connection to the past was mediated and imagined according to the story they had heard from their parents or at school. As for young local Taiwanese intellectuals, the nationalist education was as effective for them, and they had imbibed exile at school. They were supposedly in exile from a territory their ancestors had left centuries before and could be described as having a "semi-quasi-exilic mentality" or "semi-postmemory."

The Fad for Existentialism and the Isolated, Impotent Intellectual

College graduates mostly hoped to go to America, and maybe they were culturally Americanized, but two of the European philosophers they were reading had a profound influence on their state of mind, particularly later in the decade. Those two philosophers were Jean-Paul Sartre and Bertrand Russell. The fashion for existentialism and logical positivism was satirized in Chen Yingzhen's short story "Tang Qian's Comedy" (Tang Qian de xiju, 1967). A young woman named Tang Qian switched lovers frequently, including a pretentious follower of existentialism and an aggressive logical positivist. "From that moment, existentialism swept through the capital [Taipei] like a sudden hot wind; it became the current rage among young intellectuals, exactly like one of the new dance steps that was just then popular on the nightclub circuit," Chen Yingzhen wrote. When the intellectual wind changed, "the new positivists spoke the abstruse language of mathematics and physics" and "their attack was felt as a sharp stab by the circle of existentialism's adherents, none of whom had ever passed math." Chen continued: "Sometimes they went so far as to stake out a place within the old Vienna school, and to suffer from the illusion that they were on the same level as white-haired scholars like Carnap and Hans Reichenbach."[54] Zhang Xiguo comments:

The two most powerful currents of thought in Taiwanese intellectual circles are logical positivism and existentialism. At least to us,

Russell and Sartre are the patriarchs of two schools of thought . . . which more or less tell us: the intellectual is lonely and should be proud of it. . . . There is no objecting to these two thinkers, but is the influence they have on us really a good one? Undeniably, we all more or less were influenced by Russell or Sartre: we liked to stress the responsibility and pride of the intellectual.[55]

Existentialism in particular contributed to a mentality of isolation; the proud, responsible intellectual was solitary. Like Yu Lihua, the Mainlander writer who died young, Wang Shangyi (1936–1963) was deemed to be another spokesperson of their generation. While Yu was widely regarded as giving voice to "the rootless generation," Wang was considered as representative of a Taiwan version of "the Lost Generation."[56] Profoundly shaped by existentialism, his posthumous works enjoyed popularity among young intellectuals. In an essay comparing the existentialist writer Albert Camus with Ernest Hemingway, the representative writer of "the Lost Generation," and discussing their novels, especially *The Stranger* and *The Old Man and the Sea*, respectively, Wang characterized his generation as wandering in a desperate condition of "estrangement" and "loss." He encouraged his generation to follow Camus and his character Mersault, unyielding fighters for life who defied the absurdity of existence, rather than Hemingway and his characters, who were weaker and more negative.[57] Similarly, a contemporary Taiwanese interpreter of Sartre asserted: "It is because people do not have an innate nature that when they come into this world they are as if thrown in a vast wilderness beyond the possibility of assistance. For everything they depend on themselves. They must create their own worlds and value systems, and at the same time give their worlds meaning." He summed up: "An enlightened person. A solitary but proud hero. This is Sartre's message."[58] This may have resembled Sartre's message, but for most reform-minded young intellectuals, it was existentialism with Chinese characteristics. The solitary but proud hero was combined with the traditional Confucian's high-minded commitment to social betterment. Hence the irony of the man for the people who is not of the people. Again, Zhang Xiguo: "We modern Chinese intellectuals solitarily bear our crosses in order to save the world and rescue humanity. How lofty and great!"[59] Chen Guying (see chapter 3), a young intellectual leader in the political activism in the wake of the Baodiao movement, had a similar experience. His wife recollects:

My husband got all his basic education here [in Taiwan]. . . . To put it grandly, he is an optimist and an idealist. To put it plainly, his views are bookish. He is overly idealistic, as many critics say. But he can't help it, he has internalized the social responsibility of the traditional Chinese intellectual, and is yet at the same time always eager to transplant many of the positive aspects of Western liberal society onto our social foundation.[60]

When would this graft of liberalism/existentialism onto the Chinese branch finally happen, and if so, how? *Free China* and *Apollo* first raised the banner of democratization and modernization of traditional Chinese culture from the 1950s to the mid-1960s. Founded in January 1968, *The Intellectual* echoed the reformist agenda of the two earlier publications and was similarly a venue for self-criticisms of the exilic mentality. What was different in *The Intellectual*, in a way that makes it seem like a herald of the return-to-reality and return-to-native-soil movements that appeared after the Baodiao movement in the early 1970s, was attention to the common man, from whom the eponymous intellectual was isolated. To some writers who contributed to *The Intellectual* in the late 1960s, the lifeworlds of workers, peasants, and other sections of the lower class rather than their own intellectual life constituted "authentic" social reality. This reality was Taiwanese, but they understood it as "modern Chinese intellectuals" (*xiandai Zhongguo zhishi fenzi*) through the Chinese nationalist narrative of history. It was the "Chinese common people" (*Zhongguo laobaixing*) that young intellectuals wanted to understand. For instance, this letter to the editor of *The Intellectual*:

I am Chinese, born into a divided China in the sixth decade of the twentieth century. During my university days there were times when I walked the dark and dirty alleys of Taipei. Several times, in turning toward the glimmering towers along Zhongshan North Road (*Zhongshan beilu*), I've seen families crammed into dilapidated shacks. In the country, I've met people who worked extremely hard every day just to get by. Why is it that the farther we intellectuals go the more distant we get from society and the less true compassion we have for ordinary people? If the "new intellectual class" is built on a confining intellectual "ideology," then I'd rather not ascend into this "class." I'd rather abandon the robes of the "intellectual." I would be happier walking unadorned in the fields and shoot the breeze with the country folk by the side of the creek.

An intellectual is someone who truly lives the life of the Chinese people, who sees what the Chinese people see, who says what the people want to say, who gives voice to the pain of the Chinese people, who shares their happiness by smiling, right? The age of the "literati" (*shidaifu*) has already passed.[61]

The author was clearly interpreting Taiwanese society within the framework of a Chinese nationalist historical narrative, and just as clearly dissatisfied with life in the ivory tower. I propose that the desire the author expresses to get closer to "the common people" was a way of bearing the impossible burden that the nation had placed on their shoulders. They were in exile from the Chinese mainland, tasked with the impossibility of retaking it. There was no way out of this geographical exile, but they could at least overcome their social exile, in theory.

But not in practice, for the time being. The eponymous character in Lin Huaimin's short story "The Boy in the Red Shirt" (Chuan hongchen-shan de nanhai, 1968) was a jack of all trades who had worked as a land surveyor, billboard painter, plumber, fisher, and so forth. The protagonist, a college graduate who felt aimless and powerless in life, was impressed by the boy's rough, scarred, and powerful hands, which were "seasoned by real life." Still, the college graduate kept planning to study in America like everyone else. In the end, he stayed in Taiwan, a bored teacher.[62]

Intellectuals in the late 1960s continued to feel alone, passive, excluded, and, of course, bored. Hence a future leftist leader of the Baodiao movement in the United States, the novelist Liu Daren, wrote:

Basically, this generation of overseas students has played no active role in modern Chinese history. Most of them grew up in the time after their parents and grand-parents had already lowered the flags and silenced the drums. Their world was books and legends. Their life experiences have been textual transplants, airy inferences and imaginings. Most of them today cannot escape these frames. They walk down the road their elders paved for them. Regardless of how they feel, they are unable to pave a new road. Perhaps for their whole lives they will have to carry the burden of the history created by their fathers. Walking in the shadows, they now proceed in a fog in the direction in which their fathers have pointed. (italics original)[63]

Liu's account is a vivid profile of a passive, melancholic generation living in exile under the shadow of the older generation.

The transfer of Taiwan's sovereignty to the KMT-ROC party-state in 1945 and the authoritarian state's relocation in 1949 with over a million Mainlander refugees were sea changes in Taiwanese society. During the 1960s a new generation, including members of local Taiwanese and Mainlander background, came to maturity. Young intellectuals grew up on narratives of exile that they had not themselves experienced and therefore were characterized by a "quasi-exilic mentality" or "semi-quasi-exilic mentality," "postmemory" or "semi-postmemory," depending on their provincial background. For the duration of the decade there seemed no way out of exile, besides another kind of exile, especially in America.

Students from Taiwan read about, and in a few cases witnessed, the student activism in the United States, Europe, Japan, and other places in the 1960s, but Taiwan itself remained tranquil, as far from the turbulent 1960s as it was possible to get. Young intellectuals in Taiwan during this decade constituted a passive generation in-itself. The major reason for their apathy was the fact that they were completely excluded from public affairs, especially politics. They had little role to play.[64] This was the case not just for local Taiwanese but also for Mainlanders. One author summed up: "A consciousness of being part of the 'lost' or 'rootless' generation was lodged in the minds of most students. All they hoped for was knowledge. All they dreamed of was studying abroad. Every day they extolled existentialism and nihilism. They even thought they were imbibing the essence of knowledge."[65]

Ambrose Y. C. King (Jin Yaoji, 1935–), a young sociologist of Mainlander origin, argued that young intellectuals "did not seem to lack confidence in their mother country's [that is, the ROC's or the Chinese nation's] future." To King, young people were passively waiting for a favorable historical opportunity. "They are just waiting—waiting for a challenge."[66] Retrospectively, it seems that the challenge that King expected was precisely the drama of Taiwan's loss of the Diaoyutais and then the seat in the United Nations.

CHAPTER III

The Rise of the Return-to-Reality
Generation in the Early 1970s

At the end of 1969, Taiwan and Japan began to dispute the sovereignty of the Diaoyutai Islands, a group of small, uninhabited islets located over potentially vast oil reserves about 120 nautical miles northeast of Taiwan. The Diaoyutais had been under American control; now, according to the reversion settlement with Tokyo, the United States would turn them, along with Okinawa and the rest of the Ryukyus, over to Japan. Although the KMT government had asserted ROC sovereignty, the United States sided with Japan.

Several months later Taiwan faced another, much more serious diplomatic crisis. Henry Kissinger made two visits to Beijing, in July and October 1971, and announced that Nixon would visit the PRC the following year. At the end of October, the UN General Assembly resolved to admit the PRC and recognize it as the only legal representative of China and the rightful holder of China's seat in the United Nations. Taiwan, under the name of the ROC, was expelled from this organization. In February 1972 Nixon made his visit to the PRC and signed the Shanghai Communiqué, in which the two sides promised to "normalize relations." In the communiqué, the PRC also asserted that "the Government of the People's Republic of China is the sole legal government of China" and that "the liberation of Taiwan is China's internal affair in which no other country has the right to interfere."

Following in Nixon's footsteps, Japanese prime minister Tanaka Kakuei visited the PRC in September 1972 and signed a joint communiqué announcing the establishment of diplomatic relations. In the communi-qué, Japan took an even more pro-PRC position than the United States, recognizing that the PRC is "the sole legal Government of China" and respecting the claim that "Taiwan is an inalienable part of the territory" of the PRC.

In chapter 2 we saw that, compared with the United States, Europe, Latin America, Japan, and other places in the 1960s, which saw widespread student and youth movements, Taiwan remained tranquil, or tranquilized; the postwar generation was by and large politically inert. Major political and cultural changes did not occur until the early 1970s, when the post-war generation finally rose up and challenged the authoritarian state. This chapter is an analysis of the rise of the postwar generation. It is obvious that this rise largely resulted from the key diplomatic failures just outlined. What needs more study is the development of the ideal that inspired politico-cultural activism: return to reality. This chapter examines the for-mation of an "actual generation" from a "generational location" around the ideal of returning to reality.

Baodiao, Calls for Reform, and Intergenerational Critique

In September 1971, on the eve of the loss of the UN seat, Guo Rongzhao, a Mainlander historian in his thirties, published an article in *United Daily News* (*Lianhebao*) entitled "A Historian's Reflection on the Present Situa-tion." In this article, he strenuously attacked the authorities for ignoring domestic and international change for more than two decades and for "meeting every change with inaction." In discussing Taiwan's internal transformation, he stated:

Over the past twenty years, there's been an increase in population and mobility; industry and commerce are flourishing; per capita income has risen along with the standard of living; exports have expanded; transportation has advanced with the development of mass communication; new talent has been emerging, along with capital-ists and a new middle class; the gateways to America and Japan are wide open; a large batch of overseas students have returned; new cur-rents of thought are stimulating new trends; there is a precocious political consciousness, and so forth. . . . These new developments, these new historical factors, speak to the fact that a new historical current is flowing this way in force. *A new epoch has been born.* (Emphasis original)[1]

In fact, the advent of this "new epoch" was not only the result of the changes in the social structure that Guo identified. It was also due to the "awakening" of the occupants of a specific generation location as a result of traumatic political and cultural events in the 1970s.

Taiwan's loss of a seat in the United Nations was obviously of greater concern than the loss of a few islets, but it was the latter crisis that was decisive for the formation of the return-to-reality generation. When the news of the U.S. decision to side with Japan reached overseas Taiwan students in America, many began organizing an overseas movement to Defend the Diaoyutais (Baodiao). They held demonstrations in major U.S. cities from January to April 1971.[2] In April college students, mainly in the North, launched a domestic version of the Baodiao movement. They held on-campus demonstrations and wrote patriotic letters to the government. On June 17, 1971, when the United States and Japan signed the transfer of sovereignty over the Ryukyus (including the Diaoyutais), students organized an off-campus protest march in Taipei that drew about a thousand people. The march culminated at the American and Japanese embassies, where letters of protest were delivered.[3]

The Baodiao movement never really ended. As one student put it, it was "a new scene unprecedented in the previous twenty years. It was the first time student interest had been so intently focused on political and social issues."[4] Hong Sanxiong, a Baodiao leader, later recalled that "the movement shocked intellectual youth in the ivory tower awake."[5] Thus awakened, the nation's youth felt intensely patriotic. Wang Xiaobo, a graduate student in philosophy at NTU who drafted "A Letter to Our National Fellows" (Gao quanguo tongbao shu), which was distributed in June 1971 during the Baodiao demonstrations, described the students' sentiments in the following manner: "Because of a series of national humiliations beginning with the Diaoyutais event, the students now feel that country and nation are close to them and very real."[6] Ma Yingjeou, president of Taiwan from 2008 to 2016, was an undergraduate at the time in the Department of Law at NTU and active in the Baodiao movement. He later recalled that "after the [Baodiao] movement erupted, the country became a life and blood reality in the hearts and minds of youth. It was no longer an abstraction!"[7] While Wang and Ma were Mainlanders, Hong was a local Taiwanese.

Local Taiwanese outside of university campuses were affected in the same way: they awakened to a sense of personal responsibility for national problems. He Wenzhen, a local Taiwanese member of the KMT who had just left the army, pointed out that there was "a common cry for reform, self-strengthening, and national salvation" in a time of crisis.[8] In reference to NTU students' passionate interest in sociopolitical reform after the Diaoyutai dispute, Chen Shaoting (1932–2012), who was president of *The Intellectual* and had a local Taiwanese background, wrote: "Silent for over twenty years, [students on] university campuses finally awakened at a moment of national crisis." He also considered the publication *NTU Legal Logos* (*Taida fayan*) "a sign of awakening of this generation of college students" who had "inherited the Chinese intellectual's fine tradition of taking the entire realm as his personal responsibility."[9] The response of these university students and young intellectuals, either Mainlander or local Taiwanese, was congenial toward the government in that the Baodiao protesters' position was not antigovernment and they "cast the issue in the broader historical context of China's national struggle." While to some extent the legitimacy of the KMT to control the language of Chinese nationalism was challenged, all this showed "a degree of effectiveness with which the KMT had substantiated Chinese identity in Taiwan through state institutions."[10]

But patriotism was not the main effect of awakening, whether for Mainlanders or for local Taiwanese; strident, widespread criticisms of the older generation and demands for reform were. In the fall of 1971 student publications like *NTU Legal Logos*, *University News* (*Daxue xinwen*), and *NTU Student Union Bulletin* (*Dailian huixun*), as well as student clubs like NTU Law Student Council (Taiwan daxue faxueyuan xuesheng daibiaohui) and NTU Student Union (Taiwan daxue xuesheng daibiao lianhehui), began to issue statements and hold activities that pushed for campus and wider sociopolitical reform.

The herald of these calls for reform in the late 1960s, *The Intellectual*, was relaunched at the end of 1970. More than sixty reform-minded young people from academia, politics, and commerce were added to the magazine committee. In January 1971 it began to actively call for reform. The Baodiao movement began just over three months later. During the next two years, *The Intellectual* would become the discursive center of sociopolitical critique. There was a lot of back-and-forth between the editorial office and NTU, especially after November 1971. When *The Intellectual* was reorganized once again in January 1972, five NTU students were added to the committee: Wang Xingqing (later known as Nanfang Shuo), Qian Yongxiang, Chen Lingyu, Wang Fusu, and Hong Sanxiong. At a time when the Dangwai (see chapter 6) was still in its infancy, it was students and young intellectuals in the orbit of *The Intellectual* who became the leading proponents of reform.

Students at NTU called for internal, academic reform. Special criticism was directed toward the rigid system of tutelage and ideological education and the censorship of articles in student publications. Students called for "educational independence" and "university democratization."[11] They held forums on "Freedom of Speech at NTU" and "Democratic Life at NTU."[12] But students were also concerned with national affairs. There were joint publications in *The Intellectual*, such as "A Letter to Mr. Chiang Chingkuo" (Gei Jiang Jingguo xiansheng de xin) (January 1971) and "Advice About National Affairs" (Guoshi zhengyan) (October 1971), and "Nine Essays on National Affairs" (Guoshi jiulun) (January 1972).[13] Each of these articles called on the KMT government to enact significant reform.

A long article entitled "Analysis of Taiwan's Social Forces" (Taiwan shehuili de fenxi), first printed in the July 1971 issue of *The Intellectual*, is one of the first statements by representatives of the return-to-reality generation and arguably contains the first public discussion of the mindset of the older local Taiwanese generation under KMT rule. It described the local Taiwanese intellectuals of the preceding generation as follows:

> They are mostly older than fifty-five. They received a complete education in Japanese. With few roles for them to play in actual society, they spend their days recollecting the past. Although they occasionally look on admiringly at Japan's contemporary prosperity, they know their place and obey the law, *becoming an "apathetic audience" of the government. Only when they occasionally hear someone criticize them for receiving "a slave's education" (nuhua jiaoyu) [under the Japanese] do they feel a nameless anger, only to return to a helpless silence.* They have a very good command of Japanese as a language tool but cannot use it to speak out. Because they for the most part remain silent, society has forgotten them. (Emphasis original) [14]

Whether society had forgotten the older generation, the younger generation of local Taiwanese background had the sense that their elders could not be expected to change, that their wartime and colonial experience had not toughened them but resigned them to acceptance of the status quo, while the younger generation's very lack of experience had somehow formed it into an instrument of change:

The result of the expansion of education over the past two decades is that a huge number of young intellectuals have been nurtured. This second generation, which has been reared in [a time of] stability, has transformed into a new type, totally different from the elder generation. Because they never underwent the baptism of war, the younger generation's epochal environment and educational background are completely different from the elder generation's. . . . Intellectuals of this younger generation . . . [therefore] have no awe for idols of power. They are fearless. They have a purer, less inhibited disposition than the previous generation, which has given them a strong tendency toward modernization and rationalization. This is the basic psychological trait of this generation.[15]

Note that in this paragraph, Bao Qingtian et al. are no longer writing merely about young local Taiwanese intellectuals, but about their generation as a whole.

Young Mainlanders were often more critical of KMT rule than their local Taiwanese counterparts. They were more antagonistic toward the previous generation. The sociopolitical criticism and demand for reform in the early 1970s partly reflected an intergenerational conflict within the Mainlander population. The postwar generation of Mainlanders found it hard to accept that the regime had disappointed the people yet again. A young Mainlander who was in his thirties at the beginning of the 1970s bluntly expressed "what he had on his mind" regarding Taiwan's loss of its UN seat:

Domestic governance must be immediately and totally reformed. Without reform we cannot survive. . . . From the age of fourteen, when I followed the government to Taiwan, to now, the state has fed and clothed me like a parent. So though there have been people who criticized the government, I've neither dared nor been willing to add a single word. . . . The reason why I discuss problems of domestic governance now is because the future of the country and of young people is at stake. Without comprehensive reform there is no way for us to survive the current crisis.[16]

According to people like Zhang Hongyuan, the older generation was on the defensive, or even on the way out. Picking up on the youthful wave of reformist activism, an NTU student called Chen Mingzhe anticipated a shake-up: "Every generation will experience a series of challenges over its lifetime that lead to change on many levels. Today, due to the emergence of various irresistible social forces, we firmly believe that the established order will sooner or later respond to these forces by undergoing a fundamental transformation. I hope we can dispense with all outmoded frameworks and create for ourselves a new future."[17] Another NTU student wrote: "There are stormy seas ahead. This is a historical awakening, a coming to awareness of ourselves as subjects of history and of our position in the context of history, a realization of the relatedness of past and present. Thus, it is an existential realization."[18]

These quotations show how the return-to-reality generation positioned itself in a larger historical process. This positioning was framed within a historical narrative template that, as pointed out in table 0.1, described China's miserable fate over the past century, caused by foreign bullying and civil wars, and the possibility for its redemption.

Faith in Democracy and a Rude Awakening

Throughout the 1970s members of the return-to-reality generation who rose up to challenge the status quo often sounded quite proud of themselves. They were not only considerably different from their parents in terms of life experiences and values "but also different from any generation in Chinese history." They recognized their generation as being the first in modern Chinese history to grow up in such a stable environment. They had received a more complete education than the preceding generation. Though they were living under martial law and an authoritarian regime that had incarcerated or executed an older generation of dissidents, they typically described themselves as being "change-seeking," "innocent and uninhibited," "able to think freely," "frank and practical," "global in perspective," "magnanimous and greatly ambitious," "the first generation who will welcome the twenty-first century," and "deeply influenced by Western democratic thought."[19]

With the mention of Western democratic thought, it is tempting to explain the rise of the return-to-reality generation in terms of intellectual flows, but it is important to remember that the flows were largely under the control of the KMT, and that the return-to-reality generation was a product of the Taiwan the KMT helped make, particularly the education system. In that system, students were exposed to Western ideals of liberty and democracy because the KMT-led ROC was dependent on the United States and at least nominally part of the American-led "free world." The values and political institutions of liberal democracy were introduced and applauded at different educational levels, which had great influence on the sociopolitical ideals of the postwar generation, though probably not the influence that the KMT anticipated or had in mind.

Members of the awakened generation liked to portray themselves as inspired with a naïve faith in democracy that they had internalized at school and was tested when they looked at the actual society around them. The authors of "Analysis of Taiwan's Social Forces" pointed out that a great many young intellectuals felt dispirited upon leaving school "due to the fact that a large part of the content of the educational system [was] Western," and because the media portrayed the Western world positively. They further noted about the graduates: "What they see of various backward domestic institutions are totally estranged from their ideals."[20] Similarly, NTU philosophy lecturer Chen Guying described the experience of his generation as follows:

> The authorities have founded so many schools over the past twenty years, leaving too many college graduates with a prospect of a perfect and prosperous modern country, with an incorruptible and efficient government, an ethical and just society. But after leaving the classroom and the campus, what they observe is a reality all too different from that prospect. One could either "alter" the beautiful picture painted by education or "alter" reality to make it conform to the utopian image to which young people aspire.[21]

The return-to-reality generation hoped to alter reality, to make it more democratic. For instance, in November 1971 at the student forum on

"Democratic Life at NTU," Chen Guying, made a bold appeal: "Lift the ban on student movements!"[22] In fact, faith in democracy was an essential element in young people's definition of their generational peculiarity. The postwar KMT educational system was politically repressive, but by spreading the ideal of democracy, the KMT planted the seeds of discontent. In the 1970s the seeds germinated.

Out of Exile, Return to Reality

The awakened intellectual youth were distinguished most by their "de-exilic" outlook. They came out of exile by taking Taiwan as their immediate frame of reference. The larger and long-term narrative frame the reform-minded young intellectuals had in mind was Chinese, but there was now a salient midterm subframe: Taiwan. Youth demanded that the authorities confront the fact that the territory under KMT rule was confined to the island of Taiwan. In response to Taiwan's loss of its seat in the United Nations, an editorial in the *NTU University News* made the following appeal:

> We must realize that regardless of how much territory we have, at least it is free and in the possession of a group of people who stick together through thick and thin. Before the mainland is reclaimed, we have only to cooperate in building here [on Taiwan] an advanced nation with a truly democratic constitutional government system. Then we can discuss other more distant plans. Only in this way can we keep things straight and retain a free hand.[23]

An editorial in *NTU Legal Logos* argued: "To construct the country is the key. If we want to counterattack the communists we must first construct the country. This is the proper order of root and branch. Until the Chinese mainland is regained, we must first fully realize in the free area [i.e., Taiwan] democratic governance and responsible rule, which we can capitalize on in our opposition to communism."[24] The return-to-reality spirit was also displayed in the proposals that were made in "Advice about National Affairs," a long article coauthored by Zhang Junhong and his colleagues at *The Intellectual*. They stated: "For two decades we have not faced reality enough in domestic issues. . . . We do not need to spend too much time and effort on plans we cannot carry through at our present strength. Achieving

China's unification is our greatest ideal and our fighting objective. But at present what we need to be eager to do is to [find out] how to turn Taiwan around."[25] The major diplomatic failures alerted college students and young intellectuals to the precariousness of Taiwan's position in international politics. To them, a return to reality and the demand for domestic reform meant realizing that since everyone was in the same boat, they all had to care about the land they had grown up in and knew best.[26]

Coming out of exile did not change the national narrative fundamentally, but it certainly changed people's attitudes toward the "middle" of the story. In the 1960s young intellectuals had felt caught in the middle, which was unfortunately set in Taiwan. The very essence of this mentality is a sense of loss, uprootedness, and nostalgia.[27] In the 1970s young intellectuals embraced the middle and its setting, Taiwan. This was especially true for young Mainlander intellectuals. Gao Zhun, for instance, remarked: "Born a citizen of the ROC, I arrived in Taiwan at eight years of age. Most of my life has been spent on Taiwan. I cannot but be passionately concerned about the people and society of Taiwan and hopeful for its progress."[28] After abandoning his plan to study abroad, Wang Xingqing reflected: "I am a Chinese person who was born on the mainland but who grew up on Taiwan. I have incomparable feelings and love for the land and people [of Taiwan] for having nurtured me."[29] And future president Ma Yingjeou: "We owe too much to Taiwan, this motherly society. Anyone who has grown up on Taiwan should always be thinking of giving something back by caring for it."[30]

Unlike the heralds of return to reality at the end of the 1960s, the return-to-reality generation acted on their desire to understand the reality of common people's lives. The students and intellectuals of the return-to-reality generation were similar to the intelligentsia of Russia in the late nineteenth century, who promoted the idea and practice of "going to the people." The president of the NTU Student Union, Wang Fusu, and others established the "Social Service Group" (Shehui fuwutuan). More than 150 students began surveying farming villages, the urban poor, labor, police-citizen relations, elections, and other topics. In the spring of 1973 NTU students initiated another activity, the "Million Hour Contribution Campaign" (Baiwan xiaoshi fengxian yundong), to support farming and fishing villages and aboriginal communities. For these intellectual youth who rejected the exilic mentality, crossing class lines in this manner out of a humanitarian concern was a way out of exile.

The Radical Demand to Reelect
Parliamentary Representatives

The sociopolitical activism of the return-to-reality generation was moderate for the most part, but there was a radical edge to it. Hong Sanxiong, chair of the NTU Law Student Council, called on students to "take the sword to your school and launch an attack on society" (*dui xuexiao kaidao, xiang shehui jinjun*), in other words, to "revolutionize from within the strange status quo in the struggle for a new atmosphere."[31] The slogan "take the sword to your school" spread to other campuses, including National Chengchi University, National Central University, the College of Chinese Culture (now Chinese Culture University), and other institutions.[32] The most radical proposal was the comprehensive reelection of all national representatives of the parliamentary organizations. This was an attack on the "constitutional tradition" (*fatong*) of KMT authoritarian governance.

Although a displaced regime, the KMT maintained the structure of the government that was organized according to the constitution adopted on the Chinese mainland in 1946. The representatives of the three parliamentary organizations (the National Assembly [Guomin dahui], Legislative Yuan, and Control Yuan [Jianchayuan]) were elected in 1947 and 1948 on the mainland. To justify the claim that the ROC was the sole legitimate government of all of China to the extent that it carried on the "constitutional tradition," the emergency measures created for "the period of Communist rebellion" extended the terms of the members of the three organizations and maintained their functions, even though they had no electoral constituency. The three organizations were in fact controlled by the KMT.[33] By the end of the 1960s, however, the concern that the actual number of representatives might fall short of the constitutionally defined number became serious because the seat holders in the three parliamentary organizations were dying off.

After the Baodiao movement, there was a public discussion of the problem. For instance, in September 1971 the Mainlander scholar Guo Rongzhao argued:

> 99.9% of National Assemblymen and Legislators were elected over twenty years ago on the mainland . . . and Taiwan's fourteen million people cannot have much influence on them, because there has been

no political connection or legal connection [between these representatives and the people]. Thus, government officials and policies have free reign and are unsupervised. For the past two decades, some officials have been able to do whatever they want regardless of public opinion: This is the key issue. [They carry on in this way] because they do not need to please the people, because they only have to please a small number of people or a certain group of people. . . . A political party should not simply consist of a leadership team, nor should a regime consist of only a central government which is aloof and narcissistic.[34]

In October of the same year, the members of the magazine committee of *The Intellectual* cosigned "Advice About National Affairs." They declared: "We are a group of young people who grew up here (even though our provincial backgrounds are different). . . . We have the right to speak out about our survival and destiny." After introducing themselves, they launched their attack:

For the past two dozen years, we have been maintaining a large, aging privileged faction that supposedly represents but is totally disjointed from the people. Although on the surface it maintains the constitutional tradition pro forma, it is unrepresentative of the younger generation, of people who twenty-three years ago [the last time a national election was held on the Chinese mainland] were not yet twenty years old, which is to say people less than forty-three years old today. Now roughly two-thirds of our nation's population, being younger than forty-three, has never had the chance to vote in a national election of parliamentary representatives.[35]

Against a proposed policy of "supplementary elections" or the idea of allowing people in Taiwan to elect only a small portion of representatives, these members of the magazine committee proceeded to suggest a more radical alternative, demanding a "total transformation" and regular reelections.[36]

During the months between the Baodiao movement and Taiwan's expulsion from the United Nations, the proposal for a comprehensive reelection gained widespread support among college students and young intellectuals.[37] After Taiwan was expelled, as one writer noted: "People who used to remain silent have begun to speak . . . people are saying things they dared not say before. Many people no longer blame the UN. Rather, they demand domestic reform. The need for the reelection of all national representatives has become all the more pressing."[38] On the NTU campus, in *University News*, *NTU Legal Logos*, and elsewhere, students advocated for a comprehensive reelection of the parliamentary representatives while simultaneously rebuking the previous generation.[39] They held a national affairs forum in 1971 on the rhetorical question, "Should all national parliamentary representatives be reelected?" (*zhongyang minyi daibiao yingfou quanmian gaixuan*).[40]

I will end with Chen Shaoting, who, as we shall see, played a major role in raising the profile of literary and political resistance efforts during the colonial era (see chapters 4 and 6). His criticism of opponents of reelection deserves to be quoted in detail:

The reasons for opposition are not rational but rather psychological. Clearly, the result of complete reelection would be a huge increase in local Taiwanese representation. This result should be welcomed. Why worry about it? Due to the failure of the corrupt Manchu Qing government in the war of 1894, peace was obtained by ceding territory. Taiwan fell under the alien rule of Japan. Taiwanese compatriots became scapegoats for their compatriots on the mainland. In the long half century of Japanese rule, however, local compatriots ceaselessly resisted Japanese rule by force of arms, writing an awful yet glorious page of history for the Chinese nation. They proved that they were the most patriotic and excellent of all the sons and daughters of China. For the past twenty-five years, we have been building Taiwan into a base for the restoration of national prosperity. There is no question about the competence of the government's leadership, but the contribution and sacrifice of local Taiwanese compatriots has also been essential. Thus, we should let local Taiwanese individuals have more voice in the central government organization. We must be deeply aware that Taiwan is part of China and that local Taiwanese people have a share in China!. . . Thus, [local Taiwanese compatriots] are all aware that, in the great revolutionary work of national development and national restoration, they bear a weighty, epochal mission. At the same time, with incomparable confidence, they will not disappoint the great trust the entire Chinese people is placing in them. They will support and defend the government, recover the mountains and rivers of China, and restore national integrity.[41]

Does it sound like he is protesting too much, perhaps in order to distance local Taiwanese, who were Chinese patriots, from the overseas "Taiwan Independence movement" (Taiwan duli yundong)? No, his audience had little idea of the independence movement. To them it went without saying that they were all Chinese. The problem was that some Chinese people were more Chinese than others. His demand was for political equality, and for an end to the exilic mentality under which the particular historical experiences and cultural orientations of local Taiwanese were stigmatized and suppressed. He was suggesting that Taiwan, the land the exiles were treading on, should be given priority over the Chinese mainland, to which they could only dream of returning.

Hsiao Hsinhuang's research has shown that the sense of crisis over Taiwan's predicament inspired in intellectuals by the diplomatic failures of the early 1970s contained both a nationalist "Chinese consciousness" (Zhongguo yishi) and a "Taiwanese consciousness" based on a strong social concern at the time. To the intellectuals, the two consciousnesses were not in conflict. "For the sake of both Taiwan's survival and China's prospects—or perhaps it would be clearer to say for the sake of China's prospects in the future, it is necessary to first attend to Taiwan's present problem of survival." As Hsiao points out, "Taiwan was no longer a vague image or only a shadowy existence under an abstract idea of China." Therefore "Taiwanese native-soil consciousness (xiangtu yishi) began to gain public 'legitimacy' in intellectual circles in the 1970s. This native-soil consciousness continued through the whole of the 1970s and into the 1980s."[42] During the 1970s Nativism or localism was "an attempt to proscribe [sic] Taiwanese culture and to define what constituted a Taiwanese experience"; it was not "explicitly Taiwanese nationalism, in that it did not imagine the 'local' in Taiwan in national terms."[43]

The demands of the return-to-reality generation for political reform, including the complete reelection of parliamentary representatives, ultimately fell on deaf ears. Despite the intensity of these demands, the KMT's will to maintain the status quo in governance did not waver. In April 1972, by serializing over the course of six days a long article entitled "The Voice of an Ordinary Citizen" (Yige xiaoshimin de xinsheng), the KMT-run *Central Daily News* began to fiercely attack the reformist college students and young intellectuals for holding "extremist views" and specifically expressed its opposition to the student movement proposed by Chen Guying.[44] At the beginning of December of the same year, some leading reformist students and intellectuals on the NTU campus, including Chen Guying, were arrested and interrogated by the Taiwan Garrison Command (Taiwan jingbei zongsilingbu), Taiwan's state security body. They were accused of covertly supporting the "communist bandits" (*gongfei*). Meanwhile, the KMT became less and less tolerant of *The Intellectual*, and the journal came under intense pressure. After two years of reformist discourse in the wake of the Diaoyutai incident, college students and young intellectuals lapsed into silence. In the spring of 1973 the NTU Department of Philosophy began to purge its staff: Chen Guying, Wang Xiaobo, and more than ten other faculty members were forced to leave the department, in what was later described as the NTU Department of Philosophy Incident (Taida zhexuexi shijian). The state clamped down on the social and political activism that had developed since the Baodiao movement. As J. Bruce Jacobs observes, the basic one-party structure of the KMT state "—supported by the hard, if velvet-covered, fist of the security forces—remained to remind people not to wander too far in speech or print in exploring political liberalization. Democratization was still a distant dream."[45]

Needless to say, the attempt to silence this social and political activism did not spell the end of the return-to-reality generation. On the contrary, many awakened members of the postwar generation found alternative ways to realize their reformist aspirations, such as by researching the history of the Taiwan New Literature (chapter 4), by writing or supporting Nativist literature (chapter 5), or by researching the history of colonial resistance and getting involved in politics (chapter 6). The following three chapters are devoted to analyzing the relationship between the Nativist search for historical and cultural roots and engagement with the present situation, on the one hand, and the generational identity and national narration of the return-to-reality generation, on the other.

CHAPTER IV

The Rediscovery of Taiwan New Literature

In late January 1941 the father of Taiwan New Literature, Lai He, was on his deathbed. Yang Yunping (1906–2000), an important writer in his own right, recorded his last words: "After a short while, Lai He suddenly exclaimed: 'All we did in the New Literature movement was in vain!' Shocked, I gazed at him as he sat up, pressing his left hand on his aching heart. Anxious to comfort him, I said: 'No, no! Three decades from now, or even half a century on, people will still remember what we did.'"[1] On January 31, Lai He died.

It is easy to understand his pessimism. It was wartime; the colonial government-general was promoting the Kominka, or imperialization movement, in order to turn Taiwanese people into "real" Japanese subjects who would support the war with more enthusiasm. Monitored and mobilized by the Imperial Subject Public Service Association (Huangmin fenggonghui) and the Greater East Asia Writers' Association (Dadongya wenxuezhe dahui), local writers were allowed little creative autonomy. Indeed, "the individuality and potentiality of writers individually and collectively were suppressed. A policy of forced unity was implemented in order to develop a wartime cultural apparatus on the southern advance base of Taiwan."[2]

But as we shall see, Lai He was overly pessimistic. If, from beyond the grave, he knew how his writing would be ultimately received, he would be consoled: the New Literature was ultimately rediscovered.[3] Before discussing that rediscovery, we need some background on the history of the literature in question.

A Brief History of the New Literature

Under Japanese colonial rule, Taiwanese intellectuals gained access to modern Western political and cultural ideas through Japanese sources. They were also inspired by the Chinese Revolution of 1911, the May Fourth movement in 1919, and the "new culture" of China. In 1920, starting in Tokyo, a group of Taiwanese students and intellectuals organized to promote the idea of the autonomy of the colonized people of Taiwan and to pursue equal rights for them under Japanese rule. Part of this effort was dissemination of ideas in *Taiwan Youth* (*Taiwan qingnian*), which was later turned into the *Taiwan People's Newspaper* (*Taiwan minbao*). It became the voice of the suffering and demands of the colonized.[4]

Starting in the early 1920s, under the influence of the new literature movement in China, many Taiwanese intellectuals, such as Chen Xin (1893–1947), Huang Chengcong (1886–1963), Chen Duanming (1902–1984), Huang Chaoqin (1897–1972), and Zhang Wojun (1902–1955), were interested in how literature could help enlighten their fellow Taiwanese. These writers did not think classical Chinese (*wenyanwen*) literature by traditional literati was up to the task. They accused literati of being out of touch and treating literature as an idle pursuit rather than a means of enlightening the "masses" and of facilitating national revival. They called on Taiwanese writers to write in vernacular Mandarin (*baihua*), the language of the May Fourth writers.[5]

In the early 1930s, when political resistance was suppressed, another literary trend appeared. A group of young intellectuals, including Huang Shihui (1900–1945) and Guo Qiusheng (1904–1980), advocated a "Nativist literature" (*xiangtu wenxue*) in *Taiwan huawen*, an experimental writing system for the language spoken by the majority of Taiwanese, the Hoklo people.[6] Their literary achievements were modest, however.[7] Because of the promotional efforts from the early 1920s on, the so-called *Taiwan xinwenxue*, or "Taiwan New Literature," developed into a literary movement. It lasted until the Second Sino-Japanese War erupted in 1937. An increasing number of young authors, such as Yang Kui (1905–1985), Lü Heruo (1914–1951), Long Yingzong (1911–1999), and Wu Yongfu (1913–2008), who wrote in Japanese instead of Mandarin, began to establish their careers in literary circles from the early 1930s on.[8]

Whether they wrote in Taiwanized Mandarin, the Hoklo writing system, or Japanese, they were more or less forgotten for two decades following *guangfu,* the "Retrocession" of Taiwan to ROC rule. This chapter is about their rediscovery. What was crucial in the rediscovery was how to make sense of the colonial literary legacy. Not only "Taiwanese literature" but also "Taiwan" itself "is not a self-evident, preexisting category but a discursive and political construct that is continually being constituted and contested through a multifaceted process of 'writing,' literary or otherwise."[9] This involves a "politics of referential frames."[10] I discuss these frames in terms narrative templates.

The New Literature in the First Two Decades of the ROC Era

From 1946 to the eve of the February 28 Incident of 1947, an open controversy raged about the issue of whether the Taiwanese people had become degraded into a state of "servitude" (*nuhua*) during Japanese colonial rule.[11] To those who doubted Taiwanese people's integrity and Chinese identity, including officials of the Taiwan Provincial Administration and a number of Taiwanese who had served under the KMT on the mainland,[12] it was unlikely that writers such as Lai He had written out of a spirit of resistance. With every rediscovery of the New Literature, their resistance was stressed one more time by local Taiwanese intellectuals who refuted the *nuhua* arguments, which they believed were based on province-of-origin prejudice.

In August and December 1954 in the two "New Literature and New Drama Movement in Northern Taiwan" special issues (*Beibu xinwenxue, xinju yundong zhuanhao*) of the *Taipei Historical Documents Quarterly* (*Taibei wenwu*), the official organ of the Taipei City Archives Committee (Taibei-shi wenxian weiyuanhui), there were articles on the New Literature. These articles were written by older Taiwanese authors who had been born in the first decade of the twentieth century and had launched their literary careers in the mid-1920s. The December issue, however, was banned before distribution. The first open discussion of the Taiwan New Literature in the postwar period was nipped in the bud.[13]

Many writers who had contributed to these two issues went on to write about the New Literature in other obscure venues, including Wang Shilang (1908–1984),[14] Ye Shitao (1925–2008),[15] Wu Yingtao (1916–1971),[16] and Huang Deshi (1909–1999).[17] Highlighting "anti-Japanese resistance" as the defining character of the New Literature, they thought that the main motivation for literary creation under the Japanese was resistance and that the works themselves constituted acts of resistance. In this way, they drafted the New Literature into the Chinese "anti-Japanese resistance movement." Apparently this literary resistance was inspired by Chinese nationalism, and the writers in question acted out of a conscious sense of Chinese identity. Throwing off the yoke of colonial rule and returning to Chinese rule became their ultimate aim.

Now that Chinese rule over Taiwan had in fact been restored, these older Taiwanese writers believed that the New Literature writers had accomplished their mission and could go into honorable retirement. It went without saying that the younger generation of local Taiwanese writers, who grew up under the KMT, would write Chinese literature. In a nutshell, the answers senior local Taiwanese authors of modern literature with personal experience of Japanese rule gave to the questions "What was the Taiwan New Literature of the colonial period?" and "How is the New Literature relevant today?" conformed in large part to the model of collective memory of the colonial period authorized by the KMT government. Whether grudgingly or not, these writers of the older generation accepted the KMT's narrative template of history and interpreted their experience in its terms. But to the average young intellectual, their reminiscences barely registered.

Fifteen years or so younger than the other writers that had contributed to the 1954 retrospectives, Ye Shitao had started his literary career in Japanese in the final few years of the colonial era. He spent 1951 to 1954 in prison for involvement with "seditious individuals." From 1954 to 1965 he stayed out of literary circles. Two and a half decades after Lai He's death, in 1965, Ye published "Taiwan's Nativist Literature" (Taiwan de xiangtu wenxue). In this seminal article of local literary criticism, Ye used "the Nativist literature of this province" (bensheng de xiangtu wenxue) or "Taiwan's Nativist literature" (Taiwan de xiangtu wenxue) to refer to all modern Taiwanese literature, whether written in the colonial period or after, in nonexclusive contradistinction to "Chinese literature" (Zhongguo wenxue) and "World Literature" (*shijie wenxue*). He contemplated the history of the New Literature thus:

> The Nativist literature of this province in the Japanese occupation period had to be promoted, in order to activate the national spirit and guide the resistance against the Japanese. Historically, it had a necessary existence. The brilliance of its achievement is undeniable. However, does it still need to exist now, to be cherished, nurtured, or extolled? The answer is, of course, no. In the hearts of the younger generation of "postwar" writers, the Japanese are mere specters, shadows that may still evoke hazy, bloody memories that cannot be totally wiped away but are memories of what is gone, never to return again. The younger generation . . . is definitely less regionalistic. They have naturally dissolved into Chinese literature and gone on to strive to enter the echelons of World Literature. This is the final destination of Nativist literature, a goal of which the previous generation of writers could but dream.[18]

In July 1966 Ye took one of his literary forerunners, Wu Zhuoliu (1900–1976), to task for resisting this passage to World Literature, in an essay entitled "On Wu Zhuoliu" (Wu zhuoliu lun):

> Lacking a profound universality and story elements, Wu Zhuoliu's novels call to mind many of the major works of Upton Sinclair.
>
> Seeing the fate of the Taiwanese people as part of the life of all humanity and pursuing idealistic tendencies will guide Taiwanese writers onto the broad highway leading to the gate of World Literature. This is the task that every author dreams about. A work should begin from a certain native ground, exalt the glory of humanity, and rise to the universal, to the human nature common to all people. There is no doubt that this is the way most Taiwanese writers have chosen to go. It is indeed the right path to take. It's just that now our feet have been stuck so long in the mud of excessive notions about native soil that we find it hard to extricate ourselves. Many Taiwanese writers now live in a narrow cage, thinking it a kingdom. Although almost all great novels in the world are rooted in the soil, expressive of authentic nationality and redolent of native scents, they also reveal a

common human nature and destiny. . . . There's no denying that the native soil in Wu Zhuoliu's stories is rich, that the themes of his fiction are always related to the Taiwanese people and their customs, and that his stories often uncover unique systems, conditions, characters, as well as historical and social factors in the native land. But they lack an overarching idea of the human. Thus, some of his stories are scented so strongly with the native soil that one can get drunk on them. The spark of universal reason goes out, and the characters in his stories roll around in the local Taiwanese mud, crying and hollering in their own little world.

Though *Orphan of Asia* (*Yaxiya de guer*), which has become a classic in Taiwanese literary history, is not vulgar or clichéd, though it is a magnificent narrative poem . . . it is, unfortunately, technically and compositionally outmoded. In expression it is hackneyed. It lacks a clear sense of modernity, which prevents it from entering the list of World Literature masterpieces.

. . . Wu Zhuoliu cannot transcend the age in which he grew up and the air that he has breathed his whole life. His thought has already acquired a patina of the past. His writerly spirit lives on, and his creativity has not been exhausted; but we cannot expect another forceful flight from him.[19]

At the time, however, Ye Shitao, a former political prisoner and a primary school teacher, had an extremely limited audience.

In brief, despite the sporadic efforts by such senior authors as Wang Shilang, Huang Deshi, Wu Yingtao, and Ye Shitao to promote the memory of Taiwan's colonial literary legacy in the 1950s and 1960s, they aroused little public interest under the dominance of Chinese nationalism and the exilic nostalgia for the Chinese mainland. My thesis in this chapter is that it was the return-to-reality generation, rather than older writers like Wang, Huang, Wu, and Ye, who played the lead role in the vogue for the New Literature in the 1970s. These youths were the ones who actually popularized it and turned it into a focus of historical rediscovery.[20] Their investigation of this literary past was part of an uncoordinated project of constructing the collective memory of "the resistance of the Chinese (in Taiwan) to the Japanese." What this chapter discusses is not the history of Taiwanese colonial resistance itself but rather how this past was recalled in the 1970s. I focus on how the New Literature was discursively "nationalized" by the return-to-reality generation, that is, how it was characterized as a part of the national tradition of Chinese literature by incorporating it into the Chinese nationalist historical narrative. In the process they were engaged in a Chinese nationalist "invention of [Taiwanese] tradition."[21]

Chen Shaoting's Rediscovery of the New Literature

In the early 1970s the New Literature was rediscovered by the return-to-reality generation as the historical context of the reality they wanted to return to. It all started with an article by Chen Shaoting, the Pingdong-born local Taiwanese president of *The Intellectual*. In May 1972 Chen published "May Fourth and the New Literature Movement in Taiwan" (Wusi yu Taiwan xinwenxue yundong) in that journal. Chen defined the New Literature in terms of Chinese nationalist resistance:

> In Taiwan's literary arena in the latter part of the Japanese occupation, there was a spectacular New Literature movement. This movement began under the influence of the May Fourth new cultural movement of the ancestral land. It made a huge contribution to the enlightenment movement and the national anti-Japanese movement of this province [of Taiwan]. It was part of Taiwan's new culture movement. It was also a branch of the national anti-Japanese movement, one that was launched by Taiwanese compatriots. What we should also understand is that the national anti-Japanese movement in Taiwan was a Chinese nationalist movement that identified itself with the ancestral homeland of China. Therefore, in larger context, the New Literature movement in Taiwan can be described as part of the New Culture movement in China and thus a branch of the literary revolution of the May Fourth era.[22]

Chen further indicated that "during the long period of half a century, the Taiwanese compatriots were continually engaging in a national struggle with the Japanese rulers." This resistance occurred not just in the first part of the colonial period, when "there was constant violent resistance to

Japanese alien rule by Taiwanese compatriots," who "wrote an awful yet glorious page in the history of the children of the Yan Emperor and the Huang [Yellow] Emperor (Yan Huang zisun)." It also included the non-violent resistance from 1920 on, during which time "intellectual youth groups formed one after another in Tokyo, Taiwan, and the mainland . . . with the same founding aim: to liberate their compatriots and return to the ancestral homeland of China" (18–19).

In his conclusion, Chen summed up the "historical meaning" of the New Literature: "Clearly, the Taiwan New Literature movement came to a decisive close with the Retrocession—with Taiwan's return to the bosom of the ancestral land. Since Taiwan's literature was Chinese literature, naturally there was no longer any 'Taiwanese literature' (Taiwan wenxue) to speak of ('Nativist literature' is another question). This is to say that our forefathers who devoted themselves to the New Literature movement had proudly completed their historical mission" (24).

Chen's views overlap to a significant extent with those of the senior writers cited above. Like them, Chen stressed that the New Literature was part of Chinese literature and that anti-Japanese resistance was both its raison d'être and the driver of its development in the first place. To him, the resistance mission had been completed, and it went without saying that local Taiwanese writers and their works would be incorporated into the canon of Chinese literature after 1945, with no more need for Taiwanese writers to use "Taiwanese literature" to refer to their creative efforts. In fact, at the end of his article, Chen noted that the main works he had consulted were the two issues of *Taipei Historical Documents Quarterly* as well as the writings of Wang Shilang, Huang Deshi, and others.

What sets Chen Shaoting's account apart is that he expressed a much stronger sense of Chinese identity than his predecessors, who had grown up under Japanese colonial rule. He was more conspicuously using the paradigmatic historical narrative of Chinese nationalism (see table 0.1), with particular reference to the May Fourth movement. Indeed, his "reminiscences about Taiwan New Literature movement" were to honor the dedicated forerunners in the New Literature and to "commemorate the fifty-third anniversary of the May Fourth movement" (18). What did May Fourth mean to Chen?

Two years earlier, he had written another essay, about the May Fourth movement. It was the beginning of 1970, when the Diaoyutai territorial dispute had just started, *The Intellectual* had not yet been reorganized with Chen as president, and the Baodiao movement had not gathered momentum either overseas or in Taiwan. Highly influenced by the "modernization" discourse of Taiwanese academia in the 1960s, Chen Shaoting lamented the "impact of Western culture" over the past century, "which had caused massive and unprecedented change in China." To catch up with the West politically, economically, and culturally, he felt that the aspiration of "this generation of Chinese intellectuals" should be to "take up the unfinished May Fourth mission—the modernization of China": "Establishing a modernized China is undoubtedly the goal toward which this generation of Chinese intellectuals should strive. . . . From Western culture we have obtained science and democracy to nourish and enrich Chinese culture. Modernized, China will be not just a scientific and democratic China but also a humanist and rationalist China."[23] In other words, May Fourth to Chen meant Chinese modernity. One can discuss May Fourth and its importance to Chinese modernity anywhere, but Chen was doing so in Taiwan, and in the context of local literary production. To what end? Clearly, he was trying to cast local Taiwanese in leading roles in the development of a local articulation of Chinese modernity.

After "May Fourth and the New Literature Movement in Taiwan" appeared, many young intellectuals who cherished the ideal of returning to reality and native soil followed in Chen's footsteps and began exploring the New Literature. Their explorations contributed to the canonization of the literature of the colonial era.

In a symposium on "Taiwanese Literature and the anti-Japanese Resistance Movement in the Japanese Occupation Era" held by *The Intellectual* to commemorate the twenty-ninth anniversary of the Retrocession, Chen Shaoting commented: "The younger generation of local Taiwanese people seem not to understand very well the history of their fathers' and grandfathers' generations, creating an 'intellectual gap' between the two generations."[24] This was soon to change.

The Canonization of the New Literature

When they first discovered the New Literature, the return-to-reality generation castigated themselves for their ignorance and lamented the generation gap. At the same symposium, local Taiwanese poet Zhao Tianyi (1935–2020), who had in 1963 founded the Li Poetry Society (Li shishe) with Wu Yingtao and others, expressed a similar anxiety:

What's the definition of Taiwanese literature? What works count? I think that Taiwanese literature should be a branch of Chinese literature, but unfortunately during the Japanese occupation period Taiwanese authors had to write in an alien tongue, which created a rather peculiar process of development for Taiwanese literature within Chinese literature. It has given us a sense of a great gap between the older and younger generations. I remember Wu Yongfu of the Li Poetry Society once told me, "I really envy you young people for being able to write Chinese so well."[25] This should give the younger generation a lot of encouragement.

. . . I . . . always have the feeling of being cut off from the previous generation, so that when we're starting our literary creation we have to start from scratch in many respects, unable to take advantage of the strengths of tradition. This makes it imperative for us, the younger generation, to understand the literary achievements of the previous generation.[26]

Similar sentiments were expressed throughout the rest of the decade. In 1977 a young Mainlander professor of Chinese literature, Qi Yishou, was ashamed to say that due to the influence of Western culture, including literary modernism (see chapter 5), "I only heard about Yang Kui and read his works last year: that tells you how shut off we were."[27]

Nativist writer Chen Yingzhen deplored the fact that "almost no literary youth know Lai He, Yang Kui, and Lü Heruo."[28] For this reason he stressed that "the recognition and reevaluation of Taiwanese national resistance writers of the previous generation is without a doubt the most educational way for the new generation of Chinese literary artists in Taiwan to carry on and exalt this great and glorious tradition."[29]

In fact, they had been trying to educate themselves and the whole return-to-reality generation since late 1973. The second number of *Literary Season* (*Wenji*) (see also chapter 5), published in November 1973, included a special "Examination of Modern Chinese Writers [from Taiwan]." Zhang Liangze (1939–), Shi Junmei (the pen name of Tang Wenbiao, 1936–1985), and Liu Ruojun (?–?) wrote articles on local Taiwanese author Zhong Lihe (1915–1960), who grew up in the colonial era, traveled to Northeast China, and died in Taiwan. As a tribute to Zhong, a short story of his was reprinted.[30] In addition, this issue reprinted a short story by Yang Kui, a noted local Taiwanese author ten years older than Zhong Lihe but still strong and healthy.[31] Yang wrote in Japanese and started his literary career in the early 1930s, as mentioned earlier. These two authors were the representatives of the Taiwan New Literature of the colonial period most discussed in the 1970s, and *Literary Season* led the rediscovery of them and their works by the return-to-reality generation.

The third issue of *Literary Season*, published in May 1974, printed Lin Zaijue's (1951–) "A Retrospective Review of Taiwanese Literature in the Japanese Occupation Era" (Riju shidai Taiwan wenxue de huigu).[32] Compared with Chen Shaoting's short piece from two years before, Lin's article was a much more comprehensive attempt to examine the colonial literary legacy.

From then to the end of the decade, a steady stream of articles on deceased or still living senior local Taiwanese authors from the colonial era appeared in newspaper literary sections and literary journals. These articles included introductions, criticisms, special features, stories, and poems originally composed in Chinese, translations from the Japanese, and so on. Publishers brought out dedicated commemorative collections and complete works. There were treatments of specific authors and general treatises. In addition, reprints of many of the major magazines and newspapers relating to the New Literature appeared. In 1979 two comprehensive collections of New Literature works were published, including fiction, poetry, and prose from the colonial era as well as criticism. They were *Taiwan New Literature Under the Japanese Occupation, Ming Volumes (Riju xia Taiwan xinwenxue, mingji)*, in five volumes and *Complete Pre-Retrocession Taiwanese Literature (Guangfu qian Taiwan wenxue quanji)* in eight volumes, edited by Li Nanheng and by Zhong Zhaozheng and Ye Shitao, respectively.[33]

The critics who followed in Chen Shaoting's footsteps agreed with him about national identity, both of the writers of the New Literature and the scholars who studied it. The intense rediscovery represented a process of "nationalizing" or "re-Sinifying" Taiwanese colonial literature by narrating it as part of the Chinese nationalist narrative of history. By affirming the Chineseness of the literary legacy, many cultural activists of the return-to-reality generation affirmed their own Chineseness. Another local Taiwanese writer of the postwar generation who more than anyone else

affirmed his Chineseness, Chen Yingzhen, précised the political situation
and the response of the return-to-reality generation:

After 1970, due to changes in international politics and the domestic
social structure, an era of reflection and criticism began. The "Baodiao" movement aroused an upsurge in nationalism and patriotism
and stimulated social service and social survey movements. A social
consciousness and awareness developed for the first time among youth
of the postwar generation. With these changes, the literary trend
called "Nativist literature," which was committed to realism in literary creation, inspired a critique of modernist literature's dependency
on the West. The national belonging and style of literature as well as
its social function were all addressed. In literary history, recognition
and reappraisal of the previous generation's national resistance literature of the Province of Taiwan acquainted a new generation of youth
with the anti-imperial and antifeudal implications of the national
resistance literature from the era of Japanese rule.[34]

This rediscovery of the literary past was also one of the return-to-reality
generation's primary approaches to leaving exile and returning to Taiwanese social reality. Return-to-reality activists wished to pursue a closer connection with the land (*tudi*) and people (*renmin*) through the rediscovery of
the local literary past, which they understood in Chinese context. For
instance, the editorial note on the series Examination of Modern Chinese
Writers in *Literary Season* emphasized:

Chinese writers of the twentieth century have been lucky to face so
many challenges!
    They had to face the lingering roots of illness of feudal society as
well as the colonial poison brought in during the imperialist invasion, in order to establish a Chinese foundation for their works.
    They had to face the suffering of the Chinese nation and go to
war to resist autocracy, totalitarianism, and the politics of terror, in
order to establish the Chinese spirit of their works.
    Thus, [the modern Chinese writer] is no longer a literatus in his
study, enjoying the fruits of society. He must now enter society, erad-
icate selfishness, care for others, and keep learning in the reality in
order to become Chinese.

Chinese writers of the twentieth century have been exceptionally lucky to face so many challenges![35]

The biggest challenge of all was attaining national cultural autonomy. Zhang Liangze, one of the earliest to review and edit Zhong Lihe's works, explained why he objected to interpreting Zhong's writings solely as works of "silent endurance" (*yinren*):

> Zhong Lihe not only expressed a powerful nationalist spirit in his writings. His actions also proved how active he was by showing courageous willingness to participate and take a stand. This is why his writings are filled with such powerful sentiments of love and hate. On balance, one might sense both a deep love for and a heavy criticism of our nation and also a frank hatred for the alien [Japanese] race, whom he [nonetheless] treated with forgiveness. This indeed represented the Chinese mind and was where Zhong Lihe's spirit lay in.[36]

Just as Zhong Lihe had resisted colonial rule, so return-to-reality researchers resisted cultural invasion; their research was a form of resistance to foreign hegemony. It evinced an aspiration for cultural autonomy. Yu Tiancong, one of the cofounders of *Literary Season* (see chapter 5), put it this way:

> It's been over twenty years since I came to Taiwan [from the Chinese mainland]. Every time I remember those lines [from a poem by Qiu Fengjia, a scholar-official born in Taiwan in the late Qing dynasty] in our high school Chinese textbook—"The prime minister has the power to cede territory; the lone courtier is powerless to turn the situation around" (*zaixiang youquan neng gedi, guchen wuli ke huitian*)—I am always reminded of the special meaning Taiwanese Chinese literature has in the past century of Chinese history. The ceding of Taiwan [to Japan] shows the corruption of Chinese feudal society, while the occupation of Taiwan by imperialist Japan shows the brutality of international imperialism. If one says that the past hundred years of Chinese literature is built on a foundation of anti-imperialism and anti-feudalism, then Taiwanese Chinese literature shows this best, for it has resisted both foreign enemies and internal

oppressors. In the recent *Zhang Wojun Collection* (*Zhang Wojun wenji*) there's a piece called "Taiwan's Awful Literary Scene" (Zaogao de Taiwan wenxuejie) that talks about the decadent works produced under corrosive imperialist oppression. At the time Chinese literature in Taiwan had two aspects: there was a colonial literature of anti-imperialist resistance, and a colonial literature of submission to imperialism.

And then Taiwan was restored to China! For over twenty years we've enjoyed prosperity in many respects, but within prosperity we perceive a strong influence of highly developed industry and commerce on literature, a growing literary countercurrent—a decadent, defeatist, and escapist modernism. Although Taiwan is small, it represents the fighting spirit of five thousand years of Chinese culture. We hope everyone can bring his ability into play and leave behind a historic record of the achievement of the present age.[37]

Local Taiwanese members of the return-to-reality generation were the same—Zhang Liangze, for instance, was the first to discuss Zhong Lihe at the beginning of the 1970s. He has been credited with "having inaugurated research on Taiwanese literature."[38] In a later investigation of Yang Kui, Zhang Liangze traced the roots of Nativist literature in a more inclusive way than Ye Shitao had done in his article "Taiwan's Nativist Literature," mentioned earlier. Zhang traced the history of Nativist literature back to the reign of Ming dynasty loyalist Zheng Chenggong (Koxinga, 1661–1683) and described his personal development in detail:

It is only because of heartfelt affection for my native soil, with the sentiment and wisdom of China's five thousand year cultural heritage I have cherished since childhood, that I have entered the world of Taiwanese literature written during the fifty-year Japanese imperial rule and tried to trace a lineage from China's New Literature, in order to be able to declare to posterity: the "roots" that were broken when the mainland went red were transplanted to Taiwan.

Taiwan's Nativist literature is a branch of Chinese literature. It clearly begins with the mournful heroism of the poems of Ming loyalists and continues through periods of pacification and edification under Qing rule. Japanese rule inspired the patriotism and race-love of resistance fighters. And then the KMT government has brought the Confucian tradition to Taiwan. Having undergone all these trials, tiny streams have converged into a great river, which will flow for a hundred generations.

Especially during the Japanese occupation period, when writers were persecuted by an alien race and inspired by new global trends in thought after the Great War, including our National Father Sun Yatsen's republican revolution and the May Fourth New Literature movement, Taiwanese literature became especially diverse: there was the debate on new and old literature, and the difference between "resistance" and "collaboration."

Times have changed. Later generations probably will forgive the "collaborationist writers" for not having any choice. But in the same situation, there were "rebellious writers" who upheld the Han spirit. Like the tough grass resisting a stiff gale, they inspire respect. I want to spend the rest of my life researching authors like Lai He, Yang Kui, Wu Zhuoliu, Zhang Wenhuan, Zhang Shenqie, Lü Heruo, and Zhong Lihe, who had such strength of character. . . .

In recent years . . . many people have been discussing Taiwanese literature from the colonial era, which has given me the opportunity to publish what I've learned in my researches over the years and even seems to have created a trend in academic research. On this thirtieth anniversary of the Retrocession of Taiwan, when we look around at the various developments undertaken under government leadership one can but marvel at what has been achieved. Since everyone has witnessed the development of literature over the past three decades, I don't need to ramble on about it here. As for the painful memories from the fifty years prior to the Retrocession, I can't bear to recollect: let Yang Kui represent the seven writers I have been researching and serve as a partial record of the opposition to aggression and tyranny expressed in literature by our compatriots during the Japanese occupation period.[39]

Once the Chinese nationalist historical narrative became the frame of reference for the construction of collective memory, the entire corpus of Taiwan New Literature was either assumed to simply embody Chinese identity and a spirit of anti-Japanese resistance, as in Chen Shaoting's account, or divided into a literature of resistance and a literature of nonresistance, into "anti-imperialist colonial literature" and "submissive colonial literature," or into "rebellious" and "collaborative" literature, as in Yu Tiancong's and Zhang Liangze's interpretation. In either case, "anti-Japanese resistance" was posited as the defining feature of the New Literature. For instance, Lai He, who, as indicated earlier, was called the "Father of the Taiwan New Literature," had also been described as "an anti-Japanese warrior fighting for national liberation."[40] Another writer asserted that "a spirit of critique and resistance is the defining characteristic of the New Literature under the Japanese occupation and was the mission literature bore at this turning point in history," and that "Lai He was the pioneer in the formation of this kind of literary spirit."[41] The works of Wu Zhuoliu, whose representative novel is *Orphan of Asia*, were described as "recording the spirit of Chinese national anti-imperialist resistance as well as the journey of the national soul."[42] Zhang Shenqie (1904–1965), who in 1934 had led the formation of the Taiwan Literary League (Taiwan wenyi lianmeng) and the publication of the league's organ *Taiwan Literature* (*Taiwan wenyi*, 1934–1936), was praised in the following terms: "'A thoroughgoing nationalist' is his greatest glory."[43] Similarly, a poet who had died young, Yang Hua (1906–1936), was "the same as the great majority of the anti-Japanese resistance figures."[44] As for Wu Xinrong (1907–1967), an important figure in the "regional literature of Yanfen" (*yanfen didai wenxue*) in what is now Tainan City, he was extolled as a "red-blooded patriotic poet."[45] In addition, Wu Yongfu, who had participated in the establishment of the Taiwan Artistic Study Association (Taiwan yishu yanjiuhui) in Tokyo and had in 1933 published the literary journal *Formosa* (*Fuermosha*), wrote the poem "Ancestral Land" (Zuguo), which, together with his other works, was later said to represent "a lifelong wish to return to the bosom of the ancestral land."[46]

The Consecration of Yang Kui

Yang Kui had been the author who received the most attention since exploration of the New Literature began in the early 1970s.[47] But not all his works received equal attention. Yang Kui wrote many works, including fiction, prose, plays, criticism, and songs. But after *Literary Season* reprinted his work in November 1973, almost all the attention was focused on a few stories he wrote in a few years before and after 1945. Thematically, these stories dealt with the oppression and exploitation of the Taiwanese people under Japanese rule; the protagonists expressed a longing for a free and equal society. These works were, in other words, explicitly judgmental of Japanese colonialism.[48] To the editor of *Literary Season*, Yang Kui had "inherited that great tradition of determination and courage that our ancestral land displayed in its long resistance to the Japanese invasion."[49] This is why in the first essay in the 1970s that linked Zhong Lihe and Yang Kui together, Lin Zaijue asserted that Yang's works were representative of the "spirit of protest" in Taiwanese literature.[50]

The focus on Yang was partly due to the fact that "of senior local Taiwanese authors, Yang Kui was the only one who participated directly in the national liberation movement during the Japanese occupation period."[51] For this reason, the return-to-reality generation heaped praise on him: he was "the greatest giant and warrior in cultural circles" and a Chinese patriot who was "a venerable old hero of the Taiwanese people."[52] Yu Tiancong declared that Yang was "the local Taiwanese author who most embodied the national spirit during the Japanese rule period."[53] Zhang Liangze asserted that, "Of local anti-Japanese resistance authors, the one with the most 'foolhardy courage' was Yang Kui." Zhang, whose "vocation" was "to spend [his] whole life researching Taiwan's Nativist literature [in the Japanese colonial period]," might well have been content focusing on Yang Kui alone. "Without a doubt," he wrote, "researching Yang Kui is one of my most important goals."[54] Obvious limitations in Yang Kui's stories, such as type-cast characters, stereotypical plots, and contrived endings, did not detract from his legacy and were even expressly defended as part of the Chinese literary tradition or as praiseworthy, given Yang's powerful social conscience and concern for his compatriots.[55]

There was another reason why Yang Kui received such accolades: he was still hale and hearty in the 1970s. He was a real live resistance hero who could offer wise counsel. Descriptions of him by young intellectuals were filled with excitement over his presence. To them, Yang Kui was like "an ancient excavated ruin of historic value," "a famous anti-Japanese resistance writer who was a living part of modern Taiwanese history," and "a rare surviving anti-Japanese resistance writer."[56] Zheng Hongsheng once recollected that at the time Yang was "a flesh and blood participant in history" who gave university students and young intellectuals, including himself, a sense of the labor and farmer movements in the colonial period.[57]

In 1975 Yang Kui was officially canonized as a result of promotion by the return-to-reality generation. His short story "The Uncrushable Rose" (Yabubian de meiguihua, originally "Spring Sunshine Can't Be Shut Up") was included in the junior high school Chinese textbook for its "national consciousness."[58] Many teachers and students who "came in contact with a period in Taiwanese history" by reading Yang's story visited him.[59] In this regard, a blurb heaped the following fulsome praise on him:

> Among older local Taiwanese writers, none is more deserving of the commendation [from *Mencius*, about a great man whom] "force cannot master, nor poverty move" (*weiwu buneng qu, pinjian buneng yi*). His literary works are resoundingly majestic. He is the earliest author to get international recognition and is now in Taichung tending the Donghai Flower Garden (Donghai huayuan) near Tunghai University. There, he cultivates, reads, and writes. He has become one to whom young people "make a pilgrimage."[60]

The praise continued on the back cover:

> There is an old man who lives near Tunghai University. By day he waters the vegetables and the flowers; by night he writes works of literature. Young people often visit him. They say they are "pilgrims"! Whenever Donghai is mentioned what they think of is this old man. When you write him a letter you don't need to note the address: his name is enough. He is the writer Yang Kui. As a man he is irrepressible and resounding, just like his magnanimous literary works.

A young local Taiwanese man Lin Ruiming (1950–2018), who would go on to become a prominent writer and local literary historian, contributed greatly to the consecration of Yang Kui. Starting in about 1975, he devoted himself to studying Yang Kui's life, "to try to understand through a living person the age in which he lived and reconstruct some layers of history." To do so, Lin went to live with Yang for a year in the garden.[61] What drew him to Yang Kui? Lin wrote it was that Yang's stories depict the suffering of the Taiwanese people under Japanese rule:

> This was the fate that the Chinese people had endured together. This is the larger meaning of Yang Kui's works. He wrote about the background with which he was familiar, about the grief of the sons and daughters of China. These were not simply narrowly Nativist stories.

They had the characteristics that define the literature of 1930s China, and, in a broad sense, they are originally [part of] the harvest of Chinese literature.

The spirit of Yang Kui has already been revived by the younger generation.

This newfound strength is China's hope for the future.[62]

In his essay "A Portrait of Yang Kui" (Yang Kui huaxiang, 1977), Lin Ruiming noted that since *Literary Season* reprinted a story of Yang Kui's "Mainlanders . . . and young [Taiwanese] readers could finally have the chance to encounter a complete work by Yang Kui and get a preliminary sense of his literary activity. From that time on, more people started visiting Donghai Flower Garden"; "young people came to the garden for pleasure, but also to learn about life by getting a complete sense of Yang Kui's spirit."[63] In another work, Lin described Yang's achievement in the following terms:

After ten or twenty years of loneliness, the Donghai Flower Garden has become a busy place, with frequent visitors. Writers, scholars, university and middle school students, Chinese people, and foreigners . . . all kinds of people come. There are more introductions and commentaries appearing in newspapers and magazines.

Yang Kui, who had for a time been buried in obscurity, is now seeing livelier days.

Finally Yang Kui has defeated time.[64]

In the figure of an unremarkable old man watering the flowers, many young people saw the past that they were seeking to relate to the age to which they belonged. Many claimed that they came away from a visit to Yang Kui with the courage to face the future. In 1977, using the penname Lin Wengeng, Lin Zaijue wrote an introduction, or a confession, for Lin Ruiming's *A Portrait of Yang Kui* (Yang Kui huaxiang) that is worth citing in detail:

In the sixty-first year of the ROC calendar [1972], stunned by developments in Taiwan's international situation, I was, like most deeply shocked young people, in a state of powerful intellectual confusion. What we all felt most powerfully was the continuity of China's sorrowful fate over the previous century, and what we were most unclear about was national salvation. Luckily, with everyone's input, we came through discussion and reflection to have a central objective, which was to attend to the reality of Taiwan. However, to me this objective involved a huge problem of historical identity. This problem was: How could I link the reality I was observing to history? How to follow the continuity of history and figure out the possible direction of the change of this reality? And in what sense did the history of this reality belong to Chinese history? I thought hard about these issues but got no specific or concrete answers. I still felt deeply detached from the past. If we were detached from the past, how could we understand the past? If we did not understand the past, how could we come to grips with the present and observe reality?

When I was feeling most dejected, I met Yang Kui. The first time I visited him, he quietly and gently related certain fragments of modern Taiwanese history. It was news to me. When I was leaving, I borrowed a copy of a bilingual Chinese-Japanese edition of *The Paperboy (Songbaofu)*. I'll never forget how stunned I felt after I finished Yang Kui's work that evening. I found it hard to believe that in a period of history of which I was totally ignorant there could be such an outstanding work of literature. It was like the people oppressed and humiliated in the novel were riding the wave of history. Thus the door to history was opened unto me. My present reality was linked to the past, and the past returned to the source. The age of detachment was stitched whole again.

Through Yang Kui, who had experienced so many disasters unyieldingly, this period in history appeared in concrete form. Gradually, I came to know about Lai He, Yang Hua, Lü Heruo, Zhang Shenqie, Cai Huiru, Lin Youchun, Lin Xiantang, Jiang Weishui, and others. Through these people, I got a clearer understanding of the modern Taiwanese popular anti-Japanese resistance movement, and by understanding the nature of this movement I had a deeper understanding of the Chinese republican revolution. Thus, my individual life now had a sense of historical context, as did the contemporary reality we were trying to observe.[65]

In the first essay in the 1970s that compared Zhong Lihe with Yang Kui, Lin Zaijue explained what drew him to Yang Kui's stories:

In Yang Kui's stories, we see Sisyphus indignant, while in Zhong Lihe's stories we see Sisyphus resolute. As we are tossed and dazed in the tumult of history, as we encounter more and more irrationality in the world, we may return to the spirit of protest and quiet endurance and recover the everlasting source of life and history. Then we no longer feel intimidated or lonely. Now we have dignity.

Both Yang Kui's protest and Zhong Lihe's quiet endurance grew out of the native soil. In their blood rushed the happiness and pain of the people who live on this patch of earth.[66]

If Zhong Lihe, though deceased, could inspire love for the land in the hearts of young people and a sense of connection with national history, then Yang Kui, who was still among the living, was all the more inspirational. One university student watched from behind as Yang worked in the garden at sunset and saw "a page of living modern history."[67] Another young writer voiced his excitement at being able to connect his epoch and generation to Yang's:

In fact, they too live in our age, and we more or less possess their age. Between the two ages there is actually no boundary. A nation has so much life. Every year, month, and day new life comes into the world. At each moment in time there are people old and young living and growing, without real gaps between generations. Thus, they [our elders] have not yet become part of the past. They are still our contemporaries and our friends, friends who walk, breathe, and exist among us![68]

In the presence of Yang Kui, many members of the return-to-reality generation got a sense of the past of "our nation" and were able to relate that past to the present and future, thereby feeling moved, excited, and hopeful. But their sentiments were not produced in a vacuum. Their understanding of self, society, history, and related sentiments were elicited and informed by the Chinese nationalist narrative of history—the KMT-authorized frame of reference for collective memory—they had internalized at home and/or at school. The narrative was temporal, but like all such narratives it included all nationals, however widely separated in time and space, in an "imagined community."[69]

The older generation of Mainlander writers had taken notice. Zhu Xining (1927–1998) described Yang Kui as a "senior writer I have admired for a long time." To him, Yang was a "steely man of righteousness" and a "national orphan" who deserves the utmost respect for his resistance to Japanese rule.[70] Hu Qiuyuan claimed on the occasion of the publication of the collection of Yang's works in 1975 that "only then did I know there was a writer with such pure national sentiment." He went on to stress that this "simple old warrior" and "patriot-author" wrote about "the lives of Chinese people humiliated and damaged under Japanese colonial rule." Moreover, "the value of Yang Kui's works is that they represent not only the lives of the Chinese people of Taiwan but also the lives of the Chinese people of the mainland."[71]

The older generation of local Taiwanese writers took notice, too.

The Reentry of the Japanese-Educated Generation

Since he used the term "the Nativist literature of this province" or "Taiwan's Nativist literature" to refer to all the modern literature created by local Taiwanese authors in the colonial period and after in his article "Taiwan's Nativist Literature" (1965), Ye Shitao had also usually categorized writers, especially writers of fiction, of local Taiwanese background in terms of "generation." To him, by the 1970s, postwar Taiwan had witnessed four generations of local Taiwanese writers of modern literature: the colonial or prewar generation and the first, second, and third generations of postwar writers. The colonial generation had grown up under Japanese rule and achieved a reputation by writing in Japanese—think of Wu Zhuoliu, Yang Yunping, Huang Deshi, Lü Heruo, Yang Kui, Wang Shilang, Wu Yongfu, Long Yingzong, Wu Yingtao, and Zhang Wenhuan (1909–1978). The first postwar generation of local Taiwanese writers typically grew up during wartime and received their education in Japanese. Learning Mandarin Chinese on their own during the difficult early postwar years, they did not emerge as writers until the late 1950s. They included Zhong Lihe, Chen Huoquan (1908–1999), Li Rongchun (1914–1994), Shi Cuifeng (1925–2018), Zhong Zhaozheng (1925–2020), Liao Qingxiu (1927–), Wen Xin (Xu Bingchen, 1930–1987), and so on.[72] While a few elder members of the second generation received some Japanese education in the final years of Japanese rule, in general they grew up in the early postwar period, when Taiwan transitioned from an agricultural to a nascent industrial society, and had only vague memories of Japanese colonialism. Heavily influenced by Western literary trends, they included Zheng Qingwen (1932–2017), Li Qiao (1934–), Huang Chunming (1935–), Qideng Sheng (1939–), and Zhong Tiemin (1941–2011). As for the third-generation postwar local Taiwanese writers, they were represented by the lead Nativist writers in the 1970s other than Huang Chunming, such as Chen Yingzhen, Yang Qingchu (1940–), Wang Zhenhe (1940–1990), and Wang Tuo (1944–2016), to be discussed in chapter 5.[73]

Ye's categorization was based mainly on an age cohort definition of a generation, as noted in chapter 1, and partly on when a writer started his or her writing career. It was somewhat arbitrary in application. For example, although Huang Chunming was just one year older than Chen Yingzhen, and both began their careers at about the same time, they were classified into different generations. Still, Ye's categorization has become increasingly accepted as a useful way to make sense of the generational difference among local Taiwanese writers. I draw on this categorization. But in my analytical framework, which assumes a traumatic-event definition of a generation, the key Nativist writers in the 1970s, who belonged to the third generation of postwar local Taiwanese writers in Ye's sense, together with Huang Chunming, formed a major part of the return-to-reality generation that emerged from the postwar generation. As also delineated in chapter 1, in the context of 1970s Taiwan, "the postwar generation" denotes a broader, general population of young people who grew up after the Second World War ended, and by "the return-to-reality generation" I intend a notion of a group of awakened intellectual youth that is not defined by age but rather is precipitated out of this population by major traumatic events.[74]

Before the fiction of Chen Yingzhen, Huang Chunming, and other writers was termed "Nativist literature" in the early 1970s, many senior local Taiwanese writers had been using that term to refer to the literary output of local writers from the Japanese colonial period and after, as exemplified by Ye Shitao's 1965 article.[75] Such writers had been marginalized, shut out of mainstream channels of literary affirmation. In response, they formed their own channels in the 1960s. There was one channel for poets, and one mainly for writers of fiction. In March 1964 twelve local Taiwanese poets, including colonial-period figures such as Wu Yingtao, Chen Qianwu (1922–2012), and Lin Hengtai (1924–), as well as younger poets like Zhao Tianyi and Bai Qiu (1937–), who had grown up under the KMT and gone through the Chinese nationalist education system, founded the Li

Poetry Society, which launched the first issue of the *Li Poetry Magazine* (*Li shikan* 1964–), in June.

In April 1964 Wu Zhuoliu, who belonged to the colonial generation in Ye Shitao's categorization, founded *Taiwan Literature* (*Taiwan wenyi*, 1964–2003), which bore the same name as the organ of the Taiwan Literary League in the Japanese colonial period mentioned earlier. *Li Poetry Magazine* and *Taiwan Literature* represented the first relatively organized gathering of local Taiwanese writers since the February 28 Incident in 1947. From 1964, these two magazines became the gathering places and publication forums for most local Taiwanese writers of the older colonial generation and of the younger generation, which is to say the first and second generations in Ye's sense. The Chinese of local Taiwanese writers drawn together around *Taiwan Literature* in the 1960s, especially those of the first and second generations, was plain and simple. Moreover, they drew their material from their familiar surroundings. Stylistically, they were modest and moderate. In social or political terms, these writers evinced no particular ideological concerns.[76] Intentionally or not, they stayed away from, or at least were extremely hesitant in responding to, Taiwan's postwar political and social vicissitudes, including the return-to-reality trend.[77]

The Li poets felt the influence of resurgent Chinese nationalism in the Baodiao movement in 1971 earlier than the coterie of *Taiwan Literature* writers. They responded more readily to the return-to-native-soil trend. In October 1972, just five months after Chen Shaoting's essay "May Fourth and the New Literature Movement in Taiwan" appeared, *Li Poetry Magazine* established an occasional column entitled "Taiwan New Poetry Retrospective" (Taiwan xinshi de huigu), which introduced and discussed such colonial figures as Wu Xinrong, Guo Shuitan (1907–1995), and Wu Yongfu in the hope of increasing interest in the poetic achievements of local Taiwanese poets. In introducing older works by Wu Xinrong and Wu Yongfu, *Li* editors chose the former's "The Homeland Forces Have Arrived" (Zuguo jun laile) and the latter's "Orphan's Longing" (Guer zhi lian) and "Ancestral Land." In each case, they were stressing the yearning of local Taiwanese writers for liberation by their Chinese compatriots and their joy at the time of the Retrocession.[78]

As for writers associated with *Taiwan Literature*, only after Wu Zhuoliu's death in 1976 was there any coverage of the New Literature. The editorial baton was passed to Zhong Zhaozheng, who, like his peer Ye Shitao, belonged to the first postwar generation of local Taiwanese writers, a generation younger than Wu's. The first issue Zhong edited was March 1977, a "Special Issue of Research on Zhong Lihe and His Works" (Zhong Lihe zuopin yanjiu zhuanji). It was almost four years after the special issue on Zhong Lihe in *Literary Season* in November 1973. This time lag shows the detachment of the *Taiwan Literature* coterie of writers from society and politics and their unresponsiveness to sociopolitical change.

In this March 1977 issue, Ye Shitao and Zhang Liangze engaged in a dialogue on Zhong Lihe. The moderator was Peng Ruijin (1947–), who clearly indicated that the emphasis in the discussion was on examining "the place [of Zhong Lihe's works] in Taiwanese literary history or Chinese literary history."[79] As well, in 1979 *Taiwan Literature* brought out an issue of Chinese translations of works in Japanese by Taiwanese writers, including Yang Kui, Zhang Wenhuan, Long Yingzong, and Ye Shitao, among others. To Zhong Zhaozheng, "The New Literature of the Japanese occupation period . . . is part of our Chinese national cultural heritage . . . and what is most valuable is that the Nativist literary spirit—a spirit of resistance and of love of country and compatriots—has been passed on to the present, so that two different eras reflect and illuminate each other."[80]

From them on, there would be a dialogue between these older writers and the return-to-reality generation. The rediscovery of the Taiwan New Literature culminated in Chen Shaoting's *A Basic History of the Taiwan New Literature Movement* (*Taiwan xinwenxue yundong jianshi*) in May 1977. This book expanded on Chen's "May Fourth and the New Literature Movement in Taiwan," but the thesis was the same. The significance of the book was not so much the viewpoints it expressed as the context it was published in, right before the Nativist Literature Debate (*Xiangtu wenxue lunzhan*). The debate erupted from spring 1977 to early 1978. On the one hand were pro-KMT and radically anticommunist writers and critics who in general were Mainlanders and attacked "localism" and the putative "leftism" and political "separatism" of Nativist writers. On the other hand were writers and supporters of the Nativist literature who asserted their Chinese identity and defended their commitment to concern with social reality through literary creation.[81] In this context, the patriotism of the colonial Taiwanese writers like Yang Kui was reaffirmed.

Chen Shaoting clearly states in the afterword to *A Basic History of the Taiwan New Literature Movement* that the backbone of his book is Huang Deshi's essays published in the *Taipei Historical Documents Quarterly* in the mid-1950s, and he notes that Huang Deshi commented on a draft of the book and agreed to write a preface for it.[82] In his preface, Huang stated that the book "gives a clear and to-the-point bird's eye view of the New Literature movement before the Retrocession. It shows the reader the contours of this literary movement."[83] Ye Shitao wrote a glowing book review. He agreed with Chen Shaoting that "the Taiwan New Literature movement was the most important part of the revolutionary anti-Japanese resistance movement of our nation, as well as an embodiment of the republican revolution against imperialism and feudalism on the Chinese mainland that was inspired by [Sun Yatsen's] Three Principles of the People," and that it also "bore a strong nationalist literary hue right from the start." Ye also noted that "an unrelentingly stormy period" from the beginning of the 1970s had caused "a new generation of intellectuals" to realize that American and Japanese "colonizers" were oppressing their society, which in turn led them to a "rediscovery of their own magnificent native soil." According to Ye, Chen's book compiled an ideal set of materials about the native soil for young intellectuals, that it would "guide people in understanding the ins and outs of the Taiwan New Literature movement." Admiringly, Ye Shitao continued: "This is a really good book. It traces out the way for anyone of the future generation thinking of writing a thick *History of Taiwanese Literature*."[84] As Ye was thinking of doing.

In regard to Chen Shaoting's claim that the New Literature was part of the May Fourth movement, Ye wrote:

> It is especially in the last chapter, chapter 7, entitled "The Historical Meaning of Taiwan New Literature Movement," that one witnesses Mr. Chen Shaoting's hermeneutic brilliance. He points out that the New Literature movement occurred under the direct influence of May Fourth new culture movement. Although this point has been made in writing by others several times previously, his reaffirmation of the argument is forceful. Next, he says that the Taiwan New Literature movement began with linguistic reform (advocacy of the vernacular) and continued with an attack on old-style literature. Only then was there new literary creation. However, the New Literature movement was not completely a facsimile of the May Fourth movement but had its own particularity, which, in my opinion, is precisely Taiwan's own native particularity. Chen also discusses the New Literature as a wing of the national resistance movement that later became radical after a baptism by socialism. It is gratifying that this

argument is the same as what we [who lived through it all] observed. As for his statement that "the Taiwan New Literature movement came to a decisive close with the Retrocession—with Taiwan's return to the bosom of the ancestral land . . . naturally there was no longer any 'Taiwanese literature' to speak of (Nativist literature is another question)," it really is an incisive yet balanced remark. It is a fact that after the Retrocession "Taiwanese literature" became part of the past, but the promotion of Nativist literature had just gotten started, and now writers of the next generation have inherited the spirit of resistance of the New Literature and, weathering a storm of their own, are striving to turn the situation around![85]

From 1965, when he published "Taiwan's Nativist Literature," until the early 1970s, when the New Literature became a hot topic, Ye Shitao kept his critical attention focused on the local Taiwanese writers of the colonial and postwar periods. In fact, during this period Ye became the only major local Taiwanese literary critic of stories and novels. A senior author who had turned twenty under the Japanese, Ye helped define the meaning of the New Literature for the collective "we" from 1965 on. He became one of the major contributors to the construction of collective memory of the New Literature. Thus his review of Chen Shaoting's book is of considerable significance as an affirmation by a member of the older Taiwanese generation of the manner in which the return-to-reality generation had been investigating the New Literature.

In 1979 Ye Shitao and fellow local Taiwanese writer Zhong Zhaozheng, who both were twenty in 1945 and had to learn Mandarin Chinese after the Retrocession, collaborated on the editing of the eight-volume *Complete Pre-Retrocession Taiwanese Literature*, mentioned earlier. On the first page of the first volume, the executive editorial staff (Lin Ruiming et al.) explained the editorial aims and motives, stressing that "Taiwanese compatriots resisted Japanese imperialism violently or nonviolently for fifty years, writing a chapter of heroic agony in modern Chinese history. The New Literature movement under the Japanese occupation was not just part of the Chinese national cultural struggle against Japan, but also a movement of enlightenment in Taiwanese intellectual history. It has an indelible significance in the history of the new literature of modern China."[86]

A similar case is Wang Shilang's introduction to the five-volume collection *Taiwan New Literature Under the Japanese Occupation, Ming Volumes*, which Li Nanheng edited and published in 1979.[87] One of the volumes included most of the materials about the senior New Literature writers from the two special issues in *Taipei Historical Documents Quarterly* in the mid-1950s. In his introduction, Wang summarized the origin and development of the New Literature and reiterated the view he had expressed before the 1970s, that the New Literature was a branch of the anti-Japanese new culture movement. Moreover, it "matched the May Fourth new literature on the Chinese mainland step for step," and "its baseline was national ideology and national consciousness."[88]

The appearance in the late 1970s of Chen Shaoting's book as well as the two collections edited by Li Nanheng and by Zhong Zhaozheng and Ye Shitao marked the climax of the rediscovery of the New Literature, one of the main expressions of the return-to-native-soil cultural trend, which had begun in the wake of the Baodiao movement. It was the beginning of the end, however, the point at which the force of the Chinese nationalist historical narrative, which had informed the collective memory of the New Literature in the 1970s, began to fade.[89]

Let us return to Yang Yunping by Lai He's deathbed. In a way, Yang Yunping was right: the new literature written by Lai He and others found an audience both three decades later and half a century later. Three decades later, he found a wide audience among the return-to-reality generation. For this generation, Lai He and his peers were anti-Japanese heroes that embodied Chinese national consciousness. But half a century later, Lai He was understood in a very different way, in the context of the indigenization—or Taiwanization—of Taiwan's politics and culture.[90] A champion of Taiwanese nationalism, the literary historian Peng Ruijin commented:

> One can say that the birth of Taiwan New Literature was induced by the subjective desire of the Taiwanese people to have their own culture and further to have their own literature, and that it is a literature of ethnic character. . . . In the wake of the debate on traditional versus new literature in the 1920s . . . the task of the New Literature was to awaken the Taiwanese consciousness of the people of Taiwan, which in turn was started with raising the sense of attachment of the Taiwanese people to the land.[91]

There is no mention of the Chineseness of the writers. By this point, Ye Shitao was arguing that under Japanese colonial rule "the Taiwanese people belonged to the Han nation without being Chinese and had Japanese citizenship without being members of the Japanese nation," so that "the authors of the New Literature of Taiwan, who represented the collective voice of the Taiwanese people, increasingly developed their common longing, that is to say the idea that 'Taiwan is the Taiwan of the Taiwanese people.'"[92] Ye's peer Zhong Zhaozheng defined Taiwanese literature as "growing out of this land, this people, and this cultural background," which is to say as being "unrelated to Chinese literature." In Zhong's view, the Taiwan New Literature in the colonial period "was neither Chinese literature nor Japanese literature."[93]

Like many postcolonial societies, Taiwan has being dealing with the legacy of colonialism. What compounds this problem is that postwar Taiwan, especially since the 1970s, has been vexed with a conflict over national identity: Chinese or Taiwanese. The contrasting reception of the New Literature in the 1970s and 1990s shows how this conflict evolved. We turn to another aspect of the same conflict in chapter 5.

CHAPTER V

The Reception of Nativist Literature

During the Nativist Literature Debate period, which lasted from spring 1977 to early 1978, Huang Chunming's stories had been widely acclaimed as the epitome of this literary genre and become very popular. Huang was often invited to give talks, and one day in Taipei, the venue hall for a symposium organized by the intellectual-cultural magazine *China Tribune* (*Zhongguo luntan*) was crowded with a large number of excited participants. Talking about his writing interest and career, Huang confessed sentimentally that as a writer, he liked everyone and hoped to write about everyone. He took Taiwan's indigenous people (derogatorily referred to as "mountain compatriots" [*shandi tongbao*] in general at the time) as an example, saying that when he understood their life, he felt an impulse to narrate it into his stories. Suddenly, someone in the audience spoke up: "You don't care about a billion compatriots on the Chinese mainland; you just care about a hundred thousand mountain compatriots!"[1]

This anecdote regarding Nativist literature spoke volumes about a major aspect of the zeitgeist of the 1970s: the return-to-reality and return-to-native-soil cultural trend under the dominance of Chinese nationalism and nostalgic irredentism. This chapter is about the relationship between the rise of Nativist literature and the formation of the return-to-reality generation. I will argue that Nativist literature can be understood in terms of a generation gap. The return-to-reality generation was finally able to emplot themselves in the Chinese nationalist narrative of history in a very different way from that of their parents. They came out of exile to go to the people and write stories about the people.

In doing so, they entered sensitive terrain, because they were being Chinese in a way that raised hackles in the ruling elite, who belonged to previous generations. The nationalist education the ruling elite had arranged for students who would become part of the return-to-reality generation had unintended consequences, namely, "anti-imperial and anticapitalist consciousness" that was strenuously criticized by pro-establishment figures during the Nativist Literature Debate.[2] Harshly and, it must have seemed, unfairly criticized during this debate, Nativist writers would remain staunchly Chinese in national identity for the next few years, but the debate marked the beginning of the end, an end that was a new beginning: in the final sections of this chapter I will discuss the ways in which the literary Nativism of the 1970s was reinterpreted in the 1980s and 1990s, when an explicitly Taiwanese national narrative came to the fore.

The Generation Gap in the Rise of Nativist Literature

Yu Tiancong and colleagues founded *Literature Quarterly* (*Wenxue jikan*) (October 1966–February 1970), the forerunner of *Literary Season*. It was in *Literature Quarterly* that the important stories of the three main Nativist writers, Chen Yingzhen, Huang Chunming, and Wang Zhenhe, would first be published. They were soon celebrated for their straightforward, realistic depictions of small-town folks in the 1970s. Chen, Huang, and Wang were joined in the 1970s, when Nativist literature had become an important literary trend, by the likes of Yang Qingchu and Wang Tuo.[3]

In August 1973 one of the main venues of literary Nativism was founded, *Literary Season*. As we saw in chapter 4, *Literary Season* was a venue for the rediscovery of Taiwan New Literature by the return-to-reality generation. It also nurtured Huang Chunming, Wang Zhenhe, and Chen Yingzhen, the main Nativist writers of the 1970s, all of whom were local Taiwanese. The very first issue included "Sayōnara-Goodbye" (Shayaonala-zaijian), a landmark story by Huang Chunming.[4] This story was a stylistic change of direction. In the late 1960s Huang had depicted the miseries of common people in impoverished rural villages with great affection; now, with a strong socially critical awareness, he portrayed urban life ironically.

There was a noticeable change in the literary atmosphere, as *xiangtu* (native soil) and *xianshi* (reality) became catchphrases in discussions of literature. Over the next several years, up to the start of the Nativist Literature Debate in 1977, a stream of essays supporting Nativist literature appeared in newspapers and magazines. Wang Tuo joined Chen Yingzhen and Yu Tiancong as one of the major Nativist literature theorists.

Nativist literature was mainly fiction, and the key common feature Nativist writers shared was their realist tendency. According to Joseph Lau, the major themes in Nativist literature were (1) criticism of Japanese and American "imperialism," especially economic and cultural imperialism; (2) demands for a more equitable distribution of wealth and for social welfare reform; (3) eulogizing of the basic virtues of "the little guy" or the common man from rural villages and small towns; and (4) the idea that Chinese people should uphold national pride rather than emulate the shameless and coarse behavior of "ugly Americans" or "greedy and lustful Japanese."[5]

What deserves more attention is the generational identity of the writers. All of them belonged to the return-to-reality generation. Yang Qing-chu, in an interview at the end of 1974, was asked, "Given that Taiwanese people, like you, in their thirties and forties live in a time of great social change, as an author, which do you feel has influenced you the most, China, the West or Japan?" Yang replied:

I was born in the twenty-ninth year of the ROC calendar [1940]. I was five years old at the time of the Retrocession, young and ignorant of the true countenance of the Japanese people, of whose deeds I had only heard. I've written a few stories set in the Japanese occupation period based on what I've learned from my elders. The writers Zheng Qingwen and Li Qiao are both older than me by six or seven years. They went to school in Japanese and can read Japanese literary works. They have, I imagine, absorbed something from the Japanese. I've met a lot of people in their mid-forties who got a Japanese education. These people think like Japanese people. They understand Japanese people as well as Chinese people. The change in era has given them a comparative perspective. They're always comparing the Chinese and Japanese ways of doing things and making moral judgments based on their views of the Japanese spirit. They hate how the Japanese oppressed their compatriots, but in certain respects they admire the Japanese. They are fluent in Japanese but can't use Chinese to write formal documents or even to express their views of things. Their linguistic incompetence leaves them at a loss for words. Faced with corruption in society or anything else they don't like the looks of, they follow their Japanese spirit and vent their views in conversation. I've heard enough to know. When I was young, I felt these people, these "slaves of the powerful country," were bad to the bone, but now that I'm older I can think and judge for myself. I can understand them now. They may talk about the Japanese spirit, but what they're really doing is rather pathetically trying to protect their own rice bowls. In regarding them, I see the Chineseness of my own countenance. As for Japanese literature, I've only read it in Chinese translation. What I've read seems light, soft. I don't think much of it. Japanese literature has not had much influence on me.

I've never been abroad to drink the ink of the Western ocean. I read Chinese books. Among these three [China, the West, and Japan], of course China has had the greatest influence on me. Yet I am not able to read Chinese literary works of the 1930s and have read a number of world classics in translation, so that in terms of fictional technique and certain conceptions I've been influenced quite a bit by the West.

But what's influenced me the most is not books but the Taiwan folk sentiment. I've gotten sustenance from the people. My works are written out of the folk way of life, out of the folk way of thinking, out of what ordinary people want in this life, and out of my own "basic instincts."[6]

Yang's avowal is a classic example of the effectiveness of Chinese nationalist indoctrination in the formation of the postwar generation. The KMT had tightly controlled and filtered Chinese influence. For instance, the works of leftist writers from the 1930s were unavailable to Yang. A critical perspective was unavailable to him, except the official line: his father's generation had been given a slave's education. Yang's generation believed this, and that they had had a good childhood. They had enjoyed prosperity, stability, and a proper Chinese education. Yang Qingchu's national identity was successfully Sinified, which opened a generation gap between him and his parents, to the extent that the younger generation felt no qualms at publicly censuring the older generation as no better than lackeys of imperialist Japan.[7]

But the government did not want or anticipate two things: the attraction Western culture had held for young people, and "Taiwan folk sentiment," which Yang claims influenced him the most. In this respect he, like Chen Yingzhen, Huang Chunming, Wang Zhenhe, and Wang Tuo, was different from most young Mainlanders. Indeed, provincial background was a core factor in the development of Nativist literature, as the older Mainlander literary critic He Xin (1922–1998) has remarked:

> Mr. Jiang Menglin asked writers to understand thoroughly the reality of this time and place by going to rural villages and to cities to make observations. His hope is gradually (it's impossible for it to happen overnight) starting to be expressed in the works of young writers who grew up in Taiwan's farming communities, young people who received an education enabling them to use Mandarin to aptly express their thoughts and feelings. They have deep-seated feelings about farming villages, about farmers and their way of life. If they have met more workers, then they have a deep love for workers and understand everything about them—their misery, hope, and happiness. Emotionally, writers who still see Taiwan as a place they're just visiting cannot really understand these things.[8]

From a generational perspective, writers in the 1970s such as Chen Yingzhen, Wang Zhenhe, Yang Qingchu, and Wang Tuo comprised the third generation of postwar local Taiwanese writers in Ye Shitao's classification. Huang Chunming, as noted earlier, actually shared a similar generational background with them, as he was just one year older than them. Thus far, it would seem as if the rise of Nativist literature can be explained in terms of a generation gap in the local Taiwanese population. There are two complications however: one to do with writers, the other with readers.

First, the first- and second-generation postwar local Taiwanese writers embraced Taiwan folk sentiment and accepted and even understood it in terms of a Chinese nationalist narrative of history. I will discuss Ye Shitao, who can represent senior writers like Li Qiao, Zhong Zhaozheng, Zheng Qingwen, and the like, below. Here let me say a few words about the Li Poetry Society as the main gathering place for most local Taiwanese poets. As noted in chapter 4, they responded almost immediately to the Baodiao movement by researching the New Literature of the colonial period. They also commented on current events. The Li poet Li Kuixian (1937–), who belonged to the postwar generation, even wrote a series of poems about the Diaoyutais.[9] At the end of 1980 Li Kuixian reminisced about the period of change the Li poets underwent from 1969 to 1974. He said that early on they were in favor of "vernacularized" poetry, while later they felt poetry had to intervene in or deal with daily life, believing that poetry's new objective was to record social reality. As a result, "national consciousness became even more conspicuous."[10] They also realized that they belonged to a generation distinct from their parents and grandparents. Another Li poet, Zhao Tianyi, wrote a poem called ""Sheishuo women bushi xingfu de yidai" (Who says we aren't a fortunate generation?).[11]

For the Li poets in the 1970s, an age of resurgent Chinese nationalism and a return to native soil in culture, "local culture was linked to Chinese culture," while "Taiwanese literature," including "pre-Retrocession Taiwanese literature," was all "part of Chinese literature."[12] In this period, the goals pursued by Li poets diversified. Nativism was added to ideals like "Chineseness" and "modernity" in the 1960s. Zhao Tianyi waxed lyrical about the "Nativist spirit": "In modern China, in a China fighting for democracy and freedom, a Chinese poet should be neither a blind inheritor of tradition, nor a fawning adulator of the West, but rather a defender of his native soil, a singer of a vital and steady music!"[13] Like other members of the return-to-reality generation, they accepted the prevailing Chinese nationalist narrative of history, in which they positioned themselves as modern poets dedicated to a free China and to a poetry at once Chinese, modern, and Nativist. These attitudes and ideals were typical of the return-to-reality generation, whether in terms of national identity, historical consciousness, or self-expectation.

Second, the generation gap between the return-to-reality generation and previous generations is equally important for Mainlanders, because the return-to-reality generation, regardless of provincial background, formed the readership of Nativist literature. As He Xin put it: "Young readers, no matter what home province is listed on their household registration, all grew up here. Their hearts are naturally here. As for their homelands, whether they be along the Great Wall or in the hilly country around Guilin, they've only heard about them or read about them in their textbooks. They no longer have the older generation's 'intense homesickness.' All these have helped the reception of literary works about the here and now."[14] In talking about the "reportage literature" (*baodao wenxue*), which recorded social reality and had developed under the stimulus of Nativist literature,

He Xin discussed why the awakened members of the postwar generation was such a receptive audience for it:

A new readership has formed, mainly young intellectuals and youth who are entering the middle class. It is completely different from the audience of twenty years ago, or even ten years ago. They are no longer in bondage to the past. They no longer have a sense of

Swallows who flew in front of the halls of illustrious families
Now fly through the homes of common folk.

They do not have experiences of the struggles against the Japanese and the Communists [on the Chinese mainland] which have weighed down the souls of their previous generation. To them these struggles are distant, part of history. International political changes over the past few years have sapped their confidence in the dependability of diplomatic allies. These young people no longer adulate American culture. They've turned inward. Now they are getting to know themselves. This is what people call identifying with oneself. This change has produced a powerful appeal: to understand oneself and build one's own culture. These young people in their thirties were born on Taiwan and have grown up here. This explains why they are most concerned about their native land, the place where they were born and bred.[15]

Nativist writers and their readers belonged to the return-to-reality generation. As He Xin emphasized, this generation's formation began at a time when Taiwan was confronting major international political change. The next section discusses their awakening due to this change.

Nativist Writers' Awakening, Return to Reality, and the Nationalist Historical Narrative

The main writers and supporters of Nativist literature were an important "generation unit" within the return-to-reality generation. Like the rest of the generation, they reacted against the rootlessness of young intellectuals in the 1960s, and against their Westernization. As Chen Yingzhen once wrote, intellectuals in the 1960s had "taken all standards from the West."[16] For those awakened by the national crisis beginning from the Diaoyutai incident, all this had changed ever since. For Yu Tiancong, it was a wake-up call; for Chen Yingzhen, it was "the watershed of a change in thinking," as both of them emphasized in 1978.[17] The year before, in 1977, Chen had commented:

> The eruption of the "Diaoyutai incident" was the first time the patriotic sentiments and nationalist feelings of the younger postwar generation were inspired, the first time we truly had a sense of national crisis, of dependency upon foreign powers. In the past, our feelings and ideas about China were based on the begonia leaf shape on the map. We learned about modern Chinese history in class, about imperialist incursions. We felt indignant about it for a while but quickly forget. Only after the Baodiao movement did youth truly start participating in the fate of the nation in the real movement.[18]

In an interview, Wang Tuo discussed the incidents that had influenced him the most, the "turning points in his life," the biggest of which was the Diaoyutai incident.

> Because of the incident, we came to understand how to take action and how to think theoretically. We think about how this whole nation and state has turned out like this. In looking for reasons and pursuing knowledge, we've discovered the crux of the problem. . . . At the time there were so many young people demanding social reform from so many different perspectives. Politically, they realized that the complete reelection of all national parliamentary representatives is the key to solving Taiwan's political problems.[19]

Convinced that the solution to Taiwan's travails was political, Wang, like many young return-to-reality intellectuals, sought a political solution by joining the Dangwai opposition and becoming a Dangwai candidate in the National Assembly election in 1978. But he also thought that Nativist literature was part of the solution:

> We can reach a simple conclusion about Taiwanese society in this period: due to the impact of major international incidents and unequal

domestic economic development, an intense national and social consciousness has developed in opposition to imperialism as well as economic colonialism or compradorism. It tells us we must love country and nation and show concern for the livelihood of the masses.

This is the background to the vigorous development of "Nativist literature."[20]

It was part of the solution if this literature helped people love country and nation and show concern for the common man. There is, at any rate, in the recollections of Yu Tiancong, Chen Yingzhen, and Wang Tuo a clear turn toward society, country, and nation. They had a newfound sense that social concern and nationalism should be the inspirations for literature. They oriented themselves around the issue of the role of the individual in the fate of the nation. All of which illustrates how they found agency when they cast themselves in roles in the Chinese nationalist historical narrative. They now had a well-defined position, a part to play, a sense of the meaning of individual and collective existence, a personal and generational identity.

Another major Nativist writer, Huang Chunming, in a speech in early 1978, looked back on the way his writing had changed, how he went from sympathetic depictions of the sufferings of ordinary people in impoverished villages or small towns to highly critical and analytical representations of urban life, how his new works were informed by an understanding of political and economic relations between Taiwan and the United States or Japan as being characterized by "dependency." This, along with the cases of Yu Tiancong, Chen Yingzhen, and Wang Tuo, is a clear example of "conscientization" (see chapter 1). Huang Chunming claimed that it was not until the early 1970s that he "saw [his] own past clearly and understood the relations between self and society." Only then did he find "a path of spiritual development and begin to think deeper." He admitted that only after this discovery, his stories were filled with a strong sense of "the social." He went on:

If we take the trunk of a divine tree as a metaphor for our nation and our society, then we are leaves; and the time we spend on the branch is only for photosynthesis. When we fall to the ground we are fertilizer. Our individual lives are short, but the trunk of the tree represents the striving and conscientiousness of every leaf. A tree that is five thousand years old [like the Chinese nation] has had five thousand seasons of budding and falling leaves. My writing experiences may be a total failure, but I still hope to become a writer, to be a leaf together with all the other leaves on a wondrous tree, sacrificing myself for the sake of our society, our country, and our nation.[21]

To the KMT government and (generally Mainlander) staunch anti-communist writers and critics, the development of Nativist literature was reminiscent of the leftist social-realist literature of the 1930s, which critiqued KMT rule, and of the "literature of workers, farmers, and soldiers" (*gongnongbing wenxue*) advocated by Mao Zedong. Its local color did nothing to endear it to these same critics, who attacked it in such terms during the Nativist Literature Debate from spring 1977 to early 1978.

But however "rooted in the soil of real Taiwanese society" Nativist literature was, or however critical, it was not a form of separatism that set Taiwanese nationalism against Chinese nationalism.[22] For instance, in reply to the criticism that Nativist literature was too narrow to be able to reflect the problems of China, Huang Chunming explained that, "Because Taiwan is part of China, we use the Chinese language to write about life and problems in these surroundings. This is our national literature. It is a literature born and bred in Taiwan, but it is also a literature of our China."[23] Similarly, Yang Qingchu claimed that "anything written with setting in some part of China about the social reality there is Chinese Nativist literature." He defined Nativism as follows: "Recently some intellectuals have started a trend toward writing about our native land. They all want writers to stop losing themselves by following Westerners. They want writers to instead do their own thing for their own society. There are both Mainlander and local Taiwanese proponents of this idea. This is a social need. I don't think anyone has a narrow concept of locality."[24]

In fact, Yang Qingchu and his Nativist peers felt a strong sense of Chinese national identity, particularly a spiritual kinship with the May Fourth activists, and with the writers of the New Literature of the colonial era (see chapter 4). Nativist writers of the postwar generation like Chen Yingzhen, Huang Chunming, Wang Zhenhe, Yang Qingchu, and Wang Tuo, on the one hand, and New Literature writers in the 1920s and 1930s under the Japanese, on the other hand, were linked together by being written into the same Chinese nationalist historical narrative. Hence Qi Yishou, in discussing the social concern of Taiwanese Nativist writers in the early

1930s as well as the debate about experiments with writing in Taiwanese, emphasized:

> Though there was no conclusion to the "Nativist literature" debate, which lasted for over two years during the Japanese occupation era, both sides in the debate evinced opposition to the corrosive assimilation of foreign colonial culture and stressed a self-respecting national spirit. It cannot be denied that writers of the new generation who grew up after the Retrocession and who are about forty years old now, such as Wang Zhenhe, Huang Chunming, Chen Yingzhen, Yang Qingchu, and Wang Tuo, have a certain kindred closeness [to their predecessors in the Japanese colonial period]. Although these authors got lost in flashy, foreign culture as they were growing up, it was only for a short time, after which they quickly corrected themselves and rooted themselves in the soil of the nation. In this way, their works, in comparison with those by writers who have gotten caught up in the psychology of a traveler or an immigrant, have a distinctive flavor. Perhaps this is why they are called contemporary Nativist writers.[25]

Nativist writers themselves in the 1970s also used this narrative frame of reference to understand their nativist predecessors, whether on the mainland or in Taiwan. Chen Yingzhen felt that "Chinese literary works . . . from 'Country Village in August' (*Bayue de xiangcun*) by a writer from northeastern China [called Xiao Jun] to Taiwanese works like 'Sayōnara-Goodbye' [by Huang Chunming] and 'Little Lin Comes to Taipei' (*Xiaolin lai Taibei*) [by Wang Zhenhe] were written at different periods in history in service of the great Chinese anti-imperialist nationalist movement."[26] Also for instance, Wang Tuo: "From the Japanese colonial period to the victory in the Anti-Japanese War, Chinese literature on Taiwan" was "a typically Taiwanese Nativist literature," in that spiritually it expressed "a national spirit and a sense of social justice in opposition to imperialism, feudalism, and oppression." Taiwanese literature's "resistance to imperialist incursion and domestic feudal exploitation was the same as that of the May Fourth new cultural movement and all subsequent movements" in the same tradition.[27] Finally, another prominent Nativist writer, Yang Qingchu: "Taiwan's Nativist literature can be traced back to local writers in the Japanese occupation period like Yang Kui, Lai He, and so on. . . . Now, twenty or thirty years [after the Retrocession,] a new generation who have grown up here and put roots down in Taiwanese soil wants to write about this land and depict the loves and hates" of people living here.[28]

The accusation made by the KMT or by individual critics that there was political separatism lurking in the localism of Nativist literature was baseless. Hsiao Hsinhuang's research on the background of the participants in the Nativist Literature Debate has shown that as in the case of the influences of literary modernism on writers in the 1960s (see also chapter 2), "provincial background was not a crucial defining factor. The most important sociological variable was literary and societal ideology and identity." In the debate, many Mainlander writers or even political commentators who embraced Chinese nationalism supported the mainly local Taiwanese Nativist writers. The Nativist consciousness expressed in the debate was actually "a kind of blending of 'Taiwanese consciousness' (social consciousness) and 'Chinese consciousness' (nationalism)."[29] Obviously, the return-to-reality and return-to-native-soil ideals laid a foundation for indigenized consciousness or Taiwanese consciousness oriented toward Taiwan nationalism, which eventually emerged in the 1980s, but were not themselves inspired by Taiwanese nationalism.

The Critique of Literary Modernism

I noted in chapter 1 that the generation units Karl Mannheim studied were, for him, ideologically defined, for instance, conservatives versus progressives. The three generation units I have studied in this book can be seen as both conservative and progressive. They sought their cultural roots, but they also challenged the state as much as they could in the 1970s. Many of the literary Nativists' opponents were modernists. They were modernists partly in the sense of being in favor of modernization, and they tended to be degraded as being aligned with the authorities, whom they saw as the agents and orchestrators of modernization. As Sung-sheng Yvonne Chang noted, in the Nativist-modernist contention, the modernists "had been used as scapegoats for an unbridled outburst of antigovernment sentiment."[30] However they are to be characterized on the conservative-progressive spectrum, the Nativists and the modernists as literary figures came into open conflict at two times in the 1970s, in the Nativist attack on modernist poetry in 1972–1973 and in the modernist/establishment counterattack on Nativist literature in the Nativist Literature Debate in 1977–1978. This section is mainly concerned with the first conflict.[31]

The first conflict was mainly over poetry. In the first issue of *Literary Season* in August 1973, there were some critiques of Ouyang Zi, who wrote stories inspired by soap operas and Freud and had nothing particularly Taiwanese to them,[32] but most of the criticism was directed at poetry. The editorial statement of this issue evinces a discontent with modernist literature.[33] The issue included Tang Wenbiao's well-known attack on modern poetry in Taiwan and Hong Kong.[34]

Critics continued to eviscerate literary modernism for years. For instance: "Modernist literature, especially modern poetry, is a spiritual colonization by Western modernism and individualism. In expression and content it is muddled and escapist; in language it is obscure, peevish, and very hazy. In poetic circles, it indulges in its jargonistic taste, and it backs away from the popularization of the tool of language in the May Fourth literary revolution."[35] Such attacks were launched against modern poetry, but they also broached the fundamental meaning of literature's existence, especially creative motivation and the relationship between literature and its wider context, including society, nation, and state.

For Zhao Zhiti, modernist poetry raised questions like, "Is literature created for the public? Can its mimesis and critique lead to social progress? What has it contributed to the development of our nation?"[36] Another critic asked, "What have the poets achieved? Where's the accomplishment? What role does their poetry play and what place does it have in the hoary Chinese literary tradition? What witness, true and heartfelt, has it borne of our lives here and now?"[37] In a nutshell, all these critiques were accusing modernist poets of not being "national" and "social" enough. The critics were mainly members of the return-to-reality generation.[38]

It was felt that the "Special Commentary Issue" (*pinglun zhuanhao*) (July 1973) of *Poetry Journal of the Dragon Nation* (*Longzu shikan*), the magazine of the Dragon Nation Poetry Society (Longzu shishe), founded in January 1971 mainly by a group of young local Taiwanese poets with a strong Chinese national consciousness and concern about social reality, had "spent the most time and effort reflecting on modernist poetry and had done the best job of it."[39] The planner and editor of this issue was Gao Xinjiang, a Mainlander. He had served on the magazine committee of *The Intellectual*.[40] Gao related that

> as if jolted awake by spring thunder, we heard critical voices everywhere, from different levels and directions in society; it was like

everyone was waking up and confronting the features and meanings of modern poetry. There was general and extended discussion in academic and artistic circles, and even the poets themselves joined in. . . .
. . . This discussion was significantly different from every previous debate on new poetry—most of the critics were young generation scholars, poets, or academics closely connected with the poets and concerned about new poetry.[41]

He argued that "a major trend is that readers and writers are together demanding that modern poetry have a sense of 'belonging.' Temporally, they expect a certain connection to tradition. Spatially, they hope for a true response to reality."[42] In asking writers of modern poetry to attend to tradition and reality, he was emphasizing the "national" and the "social" in literature—the twin values that emerged during the Modern Poetry Debate (*Xiandaishi lunzhan*) of 1972–1973 and throughout the 1970s were the characteristic qualities that advocates of social reform and a return to the culture of native soil aspired to achieve.[43]

What was the referent of "native soil"? Under the prevailing exilic mentality characterized by the nostalgia for Chinese mainland in postwar Taiwan, its meaning was not necessarily clear for many. For Mainlander literary critic He Xin, who came of age in China, it was in China. "Where is the 'native soil'?" he asked, with rhetorical irony. "Maybe over four thousand years of [traditional Chinese] culture is too distant and too grand? All we can do is return to our 'native soil' here and now, which is a return to the folk narrowly conceived."[44] For the return-to-reality generation, the native soil of the here and now was not narrow and was every bit as grand as places in China. Regardless of provincial origin, Taiwan was the only "Chinese" social reality they were familiar with. For them, concern for Taiwan was concern for China. Gao Xinjiang castigated the writers of modern poetry for "blindly abandoning tradition and refusing to recognize social reality," by which he meant the Taiwanese corner of China:

Over a hundred years of disaster, imperialist invasion and oppression, and the shame of history and present reality, the common people have experienced the pain of migration and destitution. . . . What can we do to cherish this broken land and these flesh and blood compatriots? When we see how gentle and decent Chinese people stumble under the weight of history and stand up again, how they bleed and sweat silently while building our national civilization which has continued for thousands of years, what do we feel in our hearts? When we enter the coal mines at Ruifang [Taipei County at the time] or the salt fields at Eliao [then-Tainan County] or when we confront the site of a shipwreck at Yunlin, how humble and careful should we be in our written expressions? When we remember that right now across the narrow [Taiwan] Strait we have so many suffering fathers and brothers with the same blood flowing in their veins, compatriots who have been deprived of dignity, who have gritted their teeth and held in their tears of hatred while living meanly and dying meanly, how could we follow people [like the modernist poets] in fooling around, making jokes, going in for vapid obscurity or even aggressive absurdity? How could we bear to do this? Especially in the past two years, with the changes in the international situation and the domestic social structure, we have been smelling something new in the air. The younger generation has become aware of the importance of facing reality and getting closer to the social and national background. Young people believe more and more that if we do not love this land which has borne and nourished us, if we do not get to know it and shed blood and sweat in hard work, we are fated to become the most pitiful, shame-faced, and irresponsible people in history.[45]

Gao Xinjiang affirmed the Chineseness of Taiwan's domestic political and social problems, just as the local Taiwanese Chen Shaoting had constructed the Chineseness of the colonial New Literature as part of the native cultural tradition. Chen wondered about writers of literature in general, Gao about poetry. Both drew on the same narrative model of national history.

The rest of this chapter, by reviewing the literary criticism of senior writer Ye Shitao from the 1960s to the 1990s, deals with how this model was used to make sense of the Nativist literature of the 1970s and its displacement by a competing model.

Ye Shitao's Reception of Nativist Literature
Before the 1980s

As noted in chapter 4, from 1965, when he published "Taiwan's Nativist Literature," to the early 1970s, Ye Shitao was the only major local Taiwanese literary critic who focused on stories and novels created by local Taiwanese writers. To the local Taiwanese writers who were marginalized until the 1970s, Ye's many introductory and review articles were of great encouragement. To many local Taiwanese fiction writers in the orbit of *Taiwan Literature*, Ye was their champion. For example, Zhong Zhaozheng once said he had always depended on Ye Shitao: "I always felt that as long as Ye Shitao was with us—as a group we had nobody to help us or listen to us complain—it was as if there was a massive column propping up the sky. At the least, he supported a small, rather pathetic literary scene. I was willing to believe that with his critical and creative pen there would come a day when we could win a place in the literary firmament."[46]

In his pioneering essay in 1965, Ye Shitao conceived of the distinctiveness and the potential of "the Nativist literature of this province" in this way:

The province's specific historical background, local conditions shaped by the subtropical climate subject to typhoons, linguistic and cultural marks left by the Japanese, customs and practices developing under separation from the mainland, and so on are not completely the same as those of the mainland. Therefore, is this not a rich source of materials for an author? I feel that excavating this distinctiveness and probing this particularity can add new territory to this Chinese literature of ours.[47]

In another article Ye wrote in this period, he reviewed the local Taiwanese writers and works he had covered in the two years from 1966 to 1967 in *Taiwan Literature*:

Over the past two years, this province's writers and works have shaken off the tendency to regionalism. In description, some works have gone beyond the scope of the province, of the sociopolitical and moral problems of a single area. They have reached the point of symbolizing Chinese national commonality. In the future, as we put our hands to rebuilding our country [when the mainland is retaken], the more outstanding works of literature of this province may in this way become a kind of standard or beacon.

Yet although our provincial literature is gradually breaking away of regionalism and rising into universality, this in no way implies that it has lost its local color. While considerable progress has been made in literary technique and expression, local color can still pulsate in each and every work. . . . We are not attacking innovation and modernization in fiction; nor are we encouraging everyone to bury his head in the sand like an ostrich and shut himself up in the old ways. Yet to overlook native soil consciousness is to lose the national style, without which literature has no reason to exist.

In the tide of World Literature, our provincial literature is still limited to a small corner space, extremely inferior in quality and quantity. This is the time to develop our strengths and correct our weaknesses, to strive to put tradition and modernity into a crucible in which we forge our own unique style: this is the correct direction to take.[48]

These quotations show that in this period the advice Ye Shitao frequently gave local Taiwanese fiction writers was to continue finding and representing local color, but not to the point of narrow regionalism. To his mind, creation should begin, not end, with the native environment. The more general, national or universal existential quality should not be sacrificed on the altar of the specific.[49] To Ye Shitao, Taiwan's local culture was a branch of Han Chinese culture, so that to preserve local culture was to illustrate the national style. As for "local color," it was actually "the concentration of the local sentiments of all of China." Ye felt that the difference in historical situation between Taiwan and China—the former ruled directly by Japan, the latter carved up into spheres of influence—was immaterial, that the same anti-imperialism and antifeudalism was operating in writers (and in people in general) on both sides of the Taiwan Strait. To him, the ultimate aim of local Taiwanese writers should be to raise Nativist literature to the levels of Chinese and then of World Literature. In the mid-1970s, when he and Yang Qingchu were interviewed together, Ye Shitao put it even more directly, warning of the danger of a mode of thinking that came naturally to any local Taiwanese writer, of taking the here and now as one's home: "if Nativist consciousness does not expand to include China and the world then these works will be nothing more than 'songs of self-consolation.'"[50]

At the end of his 1966 essay "On Wu Zhuoliu," cited in chapter 4, Ye Shitao wrote: "A younger generation of Taiwanese writers has come onto the stage: the curtain has been raised on a new golden age."[51] Ye did not indicate who the young writers coming onto the stage were, but he must have been thinking of Chen Yingzhen, Wang Zhenhe, and Huang Chunming. He regarded the mainly third generation postwar local Taiwanese writers as distinct from his generation, the last to experience Japanese colonialism, and the first and second generations in the postwar period:

> The society in which the third generation of authors have grown up is a society in which primary industrialization had already achieved a success. Gradually, they enjoyed richer material lifestyles and a more complete education. They started to reflect on the problems and spiritual poverty of industrial society. They went back to the roots of their national cultural tradition. Thus protests and accusations arising out of their nationalism fill their souls. Even if they have returned to the *xiangtu* principles of writing of the first generation of writers, they are different: their concern is aspects of real life here and now and not the departed spirits of past [Japanese] rulers. They oppose economic invasion and neocolonialism. They are a group of staunch nationalists.[52]

In the early 1980s Ye Shitao was, in retrospect, even more forthright about, and also somewhat admiring of, the Nativist fiction of the 1970s, which he claimed was not as "hackneyed" as earlier Nativist fiction: "It may be that the new generation of writers does not quite approve of the Nativist literature of older authors whose Taiwanese indigenized consciousness was stronger, and that these younger writers are better able to think about the way ahead for Taiwanese literature in terms of China's destiny as a whole. This might be progress."[53] That Ye was still appealing to China's destiny in 1984 attests to the endurance of the Chinese nationalist narrative of history in terms of which he and several generations of Taiwanese writers understood themselves. As applied to literature, the narrative can be analyzed as table 5.1, whose theme can be said to be "seeking national Chineseness in local Taiwaneseness." This literary narrative template was obviously shaped by the Sinocentric or "grand China" historical outlook sanctioned by the KMT, as summarized in the table. In this narrative, Nativist literature of the 1970s and colonial Taiwan New Literature were linked together because they were emplotted in a broader context of objectives and beliefs into episodes of the dominant master narrative.

TABLE 5.1

The Chinese Nationalist Narrative Template of Taiwan's
Nativist Literature

Narrator/protagonist	The Chinese people or nation
Time frame	From the Japanese occupation period
Theme	Nativist literature's journey from Taiwan to China: seeking the national style in local color, seeking the national character in regional particularity, and seeking modernity in tradition
Plot	**Beginning:** Taiwan New Literature, a form of Nativist literature by Taiwanese authors, as part of the anticolonial resistance against Japan displayed the intent to return to the national fold and embodied the national spirit.
	Middle: After the Retrocession of Taiwan, Nativist literature is again a branch of Chinese literature. At the beginning of the 1970s there is the rise of the third generation of local Taiwanese Nativist writers as committed Chinese nationalists.
	End: Having found a balance between "native soil" and "nation," Nativist literature naturally becomes part of Chinese literature and is even raised to the level of World Literature.

Nativist Literature in the 1980s: Inclusion

To the members of the *Li Poetry Magazine* and *Taiwan Literature*, the call at the beginning of the 1970s for a literature of social concern as well as the attention to Chen Yingzhen and other Nativist writers amounted to an affirmation of their approach, employing the plain style to deal with the local materials (see chapter 4). When they understood the writings of local Taiwanese authors since the colonial period according to their own local consciousness, which was informed by Chinese national identity, they came to value themselves more highly. By the late 1970s the first- and second-generation postwar local Taiwanese writers associated with both the *Li Poetry Magazine* and *Taiwan Literature* had started to portray themselves as the source of Taiwanese Nativism in general. Peng Ruijin, an editor at *Taiwan Literature*, wrote: "Submerged for three decades, the New Literature of the Japanese occupation period is now getting a chance at reaffirmation. A Nativist undercurrent that had been flowing for thirty years finally gushed out as a great literary convulsion in the 1970s. We might as well ask ourselves whether we have any reason to lack confidence. Creation is the greatest truth. The seeds of literature can remain dormant indefinitely, lying buried in the earth."[54]

In praising the first- and second-generation writers as the source of Nativist literature, the people at the *Li Poetry Magazine* and *Taiwan Literature* were taking credit where credit was not due. They were ignoring the fact that colonial period and first- and second-generation postwar authors played little role in starting either the vogue for the New Literature of the 1920s and 1930s or the Nativist literary trend of the 1970s.

The *Li Poetry Magazine* and *Taiwan Literature* coteries felt they represented the true Nativist literature, a tendency that got stronger in the first half of the 1980s when their political orientations began changing. My earlier research has shown that the Kaohsiung Incident at the end of 1979 (see chapter 6) and the radical Dangwai challenge to KMT rule in the early 1980s, including the promotion of a nationalist "Taiwanese consciousness," stimulated criticism of the KMT in the literary field.[55] In fact, *Li Poetry Magazine* and *Taiwan Literature* members developed a close relationship with the Dangwai in this period and participated in the opposition movement.[56] Also in this period, they started trying to "de-Sinify" (*qu Zhongguohua*) the literature of local Taiwanese writers, interpreting it as a Taiwanese tradition. This tradition, they argued, had little or no connection with modern Chinese literature from the May Fourth period on. Thus for both groups, *xiangtu wenxue* (Nativist literature) was gradually recharacterized as *bentu wenxue* (indigenized literature) and then as *Taiwan wenxue* (Taiwanese literature).[57] In this process, especially the members of the Li Poetry Society, who had played little role in initiating literary Nativism in the 1970s, rationalized their nonparticipation: they "had always been walking this [Nativist literary] road, so why engage in pointless disputation." The

Li poets felt that the awareness and practice of the "true Nativist poetry"—a plain style, social content, sensitive to the age—had emerged before the 1970s with the founding of the *Li Poetry Magazine* in 1964, because the Li poets "from the start proceeded from a realist poetic outlook firmly rooted in native soil and originating in life." Thus they declared that the "true Nativist literature began with *Li Poetry Magazine*," that the magazine "planted the seeds for the Nativist Literature Debate of the 1970s, seeds that also caused Taiwan's new poetry to grow away from internationalization and towards nativization." Thus the *Li Poetry Magazine* and *Taiwan Literature* came to be called "two literary bases rich in Nativist spirit" by their own members or supporters.[58]

In the discourse of de-Sinification expounded by members of the *Li Poetry Magazine* and *Taiwan Literature*, the "Taiwanese people" (*Taiwanren*) were gradually constructed as victims of a series of harsh periods of alien colonial rule and as "orphans" abandoned by China as the ancestral land. Taiwanese literature was described as the reflection of the experience of the Taiwanese people, as a tradition characterized by engagement, resistance, and indigenization.[59] As part of the construction of collective memory of Taiwanese literature in a Taiwanese nationalist framework, the Nativist literature of the 1970s was appropriated into the distinctive new historical narrative.

In fact, the first people to use this kind of Taiwanese nationalist reference framework to reposition Nativist literature of the return-to-reality generation may well have been proponents of Taiwanese consciousness in the Dangwai. The Taiwanese consciousness they advocated was no longer simply a natural love of native soil but a nationalist political stance. In the first half of the 1980s Dangwai proponents of Taiwanese consciousness attacked the Chinese consciousness of the KMT and of leftist opponents to the KMT, especially Chen Yingzhen and his colleagues at *China Tide Review* (*Xiachao luntan*). Chen had always maintained that Taiwan's history and literature should be understood from an anti-imperialist and antifeudal Chinese nationalist perspective and had argued that what people like Ye Shitao called "Taiwan's Nativist literature" should actually be termed "Chinese literature in Taiwan" (*zai Taiwan de Zhongguo wenxue*).[60] Because of his position of strident Chinese nationalism, Chen became a frequent target for Dangwai proponents of Taiwanese consciousness in the 1980s. For instance, in July 1983 the journal *Roots* (*Shenggen*), which was part of the main vehicle for the Dangwai's discourse of Taiwanese consciousness, the *Cultivate* (*Shengeng*) magazine network, published Chen Shuhong's article criticizing Chen Yingzhen's view of Taiwan history and Taiwan's Nativist literature. This article paralleled Nativist literature of the 1970s with the Dangwai opposition movement and described both as inevitable results of the long development of Taiwanese consciousness.[61]

Later, in January 1984, Chen Fangming (using the pen name Song Dongyang), a local Taiwanese member of the Dragon Nation Poetry Society who underwent a change in national identity toward Taiwanese nationalism in the late 1970s when he was studying in Seattle,[62] published the oft-cited article "The Present Problem of the Indigenization of Taiwanese Literature" (Xianjieduan Taiwan wenxue bentuhua de wenti) in *Taiwan Literature*. This article attacked Chen Yingzhen and accepted Chen Shuhong's definition of Taiwanese consciousness. It also identified the Nativist Literature Debate as a watershed in the development of Taiwanese literature. To Chen Fangming, the significance of the debate was that it defined two opposing positions in the field of postwar Taiwanese literature, represented by the "exilic mentality" (*liuwang xintai*) and "lone-minister consciousness" (*guchen yishi*) in "anticommunist literature" (*fangong wenxue*) of Mainlander writers, on the one hand, and by the sense of loss, of "orphan consciousness" (*guer yishi*) in literature of local Taiwanese writers, in which resistance to the Japanese is a frequent theme, on the other.[63] According to Chen, "the orphan consciousness [of local Taiwanese authors] was filtered and purified in the Nativist Literature Debate. As a result, the mentality of vacillation and friendlessness was transformed into a strong identification with the native land of Taiwan."[64] In another article in the same period, Chen Fangming affirmed even more confidently that the "orphan literature" (*guer wenxue*) of Wu Zhuoliu, Zhong Lihe, Zhong Zhaozheng, and others in the 1950s and 1960s was important to the spiritual development of Nativist literature in the 1970s.[65]

In the latter half of the 1980s, after the DPP was founded in 1986, members of *Li Poetry Magazine* and *Taiwan Literature* formed closer and closer relationships with the political opposition movement, in which many of them took part. At a time when the Taiwan Independence movement was making clear gains, members of these two groups played a leading role in constructing the cultural discourse of Taiwanese nationalism in the latter half of the 1980s and in the 1990s. Their ideas about Taiwanese literature became more radical in the 1990s. They de-Sinified Taiwanese literature and at the same time "nationalized" it in an alternative way, postulating an origin for Taiwanese literature thousands of years ago in the myths, legends, and songs of the Taiwanese aborigines, so that Taiwanese literature became a multiethnic literary tradition. They also interpreted the entire development of modern Taiwanese literature of local Taiwanese writers as the expression of an evolving Taiwanese national identity. In other words, Taiwanese literature was given a national character and represented as the literary tradition of a distinct Taiwanese people. In this way, they constructed the concept of *Taiwan minzu wenxue*, a "Taiwanese national literature."[66]

Two classic expressions of the transformation stage from de-Sinification to (Taiwanese) nationalization in the late 1980s and early 1990s were Ye Shitao's *An Outline History of Taiwanese Literature* (*Taiwan wenxue shigang*) and Peng Ruijin's *Forty Years of Taiwan's New Literature Movement* (*Taiwan xinwenxue yundong sishi nian*).[67] In this period, the Taiwanese literary discourse constructed by members of the Li Poetry Society and *Taiwan Literature* linked Nativist literature and the political opposition movement more clearly than before, seeing the former as an organic part of the latter and an embodiment of Taiwanese consciousness. To them, the emergence in 1964 of *Li Poetry Magazine* and *Taiwan Literature* represented the clear establishment of a Taiwanese consciousness with a clear anti-KMT and anti-Chinese nationalist tendency. They believed that on the eve of the Nativist Literature Debate, this consciousness had matured.[68] The focus of the debate was viewed as "national identity."[69] They even claimed that the debate "led to the ascendance of indigenized local consciousness and the Kaohsiung Incident" of 1979 as well as the various social and political movements in the late 1980s and early 1990s.[70] As for the setback Taiwan's political opposition movement faced in the Kaohsiung Incident (see chapter 6), it was explained that it was like "the severe setbacks and attacks Taiwanese literature encountered when it desired to indigenize itself through the Nativist literary movement" in the 1970s.[71] By this time, Ye Shitao's national identity had changed. He now claimed that "the Nativist Literature Debate was but the tip of the iceberg of the Taiwanese people's struggle for liberty and democracy."[72]

From the 1980s to the early 1990s, members of the Li Poetry Society and *Taiwan Literature* underwent a change in national identity. They also changed the way they represented the developmental experience of Taiwanese literature. The two changes occurred at about the same time and were closely interrelated. In the process, the collective boundary or identity of the Taiwanese people or nation was defined. The experience of literary development was represented in relation to this new historical subject, the Taiwanese people or nation. It was given significance by being linked to the particular collective identity. Indeed, it became a symbolic resource on which the construction of the Taiwanese people or Taiwanese national identity depended.

The place that Nativist literature of the 1970s had in the discourse of "Taiwanese (national) literature" shows that in the change in national identity experienced by the members of the Li Poetry Society and *Taiwan Literature* at this time, there was a deeper change in the reference framework that informed understanding from a Chinese nationalist one to a Taiwanese nationalist one. Nativist literature was incorporated into the collective memory of Taiwanese national literature as part of its developmental narrative. In the process, the cultural and political meaning of Nativist literature of the 1970s changed. No longer provincial or local, it was now national. This literature and the debate about it were now symbolic of the establishment of Taiwanese consciousness and the arousal of oppositional political sentiments. The narrative elements of this new nationalist understanding of Taiwanese literature and the place of the Nativist literature of the 1970s therein are presented in table 5.2.

As related earlier, what led to the stories by Chen Yingzhen, Huang Chunming, and other Nativist writers being taken seriously in the 1970s was the return-to-native-soil trend infused with Chinese nationalism. It was mainly a third postwar generation phenomenon, and local Taiwanese colonial and first- and second-generation postwar authors at the Li Poetry Society or *Taiwan Literature* did not play an active role in it, either in the wave of Nativist literature or in the Nativist Literature Debate. Be that as it may, since the 1980s, the 1970s had been gradually reinterpreted by the members of the Li Poetry Society and *Taiwan Literature* as an important part of the collective memory of Taiwanese (national) literature.

Local Taiwanese writer Chen Yingzhen, on the other hand, never changed his Chinese nationalist position. In commenting on the change in national identity of certain writers and the new construction of the collective memory of Taiwanese literature, Chen gave a description that closely

TABLE 5.2

The Taiwanese Nationalist Narrative Template of "Taiwanese Literature"

Narrator/protagonist	The Taiwanese people or nation
Time frame	From the beginning of Taiwanese history, especially since the Japanese colonial period in the 1920s
Theme	Taiwanese literature is a realist literature that describes and reflects the historical experience of the Taiwanese people, including historical experience of oppression by and resistance to foreign rulers, and their longing for liberation and quest for an independent and autonomous governmental system. Having its own unique development, Taiwanese literature does not belong to the literature of any foreign ruler, especially not to Chinese literature.
Plot	**Beginning:** The development of aboriginal literature over thousands of years and of Taiwan New Literature during the Japanese colonial period as part of the cultural resistance movement, displaying Taiwanese consciousness in pursuit of autonomy.
	Middle: After the war, local Taiwanese authors continued creation in difficult and lonely times, upholding the tradition of Taiwanese literature under the name of "Nativist literature." In the 1960s the founding of the *Li Petry Magazine* and *Taiwan Literature* represented the establishment of Taiwanese consciousness. The development in the 1970s of Nativist literature represented the maturity of Taiwanese consciousness. In the 1980s the terms "Nativist literature" and "indigenized literature" were finally rectified to "Taiwanese literature." Since the beginning of the 1990s, Taiwanese literature's "subjectivity" (*zhutixing*) has been becoming independent and autonomous.
	End: Having promoted the establishment of an independent and autonomous political system and possessing its own autonomy, Taiwanese literature becomes part of World Literature.

matches the analysis of the historical process presented in this chapter, even though in a Sinocentric, derogatory way:

> In the 1970s, Taiwan writers and intellectuals mostly believed in the connectedness and unity of Taiwan and China in history, culture, and identity and in fact. The separatist notion of a Taiwanese literature in distinction to Chinese literature pretty much did not exist in the 1970s. . . . From the Modern Poetry Debate [of 1972–1973] to the political miasma of the Nativist Literature Debate, there is almost no record direct or indirect of any current Taiwan independence leader, writer, poet, critic or theorist taking a stand on a separatist understanding of Taiwanese literature.[73]

Nativist Literature in the 1990s: Exclusion

In the early 1990s, at a time of increasing political liberalization when there was less of a taboo against public discussion of national identity, a different symbolic meaning was ascribed to the Nativist literature of the 1970s. This was a time when Taiwanese nationalists were constructing another collective memory of Taiwanese literature. This new construct can be described as "exclusionary," in contrast to the earlier "inclusionary" construct, which had interpreted the Nativist literature of the 1970s as part of the long development of Taiwanese nationalism. The new narrative construct wrote this Nativist literature off as the work of Chinese nationalists. The new narrative was more stridently Taiwanese in national identity, and Ye Shitao's and Peng Ruijin's views were representative of it.

In *An Outline History of Taiwanese Literature*, published in 1987, Ye no longer praised the Chinese nationalist Nativists of the return-to-reality generation in the 1970s so highly.[74] On the contrary, he felt that:

> Although the writers of the younger generation [such as Huang Chunming and Chen Yingzhen] at *Literature Quarterly* and *Literary Season* found creative materials in Taiwan's social reality, they dealt with the materials from a larger third-world or Chinese perspective. This approach is clearly different from *Taiwan Literature*'s deep commitment to native soil. . . . They measured Taiwanese reality in terms of changes on the Chinese mainland . . . but politically,

today's "mainland" is no longer the "ancestral land," as it was in the Japanese occupation period. Thus their thinking lacks a solid foundation in reality and is unrealizable.[75]

Apparently, roughly from 1984 to 1987, Ye Shitao had undergone a drastic reorientation in national identity. So did Peng Ruijin. In his *Forty Years of Taiwan's New Literature Movement*, he criticized *Literary Season* in the following terms:

> Although the *Literary Season*'s literary beliefs in going to the people, embracing the world, confronting the times, and participating in life . . . were not in contradiction with literature with an indigenized consciousness, they did not approve of plain and honest indigenized literature. On the one hand their literature bore the burden of "the fate of the Chinese nation." On the other hand . . . they couldn't see what was before their eyes, the Taiwanese people. Their literary humanism was just another un-self-critical pretense.[76]

Here is his take on the Nativist side in the Nativist Literature Debate: local Taiwanese writers of the Japanese colonial period and the first and second postwar generations were "authentically rooted in the earth" and remained aloof from the Nativist Literature Debate, while the "defenders of Nativist literature [i.e., Chen Yingzhen, Yu Tiancong, and his colleagues of the *Literary Season* coterie] would become obstinate opponents of the emergence of indigenized consciousness."[77] This from a critic who had, in the immediate aftermath of the Nativist Literature Debate, claimed that one of the positive meanings of that debate was that it made many realize that "Nativist literature should be developed into a new stage where a [Chinese] national literature can be affirmed."[78]

By the end of the 1990s Ye Shitao was overlooking the fact that there were both local Taiwanese and Mainlanders among the university students and young intellectuals inspired by Chinese nationalism who engaged in the Baodiao movement in the early 1970s, while it is true that Mainlanders played a leading role.[79] He seemed to think the activists were all Mainlanders. Some other facts that he overlooked were that the mainly local Taiwanese membership of the Li Poetry Society and *Taiwan Literature* (including himself) had regarded local Taiwanese writings from the colonial-period New Literature on as part of Chinese literature. This is how Ye Shitao remembered the 1970s in the late 1990s: "The Diaoyutai incident . . . led intellectuals connected with Taiwan domestically and abroad to join an upsurge of fanatic nationalist demonstrations and protest activities. This nationalism was Chinese nationalism and had nothing to do with a consciousness of Taiwan as a subject. Thus it didn't become an activity in which the Taiwanese people participated. The main leaders were Mainlander elites."[80] Furthermore:

> The third Nativist Literature Debate occurred at the end of the 1970s. . . . In it one clearly saw that Yu Tiancong, Wang Tuo, Chen Yingzhen, and other new nationalist authors were nationalists who inclined toward "Chinese literature in Taiwan."[81] They were Chinese nationalists and did not identify Taiwan as a weak, small yet emergent nation. For them, Taiwanese literature simply did not exist. All that existed was "Chinese literature in Taiwan." All the literature produced in Taiwan was [regarded by them merely as] Nativist literature. . . . In terms of identity, the old-style KMT nationalist writers were the same as the new nationalists. The only major difference was that in thinking the new nationalists were more advanced and had modernist views. They endorsed the new [communist] revolution in China, and they had a deep concern and compassion for workers, farmers, soldiers, and other disadvantaged classes living impoverished lives. . . .
>
> Looking back almost twenty years later at the third Nativist Literature Debate, we perceive that Taiwan writers and intellectuals advocating an independent and autonomous Taiwan were totally absent. The people who at the time were new nationalists or old nationalists are now all on a common road—they still long for China's reunification. The differences in opinion between them are getting smaller and smaller.[82]

In other words, Taiwan's Nativist literature in the 1970s was the work of Chinese nationalists, and the Nativist Literature Debate was simply infighting between old and new factions of Chinese nationalists. In this new construct, Nativist literature was distanced from the development of Taiwanese nationalism in politics and culture. Nativist literature was now excluded from the Taiwanese historical narrative.

To reflect this exclusion, we could rewrite the middle of the story (see table 5.2) as follows: after the war, local Taiwanese authors continued to create in difficult and lonely times, upholding the tradition of Taiwanese literature under the name of "Nativist literature." In the 1960s the founding of *Li Poetry Magazine* and *Taiwan Literature* represented the establishment of Taiwanese consciousness. In the 1970s the real indigenized writers looked on aloofly during the Nativist Literature Debate as factions of Chinese nationalists fought among themselves; instead of joining the fray, they kept creating and building solidarity, as well as researching the New Literature of the colonial period. In the 1980s the terms "Nativist literature" and "indigenized literature" were finally rectified to "Taiwanese literature." Taiwanese literature's "subjectivity" had been autonomous since the beginning of the 1990s.

From the mid-1990s, more and more Taiwanese nationalists took part in official cultural activities and policy making and received official affirmation and commendation. After the presidential election of 2000, in which DPP candidate Chen Shuibian was elected, this development became even more pronounced, especially in the literary field. For example, a series of selected local-Taiwanese-language (*Taiyu*, i.e., Hoklo language) works in five volumes, "Selected Local Taiwanese Language Works" (Taiyu jingxuan wenku), an expression of Taiwanese linguistic nationalism, received funding from the National Culture and Arts Foundation (Guojia wenhua yishu jijinhui) at the end of 1998. The series was edited by local-Taiwanese-language literature advocates Lin Yangmin, Song Zelai, and Lü Xingchang, who had been editors or consultants at *Taiwan Literature*. Also, at the beginning of 1999, the Council for Cultural Affairs, Executive Yuan (Xingzhengyuan wenhua jianshe weiyuanhui) took on the task of "exhibiting the total achievement of Taiwanese literature." The resulting institution, by Legislative Yuan resolution, was designated the National Museum of Taiwan Literature (Guoli Taiwan wenxue guan), which began operation in 2003. Thus "Taiwanese literature" was finally established by national legislative and executive act. From 1997 to 2005 eleven departments or graduate institutes of Taiwanese literature were established at universities around the country.

A further example is from August 1999, when Zhong Zhaozheng won a national award from the National Culture and Arts Foundation. Peng Ruijin and former *Taiwan Literature* editorial board member Lin Hengzhe were on the six-person nomination committee. Also on the prize review committee were Li poet Li Kuixian and two former editorial consultants at *Taiwan Literature*, Xu Daran and Chen Wanyi.[83] Li Kuixian also served as chair of the foundation's literary review committee in the second half of 1999 and in 2000. Lü Xingchang, Chen Wanyi, and a former member of *Taiwan Literature*, Wu Jinfa, were among the six other commissioners.[84] In March 2000 DPP candidates Chen Shuibian and Lü Hsiulien (Annette Lu) were elected the tenth president and vice president of the ROC, which can be viewed as the result of the thirty-year fight for representation by the political opposition and a high point in the process of political indigenization, or Taiwanization. Chen Shuibian was inaugurated in May, whereupon Zhong Zhaozheng was engaged as a presidential senior adviser. Li Qiao, another *Taiwan Literature* writer and its erstwhile general editor (from February 1994 to December 1995), then president of the Taiwan Pen Association (Taiwan bihui), was recruited as national policy adviser.[85] In May 2004 Chen Shuibian and Lü Hsiulien were elected to a second term, and Ye Shitao and Yang Qingchu were added to the roster of advisers.

The rise of Nativist literature in the 1970s was related to the formation of the return-to-reality generation. Like the young intellectuals who investigated the Taiwan New Literature of the Japanese colonial period, Nativist writers and their supporters were an important generational unit within the return-to-reality generation, sharing a common generational consciousness, national identity, and historical narration. Under the stimulus of political trauma, they began reflecting on the contemporary situation in terms of larger power networks or structures in society, developed a critical consciousness, and stressed the importance of social concern and national character in literature. The local Taiwanese background of Nativist writers made them especially sensitive to Taiwan's social reality and sentimental about local life. They not only defined their creative objectives in terms of the Chinese national narrative but also sought the meaning of their personal and generational existence in it. Many Nativist writers and readers linked the New Literature to Nativist literature within this historical narrative and affirmed the Chinese nationalism of both. By analyzing these phenomena, this chapter has revealed a close relationship between historical narrative, on the one hand, and collective identity and activism, on the other hand.

This chapter has also analyzed the relationship between the return-to-reality trend and another Nativist literature, associated with the first- and mainly second-generation postwar local Taiwanese writers of *Li Poetry Magazine* and *Taiwan Literature*, which formed in 1964. They identified themselves as being Chinese all through the 1960s and 1970s. And as time went on they tended to want to take credit for the vogue for the Nativist literature of the 1970s. I argued that they were not at the forefront of these developments. But in the 1980s they would be at the forefront of another trend: radical indigenization or Taiwanization in literature and culture. And in the 1990s they would distance themselves from the return-to-reality Nativism they had affirmed not so very long before.

My analysis revealed a contrast between the interpretive framework local Taiwanese writers and critics of *Li Poetry Magazine* and *Taiwan Literature* coteries used in the 1970s to understand the New Literature and Nativist literature and the one they used from the 1980s on. The Chinese nationalism of the former was replaced by Taiwanese nationalism in the latter.[86] In the conclusion to this monograph, I will argue that this gradual transformation should be understood in terms of narrative identity theory rather than instrumentalism. But first, in chapter 6, I will deal with the Dangwai, the final unit on which I focus within the return-to-reality generation.

CHAPTER VI

Dangwai Historiography

I n August 2001 a conference was held at the College of Medicine at
National Taiwan University to commemorate the seventieth anniversary of Jiang Weishui's death. It was organized by Huang Huangxiong,
a "scholar-politician" who was known in the Dangwai and later in DPP
circles as a scholar of resistance activities during the Japanese colonial period.
President Chen Shuibian gave the opening address.[1] It was a high-profile
event.

One of Taiwan's first Western-style doctors, Jiang Weishui (1888–1931)
had studied at the Medical School of the Government-General of Taiwan
(Taiwan zongdufu yixuexiao), a precursor of the NTU College of Medicine, in the 1910s. Jiang treated the sick in a hospital he founded later in
Taipei. He also tried to find a political cure for society's ills. In the spring
of 1921 he joined the Petition Movement for the Establishment of a Taiwanese Parliament (*Taiwan yihui shezhi qingyuan yundong*) (1921–1934). He
and others promoted the idea of the autonomy of the colonized people of
Taiwan and pursuing equal rights for them under Japanese rule. Autonomy had a cultural side: in autumn of that same year Jiang cofounded the
Taiwan Cultural Association (Taiwan wenhua xiehui) (1921–1931). He
also helped found the Taiwan People's Party (Taiwan minzhondang) in
1927 (1927–1931).

For a time during the 1920s it seemed that a gradual, reformist
approach might make some headway with the authorities, but when very

little headway was made, some intellectuals embraced more radical forms of resistance. In the early 1930s the Japanese colonial government almost completely suppressed the reformers and radicals alike.[2] The Taiwan People's Party was shut down in 1931, the year Jiang Weishui died of typhoid fever, yet to achieve any of his political or medical aims. He died a failure.

But in Jiang's afterlife he has become a success, a Chinese or Taiwanese hero. His most famous saying, a simple but powerful anadiplosis, speaks to us across the decades: "We compatriots must unite, for in unity there is truly strength" (Tongbao xu tuanjie, tuanjie zhen youli). As I will show in this chapter, Jiang Weishui has had different things to say to Chinese and Taiwanese people ever since his death. He has meant very different things to different people at different points in time, from the 1970s to the conference in 2001.[3] Jiang Weishui's reception is a central thread in the story of what I will call Dangwai historiography. Just as the Nativist writers discussed in chapter 5 looked back at writers of the New Literature to try to find support for their approach in a decades-long tradition, so Dangwai activists looked back at figures like Jiang Weishui, trying to draw strength from tradition as they sought to achieve their contemporary political aims. Before documenting the consecration of Jiang Weishui by a unit within the return-to-reality generation, however, we first need to detail that generation's role in the Dangwai.

The Return-to-Reality Generation in the Dangwai

In an article published in 2000, Wu Naiteh discussed the rise of the opposition in the 1980s after the Kaohsiung Incident of 1979 (see later discussion) in terms of "generational politics." The younger generation had not experienced the horrifying February 28 Incident, had been better educated than the older generation, and had a faith in democracy as a universal value. As a result, they were more positive about political activism.[4] Wu was speaking of the 1980s and beyond. I will show that the new generation had appeared in the first half of the 1970s, playing an important role especially from 1975 to 1978.

In the 1950s and 1960s there were independents on local government councils, people who refused to join the KMT or toe the KMT line, such as Guo Guoji, Li Wanju, Guo Yuxin, and Xu Shixian.[5] Only at the end of the 1960s were there independents at higher levels of government. At the end of 1969 Huang Xinjie and Kang Ningxiang, both younger than Guo Guoji's generation but still older than the members of the return-to-reality generation who would appear in the early 1970s, were elected as independents. Huang was elected legislator in the first elections for added or replacement seats in the National Assembly and Legislative Yuan, and Kang was elected city councilor in the first city councilor election after Taipei became a centrally administered "special municipality."[6] The election of Huang and Kang was the beginning of the Dangwai—literally "outside the party"— movement that culminated in the founding of the DPP in 1986. In the following years—every four years for local elections, every three for legislator elections, and every six for national assembly elections—anti-KMT political dissent slowly coalesced. The Dangwai opposition movement gathered momentum. Huang and Kang were its first leaders.

The Intellectual gave members of the return-to-reality generation a brief opportunity to vent and to get involved in politics. A KMT member, He Wenzhen, for instance, started out as a so-called "literary youth" (wenyi qingnian). The ROC's loss of its seat in the United Nations aroused in him a deep social and political concern. In the sixty-second issue of The Intellectual in the spring of 1973, He Wenzhen gave an account of how he got involved by helping out on the campaign at the end of 1972 for Xu Xinliang, still a member of the KMT at the time but soon to be Dangwai. He dwelled on the circumstances of other young intellectuals like him:

I'd had a phobia of politics. I've been afraid to discuss it. I've silently and solitarily idled my time away in coffee shops, sitting vacantly, without a future, with only painful memories. I was alive but had no life. I sat without thinking.

I can no longer describe the shock that book gave me because the authors . . . rekindled the life inside me.[7] This is why I decided to help him [Xu Xinliang] campaign. More accurately, it is some hope, some dream I am seeking. . . .

We've been joined on the front lines in the streets by more and more university students. . . .

Yes! I can't help but shout it out: I am helping Xu Xinliang campaign not only because he is a party comrade but also because he gives voice to my pain and he can bring hope to our bitter lives! Be that as it may, anyone who gives us hope transcends party lines. There's a certain young person, for instance, who is campaigning for both Xu Xinliang and Kang Ningxiang at the same time: his standpoint is neither KMT nor Dangwai. His standpoint is idealism and the national interest!

. . . An image of this young person I saw in Chungli [in Taoyuan County at the time] suddenly reappears in my mind's eye! I kept looking for him in the departing crowd, but there were so many young people who seemed familiar: There was no longer just one of him! "He" had been born in the midst of this election—a new breed whose only stance is idealism—a new youth.[8]

In the second half of the 1970s, these new youth, these members of the return-to-reality generation, would attempt to go into politics themselves. These younger, well-educated dissidents referred to Kang and Huang as "traditional Dangwai." By contrast, they were usually termed the "Dangwai new generation" (*Dangwai xinshengdai*) by themselves and others. In late 1975 a writer for the Dangwai political magazine, *Taiwan Political Review* (*Taiwan zhenglun*), described the experiences and feelings of this younger generation:

How many children have been schooled since the thirty-eighth year [of the ROC calendar, that is, 1949], when the government relocated to Taiwan? From the age they learned to sing the national anthem, these children knew the Three Principles of the People [of Sun Yat-sen]. From class elections in elementary school they began to receive training in democratic governance. From newspapers, the radio, and television they learn about the dynamics of civil rights in democratic nations. They have gotten educated, served in the military, and taken jobs at various levels of society. They now pay taxes and fulfill all their civic duties. Can they remain aloof from the unfolding political situation? When they observe the social kaleidoscope don't they compare what they see with what's in the constitution and with what they know of the situation in other countries? Although situational constraints or hardships leave them without many opportunities for self-expression, sooner or later they will need to vent the resentment and dissatisfaction that has been building up in their hearts. They will have to get it off their chests by speaking out. In the final analysis, what's brought us to this juncture? Why have we come here?[9]

Many of the members of the Dangwai unit within the return-to-reality generation expressed similar sentiments.[10]

At the end of 1978 He Wenzhen became a Dangwai candidate for the first time, in the election for additional seats in the National Assembly. Right before the campaign, he took a retrospective look at his experience in the Dangwai from 1971 to 1973:

In the sixtieth year of the ROC calendar [1971] we were out of the UN. In those heady days many intellectuals, grassroots civil rights activists, and youths banded together to save Taiwan. It was magnificent—so much like the glorious, heroic, and everlasting epic of the May Fourth Movement. But I'd just gotten out of the army that year. I was unemployed . . . and lonely. I was surviving, but felt helpless. There I was, a young person lingering in coffee shops, wasting time, a young life prematurely withered. . . . In middle school we'd read *Apollo, Free China, Current Democracy.*[11] We'd talked about existentialism and May Fourth. But to a youth who had walked a tortuous road, these memories only tinged the nothingness before my eyes with an intense sorrow, which deepened my painful sense of powerlessness regarding national affairs.

But the movement of awakening in the *xinhai* year [1971, the sixtieth anniversary of the 1911 Revolution] was an epic of reform in our own time. It was a powerful shock for anyone concerned about national affairs and the fate of Taiwan, and even more arresting for a person in lonely exile for long like me. . . . In the sixty-first year of the ROC calendar [1972], I started to participate in this reform movement. It got me so worked up that I felt like having a good cry, perhaps a way of relieving myself of the lingering pain of years. In the sixty-second issue of *The Intellectual* I wrote an article called "New Youths in Pursuit of Their Ideals," which might speak for some of the young people—an unrecognized and nameless young crowd—who like me were running around distributing reform leaflets.[12]

These new youths had been inspired by the likes of Kang Ningxiang and Zhang Junhong, who entered the race for Taipei city councilor in 1973:

"The images of these two civil rights activists left a huge impression in our minds. So unforgettable, they convinced me and many other young people to fight for the democratic future of Taiwan. Before we knew it, we were walking the difficult road of the champions of democracy."[13] By 1978 they were taking a more active role in the Dangwai as candidates and representatives in their own right.

From the end of 1975 to the end of 1978 there were three elections: for additional Legislative Yuan seats at the end of 1975, for five types of local government offices at the end of 1977, and for the additional Legislative Yuan and National Assembly seats at the end of 1978. In these elections, even more young intellectuals helped out on Dangwai campaigns or became Dangwai candidates.[14] The elections at the end of 1977, which provoked the Chungli Incident (*Zhongli shijian*)—the suppression of protests in Chungli City against alleged KMT manipulation of the election, were crucial. In these local elections, the largest thus far in the postwar period, Kang Ningxiang and Huang Xinjie helped Dangwai youth from around the island to liaise.[15]

After the elections, the role the postwar generation had begun to play in Taiwan politics started attracting more attention. In the summer of 1979 Xu Xinliang pointed out that "in the past the Dangwai movement consisted purely of Dangwai political figures taking part in elections basically on an individual and local basis." But "things have changed in the past two years," in which the Dangwai movement had gone nationwide: "many members of *xinshengdai* [the new generation] who are unconnected to local power brokers joined the movement enthusiastically, not only intellectuals but also masses of young workers and farmers." The ideal and objective of the new generation intellectuals was "the reform of the whole national society."[16]

Nanfang Shuo (Wang Xingqing) has mentioned a minor incident from the 1978 election campaigns that exemplified the commitment and zeal of the younger generation:

At the end of the sixty-seventh year of the ROC calendar [1978], Taiwan's young intellectuals were participating in campaign activities more passionately than they had the year before. One day, at a gathering of Dangwai candidates, there was a candidate behind whose banner a lot of young intellectuals had gathered and whose words revealed that he was rather pleased with himself for the support he was getting. But then one of his supporters, a university student, began to speak:

—"Don't assume we're supporting you. What we're defending is our own ideals!"

He was speaking on behalf of a new generation of intellectuals in Taiwan in a voice that was candid, courageous, knowledgeable and touching. It was filled with aspiration. It was a voice that inspired respect. And they were not a minority.[17]

Like the larger return-to-reality generation, the Dangwai often heaped praise on themselves in the late 1970s: "[We] are without a doubt the most outstanding generation in modern China."[18] Wu Jiabang, who was chief campaign strategist for Zhang Junhong in 1973 and 1977 and who himself became a Dangwai candidate for legislator at the end of 1978, described his generational belonging in the following way:

Taiwanese society has experienced many years of stability, economic prosperity, and rapid industrial and commercial development, allowing the younger generation to enjoy a better material environment and a more complete education. They are better able than their elders to tackle problems with an open mind, accepting new ideas and views. They tell right from wrong and uphold truth. They have lofty ideals and a strong sense of justice. They are also fearless in the face of danger and authority. Even more important, they have a powerful affection for the things of their native soil and a keen desire to participate. Most of the campaign workers for Zhang Junhong's two campaigns came from this group. They did everything from grunt work to leaflet design and campaign event organization. They expected no recompense. They unhesitatingly contributed their energy and zeal. They were a generation fighting for their ideals, and they mobilized a matchless spiritual power. . . .

The liberated awareness and strong desire to participate of the new generation represent a current that should be rationally and soberly channeled. Establishing a system of great grandeur, one that bolsters democracy and buttresses the rule of law, is the most important and pressing issue in Taiwan today.[19]

Wu Jiabang's description was a typical statement of the self-regard and aspiration of this generation within the Dangwai.[20] Indeed, Dangwai youth had high hopes for themselves. For instance, at the end of 1978 Chen Wanzhen, who had KMT membership but was slowly entering the Dangwai orbit, wanted to campaign for legislator. When she told her story, she began with the "thousands of years of autocratic misery" suffered by the people of China and moved on to her own aspiration, to "bring a new spirit into the Legislative Yuan, to play a catalyzing and leading role in the democratization of China."[21]

In December 1978 elections were held for additional representative seats of the Legislative Yuan and the National Assembly. Led by the "Taiwan Dangwai Election Assistance Team" (Taiwan dangwai renshi zhuxuantuan) established by Huang Xinjie, the Dangwai started campaigning at the beginning of autumn.[22] They hoped to repeat the unprecedented successes of the previous year's local elections for five types of local government offices by taking advantage of the popular distrust of the KMT that had become apparent in the Chungli Incident.[23] In the middle of the campaign, the United States announced the establishment of diplomatic relations with the PRC that would start from New Year's Day, 1979, the severance of formal relations with Taiwan, and the cancellation of the Mutual Defense Treaty Between the United States and the Republic of China that had provided a security umbrella since 1955. This turn of events forced President Chiang Chingkuo, who had been in office for only seven months, to issue an emergency delay of the election. Having no traditional channels for political participation, the Dangwai turned to more conspicuous forms of resistance: mass public assemblies and street protests.[24]

In January 1979 the Taiwan Garrison Command arrested Yu Dengfa, a senior dissident from southern Taiwan, and his son for sedition. Dangwai dissidents took to the streets in protest in Qiaotou Township, then-Kaohsiung County. By summer, Xu Xinliang, who had won the election in 1978 for then-Taoyuan County magistrate, was impeached and subsequently suspended by the Control Yuan for demonstrating. Xu consequently became the "most controversial core member of the Dangwai movement." The conclusion of an interview Xu Xinliang gave after his suspension was that "for the past seven or eight years all my effort, all my striving has been in order to rouse the new generation to a movement of political reform, in order to win the right to speak or even to lead in politics." He then took this one step further:

In the past, the Dangwai only had local influence, and limited support. But now the public supports the new generation, because they have faith in and expectations for the new generation. That is why I stress that this is a "new generation political movement"— which is of far greater significance than a plain old "Dangwai movement"!

. . . One can say that the people in power today have been enjoying the fruits of China's social reform movement over the past century without making any contributions themselves. But we of the new generation are different. We want to be a generation that is happy to make a devotion, and this is a time of too many problems awaiting resolution. We are the problem-solving generation!

For Xu Xinliang the lesson of Chinese history over the past century was that an outstanding nation cannot do without democracy, because a democracy does not countenance oppression of fellow nations or "a minority of one's own people scorning and bullying the great majority in politics. . . . This is the understanding we should have today. This is about the desire for democracy!"[25]

In August 1979 the Dangwai publication *Formosa* (*Meilidao*) was founded. Huang Xinjie was the publisher, Xu Xinliang president, and Zhang Junhong chief editor. Contemporary political commentators noted a split between the moderate line taken by Kang Ningxiang and the intense mass movement stance of *Formosa*.[26] But this "split" never became an open conflict. As the Dangwai's "official organ" in the late 1970s, *Formosa* came to symbolize Dangwai unity but also the high point of the 1970s opposition movement.[27] Lin Zhengjie, a young Mainlander who joined the Dangwai in the mid-1970s when he was a graduate student at Chengchi University, later reminisced: "The entire 1970s was actually a period of history from the launch of *The Intellectual* to the forced end of *Formosa* [after the Kaohsiung Incident in December 1979]."[28]

In fact, *Formosa*'s core members held a view similar to Xu Xinliang's, that this high point was a great forward push by the "political reform movement of the new generation." For instance, Huang Xinjie's "Inaugural Statement" for the magazine was entitled "Come and Support the Political Movement of a New Generation!" (Gongtong lai tuidong xinshengdai zhengzhi yundong!). Moreover, "*Formosa*'s objective is to drive the political movement of the new generation", and for the core members of *Formosa*, the prime of objective of this movement was democracy.[29] The cover story declared, provocatively:

> Riding on the success of the local elections at the end of the sixty-sixth year of the ROC calendar [1977] and the aftermath of the Chungli Incident, the political movement of the new generation has been surging, propelling the upsurge in popular political participation in the elections at the end of last year, an upsurge which represents the total expression of the people's high desire for political participation after thirty years of KMT rule, the first time the eighteen million people of Taiwan have specifically challenged the KMT regime after thirty years of autocratic rule![30]

To *Formosa*, the Dangwai was a movement of "intellectuals of the new generation—which represents the majority of the population but has been ignored—who have engaged themselves in politics one after another and invigorated Taiwan's democratic movement."[31] The title story in the inaugural issue emphasized the newness of the Dangwai by comparing the postwar intellectuals who had joined the Dangwai since 1977 with Lei Zhen and others at *Free China* who mounted an opposition to the KMT in the late 1950s. Lei Zhen and the others were "basically a group which had split off from the KMT, a group of Chinese old-style liberals who were trying to put down roots in a new land after defeat on the Chinese mainland." By contrast, though the elections at the end of 1978 were unfinished, there had been a "great coming together," "a great banding together of an awakened new generation, a generation that has been nurtured by change in Taiwanese society over the past three decades!"[32]

The cancellation of the 1978 elections made the Dangwai more strident, but it did not shake the group's sense of the role it was playing in Chinese history:

> We believe that today we have reached a turning point in history, at which supporting the political movement of the new generation is the greatest contribution the eighteen million people of Taiwan can make to the Chinese nation, so that democracy will become for once and forever our permanent political system. This is the direction in which we of the new generation are moving.[33]

We believe that given that China has experienced over a hundred years of turmoil . . . we should learn the lessons of history and strive for democracy, for only democracy can help us achieve the objectives of the political movement of the new generation—invigorating the new generation and realizing a more reasonable society!

. . . For over a century, courageous sons and daughters of China have had hurt and humiliated souls in their own land. With resolute confidence, they have even been willing to spill their own blood in order to shatter:

—imperialist invasions;
—the accumulated darkness and decay of history [of old China];
—the nonsense of the fawning literati [who say] China is not suited to democracy.

We believe that democracy is a global trend . . . and that to nourish suspicions of the democratic potential of our nation is to doubt its excellence. For over a century courageous sons and daughters of China have never doubted this [potential]. Thus, for over a hundred years the blood-and-tears dream of the Chinese people has been democracy.[34]

In sum, the founders of *Formosa* had a sense of generational identity that distinguished them from their parents, but they understood themselves as Chinese in terms of the Chinese nationalist narrative of history prevailing in postwar Taiwan.

Therefore, when He Wenzhen discussed Taiwan's contemporary land problems, he naturally began with issues related to the "tragic cycle of ancient Chinese history."[35] Pointing out that the elections for five types of local government offices at the end of 1977 were the most large-scale in postwar Taiwanese election history, Huang Huangxiong also described them as "the most deeply meaningful elections in Chinese history."[36] In criticizing the KMT government for excessive use of the charge of "sedition" in dealing with dissidents, Yao Jiawen held that "our country has been republican for sixty-eight years and the imperial notion of the emperor treating the empire as his 'family-governed world' (*jiatianxia*) is long gone," and he appealed to the KMT to "prosecute the harsh charge of 'treason' with caution and to institute republican governance fully, for only then will the blood of the republican martyrs not have flowed in vain."[37] Also, when he discussed "patriotism," Yao began with the traditional national idea of "we the Chinese nation."[38]

Another example of Dangwai Chinese consciousness at this juncture is a selection of articles from *Free China* by the editorial board of *The Eighties* (*Bashi niandai*), a magazine established by Kang Ningxiang and others in 1979. Its stated intention was to "evaluate history and meditate on the current situation" in order to realize that "it is a historical truth . . . that it is no longer the right of any regime and its affiliated intelligentsia to decide China's future or the fate of the Chinese people," that this right now belongs to the "popular multitude."[39] In the article expressing their "thoughts on Double Ten Day," the staff at *Formosa* claimed that "the 'Double Ten spirit' is the ability to reverse the course of modern Chinese history and make a turn for the better, but these days this spirit is kept more or less under wraps." With the recent crackdown in Chungli in mind, the editors at *Formosa* called on the authorities to uphold the spirit of the republican revolution. "The lesson of the Wuchang Uprising (Wuchang qiyi) on October 10, 1911, is that if we are unable to reform, we have no future." They therefore urged the authorities "to accelerate reform to commemorate the Wuchang Uprising and the National Day on October 10."[40]

That Dangwai dissidents frequently made statements critical of Mainlanders might be taken as evidence of a nascent Taiwanese consciousness. Examples of such criticisms abound. In stumping for Kang Ningxiang at the end of 1975, for instance, Zhang Junhong refuted the accusation that the Dangwai is "localist" and then accused Mainlanders of ignoring "the aspirations of their local Taiwanese compatriots who were pleading for equality." But such criticisms should not be understood in terms of a Taiwan nationalist narrative of history. Zhang Junhong said that he believed the provincial origin question would "as a matter of course gradually resolve itself after a long period of coexistence and intermarriage."[41] Lin Zhuoshui, a Dangwai dissident who was on the board of *The Eighties*, was critical of the Taiwan Provincial Administration under Chen Yi (August 1945 to March 1947), whose attitude was that "Taiwanese people are not members of the Chinese nation."[42] In a nutshell, for the length of the 1970s, members of the Dangwai, and the return-to-reality generation in general, were Chinese in spirit.

What I will show in my analysis of Dangwai historiography that follows is that they made a place for Taiwan's history within Chinese history, starting with Chen Shaoting's articles on colonial resistance activism in *The*

Intellectual in the early 1970s and Kang Ningxiang's high-profile citation of Taiwanese anticolonialism. It should be emphasized from the start that Chen and Kang were both, like most Dangwai dissidents in this decade, "loyal dissidents" whose main demand was "democratization."[43]

Chen Shaoting and Kang Ningxiang: The Resistance as Part of the Riches of ROC History

Growing up, Kang Ningxiang had met activists from the Japanese era like Wang Shilang and Guo Guoji.[44] From them he received materials that would have otherwise been difficult to obtain.[45] He used his knowledge of the era in campaign speeches. He began a stump speech for Huang Xinjie in Taipei in 1969 with Jiang Weishui and the Taiwan Cultural Association and emphasized Jiang Weishui's pride in being Taiwanese and his spirit of social reform.[46]

This speech and others like it made quite an impression. A student at NTU, Zheng Hongsheng later recollected his experience of Kang's stump speech at the main gate of the NTU campus during the election for additional national parliamentary seats in 1972: "At the beginning of the 1970s, to put NTU in the historical perspective of Taihoku Imperial University in the colonial period was rather shocking, especially when a grass-roots democracy activist was pointing out the connection. At the time we were absorbing and digesting leftist ideas, and we had just rediscovered [the writer] Yang Kui. We were moved by the declaration and appeal he was making. One felt as if Jiang Weishui had been resurrected."[47]

Chen Shaoting was the first among the return-to-reality generation to publish on the resistance to the Japanese in the 1920s, in his article "Mr. Lin Xiantang and the 'Ancestral Land Incident'—Also on the Historical Significance of the Anti-Japanese Movement of Taiwanese Intellectuals" (Lin Xiantang xiansheng yu 'zuguo shijian'—jianlun Taiwan zhishi fenzi kangri yundong de lishi yiyi), published in 1971 in *The Intellectual*.[48] This was the first of several feature articles on the "July 7th Incident and the Anti-Japanese Movement" (*Qiqi shibian yu kangri yundong*) in this issue of *The Intellectual*. The occasion was the thirty-fourth anniversary of the July 7th Incident.[49] In spring 1936 Lin Xiantang led a delegation on a study tour organized by *Taiwan New People's Daily* (*Taiwan xinmin bao*), of which he was the president, to South China. After his return to Taiwan, Lin was bitterly criticized and humiliated by the Japanese colonial authorities because he called China "the ancestral land" during the tour. In retrospect, Chen Shaoting concluded that "the ultimate goal of the Taiwan Anti-Japanese movement was to 'return to the ancestral land.' The ancestral land recognized by the Taiwanese compatriots was China, so the mainstream of the anti-Japanese ideology was Chinese nationalism. Only by grasping this point can we understand the historical significance of Taiwanese five-decade-long resistance to Japan." He further remarked: "Taiwan's history is part of Chinese history; Taiwan's Anti-Japanese movement is part of the history of China's resistance to Japan." Finally, Lin Xiantang was "a model for today's Taiwanese youth" to follow.[50] This was quite similar in spirit to his "May Fourth and the New Literature Movement in Taiwan," published less than a year later (see chapter 4).

Chen was the first among the return-to-reality generation to publish on the nonviolent anticolonial activism and Lin Xiantang, but as noted earlier, Kang Ningxiang was the first Dangwai figure to declare the importance of Taiwanese history in a political setting. In 1972 he did so at such places as the main gate of the NTU campus; in 1975 he would do so in the most important political body in the nation. On February 21, 1975, as a Taipei legislator, Kang listened to Chiang Chingkuo's "Policy Report," in which Chiang reaffirmed the policy of anticommunism. Chiang explained that the fate of "our seven hundred million compatriots on the mainland and the fate of the ROC are inseparable! China will continue to exist as long as the ROC exists. . . . The ROC exists today and will exist tomorrow: and we will recover the mainland."[51]

The following month, during an interpellation session in the Legislative Yuan, Kang criticized the Chiang report in a return-to-reality spirit. He urged the KMT to confront the crisis of the ROC's diminishing international recognition and loss of legitimacy. Then he turned to domestic affairs. He attacked the government as a gerontocracy, asking how much longer 3.2 percent of the population—people over sixty-five—could dominate the leadership levels of government. He stressed that 87.8 percent of the population was composed of the postwar generations, people under fifty years of age who "in the past twenty years have grown up in the era of a global explosion of knowledge and rapid technological progress." He asked the authorities to pay attention to "this demographic that will decide the fate of the ROC" and respect their "knowledge of and perspective on the world, their views and decisions concerning the future of the

ROC, and their views on and demands for society, on which their survival depends."[52]

Kang proposed four major reforms: (1) adjust the national budget to meet the actual needs of Taiwan society, (2) draft a "political party law" (*Zheng-dang fa*) to catalyze the formation of "vigorous" opposition parties, (3) normalize local governance according to the principle of rule of law, and (4) "reaffirm the value and position of Taiwan's 'historical culture,'" placing particular stress on this final point. He recounted how Ming dynasty loyalist Koxinga took Taiwan as his base for opposing the Qing dynasty and reinstating the Ming, demonstrating that "earlier generations [of Taiwanese people] vowed to restore the nation." These earlier generations included especially Taiwanese people who sacrificed their lives in the armed resistance against Japan for two decades after 1895. He then emphasized how in the 1920s Cai Huiru (1881–1929), Lin Xiantang, and other vanguard activists under the influence of the Wilsonian ideal of the right of nations to self-determination and the Chinese May Fourth movement engaged in a nonviolent struggle against colonial rule.

At this point, Kang introduced the Petition Movement for the Establishment of a Taiwanese Parliament, the Taiwan Cultural Association, the Taiwan People's Party, and the Taiwan Local Self-Government League (Taiwan difang zizhi lianmeng) (1930–1937). Concerning the Taiwanese resistance against Japan, Kang felt that two points needed to be recognized: First, "In fifty years of Japanese rule, the Taiwanese people, insulted, oppressed, and killed by the Japanese, suffered and sacrificed no less than their compatriots on the mainland during the eight-year-long Anti-Japanese War." Second, "the Taiwanese people under Japanese rule had a resolute [Chinese] national consciousness," and Taiwanese patriots were tireless in resistance. "In the brutal revolutionary resistance against Japan, the Taiwanese people 'longed for the ancestral land' and placed their faith in that longing, which was their greatest support." Then he made a suggestion:

The exploits of the Taiwanese people in the resistance to the fifty-year-long Japanese occupation should be included in the history textbooks, to inform every young student about this valuable history, to let students know that their fathers and mothers, grandfathers and grandmothers and their earlier ancestors shed blood and tears on this our native ground in brutal struggle with the Japanese empire. Why? For the sake of "longing for the *patria* and the dignity of the nation."

This history is the ultimate treasure for the younger generation of students. It is a vein of riches in the history and culture of the ROC.
... Affirming the value and place of Taiwan's "history and culture" is the way to express respect for the sacrifices the Taiwanese people made for the sake of "longing for the *patria* and the dignity of the nation" and for the persecutions they suffered in their struggle against an alien race. It is also the way to inspire and cultivate in the entire people a traditional historical spirit, a spirit of love for the native land, the nation, and the country. If this is possible, then the lives of the people and the destiny of the state will be inextricably intertwined and this nation and state of ours will have a glorious future.[53]

In this speech, Kang Ningxiang emphasized the importance of Taiwan's history in education and national culture. Over the following years, members of the Dangwai came to have a stronger and stronger sense of history, by and large thanks to Kang Ningxiang. As a Dangwai leader, he consciously linked his participation in the opposition movement, on the one hand, and his awareness of his postwar generational identity and Taiwanese history, on the other.

This was the first time in postwar Taiwan that a member of any kind of political opposition stood in a national parliamentary body to present a local perspective with a view to reappraising post-1920 Taiwanese anticolonial history and to make appeals to the upper echelons of the KMT administration, to Chiang Chingkuo himself. On the other hand, Kang's challenge to KMT ideological control was moderated by its context—the Chinese nationalist historical narrative in which he recounted Taiwanese history—and by the reformist orientation of his suggestions for educational, social, and political renewal.

To some extent Kang Ningxiang helped the KMT maintain ideological control, especially as regards Chinese identity and anticommunism. In the conclusion, when Kang Ningxiang affirmed that the value of Taiwanese history and culture lies in its capacity to "inspire and cultivate in the entire people a traditional historical spirit, a spirit of love for the native land, the nation, and the country," he meant China. This spirit would carry the Chinese nation forward to "a glorious future."

At the time the KMT administration was faced not only with serious diplomatic setbacks but also with the conspicuous development of the overseas Taiwan Independence movement, both of which threatened its legitimacy. The presence of reformers looking for Chineseness in their construction of local collective memory was a relief for the KMT. Chiang Chingkuo was happy to endorse Kang's proposal to include the history of the Taiwanese colonial resistance in history textbooks:

> Our compatriots of Taiwan, Penghu, Kinmen, and Matsu have been our anticommunist warriors on the base [of Taiwan] from which we will restore the nation. In particular, they have in the past conducted themselves with great vigor and extraordinary bravery. They have made a huge contribution to the [Chinese] national revolution and to the anti-Qing, anti-Japanese, and anticommunist movements. I, Chingkuo, wholeheartedly endorse Legislator Kang's proposal to include the combat exploits of our Taiwanese compatriots in our school textbooks, so that young people can realize just how anti-Qing, how anti-Japan, and how anticommunist our Taiwanese compatriots have really been! And today in the present stage our Taiwanese compatriots bear a greater responsibility: everyone must unite in fulfilling the sacred mission to oppose communism and restore the nation![54]

Kang kept invoking his favorite anti-Japanese patriot of them all, Jiang Weishui, for the rest of the decade. In 1977 Zhang Junhong described Kang Ningxiang's campaigning: "In his speeches at the Far East Theatre (Yuandong juchang) and the gate at NTU [at which he held Jiang Weishui up as a resistance hero], he declared his 'Taiwanese historical mission' as the theme of his campaign. This declaration gave the Dangwai movement an exalted sense of historical mission. It had a big impact and lifted the Dangwai mass movement to a new level."[55] By the summer of 1977 the investigation of Taiwan's history during the Japanese colonial period had become a hot topic. At a symposium held by Dangwai dissidents in honor of Jiang Weishui, Kang Ningxiang claimed that "so much of my motivation has come from Jiang Weishui" and that "I have drawn on Jiang Weishui's own political views for many of the political statements I made in my various election campaigns."[56]

In 1977 Kang Ningxiang remarked on the public's historical amnesia. To Kang, it was a tragedy that most people did not know about Jiang Weishui: "the saddest thing . . . is that Taiwanese people don't cherish the memory of generations past—our forebears had that spirit of affection which makes you glow and illuminates others—and they even turn cold, irreverent, or forgetful."[57] Because of people like Kang, everyone in the Dangwai had heard of the guy. Listen to Zhang Junhong tell it in terms of a generational categorization of dissidents under the Japanese and the KMT defined as age cohorts (which was similar to Ye Shitao's classification of local Taiwanese writers):

> The people of a country can draw passionate strength from their identification with a practical and lofty national goal and with a national system of institutions; through the precious legacy of history they can realize a sense of historical mission or pride that in turn produces a powerful self-assurance. But due to various linguistic obstacles the first generation of modern Taiwanese visionaries was not fully able to hand down their historical legacy to be celebrated by the next generation. The connection was broken, the legacy lost, and by the third generation there was no longer any sense of this kind of strength. Faith in democracy should be able to give people this kind of strength, too, but it is a shame that for many years, third- and fourth-generation youth have been losing confidence in the feasibility of democratic politics. They no longer have the passion of idealism. Mr. Kang's greatest contribution is that during his campaign he earnestly gave a solemn sense of historical mission to a confused and diffident public. In his popular activities he projected a resonant historical voice, a voice that allowed people to discover themselves, realize a sense of dignity, and understand the significance of protecting land and country. This solemn voice marked a new milestone in Taiwan's electoral history.[58]

Zhang further indicated that by incorporating Taiwanese history—especially anti-Japanese political and social activism—into his campaign speeches in the early 1970s, Kang "gave the Dangwai mass movement a noble sense of inheriting a historical mission," a sense that distinguished the Dangwai from the earlier opposition movement led by Guo Guoji and others and that even became an important factor in the decisions of many postwar generation intellectuals to join the Dangwai. Zhang explained: "intellectuals used to think that elections were for scoundrels or Robin Hood-types and couldn't be bothered. Kang Ningxiang has changed their minds. Intellectuals are now eager to join the mass movement that is Dangwai."[59]

Legitimating the Dangwai Movement Historiographically

Kang Ningxiang's encounter with an older generation of Taiwanese intellectuals, his familiarity with the history of the Japanese colonial period, and his statements during elections all established a connection between the anticolonial movement in 1920s Taiwan and the Dangwai political opposition movement in the 1970s. This connection was made in print in *Taiwan Political Review*, the very first Dangwai journal, founded in August 1975 by Huang Xinjie, Kang Ningxiang, Zhang Junhong, and others and forced to shut down by the KMT government at the end of the year, after only five issues. Four of the issues included articles on the history of the Japanese colonial period, as displayed in table 6.1.

These four articles covered the nonviolent period of the Taiwanese colonial resistance, namely, political and social activities from the early 1920s led by Cai Huiru, Lin Xiantang, and others who were influenced by trends in Western thought and political developments in China. The article "The Taiwanese Anti-Japanese Movement Seen Through Japanese Eyes," was translated from the Government-General of Taiwan's *The History of the Police of the Government-General of Taiwan* (*Taiwan zongdufu jingcha yangezhi*). It included materials on the worker and farmer movements and the Taiwanese Communist Party. The author of the other three articles was Ye Rongzhong, whose pen name was Fanfu. Ye, along with Lin Xiantang and others, had participated in the Petition Movement for the Establishment of a Taiwanese Parliament, the Taiwan Cultural Association, and the Taiwan Local Self-Government League. In his three articles, Ye looked back at Cai Huiru's and Lin Youchun's strong identification with the ancestral land, China, and Jiang Weishui's great interest in the republican revolution led by the "National Father," Sun Yatsen.[60] In doing so he made a place for Taiwan in the republican revolution.

For the Dangwai, colonial and KMT rule were both oligarchic, the few unfairly overriding the many. This was not just unfair, it was undemocratic, according to Dangwai activists like Xu Xinliang, as mentioned earlier. In developing their collective identities or justifying their opposition

TABLE 6.1

Articles on the Japanese Colonial Period in *Taiwan Political Review*

No.	Author	Publication date	Title	Vol.	Pages
1	Ye Rongzhong	August 1975	"Taiwan minzu yundong de puluren Cai Huiru" (Cai Huiru, the man who paved the way for the Taiwanese national movement)	1	56–58
2	Fanfu	October 1975	"Taiwan minzu shiren Lin Youchun" (Taiwan's national poet Lin Youchun)	3	66–69
3	Zhenghong, trans.	November 1975	"Ribenren yanzhong de Taiwan kangri yundong" (The Taiwanese anti-Japanese movement seen through Japanese eyes)	4	48–52
4	Fanfu	December 1975	"Gemingjia Jiang Weishui" (Revolutionary Jiang Weishui)	5	76–79

actions, Dangwai dissidents therefore found the recent tradition of anti-colonial activism in Taiwan a valuable resource of historical experience for them to draw on. In the fall of 1975 Huang Hua, who had served eight years in prison on the charge of sedition until his release in the amnesty following Chiang Kaishek's death, began writing articles for *Taiwan Political Review* (see chapter 2). Huang Hua had already been canonized by the Dangwai as a "saint" of the opposition movement and "a leading icon in Dangwai politics." In discussing why he refused to change his mind about joining the Dangwai, he asked, rhetorically:

Were not Jiang Weishui, Guo Guoji, and other Taiwanese heroes from the Japanese occupation period imprisoned because they strove for freedom and equality for Taiwan? After they came out of prison, they kept up their political activities. As long as they did not break Japanese law, the colonial government would not arrest them for continuing to engage in politics. Think about it: the alien Japanese imperial government allowed many Taiwanese former political prisoners to continue acting for Taiwanese freedom. How could our own democratic government forbid us?[61]

In another issue of *Taiwan Political Review*, Zhenghong, who translated *The History of the Police of the Government-General of Taiwan* as an introduction to the Taiwanese workers and farmers movements and the Communist Party of Taiwan under colonial rule, wrote: "Under harsh Japanese rule, almost a century [*sic*] ago, there were actually many Taiwan visionaries fighting for the survival and future of their Taiwanese compatriots."[62] Both men revealed that the tradition of anticolonial activism under the Japanese had played an important part in the formation of collective identity and the legitimation of political dissent and activism in the 1970s.

The impact of *Taiwan Political Review* on its readers, especially the younger generation, was palpable. Lin Zhengjie related his experience during his graduate student years:

One day, I bought a copy of *Taiwan Political Review* at a roadside stand. That's the first time I knew the names of Huang Xinjie, Zhang Junhong, Yao Jiawen, Huang Hua, Kang Ningxiang, and others. While unlike both *Free China*, which had deep political theories, and *Apollo*, which was loaded with rich knowledge, this publication had a strong grassroots nature, offering analysis of and commentary on current affairs. Reading this magazine was just like chewing a betel nut from southern Taiwan.[63]

Obviously, the magazine's coverage of the local anticolonial history also contributed to its grassroots, indigenized character as symbolized by the betel nut, a popular stimulant for working-class folks. Lin's experience gradually led him to the Dangwai.[64] Another example was Chen Fangming. Reading *Taiwan Political Review* prompted him to participate in a demonstration for the first time when he studied in Seattle—a demonstration against the KMT government's order to suspend publication. This precipitated his change in national identity from Chinese to Taiwanese, as mentioned in chapter 5.[65]

The Dangwai focused on anticolonial social and political movements in the 1920s, as is obvious in all four major Dangwai political magazines that appeared in the 1970s before the Kaohsiung Incident: *Taiwan Political Review* (August 1975–December 1975), *New Generation* (*Zheyidai zazhi*, July 1977–December 1978), *The Eighties* (June 1979–December 1979), and *Formosa* (August 1979–November 1979).[66] As mentioned earlier, *Taiwan Political Review* published four articles on the anticolonial movements or leaders in the 1920s in five issues. *New Generation, The Eighties*, and *Formosa* had three, five, and three articles, respectively, about other periods in Taiwanese history besides the Japanese era (see tables 6.2, 6.3 and 6.4). By comparison, each journal had nine, six, and four articles, respectively, exclusively concerned with the Japanese colonial period (see tables 6.5, 6.6, and 6.7). In total, there were nineteen articles on the colonial period, all but three or four of which dealt with Taiwanese resistance to colonial rule in the 1920s.

TABLE 6.2

Articles on Taiwanese History (Excluding the Japanese Colonial Period) in *New Generation*

No.	Author	Publication date	Title	Vol.	Pages
1	He Wenzhen	October 1977	"Taiwan de lishi chulu" (A historical outlet for Taiwan)	4	11–16
2	Zai Shizheng	October 1977	"Ji Taiwan guangfu de lishi jingtou" (Record of the historical image of the Retrocession of Taiwan)	4	40–42
3	Zhong Xiaoshang	November 1978	"Du Taiwan lishi yougan" (A reading report on Taiwanese history)	15	45–46

TABLE 6.3

Articles on Taiwanese History (Excluding the Japanese Colonial Period) in *The Eighties*

No.	Author	Publication date	Title	Vol.	Pages
1	Lin Zhuoshui	September 1979	"Taiwan shi meilidao" (Taiwan is a beautiful island)	1(4)	20–24
2	Wang Shilang	September 1979	"Taiwan tuozhi de guocheng" (The process of developing and settling Taiwan)	1(4)	84–87
3	Li Qinxian	October 1979	"Qiantan sanbainian lai Taiwan meishu de shidai yiyi" (Preliminary discussion of the epochal meaning of Taiwanese fine arts over the past three centuries)	1(5)	82–87
4	Zhang Xucheng (trans. Hu Yifeng)	December 1979	"Meili zhi dao" (A beautiful island)	2(1)	7–10
5	Yang Zujun	December 1979	"Kudan gezi de cangsang" (The trials and tribulations of the tragic female lead in traditional Taiwanese opera)	2(1)	91–94

TABLE 6.4

Articles on Taiwanese History (Excluding the Japanese Colonial Period) in *Formosa*

No.	Author	Publication date	Title	Vol.	Pages
1	Wei Tingchao	September 1979	"Hsinchu yiminmiao de jidian—kejiaren zuida de baibai" (Ceremony at the Righteous Citizen Temple in Hsinchu: the biggest Hakka festival)	1(2)	77–78
2	Liu Fengsong	October 1979	"Yiqian babai wan ren de Taiwan shi" (A Taiwan history for eighteen million people)	1(3)	69–76
3	Xie Taixin	November 1979	"Gemingjia ne? haishi liukou? (shang)—'Lin Shuangwen qiyi' de yixie guancha" (Revolutionary? or bandit? (part 1): Observations concerning the "Lin Shuangwen Revolt")	1(4)	99–104

During the 1970s, the historical interpretations in these articles contributed greatly to the de-exilic and de-Sinocentric understanding of Taiwan's history and culture because they celebrated local experiences and advocated local perspectives. In addition to articles, there were book-length historical works by two major dissidents of the new generation that was Dangwai, Huang Huangxiong and Lü Hsiulien, to whose writings the rest of this chapter is dedicated. Theirs were the

TABLE 6.5
Articles on the Japanese Colonial Period in *New Generation*

No.	Author	Publication date	Title	Vol.	Pages
1	Staff	August 1977	"Jinian geming xianxian Jiang Weishui xiansheng shishi 46 zhounian zuotanhui" (Symposium commemorating the forty-sixth anniversary of the death of the revolutionary sage Mr. Jiang Weishui)	2	54–63, 46
2	Staff	September 1977	"Taiwan jindai "xianjuezhe" de jingshen yichan zuotanhui" (Symposium on the spiritual legacy of modern Taiwanese "visionaries")	3	17–24
3	Jiang Weishui	October 1977	"Jinnian yao zuo shenmo?" (What are we going to do this year?)	4	36–37
4	Huang Huangxiong	November 1977	"Taiwan jindai 'xianjuezhe' de minzu qingcao" (The nationalist sentiment of modern Taiwanese "visionaries")	5	27–29
5	Taiwan minbao	December 1977	"Taiwan qingnian de shiming (The mission of Taiwanese youth)	6	52–53

(*continued*)

TABLE 6.5 (Continued)

No.	Author	Publication date	Title	Vol.	Pages
6	Huang Huangxiong	December 1977	"Zanzhu Taiwan jindai minzu yundong de riben renshi de pingjia" (Evaluation of Japanese individuals who sponsored the modern Taiwanese nationalist movement)	6	57–63
7	Lin Xixiong	August 1978	"Huang Shiqiao xiansheng tan "geming xianxian" Jiang Weishui" (A discussion of the "revolutionary sage" Jiang Weishui by Mr. Huang Shiqiao)	12	12–13
8	Huang Huangxiong	August 1978	"Yixiang zhuangyan de jianyi—jinian Jiang Weishui xiansheng shishi sishiqi zhounian" (A solemn proposal: In memory of the forty-seventh anniversary of Mr. Jiang Weishui's death)	12	19–21
9	Huang Huangxiong	December 1978	"Cong Jiang Weishui jingshen tanqi: jianlun Taiwan de zuotian jintian yu mingtian—minguo liushiqi nian shiyi yue shiqi ri zai	16	44–45

No.	Author	Publication date	Title	Vol.	Pages
			'Jiang Weishui jiniange fabiaohui' shang zhuanti yanjiangci" (A discussion beginning with the Jiang Weishui spirit: Also on Taiwan's yesterday, today, and tomorrow—keynote speech at the "Launch of Tribute Song in Memory of Jiang Weishui" on November 17, sixty-seventh year of the ROC calendar)		

most systematic and articulate historical rewritings by the dissident activists in this decade.

Huang Huangxiong's De-exilic Historiography and Assimilationism

The author of many of the articles in tables 6.5, 6.6, and 6.7, Huang Huangxiong played a leading role in the Dangwai investigations of the history of Taiwanese anticolonialism. He was from Yilan County in northeastern Taiwan—just like Jiang Weishui. After receiving his Master's degree in Political Science from NTU in 1970, Huang worked in business and taught college for several years. Later he quit his jobs to devote himself to writing. From around 1976 he began to publish works on the history of Taiwanese anticolonial social and political movements, which he understood

TABLE 6.6

Articles on the Japanese Colonial Period in *The Eighties*

No.	Author	Publication date	Title	Vol.	Pages
1	Li Nanheng	July 1979	"Riju shidai Taiwan de yanlun ziyou" (Freedom of speech in the Japanese occupation era)	1(2)	15–18
2	Zhuo Guohao	September 1979	"Buzhun jinian Jiang Weishui?" (Not allowed to commemorate Jiang Weishui?)	1(4)	73–74
3	Editors	September 1979	"Jiang Weishui huo zai women xinzhong" (Jiang Weishui, alive in our hearts)	1(4)	79–80
4	Huang Huangxiong	September 1979	"Jiang Weishui xiansheng yixun" (Mr. Jiang Weishui's teachings)	1(4)	80–82
5	Li Xiaofeng	September 1979	"Riben zhimin xia Taiwan de zongjiao ziyou—kan wushinian qian jinquan jieji mouduo jiaochan, jiaoquan de liangge gean" (Freedom of religion in Taiwan under Japanese colonialism: Two cases from fifty years ago about how members of the economically privileged class sought to appropriate temple assets and religious authority)	1(4)	83–84

No.	Author	Publication date	Title	Vol.	Pages
6	Editors	November 1979	"Weida de yizhe—Sun Zhongshan xiansheng danchen jinian tebie baodao—xiri Taiwan shehui zhong jiechu de yishi" (Great healers: A special report on the anniversary of Mr. Sun Yatsen's birthday— outstanding Taiwanese doctors in history) 1. "Wu Haishui yishi— Taiwan zhen qingnian, wenhua yundong xianjuezhe" (Dr. Wu Haishui: A true Taiwanese youth and a visionary in the cultural movement) 2. "Lai He yishi—beitian minren huaibao cangsheng de Taiwan wenxue zhi fu" (Dr. Lai He: Humanitarian father of Taiwanese literature) 3. "Han Shiquan yisheng—tachangfu pu wei liangxiang tang wei liangyi" (Dr. Han Shiquan: A great man who cannot become a virtuous minister should be a good doctor)	1(6)	77–83

(*continued*)

TABLE 6.6 (Continued)

No.	Author	Publication date	Title	Vol.	Pages
			4. "Xie Wei yishi—yi ren routi jiu ren linghun de Taiwan Shi Huaizhe" (Dr. Xie Wei: Taiwan's Albert Schweitzer, who cured bodies and saved souls)		
			5. "Wu Xinrong yishi—ai tongbao, ai xiangtu ai minzu de shiren zuojia" (Dr. Wu Xinrong: Poet who loved his compatriots, native land, and nation)		
			6. "Chen Xinbin yishi— weiwu buqu, shisi rugui de rengezhe" (Dr. Chen Xinbin: A man of indomitable and fearless character)		

in terms of a strong identification "with the Chinese nation." He claimed activists like Jiang Weishui placed their hopes in "the government of ROC, of which the KMT is the principal part." He went on to portray colonial activists as "anti-Japanese resistance heroes" who made the great historical contribution of arousing Chinese national sentiments in the Taiwanese people. What a shame they had been forgotten over the postwar three decades, creating a "'discontinuity' in modern Taiwanese history."[67] In light of this discontinuity, Huang Huangxiong argued that "Taiwanese history is waiting for urgent examination, especially the history of modern Taiwanese anti-Japanese movements."[68]

In rediscovering Taiwan's anticolonial history, Huang got to know Dangwai dissidents. Here is his retrospective:

TABLE 6.7

Articles on the Japanese Colonial Period in *Formosa*

No.	Author	Publication date	Title	Vol.	Pages
1	Huang Huangxiong	August 1979	"Dajia lai jinian Jiang Weishui xiansheng" (Everyone should commemorate Mr. Jiang Weishui)	1(1)	93
2	Wang Shilang	August 1979	"Riren zai Tai zhimindi tizhi zhi dianding— wei jinian jiufu Liao Jintai xiansheng er zuo" (The building of the foundation of Japanese colonialism in Taiwan: In remembrance of my uncle Liao Jintai)	1(1)	94–95
3	Wen Chaogong	October 1979	"Taiwan ren you weisheng, bu shizi!?—yu Lin Yanggang xiansheng tan Taiwan jiaoyushi shang zuiqima de changshi" (Taiwanese people are sanitary but illiterate!? A discussion with Mr. Lin Yanggang about the most common sense regarding Taiwanese educational history)	1(3)	87–92

(continued)

TABLE 6.7 (Continued)

No.	Author	Publication date	Title	Vol.	Pages
4	Wen Chaogong	November 1979	"Qing zhengque renshi lishi de shishi—xiang Su Nancheng shizhang jinyan" (Please correctly understand the facts of history: A word for Mayor Su Nancheng)	1(4)	91–98

In that period I wrote several books, which gave me a great deal of consolation. In writing, I was getting into modern Taiwanese history, and as it happened Dangwai figures were also talking about Taiwanese history at the time. Our interests coincided, so we were able to communicate. It seemed to me their demands were reasonable, because the ruling party's power was too great—it drew a young justice seeker [like myself] to support the Dangwai. In school we had been taught about the spirit of democracy, and now the Dangwai added an additional element. Together the two were a potent mix that inspired many young people to contribute their time and money, to volunteer to assist Dangwai leaders in the fight for liberty and democracy. . . . And so through this contact with the Dangwai, I moved closer and closer, until I became united with them.[69]

Like many of his Dangwai colleagues, Huang had a strong awareness of his postwar generational identity. Talking about the historical significance of the local elections for five types of local government offices in 1977, he emphasized:

With united support of new generation voters and voters who have placed their hope in the new generation, new generation candidates have not only won elections but also garnered the most votes, which was unforeseen given that they had the smallest campaign purses.

This attests to the fact that the strength of the new generation is starting to be felt in the political arena all around Taiwan. Their future is getting brighter and brighter, and more and more they are going to be a force to reckon with.[70]

Huang saw himself as one of the most informed voices of this generation. By 1978 he was already regarded as "an expert in Taiwanese history."[71] As an amateur researcher, he had published serials on the history of the Japanese colonial period in the *Taiwan Shin Sheng Daily News* (*Taiwan xinsheng bao*) and the overseas editions of *China Times* (*Zhongguo shibao*). His writing focused on anti-Japanese resistance in the 1920s, on which he published three books: *Taiwan's Visionary Prophet—Mr. Jiang Weishui* (*Taiwan de xianzhi xianjuezhe—Jiang Weishui xianshen*), *A Historical Story of Taiwanese Compatriots' Anti-Japanese Resistance* (*Taibao kangri shihua*), and *The Roar of the Oppressed—A Selection of Mr. Jiang Weishui's Writings* (*Beiyapozhe de nuhou—Jiang Weishui xiansheng xuanji*).[72] In these books, Huang made the explicit connection between anticolonial activists like Jiang Weishui, on the one hand, and anti-KMT dissidents, on the other, allowing him to interpret his generation and the Dangwai movement in the subcontext of Taiwanese history.

Huang investigated the "visionaries" (*xianjuezhe*), as he called them, who took part in the so-called "modern Taiwanese nationalist movement" (*Taiwan jindai minzu yundong*), mainly in the 1920s. The nonviolent anticolonial movement in the 1920s was "the first native-soil-loving movement in Taiwanese history in which intellectuals expressed collective zeal."[73] His own generation was the second. Huang felt that his generation could "obtain energy and power from the spiritual legacy of these 'visionaries.'"[74]

Like Dangwai activists, the "visionaries" Huang studied were Chinese nationalists, according to Huang. Their activities "aroused the Han national spirit of the Taiwanese people" and "made the Taiwanese compatriots proud of the Chinese nation." For this reason, they "had nothing to apologize for to the ancestral land, much less to the Chinese nation." This, he concluded, is "the necessary cognitive foundation and psychological information needed on which to build an understanding of Taiwanese compatriots." They were confident that "the power of revolution under Sun Yatsen's influence would complete the great work of uniting China."[75]

Like Kang Ningxiang, Huang Huangxiong had a sense of national crisis, which he hoped to help the nation weather. He hoped in particular that his *Taiwan's Visionary Prophet—Mr. Jiang Weishui* "would help the

Chinese nation unite" by conveying the spiritual legacy of Taiwan's proudest son.[76] Huang believed that the tradition of anticolonial activism in Taiwan could become "an important force for social stability, particularly concerning situation the country faced at the present stage." He also hoped this tradition could give people "a sense of connection and identity with the Chinese nation."[77]

Huang focused most of his research on Jiang Weishui because Jiang's "spirit and fate sum up the whole significance of the modern nationalist movement in Taiwan."[78] He concluded his biography of Jiang with an assessment of the "historical significance" of Jiang's decade of anticolonial activism, underlining that Jiang showed deep "affection for the native soil" of Taiwan but was nonetheless "a great Chinese national hero in the resistance against the Japanese." He stressed Sun Yatsen's profound influence on Jiang's outlook by arguing that the latter followed the former's every move. To him, Jiang was "Taiwan's Sun Yatsen" (*Taiwan de Sun Zhongshan*).[79]

Huang lamented that while Sun Yatsen had been commemorated with zeal, Jiang had been forgotten by his own people.[80] He parallelized the anticolonial resistance represented by Jiang Weishui's struggle with Sun Yatsen's Chinese republican revolution, noting that the Dangwai opposition movement was a continuation of the former, with the goal of realizing "the first democratic system in the five thousand years of the Chinese nation on this earth."[81]

Huang Huangxiong became a Dangwai candidate for the election at the end of 1978, which was postponed when the United States broke off diplomatic relations. One year later, in December, the Kaohsiung Incident occurred. On December 10, 1979, Dangwai dissidents held a demonstration in Kaohsiung city in southern Taiwan to celebrate "Human Rights Day," intended to honor the UN General Assembly's adoption and proclamation of the Universal Declaration of Human Rights in 1948. Interrupted and suppressed by the KMT government, the celebration turned out to be a bloody conflict between Dangwai supporters and the police. Soon after, many major Dangwai leaders, such as Huang Xinjie, Zhang Junhong, Lü Hsiulien, Wang Tuo, and Yang Qingchu, were imprisoned. This event was later known as the "Kaohsiung Incident," or "*Formosa* Incident" (*Meilidao shijian*), because the march was organized by the *Formosa* magazine crew led by Huang Xinjie and other codissidents.

When the election was finally held at the end of 1980, Huang was elected legislator. He was seen as following in the footsteps of Guo Yuxin and Lin

Yixiong as being "the Dangwai's leader in Yilan."[82] But even after he went into politics, he continued to write and speak about the Taiwanese anticolonial resistance. For this reason, he was regarded as a "Dangwai scholar-theorist."[83] Reviewing Huang's long investigation of the history of Taiwanese anticolonialism, Zhang Junhong praised his greatest contribution to Taiwanese society as being "a devotion to digging up and sorting out the ancestral legacy." He stressed that Huang's research helped Taiwanese compatriots, who were plagued with a sense of inferiority and inequality after periods of Japanese oppression and KMT domination, "rediscover dignity and hope."[84]

At the beginning of the 1980s, Huang Huangxiong, now a legislator, put his preliminary contributions to the Dangwai in context in an interview, which is worth quoting at some length:

From when I first started to encounter Dangwai figures to when I stood for election as a Dangwai candidate, my main work was theoretical construction and study of Taiwanese history. I connected and combined the striving of the Dangwai movement and the striving of our ancestors, explaining the connections and contexts to give the current movement a sense of its historical significance. At that time in this respect, I was working the hardest. I introduced modern Taiwanese history to make the Dangwai's objectives more coherent and concrete, so that we would not seem so disorganized, isolated, and fragmented. I wanted to highlight the spiritual connection we in the Dangwai had with our ancestors. . . . When I first met Dangwai people, they were pretty much putting their whole lives and all their energy into election campaigns. At that stage, election campaigning [for them] was all there was to politics. . . . At that time, the KMT dominated everything and the atmosphere was really bad. The pressure Dangwai campaigners were under forced them to see each election as life, otherwise they wouldn't be able to keep going. It was a mistake to look no farther than election day, to "see politics as elections." I thought about this mistake and its background for a long time and, with a very heavy heart, pointed it out. . . . To give a conceptual reminder, to introduce the study on Taiwanese history, and to think about what the Dangwai was fighting for as a part of a larger historical trend and from a more global perspective—all these intellectual efforts gave me some encouragement. It seemed worthwhile.

That's what I was doing from the time I joined the Dangwai to when I became a candidate.[85]

However exceptional he was as a historian, Huang was a typical return-to-reality Dangwai intellectual. He hoped for the Chinese people living in Taiwan to come "out of exile" and accept Taiwan as their home. Highlighting the Chineseness of the anticolonial activists in particular and the Taiwanese people in general, his historical reexamination, like Kang Ningxiang's address to Chiang Chingkuo, had an explicitly "assimilationist" orientation. He assimilated Jiang Weishui to Sun Yatsen. Still, by highlighting Taiwan's unique historical experience of Japanese colonialism from a local Taiwanese perspective, he challenged the "grand China" outlook and the Sinocentric view of the Taiwan-Chinese mainland relationship that buttressed the KMT's political control, cultural ideology, and exilic mentality. His demand for appreciation of Taiwan's uniqueness and for equal status for local Taiwanese obviously contested the perceptions of Taiwan/local Taiwanese as peripheral/inferior and the Chinese mainland/ Mainlanders as central/superior.

Huang's Chinese identity would change in the 1980s, though not as radically as Lü Hsiulien's. Lü's particular narration of Taiwanese history published in 1979, *Taiwan's Past and Future* (*Taiwan de guoqu yu weilai*), marked the beginning of most Dangwai dissidents' shift to Taiwanese national identity in the post–Kaohsiung Incident years.

Lü Hsiulien's Decolonialization and Embryonic Taiwanese Nationalism

Lü Hsiulien was born in Taoyuan in 1944. In the summer of 1971 she returned to Taiwan after obtaining a Master's degree in comparative jurisprudence from the University of Illinois at Urbana-Champaign. Advocating a "new feminism" (*xinnüxing zhuyi*), Lü became a very energetic social activist. At this time she had a Chinese national identity. She described herself as "a woman who had received twenty years of proper Chinese education" while growing up in Taiwan and saw herself as heir to the Chinese women's movement at the end of the Qing dynasty.[86] In spring of 1974 she wrote a preface to the second edition of a collection of her newspaper columns, in which she earnestly professed her national identity and revealed a strong sense of mission:

> A friend of mine once described me as "strong but charming and mischievous, revolutionary but peaceful and moderate." A reader described this book as being "full of Chinese, Confucian thought." I don't deserve the former description, but the latter I accept gladly. I hope I don't sound conceited. All I mean is that I appreciate the fact that I was born Chinese and will roam a Chinese ghost after I die. Therefore I have been trying hard to be Chinese—in a more modern, logical, and dynamic way. Perhaps this is the reason why this book has resonated with readers? Here and now, are we not all searching for a way of being Chinese that is modern, logical, and dynamic? Isn't this what we need to search for?[87]

Despite her popularity, Lü came under fire for her feminist views. When she was harassed by security agents, she realized that there were deeper, political issues at stake.[88] In the summer of 1977 she went to the United States to study again. At the Harvard-Yenching Library Lü found many works on Taiwanese history that she had never seen and realized how little her compatriots knew about it. Judging by the book she wrote as a result of this realization, *Taiwan's Past and Future*, she was probably reading publications by overseas Taiwanese nationalists like Su Beng's (Shi Ming) *Four Hundred Years of Taiwanese History* (*Taiwanren shibainian shi*) and Ong Joktik's *Taiwan: A Depressing History* (*Taiwan: kumen de lishi*).[89] Lü later claimed that hers was "the first book ever to examine Taiwan's history from a Taiwanese perspective." That is an overstatement, but it is certainly the case that it represented "a pathbreaking departure from the China-centric texts printed under martial law."[90] What really distinguishes her approach is her feminism. In the book she relates how she came to see "a similarity between the basic problems of women and the historical fate of Taiwanese people."[91] And while her message might have been similar to that of the overseas historians, she was saying these things in Taiwan.

Lü returned to Taiwan again after receiving her second Master's degree in jurisprudence from Harvard. At the end of 1978 she entered the National Assembly election race as a Dangwai candidate in then–Taoyuan County. During the campaign she observed: "Actually, the 'Dangwai figures' are a group of non-KMT people who are interested in politics and have their own views and who hope to participate in politics peacefully and democratically to change the status quo. . . . This group has received formal schooling under KMT rule, and the faith in democracy they espouse and the democratic burden they bear speak to the good the KMT has done economically and educationally on Taiwan over the past three decades."[92] Lü described a young generation dissatisfied with the political status quo and daring to challenge the KMT. Moreover, their challenge was predicated on the KMT's declared membership in the U.S.-led free world and on the ideals of liberty and democracy.

During this campaign, Lü also published her book about the significance of Taiwan history as *Taiwan's Past and Future*. She announced that previous records and expositions of Taiwan had been written from the perspective of traditional Chinese official historiography (*Zhongguo zhengshi*) and that few works had ever really treated Taiwan in itself as the "subject" (*zhuti*) of history. She decided to "boldly transcend the traditional Sinocentric position by adopting the standpoint of Taiwan *per se* and the people who live in Taiwan" (58–59).

Lü described Taiwan's development as a continuous stream of immigration and colonization. The immigrants sought a place to make a fresh start. They "identified with Taiwan and died in old age on Taiwan." The colonizers, by contrast, exploited the people and resources of Taiwan. They did not identify with Taiwan and took off as soon as the going got tough. The Spaniards (1626–1642), the Dutch (1624–1662), Chinese Ming loyalists under Koxinga, the Qing (1683–1895), and the Japanese were all colonizers, establishing "foreign regimes" (*wailai zhengquan*) that "governed oligarchically" (59, 105–6). She emphasized that "the basic character of Taiwan's history is tragic, in that for three hundred years Taiwanese people have suffered a lack of sovereignty, a loss of control over self, and complete manipulation by others!" (108). Lü looked back at the past and forward to the future, believing that in a time of international isolation and extreme doubt about the way ahead, it was necessary "to examine the significance of all periods in Taiwan's history and to develop ways of dealing with diplomatic setbacks." The only way to deal with such setbacks was for the people of the island to "rule the roost" (*dangjia zuozhu*) and transcend their fate—the cruel fate similar to that of traditional orphaned sons (*guer*) and adopted daughters (*yangnü*). They must fight for control of land and government. They must be self-supporting and self-liberating (61, 105, 107, 161).

Who were "the people of Taiwan?" Lü definition was inclusive: "Taiwan's history shows that as for the residents of the island of Taiwan, there is no such thing as the so-called distinction between local Taiwanese and Mainlanders. The only difference lies in the mere fact that some immigrated earlier and others later. Anyone who identifies with Taiwan, anyone who is willing to live and die with Taiwan, to share all joy and sorrow, is a Taiwanese" (161). She underlined Taiwan's positioning within China: "Yes, Taiwan is a province of China. Most Taiwanese people's ancestors came from the Chinese mainland. And this is exactly why to love Taiwan is to love China, to talk Taiwanese is to talk Chinese, to cherish Taiwanese culture is to cherish Chinese culture! And to explicate Taiwanese history is of course to explicate Chinese history." But at the same time she insisted on a Taiwanese perspective on China:

> Besides, my love for Taiwan in no way means that I do not love China, much less that I do not love the world. It is just because we love the world and China that we must love Taiwan. . . .
>
> That "I love Taiwan" (*wo ai Taiwan*) does not imply a narrow conception of locality, nor does it detract from the fact that the Taiwanese people are members of the Chinese nation, that Taiwan is a model province for [Sun Yatsen's] Three Principles of the People, or that Taiwan is a base for anti-communism, which is a fundamental national policy. Didn't our National Father [Sun Yatsen] say, *without nationalism, how can there be cosmopolitanism? Similarly, without native-soil consciousness, there is no national consciousness!* To assume we must eliminate Taiwanese consciousness in order to regain the mainland or that we must suppress the Taiwanese language in order to restore Chinese culture, is to get things mixed up, to misunderstand the Three Principles of the People, and thus to betray our National Father's vision. (166–67; emphasis original)

All of this was reformist, an attempt to maneuver within the system. But if one reads between the lines, Lü's critique was radical. She hinted that the KMT, like the previous rulers in Taiwan, was a colonizer, a "foreign regime." Urging the people of Taiwan, wherever they were from, to make themselves the masters of their own destinies, she was edging toward decolonization with respect to the KMT.[93] Only in the following passage is her radicalism explicit:

If we do not attack the communists by force and if we cannot use our basic national policy—there is only one China, Taiwan is China's territory, and the ROC is the only legitimate government of China—to escape our diplomatic predicament and rejoin international society, then we have to face the decision of whether or not "to burn bridges" and announce the secession of Taiwan from the Chinese mainland and the independent autonomy of the ROC. This choice can be realized in a public way by directly announcing the independence of Taiwan or alternatively, in a practical way, by declaring that there are two Chinas (*liangge Zhongguo*) or that there is one China with two governments (*yige Zhongguo liangge zhengfu*). (241)

In her proposal of "ROC independence" (*Zhonghua minguo duli*), Lü anticipated the later radicalization of the opposition movement and its historical narrative due to the heightened suppression by the KMT government in the years following the Kaohsiung Incident of December 1979.

Three months before the Kaohsiung Incident, in the same month as the revised edition of *Taiwan's Past and Future* was published, Lin Zhuoshui's article "Taiwan Is a Beautiful Island" (Taiwan shi meilidao) was published in *The Eighties*. The editor added the following comments:

In Chinese history, Taiwan had almost no place at all. Geologically, Taiwan has lots of mountains, typhoons, and earthquakes. Politically it has a sad history of refugees and colonizers. The residents of this island have never had the chance to "rule the roost." And those in power have distorted the history of Taiwan to serve their own political needs, so that the people of the island have seldom realized their place or value, and the national temperament has generally been affected by a sad sense of orphanhood or abandonment.

But perhaps because they were the playthings of fate, the people of Taiwan—who came originally from the Central Plains (*zhongyuan*) of China and ended up here in exile—retained a high level of central Heluo culture of the Central Plains. Taiwan was ceded to Japan by the Qing court and became the colony of an alien people, sparing the people of the island from the destruction of the Chinese civil war and thereby laying the foundation for economic development today. The KMT government retreated from the mainland to Taiwan. The original intention was temporary refuge. There was absolutely no plan to settle down. Now building Taiwan has become part of the blueprint for returning to the mainland, so that Taiwan in the future bears an unprecedented military, political, and even cultural responsibility. Who would have imagined?

Taiwan, Taiwan, our beautiful treasure island: we need to brush away the dust of history, shake off cheerless memories, seize the day, create our own destiny and achieve a new standing for the Chinese nation.[94]

The historical narrative implicit in these comments is very similar to that in Lü Hsiulien's *Taiwan's Past and Future*. Take away the identity perspective of the Chinese national subject—in these comments, we would only have to delete "and achieve a new standing for the Chinese nation," which seems almost tacked on—and we have a typical version of the Taiwanese nationalist historical narrative that appeared in the post–Kaohsiung Incident years. In the next few years, the radicalism that one mostly had to read into Lü became the new normal in the Dangwai.[95] Taiwanese nationalists would go on to deny the significance of their ethnic origin.[96]

A recollection of the incident, especially of the KMT government's hunt for Shi Mingde (1941–), a key Dangwai dissident, by Jiang Xun (1947–), a famous painter-writer of Mainlander origin who supported the Dangwai in the 1970s, gives us a vivid picture of the transformative power of this dramatic event:

The *"Formosa"* [Kaohsiung] Incident made many people feel indignant and sad.

It seemed to be the last indignation and sadness in Taiwan before the end of the 1970s. . . .

Shi Mingde, who fled in the *Formosa* Incident, was like a crucified knight in ancient legends. Every day newspaper readers followed the latest developments in his daring escape, felt excited, and prayed. He epitomized the potential tension and pleasure brought about by fighting against an evil giant. Sometimes, a wanted knight is more respectable than a pampered politician. In the late 1970s "little devils" were coming out of the shadows in every corner of Taiwan to do battle with the evil giant. They went to jail. They stumbled. But they kept embarrassing and angering the evil giant.

In the 1970s they were reformers and dreamers. They had a natural indignation and sadness. They marked the 1970s with their lovely and interesting countenances.[97]

The Kaohsiung Incident, and the KMT's response—suppression, conflict, violence, bloodshed, trumped up charges, imprisonment, and murder as well as all the sacrifice these entailed—represented a decisive break. Only after this incident did Dangwai dissidents finally make the break from reformist "de-exilic" cultural and political demands to nationalist "decolonial" cultural and political demands, which was heralded by Lü's *Taiwan's Past and Future*, arguably the most systematic and powerful presentation of Dangwai dissidents' distinctive views of Taiwanese history in this decade.[98] In retrospect, one might well wonder whether they had been pretending for some time, tacking Chinese nationalism on to get their radical views past the censor, perhaps out of idealism, perhaps out of some calculus of interest.

I will argue against this instrumentalist interpretation in the conclusion, proposing my own alternative interpretation based on the theory of narrative identity. But before getting to the conclusion, we should find out what happened to Huang Huangxiong in the decades following the Kaohsiung Incident.

In historical works in the mid-1970s, Huang Huangxiong stressed the illegitimacy of Japanese rule, situating Jiang Weishui temporally in a fifty-year-long "Japanese occupation era" (*Riju shidai*). He stressed Jiang's Chinese nationalist sentiment and the influence of National Father Sun Yatsen on him. He described Jiang as Taiwan's Sun Yatsen. In his books on Taiwanese anticolonialism, he used the Republic of China calendar, in which year zero is 1911, the year of Sun's republican revolution. Jiang's ultimate desire, Huang claimed, was for Taiwan to return to the fold of the ancestral land.

A decade and a half later he would modify his remarks at a conference held to commemorate the sixtieth anniversary of Jiang's death. The conference took place in a very different political context: martial law had been lifted in 1987, and Taiwan was now a multiparty democracy. The KMT still insisted that Taiwan was part of China and that the ultimate goal was national unification, but Huang's DPP did not agree. Over the summer of 1991 Huang participated in the drafting and publicization of a "Draft Constitution of Taiwan" (*Taiwan xianfa caoan*), according to which Taiwan was an independent and sovereign nation. The conference to commemorate Jiang's death was held by the Kaohsiung county government under DPP county magistrate Yu Chen Yueying at the end of the year. This was the first time that a local government held a formal gathering in remembrance of Jiang Weishui. The paper Huang Huangxiong delivered at this 1991 conference still identified Jiang with Sun Yatsen but no longer emphasized Jiang's Chinese nationalist sentiment.[99]

Another scholar, Zhang Yanxian, one of the main proponents of "pro-Taiwan view of history" (*Taiwan shiguan*), delivered a paper in which he criticized Huang Huangxiong for his characterization of Jiang Weishui as " 'Taiwan's Sun Yatsen' and a '[Chinese] nationalist.' " He stressed that "Jiang Weishui sympathized with the [China's] republican revolution [of 1911] and studied its tactics. However, it is presumptuous to say he was a Sinophile merely for this reason. . . . In Jiang's writings, there are no words about returning to or identifying with China." Zhang concluded that "there was no way Jiang Weishui could become a return-to-China figure. He was a part of the local movement in Taiwan."[100] You can bet that Huang was listening.

The next year, Huang "rewrote" and republished the two works from the 1970s mentioned above as *Biography of Jiang Weishui—Taiwan's Visionary Prophet* and *A Historical Story of the Anti-Japanese Resistance in Taiwan*.[101] Both books had the same "Introduction to the Second Edition." In this introduction, Huang explained that political control under martial law made it extremely difficult for him (or anyone else) to describe the "original features" of colonial history and that even remaining Taiwanese anticolonial activists faced the same problem in their own writing.[102] Time had given him "a more objective and impartial perspective from which to treat the history of Taiwan's modern nationalist movement." There was, according to Huang Huangxiong, a pressing need for such a reconsideration:

The oppressed Taiwanese compatriots, whether they realized it or not, gradually developed Taiwanese consciousness. This consciousness was the starting point of a movement impelled by the "demands of the Taiwanese people," the Taiwanese nationalist movement. Thus, when the Japanese colonial authorities referred to "extreme nationalists" or "nationalist groups," they meant "Taiwanese nationalists" working from a foundation in Taiwanese consciousness or "Taiwanese nationalist groups" striving for the liberation of the whole

Taiwanese populace—political, economic, social, and educational liberation.

. . . The [members of the] modern Taiwanese nationalist movement . . . may well have been acting on a strong sense of Han national identity, or particularly a poignant esteem for the memory of Sun Yatsen. However, this does not mean that we may see "Han national sentiments" or "Han national identity" as the ultimate ends pursued by the modern Taiwanese nationalist movement. We absolutely cannot obliterate the subjective position of the modern Taiwanese nationalist movement to the point of explaining away the modern Taiwanese nationalist movement as but a tributary of "Han national identity" of the modern Chinese nationalist movement.[103]

Huang Huangxiong made many modifications to the original works. He now used the Anno Domini system instead of the republican calendar. Instead of a "Chinese national identity," he now claimed Jiang Weishui had a "Han national identity" or "Han national sentiment." Sun Yatsen was no longer "National Father" but just "Mr. Sun Yatsen of China." Passages claiming that Jiang had placed his hopes in China or identified his ancestral homeland as China were rewritten or simply expurgated.

The commemorative event in 2001 with which I began this chapter was initiated by Huang Huangxiong, who had served terms as legislator and was by this point a member of the Control Yuan. It was co-organized by the Academia Historica (Guoshiguan) and the Council for Cultural Affairs. As mentioned, President Chen Shuibian delivered the opening address. Chen had been in office for over a year. He was Taiwan's second elected president and first non-KMT president: in the first democratic transfer of power in Taiwanese history, the DPP defeated the KMT in March 2000. By August 2001, however, the DPP was frequently attacked by the two main opposition parties, the KMT and the People's First Party (Qinmindang). To alleviate the tension, the co-organizers chose as the theme of the conference a resistance slogan Jiang Weishui had used in 1927 to try to unite people against the Japanese colonizers. Huang Huangxiong thus stressed:

The seventieth anniversary of Jiang Weishui's death happens to fall after the transfer of power [from the KMT to the DPP]. The greatest significance of this conference lies in the fact that our nation's head of state has attended and delivered an address, an explicit affirmation of Jiang Weishui's place in history by the new administration. At a time when Taiwan's political arena is fraught with turmoil, we need unity. Seventy years ago, Jiang Weishui made this profound and poignant appeal: "We compatriots must unite, for in unity there is truly strength." It is a most resonant and stirring slogan from the period of Japanese rule. If it teaches us vigilance or gives us encouragement in our contemporary circumstance, then this will be the greatest significance of the seventieth anniversary of Jiang Weishui's death.[104]

In his mention of President Chen Shuibian's affirmation of Jiang Weishui's place in history, Huang was specifically referring to the claim Chen made in his address that Jiang represented "Taiwanese spirit" (*Taiwan jingshen*).[105] In this context, calling Jiang Taiwanese in spirit seems unsurprising. In the longue durée of history, it is unsurprising, too. The renarration of Jiang's significance echoes the decolonial and Taiwanese nationalist tendency of Lü Hsiulien's *Taiwan's Past and Future* and embodies the general transformation of national identity among Dangwai dissidents and their supporters since the 1980s. The renarration is to be expected if we accept the tenets of narrative identity theory, of which this book has been a defense. Theoretically, it well demonstrates that identity, narrative, and action—especially political action—are interrelated, an argument that was formulated more than six decades ago by Hannah Arendt, who helped lay the foundations of narrative identity theory.[106] I make my final defense of the theory as applied to Taiwanese sociopolitical history in the conclusion to this book.

Conclusion

The Renarration of Identity

I n the aftermath of the Baodiao movement, just two months before Taiwan lost its seat in the United Nations, Ye Hongsheng published a magazine article in which he castigated television broadcasters and newspapers for shamelessly reporting on an inconsequential activity at a time of national crisis. The activity was a public vote on the Ten Best New Pop Singers. Ye, a Mainlander university student in his early twenties whose father was a general, also rebuked the Ministry of Education for sending an official representative to attend the event. At the end of the article, he went from indignant to despondent: "I sigh as I lay down my pen, asking the part of myself in my 'subconsciousness': 'What kind of time do we live in, truly? What should we do now?' "[1]

At the beginning of the 1970s, after a long period of apathy, many young people finally awakened, rose up, and coalesced into an actual generation with a particular political and cultural outlook. But despite the challenge posed by the return-to-reality generation, throughout the 1970s the KMT continued to apply political pressure on the population. The limited reforms the KMT introduced ultimately failed to satisfy the reformist aspirations of the return-to-reality generation. At the end of the decade Wu Fengshan, a local Taiwanese in his thirties who had served as National Assembly representative for several years and was known as a political moderate, even a nonpartisan, seemed to be responding to Ye Hongsheng's self-interrogation in the following searching reflection:

Advanced education has rapidly raised the quality of the population, and a superior sort of citizen will not be satisfied with a roof over his head and enough food to eat. When he reads works of Chinese history, he will aspire to emulate the sages, and when he reads Western theories of political parties, he will think of China's future. . . .

Generation after generation, the people ceaselessly reproduce. The nation has moved already from the "previous generation" to the "next generation." Taking twenty-three [in Chinese reckoning] as the age of university graduation, "children" born after the Retrocession [of Taiwan in 1945] have already been working in society for a decade now. Taking the thirty-ninth year of the ROC calendar [1950] as a starting point, the new generation who have not seen war themselves are today almost thirty years old, which is old enough for a person to pass through the process of education, marriage, and childbearing, to become mature enough to begin seriously considering the orientation of his life, and, cool-headed after waking from dream deep in the night, to ask himself: "What path should I follow?"[2]

As Robert Wohl wrote in his masterpiece *The Generation of 1914*, "Historical generations are not born; they are made. They are a device by which people conceptualize society and seek to transform it."[3] We may also borrow Edward P. Thompson's conceptualization of class and describe generation as "an historical phenomenon," which is to say "an active process which owes as much to subjective agency as to objective environmental conditions."[4] A generational identity, shaped by provincial background and expressed through a national historical narrative, was formed as the members of the postwar generation awakened at the beginning of the 1970s and proceeded to search for the meaning of existence and stake out a clear position for themselves. Their generational identity did not arise as a matter of course in the process of awakening. It was a construct enabling them to understand self, society, and epoch and to change the status quo. The spirit and ambition of the return-to-reality ideal made them a "generation for-itself." As a generation, they were at the forefront of the conspicuous push for political, social, and cultural change in the 1970s and beyond.

The case of the return-to-reality generation shows that generational identity can be best described as a "generational discourse" in the form of a historical narrative composed by a group of people of similar age. Like many other forms of collective identity, generational identity is a discourse of empowerment that agents construct in order to facilitate action. In short, generational consciousness is both the product of specific social change and a source of agency for further social change.

In the sociological tradition, the concept of generation, especially the research orientation inaugurated by Karl Mannheim, has still not developed into a powerful analytical tool. Only recently has Western sociology started reconsidering the phenomenon of generation as an important foundation for collective identity, especially in its relation to political and cultural change. Sociologists who are exploring generational phenomena have tended to focus on the 1960s. Edmunds and Turner write that "the size and strategic location of the postwar generation has proved to be an important and highly visible aspect of social change in the twentieth century. In cultural and political terms, the social consequences of the baby boomers or Sixties Generation could not be ignored." It has been widely noted that the postwar generation who came to maturity in the 1970s has played a particularly important role in changing the social, cultural, and political climate of the contemporary world.[5]

Examining postwar historical change in Taiwan from a generational analytical perspective helps us develop a comparative historical standpoint. Taiwan is a particular example. Before the 1970s, the postwar generation in Taiwan was passive and compliant in general. They focused on their studies or other personal pursuits and were socially and politically apathetic. It was usually noted that in Taiwan there was no resistance to the existing system in the form of a youth and student movement, as in the West, in the 1960s. Yet, as I have documented in this book, there was no lack of the typical postwar generational phenomena, namely, critique and resistance, in postwar Taiwan; it is just that, due to political and cultural repression in the 1960s, they emerged over half a decade later than in the West. This is also why the members of the postwar generation who in the 1970s began promoting sociopolitical reform and a return to reality included people from their twenties to their forties, a wider age spread than youth and student movements in the West in the 1960s. Research on the role of the postwar generation in political and cultural change in Taiwan should emphasize the pivotal decade of the 1970s, not the 1960s, the decade that has received the most attention in the West.

David Schak examines the change of the state of "civility" in postwar Taiwan compared with that in the PRC, arguing that Taiwan has moved from being "a territory lacking civility and occupied by myriad inward-looking small communities," what he calls a "society in itself," to a "society for itself" in which "people's social horizons expanded from their small communities of insiders to Taiwan as a whole and in which they felt a common identity as members with other persons, mostly strangers, of that imagined community" based on civic nationalism.[6] He continues: "Seeing them as fellow human beings and as sharing a common Taiwanese identity created a basis for affording them civil treatment." As a result of this transition, Taiwan became "a civil place."[7] Schak notes that this change began to appear in the early 1990s and coincided with democratization and liberalization, the relaxation of political control. He points out the major factors contributing to the transformation into a society for itself: modernization, industrialization, active cultural and social movements, large religious (especially Buddhist) organizations' philanthropy, and political struggles for democracy.[8] As far as the factor of politico-cultural struggle is concerned, based on the findings of the previous chapters of this book, it can be said that the move of Taiwan toward a civil place, a society for itself, started with the change of Taiwan's youth of the postwar generation from being a passive "generation in-itself" into an active "generation for-itself," the return-to-reality generation.

In the mid-1990s Lü Hsiulien looked back on the 1970s in these terms: "The 1970s was not only a very difficult decade in my life but also an era when Taiwanese society was reborn in a baptism of fire." To her, this decade, which saw her transition from being a "new feminist" to becoming a member of the Dangwai, "was indispensable to the modernization of Taiwan."[9] Roughly at the same time, Nanfang Shuo (Wang Xingqing), who joined the magazine committee of *The Intellectual* when he was a NTU student, as mentioned in chapter 3, also looked back on the politico-cultural activism of his generation. He noted that "the protest movements of students and young intellectuals in 1960s America, which preceded the Taiwanese counterparts by ten years," planted the seeds for the growth of grassroots democracy, multiculturalism, environmentalism, feminism, and the like in the 1980s. "Just as the indignant love of Western youth in the 1960s planted the seeds that sprouted in the 1980s, so the 1970s in Taiwan prepared the soil for today—the 1990s."[10] The title of his recollective essay is historically and metaphorically insightful: "Only Then Did Taiwan Grow Up" (Nashi, Taiwan cai zhangda).

In a short essay, the writer-journalist Yang Zhao once succinctly, but a little sarcastically, characterized the 1970s in Taiwan as a period of "discovering China" (*faxian Zhongguo*). He wrote:

> We can use the term "discover Taiwan" (*faxian Taiwan*) to describe the core of thought in the 1970s. But people at the time in the 1970s thought what they discovered was "China," rather than Taiwan. . . .
>
> As time passed into the 1970s, the concept of "China" itself became the most important object of controversy. The question forming in people's minds, in fact, was: Could the society we had developed and the life we were living in Taiwan be regarded as "Chinese" at all? Those who gave a positive answer to this question began to cast a dubious eye on the historical and geographical symbolism used to represent China before, those by-products of nostalgia, believing that they were really empty and rootless. [They argued that] only when we grasped the present and what was close to us could we truly grasp "China."
>
> This idea ran through the major cultural debates of the time . . . the idea that "Taiwan in reality could stand for China." . . . This idea was a wellspring of the subsequent discourse of native Taiwaneseness, but it first emerged in the form of a vehement Chinese nationalism.[11]

The documentation of the zeitgeist of 1970s Taiwan in this book validates Yang's (presumably tentative) argument.

At the beginning of the 1980s, after the KMT crackdown at the end of the 1970s, many young intellectuals of local Taiwanese background who just a few years, or months, earlier had been staunchly Chinese discovered they were exclusively Taiwanese and began trying to convince everyone else that they were exclusively Taiwanese, too.[12] It is easy to understand this switch in national identity, and in national narration, in simplistic terms, in terms of essentialism or instrumentalism. On the first, essentialist reading, before it was safe to be publicly Taiwanese, people just pretended to be Chinese, but their patriotic declarations of Chinese identity were completely inauthentic. When it was safe, they authentically declared their Taiwanese identity. It should be obvious to anyone with a sense of history that this is a naïve position on principle, and to anyone who has studied the history of education in postwar Taiwan it seems to underestimate the power of ideological dissemination. On the second, instrumentalist reading, people were Chinese when it advanced their interests, and when they realized that it was advantageous to declare themselves Taiwanese, they immediately switched. This, too, seems rather naïve, and to assume a cold, calculating view of human nature that would be more at home in an economics textbook than in a sociological treatise.[13]

Neither argument is a straw man. Taiwanese nationalists would like to believe Su Beng that Taiwanese people may have been oppressed through the ages but have always been Taiwanese.[14] At most there is an epistemological misunderstanding: people who are ontologically Taiwanese were fooled for a time into thinking they were Japanese or Chinese. As for instrumentalism, there is a lot of criticism of Taiwanese nationalism issuing from both sides of the Taiwan Strait. Critics have accused the Taiwanese nationalists of having "political ambitions" (*zhengzhi yexin*), of harboring "selfish designs" (*bieyou juxin*), of being "frenzied and perverse" (*sangxin bingkuang*), or of "recounting history but forgetting their origins" (*shudian wangzu*). In such criticism is a quite common—and crude—version of instrumentalism. It is as if national identity is purely a matter of specific (political, immoral, or selfish) "interests."[15]

I have argued against either essentialism or instrumentalism throughout this book. Instead I presented my own, alternative interpretation, which was inspired by narrative identity theory. For essentialists, narratives are to be judged by whether they fit a nation. To Taiwanese nationalists, obviously, the Chinese national narrative the KMT taught the return-to-reality generation was not a good fit; no wonder it was replaced with a Taiwanese national narrative in the 1980s. For instrumentalists, narratives are "instruments" that rational agents use to achieve their "political interests or ambitions." The Chinese national narrative of history advanced the interests of the KMT and the Mainlanders in general, while the Taiwanese national narrative of history advanced the interests of the Taiwanese majority.[16] It is that simple, apparently. I have written this book to argue that it is not that simple.

Rather than a fit for an essence, or an instrument for advancing some collective's interest, I view narrative as an embodiment of human understanding that shapes human understanding and emotion in new ways with each generation. The perspective of narrative identity that I have adopted throughout this book could be described as interpretative. Historical narrative for political agents is interpretative in that it is a means of understanding the self in social and temporal context. It is a way of constructing collective identity and motivating praxis. Rather than an essence, there is a set of materials, to which new materials are continually being added, that is used to construct identity anew when the need for new kinds of action arises. There are indeed interests, but they are not calculated coldly; they are instead judged in the warmth of the chambers of the *xin*, the heart-and-mind that Chinese philosophers have been trying to understand since antiquity. On this understanding, it will not do for us to simply disbelieve the constant apparently heartfelt declarations of Chinese national identity in texts from the return-to-reality generation throughout the 1970s. We have to consider the possibility that if a person says he or she feels Chinese, he or she *is* at that moment in time.

In his classic *The Sociological Imagination*, in a passage that is deeply moving to any committed sociologist, C. Wright Mills wrote:

> The sociological imagination enables its possessor to understand the larger historical scene in terms of its meaning for the inner life and the external career of a variety of individuals. . . . We have come to know that every individual lives, from one generation to the next, in some society; that he lives out a biography, and that he lives it out within some historical sequence. By the fact of his living he contributes, however minutely, to the shaping of this society and to the course of its history, even as he is made by society and by its historical push and shove.
>
> The sociological imagination enables us to grasp history and biography and the relations between the two within society. That is its task and its promise. To recognize this task and this promise is the mark of the classic social analyst. . . . And it is the signal of what is best in contemporary studies of man and society.
>
> No social study that does not come back to the problems of biography, of history and of their intersections within a society has completed its intellectual journey.[17]

To proceed with the sociological imagination to analyze postwar Taiwanese society by using the concept of generation as an analytical perspective and attempt to grasp the relations between history and biography, structure and agency, and self and society—this book has resulted from an application of the sociological imagination to the roots of the Taiwan turn in politics and culture.

The "Taiwan turn"—the indigenization or Taiwanization of politics and culture—culminated in the victory of the DPP over the KMT in the presidential elections of 2000 and 2004. Chen Shuibian and Lü Hsiulien served as president and vice president, respectively, for two terms. Nothing is inevitable, of course. In 2008 the KMT regained the presidency. President Ma Yingjeou was eager to seek rapprochement with the PRC.

For many, the rise of China as a global power from the late twentieth century on amounts to the return of a hegemonic Chinese empire. This is especially true for people in those regions or countries that were historical peripheries of the Chinese empire. China is notorious for its extreme aversion to dissent, let alone nationalism in Taiwan, Tibet, and Xinjiang (and Hong Kong). Its recent heavy-handed approach to anti-China protesters in Hong Kong and to territorial disputes with neighboring countries has validated the fear that has haunted many in these regions or countries.

As for Taiwan, the hegemony of Chinese nationalism championed by the PRC is overwhelmingly oppressive and presumably far outstrips that of the KMT. Moreover, in Taiwan, the generation whose members initiated the de-exilic cultural politics in the 1970s and which has shaped the process of democratization and indigenization since the 1980s has yielded the stage to the next generation, to which Tsai Ingwen, the president since 2016, belongs. That the DPP regained power in May 2016, especially that Tsai won her second term by defeating the KMT candidate, Han Kuoyu, in a landslide in January 2020, presumably epitomized the will of the majority of Taiwanese voters to defend their incipient nationhood against a new Chinese empire. As always, history is testing this island country. The future of its democracy and indigenized cultural development remains threatened.

Glossary

Bai Qiu 白萩

Bai Xianyong (Pai Hsienyung) 白先勇

baihua 白話

bainian guochi 百年國恥

Baiwan xiaoshi fengxian yundong 百萬小時奉獻運動

banshan ren 半山人

Bao Qingtian 包青天

baodao wenxue 報導文學

Baodiao 保釣

Baowei diaoyutai yundong 保衛釣魚台運動

Bashi niandai 《八十年代》

"Bayue de xiangcun" 〈八月的鄉村〉

Beibu xinwenxue, xinju yundong zhuanhao 北部新文學、新劇運動專號

Beiyapo de Taibao kangri shihua 《被壓迫的台胞抗日史話》

Beiyapozhe de nuhou—Jiang Weishui xiansheng xuanji 《被壓迫者的怒吼—蔣渭水先生選集》

bensheng de xiangtu wenxue 本省的鄉土文學

benshengren 本省人

bentu wenxue 本土文學

bentuhua 本土化

bieyou juxin 別有居心

Cai Huiru 蔡惠如

Cai Peihuo 蔡培火

Chan 《蟬》

"Chan" 〈蟬〉
Changhua 彰化
Chen Duanming 陳端明
Chen Fangming 陳芳明
Chen Guying 陳鼓應
Chen Huoquan 陳火泉
Chen Jianong (Chen Fangming) 陳嘉農 (陳芳明)
Chen Kunlun 陳坤崙
Chen Lingyu 陳玲玉
Chen Qianwu 陳千武
Chen Ruoxi (Lucy Chen) 陳若曦
Chen Shaoting 陳少廷
Chen Shuhong 陳樹鴻
Chen Shuibian 陳水扁
Chen Wanyi 陳萬益
Chen Wanzhen 陳婉真
Chen Xin 陳炘
Chen Yi 陳儀
Chen Yishan 陳意珊
Chen Yingzhen 陳映真
Chiang Chingkuo 蔣經國
Chiang Kaishek 蔣介石
Chouxiang shi《愁鄉石》
"Chuan hongchenshan de nanhai" 〈穿紅襯衫的男孩〉
Chuang Shihhuan 莊世桓
Chuangshiji shishe 創世紀詩社
Chungli 中壢
"Cunguang guanbuzhu" 〈春光關不住〉
da Zhongguo 大中國
Dadongya wenxuezhe dahui 大東亞文學者大會
Dailian huixun《代聯會訊》
dangjia zuozhu 當家做 (作) 主
Dangwai 黨外
Dangwai xinshengdai 黨外新生代
Danxin hui 丹心會
Daxue xinwen《大學新聞》
Daxue zazhi《大學雜誌》
Di Renhua 狄仁華
"Diyijian chaishi" 〈第一件差事〉
Donghai huayuan 東海花園
dui xuexiao kaidao, xiang shehui jinjun 對學校開刀,向社會進軍
Duosang 多桑

Eliao 蚵寮

"Emama chujia" 〈鵝媽媽出嫁〉

Ererba shijian 二二八事件

"Fangong dalu wenti" 〈反攻大陸問題〉

fangong wenxue 反共文學

fatong 法統

faxian Taiwan 發現台灣

faxian Zhongguo 發現中國

Feibaoli de douzheng 《非暴力的鬥爭》

Fuermosha 《福爾摩沙》

Fuzhou 福州

"Gao quanguo tongbao shu" 〈告全國同胞書〉

Gao Xinjiang 高信疆

Gao Yushu 高玉樹

Gao Zhun 高準

Gaoxiong shijian (Meilidao shijian) 高雄事件（美麗島事件）

"Gei Jiang Jingguo xiansheng de xin" 〈給蔣經國先生的信〉

Gemingjia—Jiang Weishui 《革命家—蔣渭水》

gexin baoTai 革新保台

gongfei 共匪

Gonglunbao 《公論報》

gongnongbing wenxue 工農兵文學

"Gongtong lai tuidong xinshengdai zhengzhi yundong!" 〈共同來推動新生代政治運動！〉

guangfu 光復

Guangfu qian Taiwan wenxue quanji 《光復前台灣文學全集》

guchen yishi 孤臣意識

guer 孤兒

guer wenxue 孤兒文學

guer yishi 孤兒意識

"Guer zhi lian" 〈孤兒之戀〉

Guilin 桂林

Guo Guoji 郭國基

Guo Qiusheng 郭秋生

Guo Rongzhao 郭榮趙

Guo Shuitan 郭水潭

Guo Yuxin 郭雨新

guochi 國恥

Guojia wenhua yishu jijinhui 國家文化藝術基金會

Guoli bianyiguan 國立編譯館

Guoli Taiwan wenxue guan 國立台灣文學館

Guomin dahui 國民大會

"Guoshi jiulun" 〈國是九論〉

"Guoshi zhengyan" 〈國是諍言〉
Guoshiguan 國史館
Guowen 國文
Han Jue 寒爵
Heluo 河洛
Haerbin 哈爾濱
Han Kuoyu 韓國瑜
He Wenzhen 何文振
He Xin 何欣
Hong Sanxiong 洪三雄
Hong Tong 洪通
Hsiao Hsinhuang 蕭新煌
Hu Qiuyuan 胡秋原
Hu Shih 胡適
Huang Chaoqin 黃朝琴
Huang Chengcong 黃呈聰
Huang Chunming 黃春明
Huang Deshi 黃得時
Huang Hua 黃華
Huang Huangxiong 黃煌雄
Huang Mo (Mab Huang) 黃默
Huang Shihui 黃石輝
Huang Xinjie 黃信介
Huangmin fenggonghui 皇民奉公會
Hunan 湖南
huigui xiangtu 回歸鄉土
huigui xianshi 回歸現實
huigui xianshi shidai 回歸現實世代
Ji Xian 紀弦
Jianchayuan 監察院
Jiang Menglin 蔣夢麟
Jiang Weishui 蔣渭水
Jiang Weishui zhuan—Taiwan de xianzhi xianjue《蔣渭水傳—台灣的先知先覺》
Jiang Xun 蔣勳
Jianguo dang 建國黨
Jianjian fuchou yudong 建艦復仇運動
jiatianxia 家天下
"jiebang" wenti 「接棒」問題
Jin Yaoji (Ambrose Y. C. King) 金耀基
junxun jiaoguan 軍訓教官
Kang Ningxiang 康寧祥
Kaohsiung 高雄

Keelung 基隆

Kinmen (Quemoy) 金門

Lai He 賴和

Lai lai lai, lai Taida, qu qu qu, qu Meiguo 來來來，來台大，去去去，去美國

Lanxing shishe 藍星詩社

"Laonianren han bangzi" 〈老年人和棒子〉

Lee Tenghui 李登輝

Lei Zhen 雷震

Li Ao 李敖

Li Kuixian 李魁賢

Li Minyong 李敏勇

Li Nanheng 李南衡

Li Oufan (Leo Oufan Lee) 李歐梵

Li Qiao 李喬

Li Rongchun 李榮春

Li shikan 《笠詩刊》

Li shishe 笠詩社

Li Shuangze 李雙澤

Li Wanju 李萬居

Liang Shuming 梁漱溟

liangge Zhongguo 兩個中國

Lianhebao 《聯合報》

Liao Qingxiu 廖清秀

Lifayuan 立法院

Lin Hengtai 林亨泰

Lin Hengzhe 林衡哲

Lin Huaimin 林懷民

Lin Rongsan 林榮三

Lin Ruiming 林瑞明

Lin Wengeng 林問耕

Lin Xiantang 林獻堂

"Lin Xiantang xiansheng yu 'zuguo shijian'—jianlun Taiwan zhishi fenzi kangri yundong de lishi yiyi" 〈林獻堂先生與「祖國事件」─兼論台灣智識份子抗日運動的歷史
意義〉

Lin Xingyue 林惺嶽

Lin Yangmin 林央敏

Lin Yixiong 林義雄

Lin Youchun 林幼春

Lin Zaijue 林載爵

Lin Zhengjie 林正杰

Lin Zhuoshui 林濁水

Liu Daren 劉大任

Liu Ruojun 劉若君

Liu Yuxi 劉禹錫

liuwang xintai 流亡心態

liuxuesheng wenxue 留學生文學

Long Yingzong 龍瑛宗

Longzu shikan《龍族詩刊》

Longzu shishe 龍族詩社

Lü Guomin 呂國民

Lü Hsiulien (Annette Lu) 呂秀蓮

Lü Heruo 呂赫若

Lü Xingchang 呂興昌

Lüdao 綠島

Luoshui 洛水

Ma Yingjeou 馬英九

Matsu 馬祖

Meilidao《美麗島》

Meilidao shijian (Gaoxiong shijian) 美麗島事件（高雄事件）

Meinong 美濃

meiyougen de yidai 沒有根的一代

"Mengya"〈萌芽〉

Minzhu chao《民主潮》

"Minzhu wansui"〈民主萬歲〉

"Mofancun"〈模範村〉

Mou Tianlei 牟天磊

Nanfang Shuo (Wang Xingqing) 南方朔（王杏慶）

Nantou 南投

"Nashi, Taiwan cai zhangda"〈那時，台灣才長大〉

nianqing zhishi fenzi 年輕知識份子

nuhua 奴化

nuhua jiaoyu 奴化教育

Ong Joktik 王育德

Ouyang Zi 歐陽子

Peng Mingmin 彭明敏

Peng Ruijin 彭瑞金

Penghu 澎湖

Pingdong 屏東

pinglun zhuanhao 評論專號（《龍族詩刊》）

Puli 埔里

Qi Yishou 齊益壽

Qian Mu 錢穆

Qian Yongxiang 錢永祥

Qiaotou 橋頭（鄉）

Qideng Sheng 七等生
Qigu 七股
Qinmindang 親民黨
"Qiqi shibian yu kangri yundong"「七七事變與抗日運動」(專輯)
Qiu Fengjia 丘逢甲
qu Zhongguohua 去中國化
Quanguo qingnian tuanjie cujinhui 全國青年團結促進會
Quemoy (Kinmen) 金門
Renjian 人間 (副刊)
renmin 人民
Riju shidai 日據時代
"Riju shidai Taiwan wenxue de huigu"〈日據時代台灣文學的回顧〉
Riju xia Taiwan xinwenxue, mingji《日據下台灣新文學，明集》
"Ruhe shi qingnian jieshang zheyibang"〈如何使青年接上這一棒〉
Ruifang 瑞芳
sangxin bingkuang 喪心病狂
Sanmin zhuyi 三民主義
shandi tongbao 山地同胞
"Shayaonala-zaijian"〈莎喲娜拉-再見〉
Shehui fuwutuan 社會服務團
"Sheishuo women bushi xingfu de yidai"〈誰說我們不是幸福的一代〉
Shengeng《深耕》
Shenggen《生根》
shengji 省籍
shengji wenti 省籍問題
Shi Junmei 史君美
Shi Cuifeng 施翠峰
Shi Mingde 施明德
shidai 世代
shidaifu 士大夫
shijie wenxue 世界文學
shudian wangzu 數典忘祖
Song Dongyang (Chen Fangming) 宋冬陽 (陳芳明)
Song Zelai 宋澤萊
"Songbaofu"〈送報伕〉
Songbaofu《送報伕》
Su Beng (Shi Ming) 史明
Taibao kangzi shihua《台胞抗日史話》
Taibei wenwu《台北文物》
Taibeiren《臺北人》
Taibeishi wenxian weiyuanhui 台北市文獻委員會
Taida fayan《台大法言》

Taida zhexuexi shijian 台大哲學系事件

Taiwan bihui 台灣筆會

Taiwan dangwai renshi zhuxuantuan 台灣黨外人士助選團

Taiwan daxue faxueyuan xuesheng daibiaohui 台灣大學法學院學生代表會（法代會）

Taiwan daxue xuesheng daibiao lianhehui 台灣大學學生代表聯合會（代聯會）

Taiwan de guoqu yu weilai《台灣的過去與未來》

Taiwan de Sun Zhongshan 台灣的孫中山

Taiwan de xiangtu wenxue 台灣的鄉土文學

"Taiwan de xiangtu wenxue"〈台灣的鄉土文學〉

Taiwan de xianzhi xianjuezhe—Jiang Weishui xianshen《台灣的先知先覺者—蔣渭水先生》

Taiwan difang zizhi lianmeng 台灣地方自治聯盟

Taiwan duli 台灣獨立

Taiwan duli yundong 台灣獨立運動

Taiwan huawen 台灣話文

Taiwan jindai minzu yundong 台灣近代民族運動

Taiwan jingbei zongsilingbu 台灣警備總司令部

Taiwan jingshen 台灣精神

Taiwan kangri shihua《台灣抗日史話》

Taiwan: kumen de lishi《台灣：苦悶的歷史》

Taiwan minbao《台灣民報》

Taiwan minzhondang 台灣民眾黨

Taiwan minzu wenxue 台灣民族文學

Taiwan minzu yundong shi《台灣民族運動史》

Taiwan qingnian《台灣青年》

"Taiwan shehuili de fenxi"〈台灣社會力的分析〉

Taiwan shengli xingzheng zhuanke xuexiao 台灣省立行政專科學校

"Taiwan shi meilidao"〈台灣是美麗島〉

Taiwan shiguan 台灣史觀

Taiwan tongbao 台灣同胞

Taiwan wenhua xiehui 台灣文化協會

Taiwan wenxue 台灣文學

Taiwan wenxue shigang《台灣文學史綱》

Taiwan wenyi《台灣文藝》

Taiwan wenyi lianmeng 台灣文藝聯盟

Taiwan xianfa caoan 台灣憲法草案

Taiwan xinmin bao《台灣新民報》

Taiwan xinsheng bao《台灣新生報》

Taiwan xinshi de huigu 台灣新詩的回顧（專欄）

Taiwan xinwenxue 台灣新文學

Taiwan xinwenxue yundong jianshi《台灣新文學運動簡史》

Taiwan xinwenxue yundong sishi nian《台灣新文學運動40年》

Taiwan yihui shezhi qingyuan yundong 台灣議會設置請願運動

Taiwan yishi 台灣意識

Taiwan yishu yanjiuhui 台灣藝術研究會

Taiwan zhenglun《台灣政論》

Taiwan zhutixing 台灣主體性

Taiwan zongdufu jingcha yangezhi《台灣總督府警察沿革誌》

Taiwan zongdufu yixuexiao 台灣總督府醫學校

Taiwanhua 台灣化

Taiwanren 台灣人

Taiwanren shibainian shi《台灣人四百年史》

Taiwansheng xingzheng zhangguan gongshu 臺灣省行政長官公署

Taiyu 台語

Taiyu jingxuan wenku 台語精選文庫

"Tan zhongguo xinwenyi yundong—wei jinian wusi yu wenyijie er zuo"〈談中國新
  文藝運動—為紀念五四與文藝節而作〉

Tang Qian 唐倩

"Tang Qian de xiju"〈唐倩的喜劇〉

Tang Wenbiao 唐文標

Taoyuan 桃園

Tian Qiujin 田秋菫

Tianjin 天津

Tongbao xu tuanjie, tuanjie zhenyouli 同胞須團結，團結真有力

Tsai Ingwen 蔡英文

tudi 土地

wailai zhengquan 外來政權

waishengren 外省人

Wang Fusu 王復蘇

Wang Hongjun 王洪鈞

Wang Shangyi 王尚義

Wang Shilang 王詩琅

Wang Tuo 王拓

Wang Wenxing 王文興

Wang Xiaobo 王曉波

Wang Xingqing (Nanfang Shuo) 王杏慶（南方朔）

Wang Zhenhe 王禎和

weiwu buneng qu, pinjian buneng yi 威武不能屈，貧賤不能移

Wen Xin (Xu Bingcheng) 文心（許炳成）

wenhua Taidu 文化台獨

Wenji《文季》

Wenxing《文星》

Wenxue jikan《文學季刊》

wenxue Taidu 文學台獨

Wenxue Taiwan《文學台灣》

Wenxuejie《文學界》

wenyanwen 文言文

wenyi qingnian 文藝青年

wo ai Taiwan 我愛台灣

Wu Che 吳哲

Wu Fengshan 吳豐山

Wu Jinfa 吳錦發

Wu Jiabang 吳嘉邦

Wu Naiteh 吳乃德

Wu Nairen 吳乃仁

Wu Nianzhen 吳念真

Wu Sanlian 吳三連

Wu Xinrong 吳新榮

Wu Yingtao 吳瀛濤

Wu Yongfu 巫永福

Wu Zhuoliu 吳濁流

"Wu zhuoliu lun"〈吳濁流論〉

Wuchang qiyi 武昌起義

"Wusi yu Taiwan xinwenxue yundong"〈五四與台灣新文學運動〉

Wuwang zaiju yundong 毋忘在莒運動

"Wuyicun"〈無醫村〉

Xiachao luntan《夏潮論壇》

Xi'an 西安

Xiandai shishe 現代詩社

Xiandai wenxue《現代文學》

xiandai Zhongguo 現代中國

xiandai Zhongguo zhishi fenzi 現代中國知識份子

Xiandaishi《現代詩》

Xiandaishi lunzhan 現代詩論戰

"Xiangchou siyun"〈鄉愁四韻〉

xiangtu 鄉土

xiangtu Taiwan 鄉土台灣

xiangtu wenxue 鄉土文學

Xiangtu wenxue lunzhan 鄉土文學論戰

xiangtu yishi 鄉土意識

"Xianjieduan Taiwan wenxue bentuhua de wenti"〈現階段台灣文學本土化的問題〉

xianjuezhe 先覺者

xianshi 現實

Xiao Jun 蕭軍

Xiao Yuzhen 蕭裕珍

"Xiaolin lai Taibei"〈小林來台北〉

xin 心

Xingzhengyuan wenhua jianshe weiyuanhui 行政院文化建設委員會

xinhai 辛亥

Xinjiang 新疆

xinnüxing zhuyi 新女性主義

xinshengdai 新生代

Xu Caode 許曹德

Xu Daran 許達然

Xu Fuguan 徐復觀

Xu Shixian 許世賢

Xu Xinliang 許信良

Xundaochu 訓導處

xungen 尋根

"Yabubian de meiguihua" 〈壓不扁的玫瑰花〉

Yan Yimo 顏尹謨

Yan Huang zisun 炎黃子孫

yanfen didai wenxue 鹽分地帶文學

Yang Hexiong (Yang Qingchu) 楊和雄 (楊青矗)

Yang Hua 楊華

Yang Kui 楊逵

"Yang Kui huaxiang" 〈楊逵畫像〉

Yang Kui huaxiang 《楊逵畫像》

Yang Qingchu 楊青矗

Yang Xian 楊弦

Yang Yunping 楊雲萍

Yang Zhao 楊照

yangnü 養女

Yao Jiawen 姚嘉文

Yaxiya de guer 《亞細亞的孤兒》

Ye Hongsheng 葉洪生

Ye Rongzhong 葉榮鐘

Ye Shitao 葉石濤

Ye Yunyun 葉芸芸

"Yige xiaoshimin de xinsheng" 〈一個小市民的心聲〉

yige Zhongguo liangge zhengfu 一個中國兩個政府

Yilan 宜蘭

Yin Di 隱地

Yin Haiguang 殷海光

yinren 隱忍

Youjian zonglü, youjian zonglü 《又見棕櫚‧又見棕櫚》

Yu Chen Yueying 余陳月瑛

Yu Dengfa 余登發

Yu Guangzhong 余光中

Yu Lihua 於梨華

Yu Shuping 俞叔平

Yu Tiancong 尉天驄

Yuandong juchang 遠東劇場

Yunlin 雲林

Yunmen wuji 雲門舞集

zai Taiwan de Zhongguo wenxue 在台灣的中國文學

zaixiang youquan neng gedi, guchen wuli ke huitian 宰相有權能割地，孤臣無力可回天

"Zaogao de Taiwan wenxuejie" 〈糟糕的台灣文學界〉

Zeng Guihai 曾貴海

Zhang Ailing (Eileen Chang) 張愛玲

Zhang Junhong 張俊宏

Zhang Liangze 張良澤

Zhang Shaowen 張紹文

Zhang Shenqie 張深切

Zhang Wenhuan 張文環

Zhang Wojun 張我軍

Zhang Wojun wenji 《張我軍文集》

Zhang Xiaofeng 張曉風

Zhang Xiguo 張系國

Zhang Yanxian 張炎憲

Zhao Tianyi 趙天儀

Zhao Zhiti 趙知悌

Zheng Chenggong (Koxinga) 鄭成功

Zheng Hongsheng 鄭鴻生

Zheng Jiongming 鄭炯明

Zheng Qingwen 鄭清文

Zhengdang fa 政黨法

Zhenghong 正宏

zhengzhi yexin 政治野心

Zheyidai zazhi 《這一代雜誌》

Zhiyuan Wuhan qingnian xuesheng fangong kangbao yundong 支援武漢青年學生反
    共抗暴運動

"Zhong digua" 〈種地瓜〉

Zhong Lihe 鍾理和

Zhong Lihe zuopin yanjiu zhuanji 鍾理和作品研究專輯

Zhong Tiemin 鍾鐵民

Zhong Zhaozheng 鍾肇政

Zhongguo laobaixing 中國老百姓

Zhongguo luntan 《中國論壇》

Zhongguo minzhu shehui dang 中國民主社會黨

Zhongguo qingnian fangong jiuguotuan 中國青年反共救國團
Zhongguo qingnian ziqiang yundong 中國青年自強運動
Zhongguo qingniandang 中國青年黨
Zhongguo shibao《中國時報》
Zhongguo wenxue 中國文學
Zhongguo wenyi fuxing yundong《中國文藝復興運動》
Zhongguo wenyi xiehui 中國文藝協會
Zhongguo xiandai minge ji 中國現代民歌集
Zhongguo xiandai minge yundong 中國現代民歌運動
Zhongguo xiandaiwu 中國現代舞
Zhongguo yishi 中國意識
Zhongguo zhengshi 中國正史
Zhongguohua 中國化
Zhonghua minguo duli 中華民國獨立
Zhonghua wenhua fuxing yondong 中華文化復興運動
Zhongli shijian 中壢事件
Zhongshan beilu 中山北路
Zhongxi wenhua lunzhan 中西文化論戰
zhongyang minyi daibiao yingfou quanmian gaixuan 中央民意代表應否全面改選
Zhongyang ribao《中央日報》
zhongyuan 中原
Zhu Ming 朱銘
Zhu Xining 朱西寧
Zhu Yunhan 朱雲漢
zhuti 主體
zhutixing 主體性
Zijue yundong 自覺運動
Zili wanbao《自立晚報》
Ziyou qingnian《自由青年》
Ziyou Zhongguo《自由中國》
zuguo 祖國
"Zuguo"〈祖國〉
"Zuguo jun laile"〈祖國軍來了〉
zuguo yishi 祖國意識

Notes

Preface

1. C. Wright Mills, *The Sociological Imagination* (Oxford: Oxford University Press, 1959), 6.
2. Alexis de Tocqueville, *The Old Regime and the French Revolution*, trans. Stuart Gilbert (New York: Anchor, 1955 [1856]), xi–xii.
3. Richard Madsen, *Democracy's Dharma: Religious Renaissance and Political Development in Taiwan* (Berkeley: University of California Press, 2007), xxii.

Introduction

1. E.g., Thomas B. Gold, "Taiwan's Quest for Identity in the Shadow of China," in *In the Shadow of China: Political Developments in Taiwan since 1949*, ed. Steve Tsang (Honolulu: University of Hawai'i Press, 1993), 169–92; Alan M. Wachman, *Taiwan: National Identity and Democratization* (Armonk, N.Y.: M. E. Sharpe, 1994); Steven J. Hood, *The Kuomintang and the Democratization of Taiwan* (Boulder, Colo.: Westview Press, 1997); Pelle Wennerlund, *Taiwan: In Search of the Nation* (Stockholm: Department of Chinese Studies, Stockholm University, 1997); A-chin Hsiau, *Contemporary Taiwanese Cultural Nationalism* (London: Routledge, 2000); Stéphane Corcuff, ed., *Memories of the Future: National Identity Issues and the Search for a New Taiwan* (Armonk, N.Y.: M. E. Sharpe, 2002); John Makeham and A-chin Hsiau, eds., *Cultural, Ethnic, and Political Nationalism in Contemporary*

Taiwan: Bentuhua (New York: Palgrave Macmillan, 2005); J. Bruce Jacobs, *Democratizing Taiwan* (Leiden: Brill, 2012); Yachung Chuang, *Democracy on Trial: Social Movements and Cultural Politics in Postauthoritarian Taiwan* (Hong Kong: Chinese University Press, 2013); J. Bruce Jacobs and Peter Kang, eds., *Changing Taiwanese Identities* (London: Routledge, 2017); Mikael Mattlin, *Politicized Society: Taiwan's Struggle with Its One-Party Past* (Copenhagen: NIAS Press, 2018).

2. Mark Harrison, *Legitimacy, Meaning, and Knowledge in the Making of Taiwanese Identity* (New York: Palgrave Macmillan, 2006), chap. 5.

3. Edward W. Said, "Intellectual Exile: Expatriates and Marginals," in his *Representations of the Intellectual* (New York: Pantheon Books, 1994), 48–49.

4. See, e.g., Emil Mihai Cioran, "Advantages of Exile," in *Altogether Elsewhere: Writers on Exile*, ed. Marc Robinson (Boston: Faber and Faber, 1994 [1956]), 150–52; Leszek Kolakowski, "In Praise of Exile," in *Altogether Elsewhere: Writers on Exile*, ed. Marc Robinson (Boston: Faber and Faber, 1994 [1985]), 188–92; Susan Rubin Suleiman, ed., *Exile and Creativity: Signposts, Travelers, Outsiders, Backward Glances* (Durham, N.C.: Duke University Press, 1998); Michael Hanne, ed., *Creativity in Exile* (Amsterdam: Rodopi, 2004).

5. Thomas B. Gold, "Civil Society and Taiwan's Quest for Identity," in *Cultural Change in Postwar Taiwan*, ed. Stevan Harrell and Huang Chünchieh (Boulder, Colo.: Westview Press, 1994), 47–53.

6. Doubt was voiced in *Ziyou Zhongguo* [Free China, 1949–1960], a journal established by a group of liberal Mainlanders, including such eminent figures as Hu Shih (1891–1962), Lei Zhen (1897–1979), and Yin Haiguang (1919–1969), in November 1949. One of the two editorials entitled "Fangong dalu wenti" [The issue of counterattack on the mainland], published in the August 1957 issue, asserted the impossibility of any counterattack. See Ziyou Zhongguo bianji wei-yuanhui 自由中國編輯委員會, "Jinri de wenti (er): Fanggong dalu wenti" [Today's issues (part 2): The issue of launching a counterattack on the mainland], *Ziyou Zhongguo* 17, no. 3 (1957): 69–71. In 1960 Lei Zhen was arrested on the charge of sedition and sheltering communists and the magazine was closed down.

7. John Foster Dulles, U.S. secretary of state, visited Taiwan in late October 1958 during the Second Taiwan Strait Crisis, when the PRC shelled the islands of Quemoy (Kinmen), which were and remain under ROC control. The ROC-U.S. Joint Communiqué issued at the conclusion of Dulles's visit reaffirmed that the "Mutual Defense Treaty Between the United States and the Republic of China" of 1954 was "defensive in character." It also declared that although the ROC government stated that "the restoration of freedom to its people on the mainland" was "its sacred mission," it believed that "the principal means of successfully achieving its mission" was "Dr. Sun Yatsen's Three Principles of the People and not the use of force." See United States Department of State, Bureau of Public Affairs, *American Foreign Policy, Current Documents, 1958* (Washington, D.C.: U.S. Government Printing Office, 1962), 1184–85.

8. Edwin A. Winckler, "Cultural Policy on Postwar Taiwan," in *Cultural Change in Postwar Taiwan*, ed. Stevan Harrell and Huang Chünchieh (Boulder, Colo.: Westview Press, 1994), 23, 27–28.

9. Hsiau, *Contemporary Taiwanese Cultural Nationalism*, 66, 152.

10. Hsiau, *Contemporary Taiwanese Cultural Nationalism*, 150–53.

11. See Hayden White, "The Value of Narrative in the Representation of Reality," in his *The Content of the Form: Narrative Discourse and Historical Representation* (Baltimore, Md.: Johns Hopkins University Press, 1987), 9–21.

12. The term "Axial Age" was coined by German philosopher Karl Jaspers. He used it to describe the critical period from 800 to 200 BC, when great thinkers emerged in India, China, and the Occident and laid the foundations for world civilization. It was a period in world history that gave rise to "a common frame of historical self-comprehension for all peoples." Jaspers argues: "In this age were born the fundamental categories within which we still think today, and the beginnings of the world religions, by which human beings still live, were created. . . . As a result of this process, hitherto unconsciously accepted ideas, customs and conditions were subjected to examination, questioned and liquidated. Everything was swept into the vortex. In so far as the traditional substance still possessed vitality and reality, its manifestations were clarified and thereby transmuted." See Karl T. Jaspers, *The Origin and Goal of History* (New Haven, Conn.: Yale University Press, 1953 [1949]), 1–2.

13. Molly Andrews, "Generational Consciousness, Dialogue, and Political Engagement," in *Generational Consciousness, Narrative, and Politics*, ed. June Edmunds and Bryan S. Turner (Lanham, Md.: Rowman & Littlefield, 2002), 78–80. See chapter 1 for more discussion about "conscientization."

14. E.g., Fang Hao 方豪, *Taiwan minzu yundong xiaoshi* [A brief history of the Taiwanese nationalist movement] (Taipei: Zhengzhong, 1951); Guo Tingyi 郭廷以, *Taiwan shishi gaishuo* [An outline of Taiwanese history] (Taipei: Zhengzhong, 1954); Taiwansheng wenxian weiyuanhui 台灣省文獻委員會, *Taiwan shihua* [A history of Taiwan] (Taichung: Taiwansheng wenxian weiyuanhui, 1974); Lin Hengdao 林衡道, ed., *Taiwanshi* [A history of Taiwan] (Taichung: Taiwansheng wenxian weiyuanhui, 1977); Chen Sanjing 陳三井, "Guomin keming yu Taiwan" [The Nationalist Revolution and Taiwan], in *Taiwan shiji yuanliu* [The origin and change of historical relics in Taiwan], ed. Taiwansheng wenxian weiyuanhui (Taichung: Taiwansheng wenxian weiyuanhui, 1981), 470–517; Cheng Daxue 程大學, "Taiwan de xianxian xianlie" [Sages and martyrs in Taiwan], in *Taiwan shiji yuanliu* [The origin and change of historical relics in Taiwan], ed. Taiwansheng wenxian weiyuanhui (Taichung: Taiwansheng wenxian weiyuanhui, 1981), 518–48; Li Yunhan 李雲漢, "Guomin geming yu Taiwan guangfu de lishi yuanyuan" [The historical relationship between the Nationalist Revolution and the Retrocession of Taiwan], in *Taiwan shiji yuanliu* [The origin and change of historical relics in Taiwan], ed. Taiwansheng wenxian weiyuanhui (Taichung:

Taiwansheng wenxian weiyuanhui, 1981), 396–469; Pan Jingwei 潘敬尉, ed., *Xue nong yu shui* [Blood is thicker than water] (Taichung: Taiwansheng wenxian weiyuanhui, 1981).

15. Harrison, *Legitimacy, Meaning, and Knowledge,* 120.

16. William A. Callahan, "National Insecurities: Humiliation, Salvation, and Chinese Nationalism," *Alternatives* 29 (2004): 206, 209–10.

17. Stéphane Corcuff, "Introduction: Taiwan, A Laboratory of Identities," in *Memories of the Future: National Identity Issues and the Search for a New Taiwan*, ed. Stéphane Corcuff (Armonk, N.Y.: M. E. Sharpe, 2002), xi–xxiv.

1. Generation and National Narration

1. E.g., Wang Zhenhuan 王振寰, "Taiwan de zhengzhi zhuanxing yu fandui yundong" [Political transformation and the opposition movement in Taiwan], *Taiwan shehui yanjiu jikan* [Taiwan: A radical quarterly in social studies] 2, no. 1 (1989): 90–94; Hungmao Tien, *The Great Transition: Political and Social Change in the Republic of China* (Stanford, Calif.: Hoover Institution Press, 1989), 95–96; Wakabayashi Masahiro 若林正丈, *Taiwan: fenlie guojia yu minzhuhua* [Taiwan: The divided nation and democratization], trans. Hong Jinzhu and Xu Peixian (Taipei: Yuedan, 1994): 179–91; Huang Defu 黄德福, "Xuanju yu Taiwan diqu zhengzhi minzhuhua" [Elections and political democratization in Taiwan], in *Minzhu zhengzhi de fazhan yu chengjiu* [The development and achievements of democratic politics], ed. Taiwan shengzhengfu xinwenchu (Taichung: Taiwan shengzhengfu xinwenchu, 1995), 9–11; Steven J. Hood, *The Kuomintang and the Democratization of Taiwan* (Boulder, Colo.: Westview Press, 1997), 62–64; Christopher Hughes, *Taiwan and Chinese Nationalism: National Identity and Status in International Society* (London: Routledge, 1997), 50–51. Some studies discuss class—working versus middle—in Taiwan's economic development. See Thomas B. Gold, *State and Society in the Taiwan Miracle* (Armonk, N.Y.: M. E. Sharpe, 1986); and Wakabayashi, *Taiwan,* 185–86.

2. Another important factor is gender. For example, it stands to reason that gender identity had a profound effect on activism for Lü Hsiulien (Annette Lu) (see chapter 6), but I leave that topic up to other researchers.

3. Teresa Wright, "Student Mobilization in Taiwan: Civil Society and Its Discontents," *Asian Survey* 39, no. 6 (1999): 986–1008; Shelley Rigger, *Taiwan's Rising Rationalism: Generations, Politics and "Taiwanese Nationalism"* (Washington, D.C.: East West Center, 2006).

4. E.g., Gold, *State and Society in the Taiwan Miracle,* 93–94; Li Xiaofeng 李筱峰, *Taiwan minzhu yundong sishinian* [Forty years of Taiwan's democratic movement] (Taipei: Zili wanbao, 1987), 90–108, 117, 122.

5. E.g., Sheldon Appleton, "Taiwanese and Mainlanders on Taiwan: A Survey of Student Attitudes," *China Quarterly* 44 (1970): 38–65; Sheldon Appleton, "Regime

Support Among Taiwan High School Students," *Asian Survey* 13 (1973): 750–60; Chen Yiyan 陳義彥, *Taiwan diqu daxuesheng zhengzhi shehuihua zhi yanjiu* [A study of university students' political socialization in Taiwan] (Taipei: Jiaxin shuini gongsi wenhua jijinhui, 1978); Chen Yiyan, *Woguo daxuesheng zhengzhi shehuihua zhi yanjiu—shiwunian lai zhengzhi jiazhi yu taidu zhi bianqian* [A study of political socialization of university students in our country—the change in political values and attitudes in the past fifteen years], final report of research project granted by National Science Council (Taipei: Zhengzhi daxue xuanju yanjiu zhongxin, 1991); Chen Yiyan, "Butong zuqun zhengzhi wenhua de shidai fenxi" [A generational analysis of political culture of different ethnicities], *Zhengzhi xuebao* [Chinese political science review] 27 (1996): 83–91; Liu Ichou 劉義周, "Political Support and Voting Participation of Taiwan College Students," *Journal of National Chengchi University* 41 (1979): 37–44; Liu Ichou, "Taiwan de zhengzhi shidai" [Political generations in Taiwan], *Zhengzhi xuebao* [Chinese political science review] 21 (1993): 99–120; Liu Ichou, "Taiwan xuanmin zhengdang xingxiang de shidai chayi" [Generational difference of party image among Taiwanese voters], *Xuanju yanjiu* [Journal of electoral studies] 1, no. 1 (1994): 53–73; Chen Wenjun 陳文俊, *Taiwan diqu zhongxuesheng de zhengzhi taidu ji qi xingcheng yinsu—qingshaonian de zhengzhi shehuihua* [Political attitudes of high school students in Taiwan and their formation factors—political socialization of teenagers] (Taipei: Zixun jiaoyu tuiguang zhongxin jijinhui, 1983); Chen Wenjun, "Taiwan daxuesheng de shengji yishi yu guojia rentong" [Consciousness of provincial background and national identity among university students in Taiwan], *Zhongshan shehui kexue xuebao* [Journal of Sunology: A social science quarterly] 8, no. 2 (1994): 41–91; Chen Wenjun, *Zhengzhi shehuihua yu Taiwan de zhengzhi minzhuhua: da (zhuang) xuesheng de zhengzhi taidu yu jiazhi zhi yanjiu* [Political socialization and political democratization in Taiwan: A study of political attitudes and values of college students] (Kaohsiung: Zhongshan daxue zhengzhixue yanjiusuo, 1997); Chen Wenjun, "Taiwan diqu xuesheng de zhengzhi wenhua: zhong, daxuesheng de zhengzhi taidu yu Taiwan minzhuhua de qianjing" [Political culture among students in Taiwan: political attitudes of high school and university students and the future of Taiwan's democratization], *Guoli zhongshan daxue shehui kexue jikan* [National Sun Yatsen University social science quarterly] 1, no. 3 (1998): 23–60; Chang Maukuei and Hsiao Hsinhuang 張茂桂、蕭新煌, "Daxuesheng de 'Zhongguo jie' yu 'Taiwan jie'—ziwo rending yu tonghun guannian de fenxi" [The "China complex" and the "Taiwan complex" of university students—an analysis of self-identity and idea about intermarriage], *Zhongguo luntan* [China tribune] 25, no. 1 (1987): 34–52; Zhu Quanbin 朱全斌, "You nianling, zuqun deng bianxiang kan Taiwan minzhong de guojia ji wenhua rentong" [A positional analysis of Taiwanese people's national and cultural identities], *Xinwenxue yanjiu* [Mass comunication research] 56 (1998): 35–63; Wu Naiteh 吳乃德, "Jiating shehuihua han yishixingtai: Taiwan xuanmin zhengdang rentong de shidai chayi" [Family socialization and ideology: The differences of party identification between generations among Taiwanese voters], *Taiwan shehuixue yanjiu* [Taiwanese sociological review] 3 (1999): 53–85; Chen Luhuei 陳陸輝, "Taiwan xuanmin zhengdang rentong de chixu yu bianqian" [Change and continuity of party identification among the electorate in Taiwan], *Xuanju yanjiu* [Journal of electoral studies] 7 (2000): 108–39; Sheng Xingyuan 盛杏湲, "Tongdu yiti yu Taiwan xuanmin de toupiao xingwei: yijiujiuling niandai de fenxi" [The issue Taiwan independence vs. unification with the mainland and voting behavior in Taiwan: An analysis in the 1990s], *Xuanju yanjiu* 9, no. 1 (2002): 41–80; Xiao Yangji 蕭揚基, "Taiwan diqu gaozhong xuesheng guojia rentong ji qi xiangguan yinsu" [National identity of high school students in Taiwan and related factors], *Gongmin xunyu xuebao* [Bulletin of civic and moral education] 11 (2002): 67–108; Hsung Raymay, Chang Fengbin, and Lin Yafeng 熊瑞梅、張峰彬、林亞鋒, "Jieyan hou minzhong shetuan canyu de bianqian: shiqi yu shidai de xiaoying yu yihan" [Changes of participation in voluntary associations after the lifting of martial law: Effects and implications of period and cohort], in *Taiwan de shehui bianqian 1985–2005: chuanbo yu zhengzhi xingwei* [Social change in Taiwan, 1985–2005: Mass communication and political behavior], ed. Chang Maukuei, Lo Venhwei, and Shyn Huoyan (Taipei: Zhongyang yanjiuyuan shehuixue yanjiusuo, 2013), 283–328; Lin Thunghong 林宗弘, "Zaitan Taiwan de shidai zhengzhi: jiaocha fenlei suiji xiaoying moxing de yingyong, 1995–2010" [Generational politics in Taiwan revisited: Application of a cross-classified random effects model, 1995–2010], *Renwen ji shehui kexue jikan* [Journal of social sciences and philosophy] 27, no. 2 (2015): 395–436; Liu Zhengshan 劉正山, "Shidai zhijian zhengzhi rentong chayi de tuxiang: yi duochong duiying fenxi jiehe xiguan lingyu shiye jinxing de tansuo" [Visualizing habitual domains differences across political generations: Exploring the patterns with multiple correspondence analysis], *Xiguan lingyu qikan* [Journal of habitual domains] 7, no. 2 (2016): 27–50.

6. June Edmunds and Bryan S. Turner, *Generations, Culture and Society* (Buckingham, UK: Open University Press, 2002), vii.

7. Mab Huang (Huang Mo), *Intellectual Ferment for Political Reforms in Taiwan, 1971–1973* (Ann Arbor: Center for Chinese Studies, University of Michigan, 1976).

8. Chen Guying 陳鼓應, "Qishi niandai yilai Taiwan xinsheng yidai de gaige yundong (shang)" [The reform movement of the new generation in Taiwan since the 1970s (1)], *Zhongbao yuekan* [Zhongbao monthly] 28 (1982): 27–35; Chen Guying, "Qishi niandai yilai Taiwan xinsheng yidai de gaige yundong (zhong)" [The reform movement of the new generation in Taiwan since the 1970s (2)], *Zhongbao yuekan* 29 (1982): 25–33; Chen Guying, "Qishi niandai yilai Taiwan xinsheng yidai de gaige yundong (xia)" [The reform movement of the new generation in Taiwan since the 1970s (3)], *Zhongbao yuekan* 30 (1982): 33–38; Chen Guying, "The Reform Movement Among Intellectuals in Taiwan Since 1970," *Bulletin of Concerned Asian Scholars* 14, no. 3 (1982): 32–47.

9. Hong Sanxiong 洪三雄, *Fenghuo dujuancheng: qiling niandai Taida xuesheng yundong* (The signal fires in Azalea City: Student movements at National Taiwan University in the 1970s) (Taipei: Zili wanbao, 1993).

10. Norman B. Ryder, "The Cohort as a Concept in the Study of Social Change," *American Sociological Review* 30 (1965): 843–61.

11. Robert L. Miller, *Researching Life Stories and Family Histories* (London: Sage, 2000), 30–31; Edmunds and Turner, *Generations, Culture and Society*, 6; June Edmunds and Bryan S. Turner, "Introduction: Generational Consciousness, Narrative, and Politics," in *Generational Consciousness, Narrative, and Politics*, ed. Edmunds and Turner (Lanham, Md.: Rowman & Littlefield, 2002), 1–2.

12. Glen H. Elder, Jr., *Children of the Great Depression: Social Change in Life Experience* (Chicago: University of Chicago Press, 1974); Janet Z. Giele and Glen H. Elder, Jr., eds., *Methods of Life Course Research: Qualitative and Quantitative Approaches* (Thousand Oaks, Calif.: Sage, 1998); Melissa A. Hardy and Linda Waite, "Doing Time: Reconciling Biography with History in the Study of Social Change," in *Studying Aging and Social Change: Conceptual and Methodological Issues*, ed. Melissa A. Hardy (Thousand Oaks, Calif.: Sage, 1997), 1–21; Edmunds and Turner, "Introduction," 2.

13. James J. Dowd, "The Reification of Age: Age Stratification Theory and the Passing of the Autonomous Subject," *Journal of Aging Studies* 1, no. 4 (1987): 317–35; John W. Meyer, "Levels of Analysis: The Life Course as a Cultural Construction," in *Social Structures and Human Lives*, vol. 1: *Social Change and Life Course*, ed. Matilda White Riley (Newbury Park, Calif.: Sage, 1988), 49–62; Hardy and Waite, "Doing Time," 8.

14. David I. Kertzer, "Generation as a Sociological Problem," *Annual Review of Sociology* 9 (1983): 125–49; Edmunds and Turner, *Generations, Culture and Society*, 6–7; Ron Eyerman, "Intellectuals and the Construction of an African American Identity: Outline of a Generational Approach," in *Generational Consciousness, Narrative, and Politics*, ed. June Edmunds and Bryan S. Turner (Lanham, Md.: Rowman & Littlefield, 2002), 52.

15. Robert S. Laufer and Vern L. Bengtson, "Generations, Aging, and Social Stratification: On the Development of Generational Units," *Journal of Social Issues* 30, no. 3 (1974): 185.

16. E.g., Edward R. Tannenbaum, *1900: The Generation Before the Great War* (Garden City, N.Y.: Anchor Press, 1976); Robert Wohl, *The Generation of 1914* (Cambridge, Mass.: Harvard University Press, 1979).

17. Karl Mannheim, "The Problem of Generations," in his *Essays on the Sociology of Knowledge*, ed. Paul Kecskemeti (London: Routledge & Kegan Paul, 1952 [1927]), 276–320.

18. Robert S. Laufer, "Sources of Generational Conflict and Consciousness," in *The New Pilgrims: Youth Protest in Transition*, ed. Philip G. Altbach and Robert S. Laufer (New York: David Mckay, 1972), 218–37; Laufer and Bengtson, "Generations,

Aging, and Social Stratification," 182; Kertzer, "Generation as a Sociological Problem," 127; Hardy and Waite, "Doing Time," 1, 18; Bryan S. Turner, "Outline of a Theory of Generations," *European Journal of Social Theory* 1, no. 1 (1998): 91–106; Bryan S. Turner, *Classical Sociology* (London: Sage, 1999), 246; Jacqueline Scott, "Is It a Different World to When You Were Growing Up? Generational Effects on Social Representations and Child-rearing Values," *British Journal of Sociology* 51, no. 2 (2000): 356; Edmunds and Turner, *Generations, Culture and Society*, 7–8.

19. Hardy and Waite, "Doing Time," 4.

20. Mannheim, "The Problem of Generations," 286–87, 300–301.

21. Mannheim, "The Problem of Generations," 288–91.

22. Mannheim, "The Problem of Generations," 297–98, 302–4.

23. Jane Pilcher, "Mannheim's Sociology of Generations: An Undervalued Legacy," *British Journal of Sociology* 45, no. 3 (1994): 492.

24. Edmunds and Turner, *Generations, Culture and Society*, 10.

25. Pilcher, "Mannheim's Sociology of Generations," 492.

26. Molly Andrews, "Generational Consciousness, Dialogue, and Political Engagement," in *Generational Consciousness, Narrative, and Politics*, ed. June Edmunds and Bryan S. Turner (Lanham, Md.: Rowman & Littlefield, 2002), 78–80.

27. David Wyatt, *Out of the Sixties: Storytelling and the Vietnam Generation* (New York: Cambridge University Press, 1993), 2.

28. Marxists distinguish between class membership (a "class in-itself") and class consciousness (a "class for-itself"); that is, between the objective situation of a social class and subjective awareness of common interests. Only when an objectively existing class becomes conscious of itself can it successfully act and transform from a "class in-itself" to a "class for-itself." Though the present work is not Marxist, like Edmunds and Turner (*Generations, Culture and Society*, 16–19), I have adopted the locutions "in-itself" and "for-itself."

29. Richard G. Braungart, "Historical Generations and Generation Units: A Global Pattern of Youth Movements," *Journal of Political and Military Sociology* 12 (1984): 113–14; Bryan S. Turner, "Strategic Generations: Historical Change, Literary Expression, and Generational Politics," in *Generational Consciousness, Narrative, and Politics*, ed. June Edmunds and Bryan S. Turner (Lanham, Md.: Rowman & Littlefield, 2002), 16.

30. Pilcher, "Mannheim's Sociology of Generations," 492.

31. Andrews, "Generational Consciousness," 82–85.

32. Lewis P. Hinchman and Sandra K. Hinchman, "Introduction," in *Memory, Identity, Community: The Idea of Narrative in the Human Sciences*, ed. Hinchman and Hinchman (Albany, N.Y.: State University of New York Press, 1997), xv. Like many researchers on narrative, I use "narrative" and "story" interchangeably.

33. Hinchman and Hinchman, "Introduction," xvi.

34. Roland Barthes, "Introduction to the Structural Analysis of Narrative," in *Image, Music, Text*, ed. and trans. Stephen Heath (New York: Hill and Wang, 1977 [1966]), 79.

35. Erik Ringmar, *Identity, Interest and Action: A Cultural Explanation of Sweden's Intervention in the Thirty Years War* (Cambridge: Cambridge University Press, 1996), 72–73.

36. Ringmar, *Identity, Interest and Action*, 73.

37. Andrew Bennett and Nicholas Royle, *An Introduction to Literature, Criticism, and Theory*, 2nd ed. (London: Prentice Hall Europe, 1999), 54.

38. David Carr, "Getting the Story Straight: Narrative and Historical Knowledge," in *Historiography Between Modernism and Postmodernism: Contributions to the Methodology of the Historical Research*, ed. Jerzy Topolski (Amsterdam: Rodopi, 1994), 121–22.

39. Chris Barker, *Cultural Studies: Theory and Practice* (London: Sage, 2000), 167.

40. Anthony Giddens, *Modernity and Self-Identity: Self and Society in the Late Modern Age* (Stanford, Calif.: Stanford University Press, 1991), 53, 75–77. Giddens defines a "reflexive project of the self" as "the process whereby self-identity is constituted by the reflexive ordering of self-narratives" (244).

41. See Donald E. Polkinghorne, *Narrative Knowing and the Human Sciences* (Albany, N.Y.: State University of New York Press, 1988); Margaret R. Somers and Gloria D. Gibson, "Reclaiming the Epistemological 'Other': Narrative and the Social Construction of Identity," in *Social Theory and the Politics of Identity*, ed. Craig Calhoun (Oxford: Blackwell, 1994), 62, 74; Hinchman and Hinchman, "Introduction," xxii–xxiii; Maureen Whitebrook, *Identity, Narrative and Politics* (London: Routledge, 2001), 4, 6; Andrews, "Generational Consciousness," 80, 84.

42. Andrews, "Generational Consciousness," 81, 85.

43. Alasdair MacIntyre, *After Virtue: A Study in Moral Theory* (Notre Dame, Ind.: University of Notre Dame Press, 1984), 204–25; Charles Taylor, *Sources of the Self: The Making of the Modern Identity* (Cambridge: Cambridge University Press, 1989), 47–48.

44. Kedourie analyzes the role of the younger generation in the wake of the French Revolution and the Napoleonic wars in the rapid development of nationalism in Europe, particularly because of their challenge to tradition and conflict with the previous generation. See Elie Kedourie, *Nationalism* (Oxford: Blackwell, 1993 [1960]), chap. 5. The new consensus was "that men had the right to decide who was to govern them, and that humanity was divided, naturally, into nations. These ideas became the commonplaces of radicalism on the continent, and young men, university students, in Italy, Germany, and Central Europe found it reasonable to believe in these things, and heroic to be enrolled in a secret society dedicated to Liberty and Nationality" (91–92).

45. Braungart, "Historical Generation and Generation Units," 113–14; Edmunds and Turner, *Generations, Culture and Society*, 71–72.

46. E.g., Appleton, "Taiwanese and Mainlanders on Taiwan," 56; Appleton, "Regime Support," 759, n. 12.

47. Lin Huaimin 林懷民, "Shizu yu qibu: menwai de gaobai" [Stumble and start: Confession outside], in *Wo de diyibu (xia ce)* [My first step (vol. 2)], by Lin Huaimin et al. (Taipei: Shibao wenhua, 1979), 1–18; Lin Huaimin, "Chengzhang de suiyue" [My growing years], in *Qiling niandai—lixiang jixu ranshao* [The 1970s: Ideals continue to flame], ed. Yang Ze (Taipei: Shibao wenhua, 1994), 61–66; Lin Huaimin, *Gaochu yanliang: Lin Huaimin wudao suiyue gaobai* [Bright view from the heights: Lin Huaimin's confession about his dancing years] (Taipei: Yuanliu, 2010), 16–30, 226–35.

48. Miao Yenwei 苗延威, "Xiangchou siyun—Zhongguo xiandai minge yundong zhi shehuixue yanjiu" [Four stanzas on homesickness—a sociological study of the Chinese Modern Folk Song movement], M.A. thesis, National Taiwan University, Taipei, 1991, 43–51; Yang Zujun 楊祖珺, *Meigui shengkai: Yang Zujun shiwunian laishilu* [The rose blossoms: The path Yang Zujun trod in the past fifteen years] (Taipei: Shibao wenhua, 1992), 13–7; Lu Hanxiu 路寒袖, "Qiling niandai wenhua shishi" [The ten major events in the cultural circles in the 1970s], in *Qiling niandai—lixiang jixu ranshao* [The 1970s: Ideals continue to flame], ed. Yang Ze (Taipei: Shibao wenhua, 1994), 265–66; Zhang Zhaowei 張釗維, *Shei zai nabian chang ziji de ge* [Who is singing their own songs over there] (Taipei: Shibao wenhua, 1994), chaps. 2, 3.

49. A related phenomenon was the vogue for Hong Tong's folk paintings and Zhu Ming's wooden sculptures, which, however, involved much less youth activism than the Cloud Gate Dance Theater and the Chinese Modern Folk Song movement, let alone than the three generation units I analyze. See Lin Xingyue 林惺嶽, *Taiwan meishu fengyun sishinian* [Forty years of vicissitude of fine arts in Taiwan] (Taipei: Zili wanbao, 1987), 201–28.

50. I am indebted to one of my reviewers for prompting me to clear up any confusion about the age range.

51. Nanfang Shuo 南方朔 (Wang Xingqing 王杏慶), "Nashi, Taiwan cai zhangda" [Only then did Taiwan grow up], in *Qiling niandai—lixiang jixu ranshao* [The 1970s: Ideals continue to flame], ed. Yang Ze (Taipei: Shibao wenhua, 1994), 119; Yang Zhao 楊照, "Faxian 'Zhongguo': Taiwan de qiling niandai" [Discovering "China": The 1970s in Taiwan], in *Qiling niandai—lixiang jixu ranshao* [The 1970s: Ideals continue to flame], ed. Yang Ze (Taipei: Shibao wenhua, 1994), 129.

52. Thomas B. Gold, "Civil Society and Taiwan's Quest for Identity," in *Cultural Change in Postwar Taiwan*, ed. Stevan Harrell and Huang Chünchieh (Boulder, Colo.: Westview Press, 1994), 53.

53. A-chin Hsiau, "Language Ideology in Taiwan: The KMT's Language Policy, the Tai-yü Language Movement, and Ethnic Politics," *Journal of Multilingual and Multicultural Development* 18, no. 4 (1997): 302–15; Hsiau A-chin 蕭阿勤, "Yijiu baling niandai yilai Taiwan wenhua minzu zhuyi de fazhan: yi 'Taiwan (minzu) wenxue' weizhu de fenxi" [The development of Taiwanese cultural nationalism since the

early 1980s: A study on Taiwanese (national) literature], *Taiwan shehuixue yanjiu* [Taiwanese sociological review] 3 (1999): 1–51; A-chin Hsiau, *Contemporary Taiwanese Cultural Nationalism* (London: Routledge, 2000); Hsiau A-chin 蕭阿勤, *Chonggou Taiwan: dangdai minzu zhuyi de wenhua zhengzhi* [Reconstructing Taiwan: The cultural politics of contemporary nationalism] (Taipei: Lianjing, 2012).

54. Wu Naiteh, "Jiating shehuihua han yishixingtai," 55–56, 62, 78.

55. Anthropologist Edward M. Bruner has analyzed the ethnography of the American Indian conducted by American anthropologists in the twentieth century. One of his conclusions about the conspicuous change in their ethnographic narrative structure before and after the Second World War is similar to my view here. See Edward M. Bruner, "Ethnography as Narrative," in *Memory, Identity, Community: The Idea of Narrative in the Human Sciences*, ed. Lewis P. Hinchman and Sandra K. Hinchman (Abany, N.Y.: State University of New York Press, 1997 [1986]), 267.

56. Chang Maukuei and Wu Xinyi 張茂桂、吳忻怡, "Guanyu minzuzhuyi lunshu zhong de rentong yu qingxu—zunzhong yu chengren de wenti" [On identity and emotion in nationalist discourse—issues about respect and recognition], in *Minzuzhuyi yu liangan guanxi: hafo daxue dongxifang xuezhe de duihua* [Nationalism and the relations across the Taiwan Strait: A dialogue at Harvard University between scholars from the East and the West], ed. Lin Jialong and Zheng Yongnian (Taipei: Xin ziran zhuyi, 2001), 148–49, 152.

57. On the definition of "text," see Norman Fairclough, *Critical Discourse Analysis: The Critical Study of Language* (New York: Longman, 1995), 4–5.

58. Linda A. Wood and Rolf O. Kroger, *Doing Discourse Analysis: Methods for Studying Action in Talk and Text* (Thousand Oaks, Calif.: Sage, 2000), 4; Louise Philips and Marianne W. Jørgensen, *Discourse Analysis as Theory and Method* (London: Sage, 2002), 1.

59. Fairclough, *Critical Discourse Analysis*, 187; Chris Barker and Dariusz Galasiński, *Cultural Studies and Discourse Analysis: A Dialogue on Language and Identity* (London: Sage, 2001), 62; Jay L. Lemke, *Textual Politics: Discourse and Social Dynamics* (London: Taylor & Francis, 1995), 1, 7; cf. Gilbert Weiss and Ruth Wodak, "Introduction: Theory, Interdisciplinarity and Critical Discourse Analysis," in *Critical Discourse Analysis: Theory and Interdisciplinarity*, ed. Weiss and Wodak (New York: Palgrave Macmillan, 2003), 13.

60. Philips and Jørgensen, *Discourse Analysis as Theory and Method*, 1.

61. Barker and Galasiński, *Cultural Studies and Discourse Analysis*, 63.

2. Education, Exile, and Existentialism in the 1960s

1. Diana Sorensen, *A Turbulent Decade Remembered: Scenes from the Latin American Sixties* (Stanford, Calif.: Stanford University Press, 2007), 2–3; see also Gerard J.

DeGroot, *The Sixties Unplugged: A Kaleidoscopic History of a Disorderly Decade* (Cambridge, Mass.: Harvard University Press, 2008), 14–15.

2. Paul Johnson, *Modern Times: A History of the World from the 1920s to the Year 2000* (London: Phoenix Press, 1997), 641–42; see also David Burner, *Making Peace with the 60s* (Princeton, N.J.: Princeton University Press, 1996), 136; John C. McWilliams, *The 1960s Cultural Revolution* (Westport, Conn.: Greenwood Press, 2000), 11; Sorensen, *A Turbulent Decade Remembered*, 6; Jeremi Suri, *Power and Protest: Global Revolution and the Rise of Détente* (Cambridge, Mass.: Harvard University Press, 2003), 3, 88–92.

3. Suri, *Power and Protest*, 3–4.

4. Hungmao Tien, *The Great Transition: Political and Social Change in the Republic of China* (Stanford, Calif.: Hoover Institution Press, 1989), 87; Wu Naiteh 吳乃德, "The Politics of a Regime Patronage System: Mobilization and Control within an Authoritarian Regime," Ph.D. diss., University of Chicago, 1987, 135.

5. Shih Chiayin 石佳音, "Zhongguo guomindang de yishi xingtai yu zuzhi tezheng" [The ideology and organizational traits of the Chinese Nationalist Party], Ph.D. diss., National Taiwan University, 2008, 126, n. 26; Wu, "The Politics of a Regime Patronage System," 141.

6. Shih Chiayin, "Zhongguo guomindang," 125–27.

7. E.g., Fu Jianzhong 傅建中, "Meiguo xuechao ji qi fanji" [The trend of student movements in America and its counteraction], *Minzhong ribao* [Commons daily], May 19, 1969; Minzu wanbo 民族晚報, "Meiguo qingnian fan yuezhan yundong de muhou" [The inside story of the anti–Vietnam War movement of American youth], *Minzu wanbo* [National evening news], October 18, 1965; Mu Xiabiao 木下彪, ed., "Riben de xuechao" [The trend of student movements in Japan], *Zhonghua zazhi* [China journal] 7, no. 2 (1969): 6–8; Su Yuzhen 蘇玉珍, "Moxige xuechao qianhou" [The antecedents and consequences of the student movements in Mexico], *Zhongyang ribao* [Central daily news], October 16, 1968; Taiwan ribao 台灣日報 "Meiguo ying su zhizhi xuesheng shiwei yundong" [America should stop student protests as soon as possible], *Taiwan ribao* [Taiwan daily], May 13, 1970; Tang Zemin 唐澤民, "Riben xuesheng yundong de dongxiang" [The direction of student movements in Japan], *Fanggong* [Counterattack magazine] 330 (1969): 27–29; Zeng Xubai 曾虛白, "Cong Meiri xuechao tanqi" [A discussion beginning with student movements in America and Japan], *Dongfang zazhi* [Eastern miscellany] 3, no. 6 (1969): 6–9; Zhang Dongcai 張棟材, "Faguo de xuegongchao yu daxuan" [Student and labor movements and the general election in France], *Wenti yu yanjiu* [Issues & studies] 7, no. 10 (1968): 1–4; Zhang Dongcai, "Riben zuopai xuesheng zouxiang baolihua" [Japanese leftist students are moving toward violence], *Wenti yu yanjiu* 7, no. 9 (1968): 15–19; Zhongyang ribao 中央日報, "Meiguo xuechao yu feibang shentou" [Student movements in the United States and the communist gang's infiltration], *Zhongyang ribao* [Central daily news], May 17, 1970.

8. E.g., Hong Liande 洪鎌德, "Deguo dazhuan xuesheng saodong de fenxi" [An analysis of the unrest of college students in West Germany], *Dongfang zazhi* [Eastern miscellany] 2, no. 6 (1968): 12–15; Huang Mo (Mab Huang) 黃默, "Cong jin jinianlai meiguo qingnian canjia shehui zhengzhi huodong kan minzhu zhengzhi" [Viewing democracy in terms of American young people's participation in social and political activities in recent years], *Si yu yan* [Thought and words] 5, no. 3 (1967): 1–2, 7.

9. E.g., Su Junxiong 蘇俊雄, "Lun daxue de renwu yu zhengzhi gexin" [On the mission of universities and political reform], *Daxue zazhi* [The intellectual] 37 (1971): 40; Wang Wenxing 王文興, "Wo dui 'Yige xiaoshimin de xinsheng' de kanfa" [My views on "The Voice of an Ordinary Citizen"], in *Pian'an xintai yu zhongxing xintai—ping "Yige xiaoshimin de xinsheng"* [The mentality of false ease and the mentality of rejuvenation—on "The Voice of an Ordinary Citizen"], ed. Yang Guoshu et al. (Taipei: Huanyu, 1972), 121–22; Wen Rongguang 文榮光, "Wuxin you 'qiqi' yan—'xiaoshimin' xinsheng duhou" [There is "compassion" in my heart—my thoughts after reading "The Voice of an Ordinary Citizen"], in *Taidaren de shizijia* [The cross that National Taiwan University people carry], by Taida xuesheng (Taipei: Taida daxue xinwenshe, 1972), 224; Ye Hongsheng 葉洪生, "Niannian yijue piaohuameng—cong yige nianqingren de shidai ganshou tanqi" [Awaking from a twenty-year blossoming dream: speaking from a young person's feeling for the present era], *Daxue zazhi* 47 (1971): 35–36.

10. E.g., Li Ao 李敖, "Laonianren han bangzi" [The old man and the baton], *Wenxing* [Apollo] 49 (1961): 5–9; Li Ao, "Shisan nian han shisan yue" [Thirteen years and thirteen months], *Wenxing* 63 (1963): 7–12; see also Bai Xianyong (Pai Hsienyung) 白先勇, "Liulang de Zhongguoren—Taiwan xiaoshuo de fangzhu zhuti" [The wandering Chinese—the exile theme of Taiwanese novels], trans. Zhou Zhaoxiang, *Mingbao yuekan* [Mingbao monthly] January (1976): 152–55; Ye Hongsheng 葉洪生, "Zixu" [Preface by the author], in *Zheyidai de fangxiang* [The direction of this generation], by Ye Hongshen (Taipei: Huangyu, 1976 [1972]), 1–4; Ling Shuru 凌淑如, "Budong liulei de yidai" [A generation that doesn't understand tears], in *Sheilai jingli Zhongguo* [Who will be in charge of China], ed. Lai Zhiming (Taipei: Xiangcaoshan, 1977 [1975]), 13–24.

11. Wang Hongjun was born in 1922 in Tianjin and came to Taiwan at age twenty-seven. He went to the United States in 1954 and did an MA degree in journalism at the University of Missouri-Columbia. He returned to Taiwan in 1957.

12. Wang Hongjun 王洪鈞, "Ruhe shi qingnian jieshang zheyibang?" [How to get young people to take the baton?], *Ziyou qingnian* [Free youth] 25, no. 7 (1961): 7.

13. Li Ao was born in 1935 in Haerbin in northeastern China and came to Taiwan at age fourteen.

14. Li Ao, "Laonianren han bangzi," 9.

15. Li Ao 李敖, *Li Ao huiyilu* [Memoir of Li Ao] (Taipei: Shangye zhoukan, 1997), 162.

16. Li Ao, "Shisan nian han shisan yue," 11.

17. Qiu Weijun 丘為君 et al., eds., *Taiwan xuesheng yundong, 1949–1979 (zhong)* [Student movements in Taiwan, 1949–1979, vol. 2] (Taipei: Longtian, 1979), 333–85; Wu Guodong 吳國棟, "Wu ershi qingnian zijue yundong" [The May Twentieth Youth Self-Awakening movement], in *Taiwan xuesheng yundong 1949–1979 (shang)* [Student movements in Taiwan, 1949–1979, vol. 1], ed. Qiu Weijun et al. (Taipei: Longtian, 1979[?]), 35–48; David C. Schak, *Civility and Its Development: The Experiences of China and Taiwan* (Hong Kong: Hong Kong University Press, 2018), vi, 1–4.

18. Yin Ying 殷穎, "You meiguo liuhua xuesheng suo dianran de Zhongguo qingnian zijue yundong" [The Self-Awakening movement of Chinese youth stimulated by an American student studying in China], in *Taiwan xuesheng yundong 1949–1979 (zhong)* [Student movements in Taiwan, 1949–1979, vol. 2], ed. Qiu Weijun et al. (Taipei: Longtian, 1979[?]), 362–63.

19. See also introduction of this book, n. 6.

20. Peng Mingmin, *A Taste of Freedom: Memoirs of a Formosan Independence Leader* (New York: Holt, Rinehart, and Winston, 1972), 124–29.

21. Peng escaped to Sweden and spent decades in exile in the United States before returning to challenge Lee Tenghui for the presidency in 1996.

22. Huang Hua 黃華, "Huang Hua xiansheng fangtanlu" [Interview with Mr. Huang Hua], in *Yijiu liuling niandai de duli yundong—quanguo qingnian tuanjie cujinhui shijian fangtanlu* [The Taiwan Independence movement in the 1960s—collected interviews about the Incident of Association for Promoting Nationwide Youth Solidarity], interviewed by Zeng Pincang and Xu Ruihao, transcribed by Zeng Pincang (Taipei: Guoshiguan, 2004), 118–21; Huang Hua 黃華, *Biewu xuanze—geming zhengzha* [There is no alternative: A revolutionary struggle] (Taipei: Qianwei, 2008), 286–320; Zeng Pincang 曾品滄, "Yijiu liuling niandai zhishi qingnian de duli yundong—yi 'Quanguo qingnian tuanjie cujinhui shijian' weili" [The Taiwan Independence movement initiated by intellectual youths in the 1960s—the case of "the Incident of Association for Promoting Nationwide Youth Solidarity"], in *Yijiu liuling niandai de duli yundong—quanguo qingnian tuanjie cujinhui shijian fangtanlu* [The Taiwan Independence movement in the 1960s—collected interviews about the Incident of Association for Promoting Nationwide Youth Solidarity], interviewed by Zeng Pincang and Xu Ruihao, transcribed by Zeng Pincang (Taipei: Guoshiguan, 2004), 6–7, 22–35.

23. Chen Guying 陳鼓應, "Rongren yu liaojie" [Tolerance and understanding], *Daxue zazhi* [The intellectual] 37 (1971): 6; Chen Zhangsheng 陳漳生, "Jinri zhishi qingnian zhi chujing" [The situation of intellectual youths today], *Daxue zazhi* 46 (1971): 33.

24. Chen Zhangsheng, "Jinri zhishi qingnian zhi chujing," 33. In 2013, during the KMT's Ma Yingjeou administration, the Legislative Yuan (Lifayuan), the supreme national legislature, passed a resolution demanding that military instructors be

removed from school and university campuses in eight years. It was not until January 2018, however, under the DPP's Tsai Ingwen administration, that the Ministry of Education eventually directed that the complete removal should be made by August 2023.

25. Wenli Mei, "The Intellectuals on Formosa," *China Quarterly* 15 (1963): 66.

26. Wang Hongjun 王洪鈞, "Jingshen shang de diqiya" [Low in spirits], *Wenxing* [Apollo] 1, no. 1 (1957): 24.

27. Wang Hongjun 王洪鈞, "Butaoteng han dapao" [The grapevine and the cannon], *Wenxing* [Apollo] 5, no. 1 (1959): 11.

28. Bai Xianyong (Pai Hsienyung) 白先勇, *Taibeiren* [Taipei people], 12th ed. (Taipei: Chenzhong, 1975 [1971]); Joseph S. M. Lau, " 'How Much Truth Can a Blade of Grass Carry?': Ch'en Ying-chen and the Emergence of Native Taiwanese Writers," *Journal of Asian Studies* 32, no. 4 (1973): 627; Chihtsing Hsia, "Foreword," in *Chinese Stories from Taiwan: 1960–1970*, ed. Joseph S. M. Lau and Timothy A. Ross (New York: Columbia University Press, 1976), xxvi.

29. George Kao, "Editor's Preface," in *Taipei People* (Chinese-English bilingual ed.), Chinese text by Pai Hsienyung, trans. Pai Hsienyung and Patia Yasin, ed. George Kao (Hong Kong: Chinese University of Hong Kong, 2000), xiv–xvi.

30. Chen Yingzhen 陳映真, *Diyijian chaishi* [My first case] (Taipei: Yuanjing, 1975), 146–47; Joseph S. M. Lau and Timothy A. Ross, eds., *Chinese Stories from Taiwan: 1960–1970* (New York: Columbia University Press, 1976), 48.

31. Yu Tiancong 尉天驄, "Xu" [Preface], in Chen Yingzhen, *Diyijian chaishi* [My first case] (Taipei: Yuanjing, 1975), 3–5.

32. Lin Huaimin 林懷民, "Chan" [Cicada], in *Chan* [Cicada], by Lin Huaimin (Taipei: Dadi, 1973 [1969]), 146–47; Lin Huaimin 林懷民, "Cicada," in *Chinese Stories from Taiwan: 1960–1970*, ed. Joseph S. M. Lau and Timothy A. Ross (New York: Columbia University Press, 1976 [1969]), 273.

33. John Israel, "Politics on Formosa," *China Quarterly* 15 (1963): 10; Mei, "The Intellectuals on Formosa," 71–73.

34. Yu Lihua 於梨華, *Youjian zonglü, youjian zonglü* [Palms again] (Taipei: Tingyun, 2015 [1967]), 314.

35. Yu Lihua, *Youjian zonglü, youjian zonglü*, 338–39.

36. Zhang Hua 張華, "Zhifu yu xiangyata de aiguoxin—shehui fuwu yundong" [The patriotism lying dormant in the ivory tower—the Social Service movement], in *Taiwan xuesheng yundong 1949–1979 (shang)* [Student movements in Taiwan, 1949–1979, vol. 1], ed. Qiu Weijun et al. (Taipei: Longtian, 1979[?]), 175.

37. Xu Fuguan 徐復觀, "Youguan Taiwan de liuxue zhengce wenti" [Problems about Taiwan's policy on studying abroad], in *Xu Fuguan wenlu (yi) wenhua* [Collected essays by Xu Fuguan, vol. 1: Culture], by Xu Fuguan (Taipei: Huanyu, 1971 [1968]), 182–83.

38. Yu Lihua, *Youjian zonglü, youjian zonglü*, 156.

39. Chen Xiaolin 陳曉林, "Fu xiaoxiao—tan nianqingren de wenti" [A reply to Xiaoxiao—on the problem of the youth], *Zhongyang ribao* [Central daily news] January 17 and 18, 1968; Ye Hongsheng 葉洪生, "Zheyidai de fangxiang—du 'Fu xiaoxiao' yougan" [The direction of this generation—my thoughts after reading "A Reply to Xiaoxiao"], *Zhongyang ribao*, January 26, 1968; Li Xiangmei 李祥枚, "Wu fei wu" [Mist, and yet not mist], *Zhongyang ribao*, February 8, 1968; Ye Guanghai 葉廣海, "Shouqi meiyougen de fennu" [Refraining from rootless anger], *Zhongyang ribao*, February 23, 1968; Wen Shou 文壽, "Qingnian qizhi" [Youth temperament], *Zhongyang ribao*, March 10, 1968; Zhang Xiguo 張系國, "Tan liuxuesheng" [On students studying abroad], *Daxue zazhi* [The intellectual] 20 (1969): 11; Wang Xiaobo 王曉波, "Zeren yu xinxin—tan liuxue wenti" [Duty and confidence—on the issue of studying abroad], *Daxue zazhi* 20 (1969): 15; He Xiuhuang 何秀煌, "Zhengfeng, jiaoyu yu liuxuesheng" [Political quality, education, and students studying abroad], *Daxue zazhi* 25 (1970): 15; Li Xuerui 李學叡, "Da jizhen qiangxinji" [Giving some injections of cardiotonic], *Daxue zazhi* 26 (1970): 1; Wang Gao 王高, "Chuishou tingxun" [Listening to instructions obediently], *Daxue zazhi* 36 (1970): 1; Sheldon Appleton, "Taiwanese and Mainlanders on Taiwan: A Survey of Student Attitudes," *China Quarterly* 44 (1970): 55–56; Sheldon Appleton, "Regime Support Among Taiwan High School Students," *Asian Survey* 13 (1973): 759–60; Sun Zhen 孫震, "Wokan 'Yige xiaoshimin de xinsheng'" [My views on "The Voice of an Ordinary Citizen"], in *Pian'an xintai yu zhongxing xintai—ping "Yige xiaoshimin de xinsheng"* [The mentality of false ease and the mentality of rejuvenation—on "The Voice of an Ordinary Citizen"], ed. Yang Guoshu et al. (Taipei: Huanyu, 1972), 40; Yang Guoshu 楊國樞, "Xinren yu zunzhong women de qingnian—yu youren tan 'Yige xiaoshimin de xinsheng' zhiyi" [Trust and respect our young people—discussing with my friend about "The Voice of an Ordinary Citizen," part 1], in *Pian'an xintai yu zhongxing xintai—ping "Yige xiaoshimin de xinsheng,"* ed. Yang Guoshu et al. (Taipei: Huanyu, 1972), 11; Wen Rongguang, "Wuxin you 'qiqi' yan," 224–25.

40. Chen Zhangsheng, "Jinri zhishi qingnian zhi chujing," 32.

41. E.g., Yu Tiancong 尉天驄, "Xihua de wenxue" [Westernized literature], in *Zhongguo xiandai wenxue de huigu* [A review of modern Chinese literature], ed. Qiu Weijun and Chen Lianshun (Taipei: Longtian, 1978), 155–66; Chen Yingzhen 陳映真, "Cong 'xihua wenxue' dao 'xiangtu wenxue'" [From "Westernized literature" to "Nativist literature"], in *Zhongguo xiandai wenxue de huigu*, ed. Qiu Weijun and Chen Lianshun (Taipei: Longtian, 1978), 174–75; Chen Guoxiang 陳國祥, *Qingnian husheng* [The call of youth] (Taipei: Siji, 1979), 11.

42. Zhang Xiguo, "Tan liuxuesheng," 11.

43. Yu Lihua, *Youjian zonglü, youjian zonglü,* 180–81, 252–53. *Palms Again* was thus seen as a representative work of the "rootless generation" and was even called

"the song of the exile." Mou Tianlei has been taken as characteristic of the root-less generation, and Yu Lihua as its spokesperson. See Bai Xianyong, "Liulang de Zhongguoren," 153.

44. Leo Oufan Lee, "'Modernism' and 'Romanticism' in Taiwan Literature," in *Chinese Fiction from Taiwan: Critical Perspectives*, ed. Jeannette L. Faurot (Bloomington: Indiana University Press, 1980), 10–13.

45. Matsunaga Masayoshi 松永正義, "Taiwan wenxue de lishi yu gexing" [The history and character of Taiwanese literature], trans. Ye Shitao, in *Caifeng de xinyuan (Taiwan xiandai xiaoshuoxuan I)* [Caifeng's wish: a selection of modern Taiwanese stories], by Hong Xingfu et al. (Taipei: Mingliu, 1986[?]), 140–41; see also Ye Shitao 葉石濤, *Taiwan wenxue shigang* [An outline history of Taiwanese literature] (Kaohsiung: Wenxuejie, 1987), 116.

46. Lin Huaimin, *Chan*.

47. Ye Yunyun 葉芸芸, "Bianji baogao" [Editorial note], in *Ye Rongzhong quanji* [Complete works of Ye Rongzhong], ed. Yu Yunyun (Taipei: Chenxing, 2000), 11

48. E.g., Chen Shaoting 陳少廷, "Zheyidai zhongguo zhishi fenzi de zeren" [The duty of the present generation of Chinese intellectuals], *Daxue zazhi* [The intellectual] 1 (1968): 4; Chen Xiaolin, "Fu xiaoxiao"; Du Weiming 杜維明, "Zai xueshu wenhua shang jianli ziwo" [Establishing the self in the academic and cultural field], *Daxue zazhi* 3 (1968): 6; Li Xiangmei, "Wu fei wu"; Ye Hongsheng, "Zheyidai de fangxiang"; Chen Guying 陳鼓應, "Shuohua shi yizhong tianfu de quanli (xu)" [Preface: Speech is an inborn right], in *Rongren yu liaojie* [Tolerance and understanding], by Chen Guying (Taipei: Baijie, 1978 [1971]), 2; Langxing 朗星, "Xingqu han tiancai de shuailuo" [The decline of taste and talent], in *Taidaren de shizijia* [The cross that National Taiwan University people carry], by Taida xuesheng (Taipei: Taida daxue xinwenshe, 1972), 61.

49. Zhu Yunhan 朱雲漢, "Lishi, shiju yu guoyun" [History, world situation, and the destiny of our nation], *Xianrenzhang zazhi* [Cactus magazine] 9 (1977): 181–82, 189.

50. Ling Shuru, "Budong liulei de yidai," 19. "Four Stanzas on Homesickness" was the NTU student Yang Xian's setting in June 1974 of Yu Guangzhong's poem of the same name, composed in spring of the same year. His creation began to arouse interest from the younger generation, especially university students. In 1976 Yang Xian released his popular first album, entitled *Zhongguo xiandai minge ji* (A collection of modern Chinese folk songs). Yang Xian and Li Shuangze, a graduate of Tamkang College of Arts and Sciences (now Tamkang University), founded the so-called Chinese Modern Folk Song movement, as mentioned in chapter 1. The movement was popular mainly with university students and young intellectuals and constituted part of the return-to-native-soil cultural trend with a strong Chinese national consciousness. The lyrics, based on Yu Guangzhong's original poem, evoked a powerful sense of longing for the Chinese mainland and for "the maternal." See Yu Guangzhong 余光中, *Baiyu kugua* [The white jade

bitter gourd] (Taipei: Dadi, 1974), 158–60; Yu Guangzhong, "Four Stanzas on Homesickness," in *China: Adapting the Past, Confronting the Future*, ed. Thomas Buoye et al. (Ann Arbor: Center for Chinese Studies, University of Michigan, 2002 [1974]), 540. Moreover, in postwar Taiwan, the household registration and personal ID card system marked one's provincial origin, which was determined by one's parents' (or father's) province of birth. It remained in use until 1992, when "provincial origin" was replaced by "birthplace." See Wang Fuchang 王甫昌, "You 'Zhongguo shengji' dao 'Taiwan zuqun': hukou pucha jibie leishu zhuanbian zhi fenxi" [From "Chinese original domicile" to "Taiwanese ethnicity": An analysis of census category transformation in Taiwan], *Taiwan shehuixue* [Taiwanese sociology] 9 (2005): 59–117.

51. Wang Fusu 王復蘇, "Wu yu" [Without words], in *Fuzhong xia de chensi* [Deep thinking under the Fu Bell], by Wang Fusu (Taipei: Maolian, 1990[?]), 63.

52. Zhang Xiaofeng 張曉風, *Chouxiang shi* [Homesick stone] (Taipei: Chenzhong, 1971), 2.

53. Marianne Hirsch, "Past Lives: Postmemories in Exile," in *Exile and Creativity: Signposts, Travelers, Outsiders, Backward Glances*, ed. Susan Rubin Suleiman (Durham, N.C.: Duke University Press, 1998), 419–20; see also Hammed Shahidian, "Sociology and Exile: Banishment and Tensional Loyalties," *Current Sociology* 48, no. 2 (2000): 72.

54. Chen Yingzhen, *Diyijian chaishi*, 56, 67–68; Lucien Miller, *Exiles at Home: Short Stories by Ch'en Ying-chen* (Ann Arbor: Center for Chinese Studies, University of Michigan, 1986), 125, 133–34.

55. Zhang Xiguo 張系國, "Zhishi fenzi de gudu yu gudu de zhishi fenzi" [The solitude of intellectuals and the solitary intellectuals], *Daxue zazhi* [The intellectual] 6 (1968): 14–15.

56. Wang Shangyi 王尚義, *Yegezi de huanghun* [Wild pigeons' dusk] (Taipei: Shuiniu, 1968), author profile page.

57. Wang Shangyi 王尚義, "Cong 'yixiangren' dao 'shiluo de yidai': Kamiu, Haimingwei yu women" [From *The Stranger* to "the Lost Generation": Camus, Hemingway, and us], in *Cong yixiangren dao shiluo de yidai* [From *The Stranger* to the Lost Generation], by Wang Shangyi (Taipei: Wenxing, 1964 [1962]), 52–56.

58. Liu Zaifu 劉載福, *Shate lun* [On Jean-Paul Sartre] (Taichung: Putian, 1968), 57, 70.

59. Zhang Xiguo, "Zhishi fenzi de gudu," 15.

60. Tang Feng'e 湯鳳娥, "Quan wode zhangfu liuzai shufang" [Advising my husband to stay in his study], in *Rongren yu liaojie* [Tolerance and understanding], by Chen Guying (Taipei: Baijie, 1978), 197–98.

61. See the letter by Liu Rongsheng published in *Daxue zazhi* [The intellectual] 7 (July 1968): 2; see also Zhang Xiguo, "Zhishi fenzi de gudu," 15. For a vivid description of Zhongshan North Road as one of most luxurious boulevards in 1970s Taipei, see Chen Chuanxing 陳傳興, "Hengtang de tongtianta" [A Babel

tower lying down], in *Qiling niandai: chanqinglu* [The 1970s: A collection of confessions], ed. Yang Ze (Taipei: Shibao wenhua, 1994), 31–35.

62. Lin Huaimin 林懷民, "Chuan hongchenshan de nanhai" [The boy in the red shirt], in *Chan* [Cicada], by Lin Huaimin (Taipei: Dadi, 1973 [1968]), 3–31.

63. Liu Daren 劉大任, "Liuxuesheng de sixiang kuangjia" [The frame of thinking of students studying abroad], *Daxue zazhi* [The intellectual] 25 (1970): 40.

64. Zhang Jinghan 張景涵 (Zhang Junhong 張俊宏), "Daxuesheng diaocha baogao, taolun yu jianyi—daxuesheng dui xuexiao de taidu" [Report, discussion, and suggestion about an investigation of university students—university students' attitudes toward their universities], *Daxue zazhi* [The intellectual] 24 (1969): 26; Lau, " 'How Much Truth Can a Blade of Grass Carry?,' " 631; Chen Guying, "Shuohua shi yizhong tianfu de quanli (xu)," 2.

65. Zhang Hua, "Zhifu yu xiangyata de aiguoxin," 175.

66. Ambrose Y. C. King 金耀基, "Gudu de yiqun—tan zai meiguo de Zhongguo zhishi fenzi" [A lonely crowd—on the Chinese intellectuals in America], *Daxue zazhi* [The intellectual] 20 (1969): 5.

3. The Rise of the Return-to-Reality Generation in the Early 1970s

1. Guo Rongzhao 郭榮趙, "Yige lishi gongzuozhe dui shiju de fanxing" [A historian's reflection on the current situation], *Lianhe bao* [United daily news], September 16, 1971.

2. Chihming Wang, *Transpacific Articulations: Student Migration and the Remaking of Asian America* (Honolulu: University of Hawai'i Press, 2013), 73–78.

3. Hsiau A-chin 蕭阿勤, "Jizhu Diaoyutai: lingtu zhengduan, minzu zhuyi, zhishi fenzi yu huaijiu de shidai jiyi" [Remember Diaoyutai Islands: Territorial dispute, nationalism, and generational memory of nostalgic intellectuals in Taiwan], *Taiwanshi yanjiu* [Taiwan historical research] 24, no. 3 (2017): 147–54; A-chin Hsiau, "Defending Diaoyutai Islands Movement and Pan-Chinese Nationalism (Taiwan)," in *The Wiley-Blackwell Encyclopedia of Social and Political Movements*, vol. 1: *A–E*, ed. David A. Snow et al., 2nd ed. (Oxford: Wiley-Blackwell, forthcoming); Alexander Bukh, *These Islands Are Ours: The Social Construction of Territorial Disputes in Northeast Asia* (Stanford, Calif.: Stanford University Press, 2020), 131–36.

4. Chen Mingzhe 陳明哲, "Women xuyao qi bian de jingshen" [We need the spirit of standing up for change], in *Zhishiren de chulu* [A way out for intellectuals], ed. Hong Sanxiong (Changhua: Xinsheng, 1973 [1972]), 73.

5. Hong Sanxiong 洪三雄, *Fenghuo dujuancheng: qiling niandai Taida xuesheng yundong* [The signal fires in Azalea City: Student movements at National Taiwan University in the 1970s] (Taipei: Zili wanbao, 1993), 56.

6. Mao Han 茅漢 (Wang Xiaobo 王曉波), "Liuyiqi xuesheng shiwei jishi" [A true record of the student demonstration on June 17], *Daxue zazhi* [The intellectual] 43 (1971): 24.

7. Wang Du 王渡, *Mayingjiu xianxiang* [Ma Yingjeou phenomena] (Taipei: Putian, 2002), 129.

8. He Wenzhen 何文振, "Gei zhishi fenzi de yaoqingshu" [An invitation to intellectuals], *Daxue zazhi* [The intellectual] 47 (1971): 25.

9. Chen Shaoting 陳少廷, "Chen xu" [Preface by Chen], in *Zhishiren de chulu* [A way out for intellectuals], ed. Hong Sanxiong (Changhua: Xinsheng, 1973), 2.

10. Mark Harrison, *Legitimacy, Meaning, and Knowledge in the Making of Taiwanese Identity* (New York: Palgrave Macmillan, 2006), 124, 129, 131.

11. Hong Sanxiong, *Fenghuo dujuancheng*, 60–61, 83–90.

12. Chen Guying 陳鼓應, "Zailun 'xuesheng yundong'" [Reexamining "student movements"], *Daxue zazhi* [The intellectual] 53 (1972): 69.

13. It was widely believed that President Chiang Kaishek was preparing to hand over power to his son Chiang Chingkuo. Many, especially reform-minded people, had high expectations for Chiang Chingkuo, and he became the premier in May 1972, about seven months after Taiwan was driven out of the United Nations.

14. Bao Qingtian 包青天 (Bao Yihong 包奕洪) et al., "Taiwan shehuili de fenxi (shang)" [Analysis of Taiwan's social forces (part 1)], *Daxue zazhi* [The intellectual] 43 (1971): 33–34.

15. Bao Qingtian 包青天 (Bao Yihong 包奕洪) et al., "Taiwan shehuili de fenxi (zhong)" [Analysis of Taiwan's social forces (part 2)], *Daxue zazhi* [The intellectual] 44 (1971): 14.

16. Zhang Hongyuan 張宏遠, "Shuo jiju neixin de hua" [Let me say some words from my heart], *Daxue zazhi* [The intellectual] 47 (1971): 18.

17. Chen Mingzhe, "Women xuyao qi bian de jingshen," 75.

18. Ka Er 卡爾, "Yishi gaizao—you Wang Xingqing de xuanze tandao dangqian lishi de juewu" [The remaking of consciousness—from Wang Xingqing's choice to the historical awakening at present], in *Zhishiren de chulu* [A way out for intellectuals], ed. Hong Sanxiong (Changhua: Xinsheng, 1973 [1971]), 47–48.

19. E.g., Li Shaoyi and Chen Jing'an 李少儀、陳景安, "Xuesheng de quanli yu yiwu" [The rights and obligations of students], *Daxue zazhi* [The intellectual] 53 (1972): 57–58; Chen Guying, "Zailun 'xuesheng yundong,'" 70; Taida daxue xinwenshe 台大大學新聞社, "Ziyou yu zeren—tan xuexiao de shengao zhidu" [Freedom and responsibility—on the censorship system on campus], in *Taidaren de shizijia* [The cross that National Taiwan University people carry], ed. Taida daxue xinwenshe (Taipei: Taida daxue xinwenshe, 1972[?]), 22; Zhang, Junhong 張俊宏, *Wo de chensi yu fendou—liangqian ge jianao de rizi* [My contemplation and struggle—two thousand tormenting days] (Taipei: Self-published, 1977), 6–12;

Hu Qingyu 胡晴羽, "Zhengchu yitiao zhanxin de lu" [Struggling for a brand new way], in *Sheilai jingli Zhongguo* [Who will be in charge of China], ed. Lai Zhiming (Taipei: Xiangcaoshan, 1977), 56; Wu Fengshan 吳豐山, *Wo neng wei guojia zuoxie shemo?* [What can I do for the country?] (Taipei: Yuanjing, 1978), 144, 158, 209; Huang Zongwen 黃宗文, "Yisheng hongliang de nahan—Huang xu" [A resounding call—preface by Huang], in *Xinshengdai de nahan* [The call of the new generation], ed. Song Guocheng and Huang Zongwen (Taipei: Self-published, 1978), 7–8; Nanfang Shuo 南方朔 (Wang Xingqing 王杏慶), "Xu—bokai misi zhi wang" [Preface—unveil the web of myth], in *Qingnian husheng* [The call of youth], by Chen Guoxiang (Taipei: Siji, 1979), 2; Zhu Yunhan 朱雲漢, "Maixiang ershiyi shiji de yidai—zhishi qingnian yu Zhongguo weilai" [A generation moving toward the twenty-first century—intellectual youth and China's future], in *Zhishi fenzi yu Zhongguo* [Intellectuals and China], ed. Zhou Yangshan (Taipei: Shibao, 1980 [1979]), 423, 426.

20. Bao Qingtian et al., "Taiwan shehuili de fenxi (zhong)," 14.

21. Chen Guying, "Zailun 'xuesheng yundong,'" 68–69.

22. Chen Guying 陳鼓應, "Kaifang xuesheng yundong" [Lift the ban on student movements], *Daxue zazhi* [The intellectual] 46 (1972): 64–68.

23. Taida daxue xinwenshe 台大大學新聞社, "'Gexin' cong 'gexin' zuoqi ["Reform" begins with "reform of heart"], in *Taidaren de shizijia* [The cross that National Taiwan University people carry], ed. Taida daxue xinwenshe (Taipei: Taida daxue xinwenshe, 1972[?]), 29, 30.

24. "*Quanmian gaixuan zhongyang minyi daibiao*" (Comprehensive reelection of the parliamentary representatives), *Taida fayan* [NTU legal logos] 14 (November 15, 1971), quoted from Hong Sanxiong 洪三雄, ed., *Zhishiren de chulu* [A way out for intellectuals] (Changhua: Xinsheng, 1973), 1–2.

25. Zhang Jinghan 張景涵 (Zhang Junhong 張俊宏) et al., "Guoshi zhengyan" [Advice about national affairs], *Daxue zazhi* [The intellectual] 46 (1971): 1.

26. E.g., Wang Xingqing 王杏慶 et al., "Zhe shi juexing de shihou le!" [This is the time for awakening!], *Daxue zazhi* [The intellectual] 47 (1971): 23.

27. For a clear, succinct description of the exilic mentality of Mainlanders, especially that of the older generation, made in the 1970s, see Zhou Qier 周棄兒, "Waishengren de kumen" [The depression of Mainlanders], *Taiwan zhenglun* [Taiwan political review] 5 (1975): 64–65.

28. Gao Zhun 高準, "Pinfu ji daigou maodun de jiejue zhi dao—xiangei suoyou zai Taiwan de guanxin guoshi de tongbao, lun Taiwan shehui de sizhong neibu maodun zhi san" [The rich/poor and generational-gap conflicts and the solutions to them—dedicated to all compatriots concerned about national affairs in Taiwan, on the third of the four internal conflicts in Taiwanese society], *Mingbao yuekan* [Mingbao monthly] 10, no. 4 (1975): 34.

29. Wang Xingqing 王杏慶, "Qianze han huyu" [Condemnation and appeal], *Daxue zazhi* [The intellectual] 48 (1971): 58.

30. Ma Yingjeou 馬英九, "Liuxuesheng de shizijia" [The cross students studying abroad carry], in *Liu xuesheng de shizijia* [The cross students studying abroad carry], ed. Boshidun tongxun bianji weiyuanhui (Taipei: Shibao, 1982 [1981]), 357.

31. Hong Sanxiong 洪三雄, "Dui xuexiao kaidao, xiang shehui jinjun" [Launch a critique against the school and mount an attack on the society], in *Zhishiren de chulu* [A way out for intellectuals], ed. Hong Sanxiong (Changhua: Xinsheng, 1973 [1971]), 135–36.

32. Nanfang Shuo 南方朔 (Wang Xingqing 王杏慶), "Zhongguo ziyouzhuyi de zuihou baolei—Daxue zazhi jieduan de liang di fenxi (si)" [The last bastion of Chinese liberalism—a quantitative analysis of the phase of *The Intellectual* (part 4)], *Xiachao* [China tide] 4, no. 6 (1978): 47.

33. Hungmao Tien, *The Great Transition: Political and Social Change in the Republic of China* (Stanford, Calif.: Hoover Institution Press, 1989), 140.

34. Guo Rongzhao, "Yige lishi gongzuozhe dui shiju de fanxing." For other Mainlander voices who spoke out on this issue, see Taida fayan she 台大法言社, "Zhichi quanmian gaixuan de qingnian xinsheng" [Voices from the hearts of the young people who support a comprehensive reelection], in *Taiwan xuesheng yundong 1949–1979 (xia)* [Student movements in Taiwan, 1949–1979, vol. 3], ed. Qiu Weijun et al. (Taipei: Longtian, 1979 [1971]), 715, 716; Gao Zhun 高準, "Taiwan quanli maodun ji qi jiejue zhi dao—xiangei suoyou zai Taiwan de guanxin guoshi de tongbao, lun Taiwan shehui de sizhong neibu maodun zhi yi" [The power clashes in Taiwan and the solutions to them—dedicated to all compatriots concerned about national affairs in Taiwan, on the first of the four internal conflicts in Taiwanese society], *Mingbao yuekan* [*Mingbao monthly*] 10, no. 1 (1975): 81.

35. Zhang Jinghan et al., "Guoshi zhengyan," 6.

36. Zhang Jinghan et al., "Guoshi zhengyan," 3.

37. E.g., see Yang Yongyi and Hong Sanxiong 楊庸一、洪三雄, "Minyi hezai?—Ping Zhongyang ribao de yipian wenzhang" [Where is public opinion?—comment on an article in the *Central Daily News*], in *Zhishiren de chulu* [A way out for intellectuals], ed. Hong Sanxiong (Changhua: Xinsheng, 1972), 64; Chen Yangde 陳陽德, "Xian jieduan qingnian qingxiang zhi fenxi—dui shuqi guojia jianshe yanjiuyuan de fanying zhi diaocha ji fenxi" [An analysis of the inclination of youth at the present stage—a survey and analysis on the reaction of researchers of the summer Workshop on National Construction], *Daxue zazhi* [The intellectual] 46 (1971): 35, 40.

38. Yanliang 彥良, "Yu you tan guoshi—yongren, dang timing yu zhengzhi gexin" [Discussing with my friend about national affairs—the promotion of talents, party nomination, and political reform], *Daxue zazhi* [The intellectual] 47 (1971): 24.

39. Yang Yongyi and Hong Sanxiong, "Minyi hezai?," 63–66; Hong Sanxiong 洪三雄, ed., *Zhishiren de chulu* [A way out for intellectuals] (Changhua: Xinsheng,

1973), 1–2, 5–6; Taida daxue xinwenshe 台大大學新聞社, "Liangxin de zijue" [The self-consciousness of conscience], in *Taidaren de shizijia* [The cross that National Taiwan University people carry], ed. Taida daxue xinwenshe (Taipei: Taida daxue xinwenshe, 1972 [?]), 27.

40. Chen Guying, "Zailun 'xuesheng yundong,' " 69.

41. Chen Shaoting 陳少廷, "Zailun zhongyang minyi daibiao de gaixuan wenti" [Reexamining the issue about the reelection of national parliamentary representatives], *Daxue zazhi* [The intellectual] 49 (1972): 97.

42. Hsiao Hsinhuang 蕭新煌, "Dangdai zhishi fenzi de 'xiangtu yishi'—shehuixue de kaocha" [The "native-soil consciousness" of contemporary intellectuals—a sociological investigation], *Zhongguo luntan* [China tribune] 265 (1986): 63.

43. Harrison, *Legitimacy, Meaning, and Knowledge*, 145–46.

44. Guying 孤影, "Yige xiaoshimin de xinsheng" [The voice of an ordinary citizen], in *Dui nianqingren de zhenxinhua* [My sincere words for young people], by Guying (Taipei: Zhongyang ribao she, 1976 [1972]), 1–68.

45. J. Bruce Jacobs, " 'Taiwanization' in Taiwan's Politics," in *Cultural, Ethnic, and Political Nationalism in Contemporary Taiwan: Bentuhua*, ed. John Makeham and A-chin Hsiau (New York: Palgrave Macmillan, 2005), 20.

4. The Rediscovery of Taiwan New Literature

1. This English translation is a relay translation from the Chinese translation by Lin Zaijue. See Lin Zaijue 林載爵, "Riju shidai Taiwan wenxue de huigu" [A review of Taiwanese literature in the Japanese occupation period]. *Wenji* [Literary season] 3 (1974): 135.

2. Ozaki Hotsuki 尾崎秀樹, "Zhanshi de Taiwan wenxue" [Taiwanese literature in the wartime period], trans. Xiao Gong, in *Taiwan de zhimindi shanghen* [Colonial scars in Taiwan], ed. Wang Xiaobo (Taipei: Pamier, 1985 [1971]), 185.

3. For the English translation of Lai He's complete fiction, see Lōa Hô (Lai He), *Scales of Injustice: The Complete Fiction of Lōa Hô*, trans. Darryl Sterk (Handforth, UK: Honford Star, 2018).

4. Edward I-te Chen, "Formosan Political Movements Under Japanese Colonial Rule, 1914–37," *Journal of Asian Studies* 31, no. 3 (1972): 477–97.

5. Ye Shitao 葉石濤, *Taiwan wenxue shigang* [An outline history of Taiwanese literature] (Kaohsiung: Wenxuejie, 1987), 19–24; A-chin Hsiau, *Contemporary Taiwanese Cultural Nationalism* (London: Routledge, 2000), 36–39; Chen Fangming 陳芳明, *Taiwan xinwenxue shi (shang)* [A history of modern Taiwanese literature (vol. 1)] (Taipei: Lianjing, 2011), chaps. 2, 3.

6. Ye Shitao, *Taiwan wenxue shigang*, 25–28; Hsiau, *Contemporary Taiwanese Cultural Nationalism*, 39–41; Chen Fangming, *Taiwan xinwenxue shi*, chap. 4; Zhao Xunda 趙勳達, *Kuangbiao shike—Rizhi shidai Taiwan xinwenxue de gaofengqi (1930–1937)* [A

Sturm und Drang moment—the peak of Taiwan New Literature in the Japanese colonial period (1930–1937)] (Tainan: Guoli Taiwan wenxueguan, 2011).

7. Hsiau, *Contemporary Taiwanese Cultural Nationalism*, 45.

8. Chen Fangming, *Taiwan xinwenxue shi*, chaps. 7, 8; Faye Yuan Kleeman, *Under an Imperial Sun: Japanese Colonial Literature of Taiwan and the South* (Honolulu: University of Hawai'i Press, 2003), chaps. 7, 8.

9. Carlos Rojas, "Introduction," in *Writing Taiwan: A New Literary History*, ed. David Der-wei Wang and Carlos Rojas (Durham, N.C.: Duke University Press, 2007), 4.

10. Sung-sheng Yvonne Chang, "Representing Taiwan: Shifting Geopolitical Frameworks," in *Writing Taiwan: A New Literary History*, ed. David Der-wei Wang and Carlos Rojas (Durham, N.C.: Duke University Press, 2007), 22.

11. Chen Cuilian 陳翠蓮, "Quzhimin yu zaizhimin de duikang: yi yijiusiliu nian 'Tairen nuhua' lunzhan wei jiaodian" [The conflict between decolonization and recolonization: The debate on "the enslavement of the Taiwanese people" of 1946 in focus], *Taiwanshi yanjiu* [Taiwan historical research] 9, no. 2 (2002): 145–201.

12. These Taiwanese who had close affiliations with the KMT were generally referred to as "Half-Mountain People" (*banshan ren*). They were recruited as a small part of higher echelon of the party-government in postwar Taiwan. For the origins of the Half-Mountain Taiwanese, see J. Bruce Jacobs, "Taiwanese and the Chinese Nationalists, 1937–1945: The Origins of Taiwan's 'Half-Mountain People' (*Banshan Ren*)," *Modern China* 16, no. 1 (1990): 84–118.

13. Fu Bo 傅博, "Riju shiqi Taiwan xinwenxue de pingjia wenti" [The problem of evaluating the Taiwan New Literature in the Japanese occupation period], *Wenxing* [Apollo] 104 (1987): 107–8; Xu Junya 許俊雅, "'Riju shiqi Taiwan wenxue' yanjiu gaikuang" [An overview of studies on "Taiwanese Literature in the period of Japanese occupation"], in her *Taiwan wenxue sanlun* [Essays on Taiwanese literature] (Taipei: Wenshizhe, 1994), 2–3.

14. Wang Jinjiang 王錦江 (Wang Shilang 王詩琅), "Riju shiqi de Taiwan xinwenxue" [Taiwan New Literature in the Japanese occupation period], *Taiwan wenyi* [Taiwan literature] 1, no. 3 (1964): 49–58.

15. Ye Shitao 葉石濤, "Taiwan de xiangtu wenxue" [Taiwan's Nativist literature], *Wenxing* [Apollo] 97 (1965): 70–73.

16. Wu Yingtao 吳瀛濤, "Gaishu guangfu qian de Taiwan wenxue (yi)" [An overview of Taiwanese literature before the Retrocession (1)], *Youshi wenyi* [Youth literary] 216 (1971): 274–82; Wu Yingtao 吳瀛濤, "Gaishu guangfu qian de Taiwan wenxue (er)" [An overview of Taiwanese literature before the Retrocession (2)], *Youshi wenyi* 221 (1972): 54–60.

17. Huang Deshi 黃得時, "Taiwan guangfu qianhou de wenyi huodong yu minzuxing" [The literary and artistic activities and national character before and after the Retrocession of Taiwan], *Xin wenyi* [New literature and arts] 190 (1972): 37–47.

18. Ye Shitao, "Taiwan de xiangtu wenxue," 73.

19. Ye Shitao 葉石濤, "Wu Zhuoliu lun" [On Wu Zhuoliu], *Taiwan wenyi* [Taiwan literature] 12 (1966): 28, 30.

20. I thank one of my reviewers for prompting me to clarify my point here.

21. Eric Hobsbawm and Terence Ranger, eds., *The Invention of Tradition* (Cambridge: Cambridge University Press, 1983).

22. Chen Shaoting 陳少廷, "Wusi yu Taiwan xinwenxue yundong" [May Fourth and the New Literature movement in Taiwan], *Daxue zazhi* [The intellectual] 53 (1972): 18.

23. Chen Shaoting 陳少廷, "Lun zheyidai zhongguo zhishi fenzi de zhixiang (daixu)" [On the ambitions of the present generation of Chinese intellectuals (in lieu of preface)], in *Zheyidai zhongguo zhishi fenzi de jianjie* [The views of the present generation of Chinese intellectuals], ed. Daxue congkan bianweihui (Taipei: Huanyu, 1970), 7–10.

24. Daxue zazhishe 大學雜誌社, "'Riju shidai de Taiwan wenxue yu kangri yundong' zuotanhui—jinian Taiwan guangfu di ershijiu zhounian" [Symposium on "Taiwanese literature and the anti-Japanese resistance in the Japanese occupation era"—commemorating the twenty-ninth anniversary of the Retrocession of Taiwan], *Daxue zazhi* [The intellectual] 79 (1974): 33.

25. Born in the early 1910s under Japanese colonialism, Wu Yongfu wrote in Japanese and jointed the Li Poetry Society at the end of the 1960s.

26. Daxue zazhishe, "'Riju shidai de Taiwan wenxue yu kangri yundong' zuotanhui," 31–32. Zhao Tianyi was born in 1935 in Taichung. Three months before this symposium was held, in July 1974, he had been fired from his teaching position in the "NTU Department of Philosophy Incident," when the administration punished people like him for participation in political and social activism in the wake of the Baodiao movement (see chapter 3).

27. Ming Fengying 明鳳英, ed., "Zhongguo wenxue wang hechu qu? Zhongxi wenyi sichao zuotanhui" [Whither is Chinese literature going? Symposium on currents of literary and artistic thought in China and the West], in *Minzu wenxue de zai chufa* [Restarting national literature], ed. Xianrenzhang zazhishe (Taipei: Guxiang, 1979 [1977]), 26. Qi Yishou was born in 1938 in Fuzhou, Fujian. At the time he was a professor of Chinese literature at NTU.

28. Chen Yingzhen 陳映真, "Guer de lishi-lishi de guer: shiping 'Yaxiya de guer'" [Orphan's history and history's orphan: A preliminary review of *Orphan of Asia*], in *Guer de lishi-lishi de guer* [Orphan's history and history's orphan], by Chen Yingzhen (Taipei: Yuanjing, 1984[?]), 95.

29. Chen Yingzhen 陳映真, "Wenxue laizi shehui fanying shehui" [Literature arises out of the society and reflects the society], *Xianrenzhang zazhi* [Cactus magazine] 1, no. 5 (1977): 77–78.

30. Zhang Liangze 張良澤, "Zhong Lihe de wenxue guan" [Zhong Lihe's views on literature], *Wenji* [Literary season] 2 (1973): 48–59; Shi Junmei 史君美 (Tang Wenbiao 唐文標), "Lai xiai Zhong Lihe" [Come to love Zhong Lihe], *Wenji* 2 (1973): 60–76; Liu Ruojun 劉若君, "Zhong Lihe duanpian xiaoshuo duhou" [Reading

report on Zhong Lihe's short stories], *Wenji* 2 (1973): 77–81; Zhong Lihe 鍾理和, "Pinjian fuqi" [A poor and lowly couple], *Wenji* 2 (1973): 82–90. "A Poor and Lowly Couple" was originally published in 1959.

31. Yang Kui 楊逵, "Mofancun" [Model village], *Wenji* [Literary season] 2 (1973): 105–42. The story was originally published in 1937 under Japanese colonial rule.

32. Lin Zaijue, "Riju shidai Taiwan wenxue," 133–65.

33. Li Nanheng 李南衡, ed. *Riju xia Taiwan xinwenxue, mingji* [Taiwan New Literature under the Japanese occupation, Ming volumes], 5 vols. (Taipei: Mingtan, 1979); Zhong Zhaozheng and Ye Shitao 鍾肇政、葉石濤, eds. *Guangfu qian Taiwan wenxue quanji* [Complete pre-Retrocession Taiwanese literature], 8 vols. (Taipei: Yuanjing, 1979). Four more volumes, edited by Yang Ziqiao and Chen Qianwu, were added to the latter compendium in the early 1980s. See Yang Ziqiao and Chen Qianwu 羊子喬、陳千武, eds., *Guangfu qian Taiwan wenxue quanji* [Complete pre-Retrocession Taiwanese literature], vols. 9–12 (Taipei: Yuanjing, 1982).

34. Chen Yingzhen, "Wenxue laizi shehui," 78.

35. See *Wenji* [Literary season] 2 (November 1973): 47. This series in *Literary Season* featured Ouyang Zi (issue 1) and Zhang Ailing (Eileen Chang) (issue 3), as well as Zhong Lihe in its second number mentioned earlier.

36. Zhang Liangze 張良澤, "Zhong Lihe zuopin zhong de riben jingyan yu zuguo jingyan" [The experiences of Japan and ancestral land in Zhong Lihe's works], *Zhongwai wenxue* [Chung Wai literary quarterly] 2, no. 11 (1974): 56–57.

37. Yu Tiancong 尉天驄, *Lu bushi yigeren zouchulai de* [A way cannot be tread out only by one person] (Taipei: Lianjing, 1976), 175–76. The *Zhang Wojun Collection* was edited by Zhang's son, Zhang Guangzhi. See Zhang Guangzhi 張光直, ed., *Zhang Wojun wenji* [Zhang Wojun collection] (Taipei: Chunwenxue, 1975).

38. Lü Zhenghui 呂正惠, "Riju shidai Taiwan xinwenxue yanjiu de huigu—qiling niandai yilai Taiwan diqu de yanjiu gaikuang" [A review of the research on Taiwan New Literature in the Japanese occupation period—an overview of the research in Taiwan since the 1970s], *Taiwan shehui yanjiu jikan* [Taiwan: a radical quarterly in social studies] 24 (1996): 147.

39. Zhang Liangze 張良澤, "Buqu de wenxue hun—lun Yang Kui jiantan riju shidai de Taiwan wenyi (si zhi yi)" [Unyielding literary soul—on Yang Kui and Taiwanese literature and art in the Japanese occupation period (part 1 of 4)], *Zhongyang ribao* [Central daily news], October 22, 1975. This essay was also collected in the volume edited by Yang Sujuan. See Zhang Liangze 張良澤, "Buqu de wenxue hun—lun Yang Kui jiantan riju shidai de Taiwan wenyi" [Unyielding literary soul—on Yang Kui and Taiwanese literature and art in the Japanese occupation period], in *Yang Kui de ren yu zuopin* [Yang Kui: The man and his works], ed. Yang Sujuan (Taipei: Minzhong ribao she Taibei guanlichu, 1979 [1975]), 209–26. Zhang Liangze was born in Puli in central Taiwan in 1939 and grew up in Changhua. From 1972 to 1978 he taught in the Department of Chinese Literature, National Cheng Kung University.

40. Wang Xiaobo 王曉波, "Taiwan xinwenxue zhi fu—Lai He yu tade sixiang" [The father of the Taiwan New Literature—Lai He and his thoughts], in *Bei diandao de Taiwan lishi* [Taiwan history turned upside down], by Wang Xiaobo (Taipei: Pamier, 1986 [1979]), 134.

41. Lin Bian 林邊 (Lin Zaijue 林載爵), "Renkan cangsheng hanru—Lai He xiansheng de wenxue" [Cannot bear to sit by and watch the people suffering and being humiliated—Mr. Lai He's literary works], in *Riju xia Taiwan xinwenxue, mingji 1: Lai He xiansheng quanji* [Taiwan New Literature under the Japanese occupation, Ming volume 1: The complete works of Mr. Lai He], ed. Li Nanheng (Taipei: Mingtan, 1979), 458.

42. Chen Yingzhen, "Guer de lishi," 95.

43. Lin Zaijue 林載爵, "Heise de taiyang" [The black sun—Zhang Shenqie's journey], *Xiachao* [China tide] 3, no. 3 (1977): 70.

44. Lin Zaijue 林載爵, "Heichao xia de beige" [Elegy under the Kuroshio current: Yang Hua the poet], *Xiachao* [China tide] 1, no. 8 (1976): 65.

45. Zhang Liangze 張良澤. "Wu Xinrong xiansheng zhuanlüe" [A brief biography of Mr. Wu Xinrong], *Daxue zazhi* [The intellectual] 105 (1977): 20.

46. Li Kuixian 李魁賢, "Wu Yongfu shi zhong de zuguo yishih han ziyou yishi" [The consciousness of ancestral land and freedom in Wu Yongfu's poetry], *Li shikan* [Li poetry magazine] 87 (1978): 4.

47. For the literature about Yang Kui published in the 1970s, see Kawahara Isao 河原功, "Yang Kui xiaoshuo pinglun yinde" [Index to reviews of Yang Kui's works of fiction], trans. Yang Jingting, in *Yang Kui ji* [Collected works of Yang Kui], ed. Zhang Henghao (Taipei: Qianwei, 1991[?]), 347–53.

48. Most of these stories are collected in the volume edited by Zhang Liangze 張良澤, *Emama chujia* [Mother Goose gets married] (Tainan: Daxing, 1975): "Emama chujia" (Mother Goose gets married), "Zhong digua" (Planting sweet potatoes), "Wuyicun" (The village without a doctor), "Mengya" (Sprouts), "Songbaofu" (The paperboy), "Mofancun" (Model village), and "Cunguang guanbuzhu" (Spring sunshine can't be shut up). This book was later reissued: Yang Kui 楊逵, *Emama chujia* [Mother Goose gets married] (Taipei: Minzhong ribao she Taibei guanlichu, 1979 [1975]).

49. *Wenji* [Literary season] 2 (November 1973): 105.

50. Lin Zaijue 林載爵, "Taiwan wenxue de liangzhong jingshen—Yang Kui yu Zhong Lihe zhi bijiao" [The two types of spirits of Taiwanese literature—a comparison between Yang Kui and Zhong Lihe], *Zhongwai wenxue* [Chung Wai literary quarterly] 2, no. 7 (1973): 4–20.

51. Ye Shitao 葉石濤, "Yang Kui de 'Emama chujia'" [Yang Kui's "Mother Goose Gets Married"], *Daxue zazhi* [The intellectual] 87 (1975): 33.

52. Yang Sujuan 楊素絹, ed., *Yang Kui de ren yu zuopin* [Yang Kui: The man and his works] (Taipei: Minzhong ribao she Taibei guanlichu, 1979 [1976]), 176, 228.

53. Lin Fan 林梵 (Lin Ruiming 林瑞明), *Yang Kui huaxiang* [A portrait of Yang Kui] (Taipei: Bijiashan, 1978), 198.

54. Zhang Liangze 張良澤, "Xulun" [Introduction], in *Emama chujia* [Mother Goose gets married], by Yang Kui (Taipei: Minzhong ribao she Taibei guanlichu, 1979 [1975]), 1.

55. For instance, Wen Meiling 溫美玲, "Tiejian dan daoyi de Yang Kui" [Yang Kui, who carries a moral burden on his iron shoulders], in *Yang Kui de ren yu zuopin* [Yang Kui: The man and his works], ed. Yang Sujuan (Taipei: Minzhong ribao she Taibei guanlichu, 1979 [1975]), 176; Liang Jingfeng 梁景峰, "Chunguang guanbuzhu—lun Yang Kui de xiaoshuo" [Spring sunshine can't be shut up—on Yang Kui's fiction], in *Yang Kui de ren yu zuopin* [Yang Kui: The man and his works], ed. Yang Sujuan (Taipei: Minzhong ribao she Taibei guanlichu, 1979 [1976]), 258.

56. Yang Sujuan, ed., *Yang Kui*, 119, 128, 178, 179, 201.

57. Zheng Hongsheng 鄭鴻生, *Qingchun zhi ge: zhuiyi yijiu qiling niandai Taiwan zuoyi qingnian de yiduan ruhuo nianhua* [Song of youth: Recalling the wild years of leftist youth in 1970s Taiwan] (Taipei: Lianjing, 2001), 151.

58. See the letter that Han Jue, who was working at the National Institute for Translation and Compilation (Guoli bianyiguan), wrote to Yang Kui, quoted in Lin Fan 林梵 (Lin Ruiming 林瑞明), "Yang Kui huaxiang" [A portrait of Yang Kui], *Xianrenzhang zazhi* [Cactus magazine] 1, no. 3 (1977): 261–62.

59. Yang Kui 楊逵, "Houji" [Epilogue], in *Emama chujia* [Mother Goose gets married], by Yang Kui (Taipei: Minzhong ribao she Taibei guanlichu, 1979 [1975]), 212.

60. See the final pages of Yang Sujuan's *Yang Kui: The Man and His Works* for the blurb.

61. Lin Fan, *Yang Kui huaxiang*, 295. Lin was born in 1950. While he was living with Yang Kui at Donghai Flower Garden, Lin was a graduate student in history at National Taiwan University.

62. Lin Fan, *Yang Kui huaxiang*, 187–88.

63. Lin Fan, "Yang Kui huaxiang," 246, 260. Lin Ruiming's account and review of Yang Kui and his works were published as Lin Fan, *Yang Kui huaxiang*.

64. Lin Fan, *Yang Kui huaxiang*, 41. At the end of the 1960s Lin Ruiming organized a club called the "Loyal Hearts Club" (Danxin hui) at Tainan First Senior High School, the "aim of which was to revive the manly manner of the Han and the Tang dynasties." In Zheng Hongsheng's opinion, Lin's act "reflected the romantic sentiments young students at the time had about the state and the nation." See Zheng Hongsheng, *Qingchun zhi ge*, 39. Lin's extolling Yang Kui was congenial to his sentiments and ambitions in his high school years.

65. Lin Wengeng 林問耕 (Lin Zaijue 林載爵), "*Lishi de gouhuo—'Yang Kui huaxiang' xu*" [The historical bonfire—preface to *A Portrait of Yang Kui*], in *Yang Kui huaxiang* [A portrait of Yang Kui], by Lin Fan (Taipei: Bijiashan, 1978), 1–2.

66. Lin Zaijue, "Taiwan wenxue de liangzhong jingshen," 20.

67. Lin Yinwen 林尹文, "Gengyunzhe Yang Kui" [Yang Kui the cultivator], in *Yang Kui de ren yu zuopin* [Yang Kui: The man and his works], ed. Yang Sujuan (Taipei: Minzhong ribao she Taibei guanlichu, 1979 [1974]), 127–30.

68. Liang Jingfeng, "Chunguang guanbuzhu," 259.

69. Benedict Anderson, *Imagined Communities: Reflections on the Origin and Spread of Nationalism*, rev. and extended ed. (London: Verso, 1991 [1983]).

70. Zhu Xining 朱西寧, "Ye lao yuanding" [Paying a call on the old gardener], *Zhong-wai wenxue* [Chung Wai literary quarterly] 3, no. 8 (1975): 18–19.

71. Hu Qiuyuan 胡秋原, "Hu xu—tan Yang Kui xiansheng ji qi zuopin" [Preface by Hu—on Mr. Yang Kui and his works], in *Yangtou ji* [Sheep's head collection], by Yang Kui (Taipei: Huihuang, 1976), 4, 8, 9, 11.

72. As for the problem of learning Chinese, Zhong Lihe was an exception. He was born in 1915 in Pingdong and died in 1960. From 1938 to 1946 he lived in northeastern China and in Beijing and began writing stories in Chinese. He relocated to Meinong, then–Kaohsiung County, after the war. Peng Ruijin has noted that "although Zhong Lihe spans the wartime and postwar periods, unlike other local Taiwanese authors he had no language problem to overcome, because in the Japanese occupation period he had already been a Chinese writer." See Peng Ruijin 彭瑞金, "Yi wenxue wei shengming zuo jianzheng— Zhong Lihe ji xu" [Use literature to bear witness to life—preface to *The Zhong Lihe Collection*], in *Zhong Lihe ji* [The Zhong Lihe collection], ed. Peng Ruijin (Taipei: Qianwei, 1991), 9.

73. Ye Shitao, "Taiwan de xiangtu wenxue"; Ye Shitao, "Zuojia de shidai" [The generational background of writers], in *Taiwan xiangtu zuojia lunji* [Collected essays on Taiwan's Nativist writers], by Ye Shitao (Taipei: Yuanjing, 1979[?]), 45–47; Ye Shitao, "Liushi niandai de Taiwan xiangtu wenxue" [Nativist literature in 1960s Taiwan], *Wenxun* [Wenhsun magazine] 13 (1984): 137–46; Ye Shitao, *Taiwan wenxue shigang*, 73, 91, 108–10, 117–18.

74. I am grateful to one of my reviewers for urging me to clarify how I use Ye Shitao's generational classification.

75. Ye Shitao, "Taiwan de xiangtu wenxue"; see also Zhong Zhaozheng 鍾肇政, "Jiankun guji de zuji—jianshu sishi niandai bensheng xiangtu wenxue" [Difficult and lonely footprints: a brief introduction to the Nativist literature of this province in the 1950s], *Wenxun* [Wenhsun magazine] 9 (1984): 122–34.

76. Ye Shitao, "Liushi niandai de Taiwan xiangtu wenxue," 139.

77. See, e.g., Ye Shitao and Peng Ruijin 葉石濤、彭瑞金, "Ye Shitao, Peng Ruijin duitan: yinian lai de xiaoshuojie" [A conversation between Ye Shitao and Peng Ruijin: Fiction circles in the recent year], *Taiwan wenyi* [Taiwan literature] 66 (1980): 195; Peng Ruijin 彭瑞金, "Cong Xiangtu wenxue dao Sanmin zhuyi wenxue—fang Ye Shitao xiansheng tan Taiwan wenxue de lishi" [From Nativist literature to Three-Principles-of-the-People literature—interview with Ye Shitao about the history of Taiwanese literature], *Taiwan wenyi* 62 (1979): 17.

78. See *Li shikan* [Li poetry magazine] 51 (October 1972): 92–97; 52 (December 1972): 5–16. Also see my earlier discussion in Hsiau, *Contemporary Taiwanese Cultural Nationalism*, 86–87.

79. Peng Ruijin 彭瑞金, "Ye Shitao, Zhang Liangze duitan: bingzhu tan Lihe" [A conversation between Ye Shitao and Zhang Liangze: On Zhong Lihe by the light of a candle], *Taiwan wenyi* [Taiwan literature] 54 (1977): 8.

80. See *Taiwan wenyi* [Taiwan Literature] 63 (July 1979): 5.

81. Hsiau, *Contemporary Taiwanese Cultural Nationalism*, 68–74.

82. Chen Shaoting, *Taiwan xinwenxue yundong jianshi* [A basic history of the Taiwan New Literature movement] (Taipei: Lianjing, 1977), 203–4. Huang Deshi's 黃得時 essays mentioned here include "Taiwan xinwenxue yundong gaiguan (yi)" [Overview of the Taiwan New Literature movement (1)]," *Taibei wenwu* [Taipei historical documents quarterly] 3, no. 2 (1954): 2–12; "Taiwan xinwenxue yun-dong gaiguan (er)" [Overview of the Taiwan New Literature movement (2)], *Tai-bei wenwu* 3, no. 3 (1954): 18–22; "Taiwan xinwenxue yundong gaiguan (san)" [Overview of the Taiwan New Literature movement (3)], *Taibei wenwu* 4, no. 2 (1955): 104–20. Despite Chen Shaoting's clear statement in the afterword of his monograph, a decade later Chen was criticized as a plagiarist by Fu Bo and by Chen Fangming in his discussion with Peng Ruijin. See Fu Bo, "Riju shiqi Tai-wan xinwenxue de pingjia wenti," 110; Chen Fangming and Peng Ruijin 陳芳明、彭瑞金, "Chen Fangming, Peng Ruijin duitan: liqing Taiwan wenxue de yixie wuyun anri [A dialogue between Chen Fangming and Peng Ruijin: Get rid of the dark clouds in Taiwanese literature], *Wenxuejie* [Literary Taiwan] 24 (1987): 34–35. See also Hsiau, *Contemporary Taiwanese Cultural Nationalism*, 112, for a brief discussion.

83. Huang Deshi 黃得時, "Huang xu" [Preface by Huang], in Chen Shaoting's *Tai-wan xinwenxue yundong jianshi* [A basic history of the Taiwan New Literature movement] (Taipei: Lianjing, 1977), 3–4.

84. Ye Shitao, "Jianjie Chen Shaoting xiansheng de 'Taiwan xinwenxue yundong jianshi'" [Introducing Mr. Chen Shaoting's *A Basic History of the Taiwan New Literature Movement*], *Shuping shumu* [Book review and bibliography] 53 (1977): 34–37.

85. Ye Shitao, "Jianjie Chen Shaoting xiansheng de 'Taiwan xinwenxue yundong jianshi,'" 37.

86. Zhang Henghao, Lin Fan (Lin Ruiming), and Yang Ziqiao 張恆豪、林梵 (林瑞明)、羊子喬, "Chuban zongzhi ji bianji tili" [Purpose of publication and principles of editing], in *Guangfu qian Taiwan wenxue quanji* [Complete pre-Retrocession Taiwanese literature], ed. Zhong Zhaozheng and Ye Shitao (Taipei: Yuanjing, 1979), 1.

87. Li Nanheng was a local Taiwanese born in 1940 in Taipei City.

88. Wang Shilang 王詩琅, "Riji xia Taiwan xinwenxue de shengcheng ji fazhan—daixu" [The emergence and development of Taiwan New Literature under the

Japanese occupation—in lieu of preface], in *Riju xia Taiwan xinwenxue, mingji 1: Lai He xiansheng quanji* [Taiwan New Literature under the Japanese occupation, Ming volume 1: The complete works of Mr. Lai He], ed. Li Nanheng (Taipei: Mingtan, 1979), 9–10.

89. For more on the reception of the Taiwan New Literature from 1973 to the end of the decade (including Japanese colonial era writers who remained active after the Retrocession), see Lin Fan, *Yang Kui huaxiang*, chaps. 1, 8 (on Yang Kui); Fu Bo, "Riju shiqi Taiwan xinwenxue de pingjia wenti"; Matsunaga Masayoshi 松永正義, "Taiwan xinwenxue yundong yanjiu de xinjieduan" [A new stage in the research on the Taiwan New Literature movement], *Xindi wenxue* [New land literature] 1 (1990): 32–51; Xu Junya, "'Riju shiqi Taiwan wenxue' yanjiu gaikuang"; and Lü Zhenghui, "Riju shidai Taiwan xinwenxue yanjiu de huigu." Xu Junya described the publication of the two compilations as "a proud finish to Taiwanese literary research in the 1970s." See Xu Junya, "'Riju shiqi Taiwan wenxue' yanjiu gaikuang," 9. Lü Zhenghui also noted that "in 1973 the 'unearthing' of Taiwanese literature began, and after 1979, when these two compilations appeared, the wave subsided." See Lü Zhenghui, "Riju shidai Taiwan xinwenxue yanjiu de huigu," 150.

90. For the development of Taiwanese cultural nationalism since the 1980s, when an increasing number of cultural elites of local Taiwanese background began to shift their national identity from Chinese to Taiwanese, see Hsiau, *Contemporary Taiwanese Cultural Nationalism*; and Hsiau A-chin 蕭阿勤, *Chonggou Taiwan: dangdai minzu zhuyi de wenhua zhengzhi* [Reconstructing Taiwan: The cultural politics of contemporary nationalism] (Taipei: Lianjing, 2012).

91. Peng Ruijin 彭瑞金, "Dangqian Taiwan wenxue de bentuhua yu duoyuanhua—jianlun youguan Taiwan wenxue de yixie yishuo" [Current indigenization and pluralization of Taiwanese literature—also on some perverse views on Taiwanese literature], *Wenxue Taiwan* [Literary Taiwan] 4 (1992): 12.

92. Ye Shitao 葉石濤, *Taiwan wenxue rumen: Taiwan wenxue wushiqi wen* [Introduction to Taiwanese literature: Fifty-seven questions about Taiwanese literature] (Kaohsiung: Chunhui, 1997), 6.

93. Zhong Zhaozheng 鍾肇政, *Taiwan wenxue shijiang* [Ten lectures on Taiwanese literature], ed. Zhuang Zirong (Taipei: Qianwei, 2000), 15, 17.

5. The Reception of Nativist Literature

1. Cai Yuanhuang 蔡源煌, "Zuihou de langman zhuyi zhe" [The last romanticists], in *Qiling niandai—lixiang jixu ranshao* [The 1970s: Ideals continue to flame], ed. Yang Ze (Taipei: Shibao wenhua, 1994), 184–85.

2. Chen Zhengti 陳正醍, "Taiwan de Xiangtu wenxue lunzhan (1977–1978)" [The Nativist Literature Debate in Taiwan (1977–1978)], in *Taiwan xiangtu*

wenxue-huangmin wenxue de qingli yu pipan [Nativist literature in Taiwan—clarifications and criticisms of the imperial-subject literature], ed. Zeng Jianmin (Taipei: Renjian, 1998 [1981]), 131.

3. Lü Zhenghui 呂正惠, *Zhanhou Taiwan wenxue jingyan* [The postwar literary experience in Taiwan] (Taipei: Xindi, 1992), 46–47, 51–52, 57.

4. Huang Chunming 黃春明, "Shayaonala-zaijian" [Sayōnara-goodbye], *Wenji* [Literary season] 1 (1973): 97–131.

5. Joseph S. M. Lau, "Echoes of the May Fourth Movement in *Hsiang-t'u* Fiction," in *Mainland China, Taiwan, and U.S. Policy*, ed. Huang-mao Tien (Cambridge, Mass.: Oelgeschlager, Gunn & Hain, 1983), 147.

6. For this conversation, see Li Ang 李昂, "Xiyue de beimin—Yang Qingchu fangwen" [Joyful sorrow and compassion—interview with Yang Qingchu], *Shuping shumu* [Book review and bibliography] 24 (1975): 84; and *Qunxiang—Zhongguo dangdai yishujia fangwen* [Profiles—interviews with contemporary Chinese artists] (Taipei: Dahan, 1976), 63–64. See also Yang Qingchu 楊青矗, *Bisheng de huixiang* [The resounding of the pen] (Kaohsiung: Dunli, 1978), 161–62. Yang Qingchu was the pen name of Yang Hexiong. He was born in 1940 in Qigu Township in what was then Tainan County.

7. The film *Duosang* (A borrowed life), released in 1994, is about this historical experience. This autobiographical movie directed by local Taiwanese Wu Nianzhen, born in 1952, told a story of conflict between a local Taiwanese miner who kept affections for Japanese language and culture and his son who was raised in the postwar anti-Japan climate. The movie vividly describes the generational tension in the postwar conflict of national identity.

8. He Xin 何欣, "Zhongguo xiandai xiaoshuo de chuantong—yige shi de kaocha" [The tradition of modern Chinese fiction—a historical investigation], in *Zhongguo xiandai xhiaoshuo de zhuchao* [The main trend of modern Chinese fiction], by He Xin (Taipei: Yuanjing, 1979 [1977]), 37–38. The Chinese Literary Association (Zhongguo wenyi xiehui) celebrated its eleventh anniversary on May 4, 1961. For the occasion, a new book was published, edited by the association: *Zhongguo wenyi fuxing yundong* [The movement of Chinese literary and artistic renaissance] (Taipei: Zhongguo wenyi xiehui, 1961). On pages 41–66, the book contained an essay by Mainlander Jiang Menglin 蔣夢麟 entitled "Tan Zhongguo xinwenyi yundong—wei jinian wusi yu wenyijie er zuo" [On China's new literary and artistic movement—in memory of May Fourth and Culture and Arts Day]. The quotation He Xin cites is from this essay. Jiang Menglin was then chair of the Sino-American Joint Commission on Rural Reconstruction, and at the beginning of the 1960s, in Taiwan's literary circles, he was progressive. What he hoped for would not emerge for another decade.

9. For Li Kuixian's poems, see *Li shikan* [Li poetry magazine] 90 (April 1979): 2–5. Li Kuixian 李魁賢 also wrote an article entitled "Wu Yongfu shi zhong de zuguo

yishih han ziyou yishi" [The consciousness of ancestral land and freedom in Wu Yongfu's poetry], *Li shikan* [Li poetry magazine] 87 (1978): 2–7.

10. Li Kuixian 李魁賢, "Li de licheng" [The journey of Li], *Li shikan* [Li poetry magazine] 100 (1980): 48.

11. The poem by Zhao Tianyi is on the inside cover of *Li shikan* [Li poetry magazine] 64 (December 1974).

12. *Li shikan* [Li poetry magazine] 81 (October 1977): 40–43.

13. *Li shikan* [Li poetry magazine] 73 (June 1976): 1.

14. He Xin, "Zhongguo xiandai xiaoshuo de chuantong," 37–38.

15. He Xin 何欣, "Baodao wenxue yu wenxue chuangzuo" [Reportage literature and literary creation], in *Zhongguo xiandai xhiaoshuo de zhuchao* [The main trend of modern Chinese fiction], by He Xin (Taipei: Yuanjing, 1979 [1978]), 184–85. He Xin cites famous lines from a poem by Liu Yuxi of the Tang dynasty of China. Bai Xianyong quoted these lines of nostalgia for the splendor of imperial past as the epigraph for his *Taipei People*. See Bai Xianyong (Pai Hsienyung) 白先勇, *Taibeiren* [*Taipei People*], 12th ed. (Taipei: Chenzhong, 1975 [1971]).

16. Chen Yingzhen 陳映真, "Cong 'xihua wenxue' dao 'xiangtu wenxue'" [From "Westernized literature" to "Nativist literature"], in *Zhongguo xiandai wenxue de huigu* [A review of modern Chinese literature], ed. Qiu Weijun and Chen Lianshun (Taipei: Longtian, 1978), 174, 175.

17. Yu Tiancong 尉天驄, "Xihua de wenxue" [Westernized literature], in *Zhongguo xiandai wenxue de huigu* [A review of modern Chinese literature], ed. Qiu Weijun and Chen Lianshun (Taipei: Longtian, 1978), 163, 165; Chen Yingzhen, "Cong 'xihua wenxue' dao 'xiangtu wenxue,'" 174–76.

18. Chen Yingzhen 陳映真, "Wenxue laizi shehui fanying shehui" [Literature arises out of the society and reflects the society], *Xianrenzhang zazhi* [Cactus magazine] 1, no. 5 (1977): 75.

19. Wang Tuo 王拓, "Wenxue yu shehui zhengyi" [Literature and social justice], in *Zhongguo xiandai wenxue de huigu* [A review of modern Chinese literature], ed. Qiu Weijun and Chen Lianshun (Taipei: Longtian, 1978), 257–58.

20. Wang Tuo 王拓, "Shi 'xianshi zhuyi' wenxue, bushi 'xiangtu wenxue'" [It is "Realist" literature, rather than "Nativist literature"], in *Xiangtu wenxue taolunji* [Collected discussions on Nativist literature], ed. Yu Tiancong (Taipei: Yuanliu, 1978 [1977]), 108.

21. Huang Chunming 黃春明, "Yige zuozhe de beibi xinling" [The despicable mind of an author], *Xiachao* [China tide] 23 (1978): 61, 62.

22. Wang Tuo, "Shi 'xianshi zhuyi' wenxue," 118–19. For similar views to Wang Tuo's, see Chen Yingzhen, "Wenxue laizi shehui," 76; and Yang Qingchu 楊青矗, "Shemo shi jiankang de wenxue?" [What is a wholesome literature?], in *Xiangtu wenxue taolunji* [Collected discussions on Nativist literature], ed. Yu Tiancong (Taipei: Yuanliu, 1978 [1977]), 297. For Yu Tiancong's view, see Ming Fengying

明鳳英, ed., "Zhongguo wenxue wang hechu qu? Zhongxi wenyi sichao zuotanhui" [Whither is Chinese literature going? Symposium on currents of literary and artistic thought in China and the West], in *Minzu wenxue de zai chufa* [Restarting national literature], ed. Xianrenzhang zazhishe (Taipei: Guxiang, 1979 [1977]), 31. For Huang Chunming's view, see Yu Tiancong 尉天驄 et al., "Dangqian de Zhongguo wenxue wenti" [Current issues about Chinese literature], in *Xiangtu wenxue taolun ji* [Collected discussions on Nativist literature], ed. Yu Tiancong (Taipei: Yuanliu, 1978 [1977]), 777. Peng Ruijin has noted that at the time, "no proponent of Nativism besides Wang Tuo clearly defined the category of native soil in Nativist literature as being limited to Taiwan." See Peng Ruijin 彭瑞金, *Taiwan xinwenxue yundong sishi nian* [Forty years of Taiwan's New Literature movement] (Taipei: Zili wanbao, 1991), 160.

23. Yu Tiancong et al., "Dangqian de Zhongguo wenxue wenti," 777.

24. Yang Qingchu, "Shemo shi jiankang de wenxue?," 297–98.

25. Qi Yishou 齊益壽, "Xiangtu wenxue zhi wojian" [My views on Nativist literature], in *Xiangtu wenxue taolunji* [Collected discussions on Nativist literature], ed. Yu Tiancong (Taipei: Yuanliu, 1978), 588–89. For the promotion of Nativist literature—*xiangtu wenxue*—and literature written in local Taiwanese language in the Japanese colonial period, see A-chin Hsiau, *Contemporary Taiwanese Cultural Nationalism* (London: Routledge, 2000), 36–47; Hsiau A-chin 蕭阿勤, *Chonggou Taiwan: dangdai minzu zhuyi de wenhua zhengzhi* [Reconstructing Taiwan: the cultural politics of contemporary nationalism] (Taipei: Lianjing, 2012), 89–109. See also chapter 4.

26. Shi Jiaju 石家駒 (Chen Yingzhen 陳映真), "Zai minzu wenxue de qizhi xia tuanjie qilai" [Unite under the banner of national literature], in *Minzu wenxue de zai chufa* [Restarting national literature], ed. Xianrenzhang zazhishe (Taipei: Guxiang, 1979 [1978]), 226.

27. Wang Tuo 王拓, "Nian shiji Taiwan wenxue fazhan de dongxiang" [The developmental trend of Taiwanese literature in the twentieth century], in *Jiexiang gusheng* [Drum sounds from the streets], by Wang Tuo (Taipei: Yuanjing, 1977), 84–85.

28. Yang Qingchu 楊青矗, "Xianshi yu wenxue" [Reality and literature], in *Zhongguo xiandai wenxue de huigu* [A review of modern Chinese literature], ed. Qiu Weijun and Chen Lianshun (Taipei: Longtian, 1978), 229–30.

29. Hsiao Hsinhuang 蕭新煌, "Dangdai zhishi fenzi de 'xiangtu yishi'—shehuixue de kaocha" [The "native-soil consciousness" of contemporary intellectuals—a sociological investigation], *Zhongguo luntan* [China tribune] 265 (1986): 65.

30. Sung-sheng Yvonne Chang, *Modernism and the Nativist Resistance: Contemporary Chinese Fiction from Taiwan* (Durham, N.C.: Duke University Press, 1993), 153.

31. For a critical discussion of the "misconceptions" about the Nativist-modernist contention, see Chang, *Modernism and the Nativist Resistance*, 153–60.

32. Yu Tiancong 尉天驄, "Manmu yanshi bu liao wugou: dui xiandai zhuyi de kaocha, jianping Ouyang Zi de 'qiuye'" [Curtains can't hide the dirt: An

examination of modernism, and a review of Ouyang Zi's "Autumn Leaves"], *Wenji* [Literary season] 1 (1973): 61–75; Wang Hongjiu 王紘久 (Wang Tuo 王拓), "Yixie youlu: tan Ouyang Zi de 'qiuye'" [Some worries: On Ouyang Zi's "Autumn Leaves"], *Wenji* 1 (1973): 76–82; He Xin 何欣, "Ouyang Zi shou le xie sheme" [What Ouyang Zi has expressed in words], *Wenji* 1 (1973): 46–60; see also Chang, *Modernism and the Nativist Resistance*, 41–42.

33. Wenji zazhishe 文季雜誌社, "Fakanci: women de nuli han fangxiang" [Inaugural statement: Our efforts and direction], *Wenji* [Literary season] 1 (1973): 1–2.

34. Tang Wenbiao 唐文標, "Shi de moluo: Xianggang Taiwan xinshi de lishi pipan" [The decline of poetry: A historical criticism of new poetry in Hong Kong and Taiwan], *Wenji* [Literary season] 1 (1973): 12–42.

35. Zhao Zhiti 趙知悌, "Xu" [Preface], in *Wenxue xiuzou—xiandai wenxue de kaocha* [Literature, don't leave—an examination of modern literature], ed. Zhao Zhiti (Taipei: Yuanxing, 1976), 1.

36. Zhao Zhiti, "Xu," 2–3

37. Gao Shangqin 高上秦 (Gao Xinjiang 高信疆), "Tansuo yu huigu—xie zai 'Longzu pinglun zhuanhao' qianmian" [Exploration and review—a note prefacing the *"Poetry Journal of the Dragon Nation*'s special commentary issue"], in *Wenxue xiuzou—xiandai wenxue de kaocha* [Literature, don't leave—an examination of modern literature], ed. Zhao Zhiti (Taipei: Yuanxing, 1976 [1973]), 164.

38. Critical essays are collected in Zhao Zhiti 趙知悌, ed., *Wenxue xiuzou—xiandai wenxue de kaocha* [Literature, don't leave—an examination of modern literature] (Taipei: Yuanxing, 1976).

39. Zhao Zhiti, "Xu," 3. See also Alain Leroux, "Poetry Movements in Taiwan from the 1950s to the late 1970s: Breaks and Continuities," *China Perspectives* 68 (2006): 11–12; Cai Mingyan 蔡明諺, *Ranshao de niandai—qiling niandai Taiwan wenxue lunzheng shilue* [A flaming era—an outline history of debates on Taiwanese literature in the 1970s] (Tainan: Guoli Taiwan wenxue guan, 2012), 50–55.

40. Gao Xinjiang's home province was Henan. He was born in 1944 in Xi'an and immigrated to Taiwan while he was a small child. Lin Xingyue described Gao's growth experience as follows: "on the eve of the fall of the mainland, he rushed to board the last air force flight, flying over discolored mountains and rivers to Taiwan. . . . In a time of hardship and destitution, Gao Xinjiang not only got on well with local Taiwanese children but also endured the test of bitterly hard life in postwar Taiwan and has the scars to show it." Gao graduated from the Department of Journalism of the College of Chinese Culture. When planning the "Special Commentary Issue" in *Poetry Journal of the Dragon Nation*, he was the chief editor of *Zhongguo shibao*'s (China times) literary section *Renjian* (Human realm). See Lin Xingyue 林惺嶽, *Taiwan meishu fengyun sishinian* [Forty years of vicissitude of fine arts in Taiwan] (Taipei: Zili wanbao, 1987), 192–99. In addition, Gao played a lead role in the 1970s in promoting "reportage literature," which also embodied the return-to-reality and return-to-native-soil spirit, by

publishing pioneer works of this literary genre in the literary section. See Cai Yuanhuang, "Zuihou de langman zhuyi zhe," 181–82; Lu Hanxiu 路寒袖, "Qiling niandai wenhua shishi" [The ten major events in the cultural circles in the 1970s], in *Qiling niandai—lixiang jixu ranshao* [The 1970s: ideals continue to flame], ed. Yang Ze (Taipei: Shibao wenhua, 1994), 262–64.

41. Gao Shangqin, "Tansuo yu huigu," 162–63.

42. Gao Shangqin, "Tansuo yu huigu," 166.

43. For the Modern Poetry Debate, see Cai Mingyan, *Ranshao de niandai*.

44. He Xin 何欣, *Zhongguo xiandai xhiaoshuo de zhuchao* [The main trend of modern Chinese fiction] (Taipei: Yuanjing, 1979), 148.

45. Gao Shangqin, "Tansuo yu huigu," 168–69.

46. Zhong Zhaozheng 鍾肇政, "Taiwan wenxue zhi gui—Ye Shitao" [The spirit of Taiwanese literature—Ye Shitao], *Taiwan Chunqiu* [Taiwan veracity] 8 (1989): 318–19.

47. Ye Shitao 葉石濤, "Taiwan de xiangtu wenxue" [Taiwan's Nativist literature], *Wenxing* [Apollo] 97 (1965): 73.

48. Ye Shitao 葉石濤, "Liangnian lai de shengji zuojia ji qi xiaoshuo" [The writers of this province and their works of fiction in the recent two years], *Taiwan wenyi* [Taiwan literature] 19 (1968): 44–45.

49. Ye Shitao 葉石濤, "Wu Zhuoliu lun" [On Wu Zhuoliu], *Taiwan wenyi* [Taiwan literature] 12 (1966): 28.

50. Liang Jingfeng 梁景峰, "Wenxue de qizi—yu Ye Shitao, Yang Qingchu changtan" [A literary banner—a free conversation with Ye Shitao and Yang Qingchu], in *Xiangtu yu xiandai: Taiwan wenxue de pianduan* [Native land and modernity: fragments of Taiwanese literature], by Liang Jingfeng (Taipei: Taibei xianli wenhua zhongxin, 1995 [1976]), 63.

51. Ye Shitao, "Wu Zhuoliu lun," 30.

52. Ye Shitao 葉石濤, "Zuojia de shidai" [The generational background of writers], in *Taiwan xiangtu zuojia lunji* [Collected essays on Taiwan's Nativist writers], by Ye Shitao (Taipei: Yuanjing, 1979[?]), 46.

53. Ye Shitao 葉石濤, "Liushi niandai de Taiwan xiangtu wenxue" [Nativist literature in 1960s Taiwan], *Wenxun* [Wenhsun magazine] 13 (1984): 146. Also see my earlier discussion in Hsiau, *Contemporary Taiwanese Cultural Nationalism*, 112.

54. *Taiwan wenyi* [Taiwan literature] 64 (November 1979): 4.

55. Hsiau, *Contemporary Taiwanese Cultural Nationalism*, and Hsiau A-chin, *Chonggou Taiwan*.

56. It has to be noted that in the first half of the 1980s, the change of heart—in terms of consciousness, practice, and national identity—of members of *Li Poetry Magazine* and *Taiwan Literature* did not happen overnight. Some writers passed through gray areas of intermediate stages. For some, the change happened earlier and more intensely than for others. For instance, the essays and statements of Li poets

Li Kuixian and Zheng Jiongming at the end of 1980, a year after the Kaohsiung Incident, still expressed a clear Chinese identity. See Li Kuixian, "Li de licheng," 38–39, 41, 48; and *Li shikan* [Li poetry magazine] 100 (December 1980): 54, 59. Even Zhong Zhaozheng in summer of 1982 opined that the values that Nativist literature, including *Taiwan Literature*, should pursue and "return to" should possess the "national character" of China's "five thousand year historical and cultural tradition." See *Taiwan wenyi* [Taiwan literature] 76 (May 1982): inside flap ("Note from the Editor"). During the 1980s Li Kuixian's national identity changed gradually. Later he joined the Taiwan Independence Party (Jianguo dang), formed in October 1996 with the stated objective of "founding a new and independent Republic of Taiwan." He even served as the vice-convener of the party's "development committee." In the 1990s Zhong Zhaozheng clearly inclined toward Taiwanese nationalism, to the point of affirming that Taiwanese literature had nothing to do with Chinese literature. See Zhong Zhaozheng 鍾肇政, *Taiwan wenxue shijiang* [Ten lectures on Taiwanese literature], ed. Zhuang Zirong (Taipei: Qianwei, 2000), 15, 17.

57. A-chin Hsiau, "The Indigenization of Taiwanese Literature: Historical Narrative, Strategic Essentialism, and State Violence," in *Cultural, Ethnic, and Political Nationalism in Contemporary Taiwan: Bentuhua*, ed. John Makeham and A-chin Hsiau (New York: Palgrave Macmillan, 2005), 135–36. At the beginning of 1982, Zheng Jiongming, Zeng Guihai, and Chen Kunlun, three senior members of the Li Poetry Society and *Taiwan Literature*, founded *Wenxuejie* (Literary Taiwan, 1982–1988) in Kaohsiung. In the 1980s the three journals, *Li Poetry Magazine, Taiwan Literature*, and *Literary Taiwan*, functioned as the main forums for local Taiwanese literary writers and critics to construct their distinctive discourse about Taiwanese literature.

58. For these statements by Li poets, see *Taiwan wenyi* [Taiwan literature] 70 (December 1980): 262; 76 (May 1982): 28; *Wenxuejie* [Literary Taiwan] 4 (Winter 1982): 182; and *Li shikan* [Li poetry magazine] 100 (December 1980): 48; 102 (April 1981): 42; 103 (June 1981): 34, 46; 120 (April 1984): 5, 6, 144; 128 (August 1985): 55; 130 (December 1985): 25.

59. Hsiau, *Contemporary Taiwanese Cultural Nationalism*, 100–101.

60. Xu Nancun 許南村 (Chen Yingzhen 陳映真), "'Xiangtu wenxue' de mangdian" [The blind spot of "Nativist literature"], *Taiwan wenyi* [Taiwan literature] 55 (1977): 107–12.

61. Chen Shuhong 陳樹鴻, "Taiwan yishi—dangwai minzhu yundong de jishi" [Taiwanese consciousness—the cornerstone of the Dangwai democratic movement], in *Taiwan yishi lunzhan xuanji* [Selected articles from the debate on Taiwanese consciousness], ed. Shi Minhui (Taipei: Qianwei, 1988 [1983]), 194.

62. Chen Fangming 陳芳明, "Jiliu luanyun" [Torrents of water and chaotic clouds], in *Qiling niandai—lixiang jixu ranshao* [The 1970s: Ideals continue to flame], ed. Yang Ze (Taipei: Shibao wenhua, 1994), 39–49.

63. The image of a lone minister derives from a passage in the traditional Confucian classic, *Mencius*: "Mencius said, 'Persons who possess the intelligence of virtue and the skills of wisdom are often those who have endured sickness and suffering. The solitary and unsupported minister or the concubine's son respond to danger by keeping control of their minds and become profound through anxiously anticipating calamities. Thus they achieve a penetrating understanding." See Mencius, *Mencius*, trans. Irene Bloom (New York: Columbia University Press, 2009), 147.

64. Song Dongyang 宋冬陽 (Chen Fangming 陳芳明), "Xianjieduan Taiwan wenxue bentuhua de wenti" [The present problem of the indigenization of Taiwanese literature], *Taiwan wenyi* [Taiwan literature] 86 (1984): 13. In March 1984, two months after this article appeared, Chen Fangming, under the pen name Chen Jianong, began to be listed as an associate of *Taiwan Literature*. See the copyright page of *Taiwan wenyi* 87 (March 1984).

65. Song Dongyang 宋冬陽, "Chaoxiang xuyuan zhong de liming: shilun Wu Zhuoliu zuopin zhong de 'Zhongguo jingyan'" [Toward the dawn we wished for: On the "Chinese experience" in Wu Zhuoliu's works], *Wenxuejie* [Literary Taiwan] 10 (1984): 128.

66. Hsiau, *Contemporary Taiwanese Cultural Nationalism*, 110–14; Hsiau A-chin, *Chonggou Taiwan*, 219–27. In December 1991 Zheng Jiongming and others who founded *Literary Taiwan* launched a new journal (bearing the same English title as their previous *Wenxuejie*), *Wenxue Taiwan* (Literary Taiwan), also in Kaohsiung. This new journal has become an important forum for Taiwanese nationalists to develop a Taiwanese (national) literary discourse in the 1990s.

67. Ye Shitao 葉石濤, *Taiwan wenxue shigang* [An outline history of Taiwanese literature] (Kaohsiung: Wenxuejie, 1987); Ye Shitao, *A History of Taiwan Literature*, trans. Christopher Lupke (Amherst, N.Y.: Cambria Press, 2020); Peng Ruijin, *Taiwan xinwenxue yundong sishi nian*. For a retrenched expression of their key argument in this period, see Ye Shitao 葉石濤, "Zhuanxie Taiwan wenxueshi yingzou de fangxiang" [The direction writing the history of Taiwanese literature should take], in *Taiwan wenxue de kunjing* [The dilemma of Taiwan literature], by Ye Shitao (Kaohsiung: Paise wenhua, 1992[?]), 13–15. Shortly after Peng Ruijin's book was published, Ye stated that it was "a strong work which succeeds in describing Taiwan's literary history from a Taiwanese perspective," to be placed among "histories from China or Taiwan of Taiwan's literature or periods therein" (21).

68. This is Peng Ruijin's view, though representative of the *Li Poetry Magazine* and *Taiwan Literature* coteries. See Chen Fangming and Peng Ruijin 陳芳明、彭瑞金, "Chen Fangming, Peng Ruijin duitan: liqing Taiwan wenxue de yixie wuyun anri [A dialogue between Chen Fangming and Peng Ruijin: Get rid of the dark clouds in Taiwanese literature], *Wenxuejie* [Literary Taiwan] 24 (1987): 39.

69. Chen Fangming 陳芳明, "Jiaguo banshiji—Taiwan de zhengzhi yu wenxue" [My native country in the past century—politics and literature in Taiwan], *Wenxue Taiwan* [Literary Taiwan] 2 (1992): 79.

70. Du Guoqing 杜國清, "'Li' shishe yu Taiwan shitan" [The "Li" Poetry Society and Taiwanese poetry circles], *Taiwan wenyi* [Taiwan literature] 118 (1987): 20.

71. Peng Ruijin, *Taiwan xinwenxue yundong sishi nian*, 195.

72. Ye Shitao, "Zhuanxie Taiwan wenxueshi yingzou de fangxiang," 22.

73. Chen Yingzhen 陳映真, "Xiang neizhan, lengzhan yishixingtai tiaozhan—qiling niandai Taiwan wenxue lunzheng zai Taiwan wenyi sichao shi shang huashidai de yiyi" [Challenging the ideology of civil war and cold war—the epoch-making significance of the 1970s literary debates in the history of Taiwanese literary and artistic trends], *Lianhe wenxue* [Unitas] 158 (1997): 64.

74. Ye Shitao, *Taiwan wenxue shigang*, 123. Also see the discussion in my earlier research, Hsiau, *Contemporary Taiwanese Cultural Nationalism*, 110; Hsiau A-chin, *Chonggou Taiwan*, 222.

75. Ye Shitao, *Taiwan wenxue shigang*, 171–72.

76. Peng Ruijin, *Taiwan xinwenxue yundong sishi nian*, 126–27.

77. Peng Ruijin, *Taiwan xinwenxue yundong sishi nian*, 166–67; Peng Ruijin 彭瑞金, "Xiangtu wenxue yu qiling niandai de Taiwan wenxue" [Nativist literature and Taiwanese literature in the 1970s], in *Taiwan wenxue tansuo* [Exploring Taiwanese literature], by Peng Ruijin (Taipei: Qianwei, 1995 [1991]), 254.

78. Peng Ruijin 彭瑞金, "Cong Xiangtu wenxue dao Sanmin zhuyi wenxue—fang Ye Shitao xiansheng tan Taiwan wenxue de lishi" [From Nativist literature to Three-Principles-of-the-People literature—interview with Ye Shitao about the history of Taiwanese literature], *Taiwan wenyi* [Taiwan literature] 62 (1979): 30.

79. For the discussion on the Mainlander background of the leaders and participants in the Baodiao movement, see Hsiau A-chin 蕭阿勤, "Jizhu Diaoyutai: lingtu zhengduan, minzu zhuyi, zhishi fenzi yu huaijiu de shidai jiyi" [Remember Diaoyutai Islands: Territorial dispute, nationalism, and generational memory of nostalgic intellectuals in Taiwan], *Taiwanshi yanjiu* [Taiwan historical research] 24, no. 3 (2017): 149.

80. Ye Shitao 葉石濤, *Taiwan wenxue rumen: Taiwan wenxue wushiqi wen* [Introduction to Taiwanese literature: Fifty-seven questions about Taiwanese literature] (Kaohsiung: Chunhui, 1997), 143.

81. Ye Shitao saw the Nativist Literature Debate in the 1970s as the third such debate. In his mind, the first debate was in the 1930s and the second was from 1947 to 1949. For these two earlier debates, see You Shengguan 游勝冠, *Taiwan wenxue bentu lun de xingqi yu fazhan* [The rise and development of the indigenization discourse in Taiwanese literature] (Taipei: Qianwei, 1996), 43–48, 105–32; and Hsiau, *Contemporary Taiwanese Cultural Nationalism*, chaps. 2, 3.

82. Ye Shitao, *Taiwan wenxue rumen*, 46–47. For a similar interpretation, see Lin Ruiming 林瑞明, "Xianjieduan Taiyu wenxue zhi fazhan ji qi yiyi" [The current development of local-Taiwanese-language literature and its significance], *Wenxue Taiwan* [Literary Taiwan] 3 (1992): 15.

83. Caituan faren guojia wenhua yishu jijinhui 財團法人國家文化藝術基金會, *Disanjie guojia wenhua yishu jijinhui wenyijiang zhuanji* [Special report on the Third National Awards for Arts from the National Culture and Arts Foundation] (Taipei: Caituan faren guojia wenhua yishu jijinhui, 1999), 75.

84. See *Guojia wenhua yishu jijinhui huixun* [Newsletter of National Culture and Arts Foundation] 14 (October 1999): 23. At the time, Li Kuixian was a member of the Taiwan Independence Party. See also note 56 of this chapter.

85. Shortly after the DPP was founded in 1986, important members of the Li Poetry Society and *Taiwan Literature*, such as Wu Yongfu, Ye Shitao, Li Qiao, Yang Qingchu, Li Minyong, and Zhao Tianyi, advocated the recruitment of anti-KMT cultural elites who possessed Taiwanese consciousness. In February 1987 the Taiwan Pen Association was founded, with Yang Qingchu as the first chairperson and members of Li Poetry Society and *Taiwan Literature* serving on the executive. *Taiwan Literature* became the official organ of the Taiwan Pen Association until February 1990. For the relation between the association and the political opposition movement after the founding of the DPP, see Hsiau, *Contemporary Taiwanese Cultural Nationalism*, 106.

86. See also Hsiau, "The Indigenization of Taiwanese Literature," 125–55.

6. Dangwai Historiography

1. Wang Yujing 王玉靜, ed., *Jiang Weishui shishi qishi zhounian jinian zhuankan* [Special volume commemorating the seventieth anniversary of Jiang Weishui's death] (Taipei: Taiwan yanjiu jijinhui, 2001).

2. Xu Shikai 許世楷, *Riben tongzhi xia de Taiwan* [Taiwan under Japanese rule] (Taipei: Yushanshe, 2006 [1972]); Weng Jiayin 翁佳音, *Taiwan hanren wuzhuang kangrishi yanjiu (1895–1902)* [A study on the history of the armed anti-Japanese resistance of the Han Chinese in Taiwan, 1895–1902] (Taipei: Daoxiang, 2007 [1986]); Yang Bichuan 楊碧川, *Riju shidai Taiwanren fankangshi* [A history of Taiwanese resistance in the period of Japanese occupation] (Taipei: Daoxiang, 1988); Taiwansheng wenxian weiyuanhui 台灣省文獻委員會, ed., *Taiwanshi* [A history of Taiwan] (Taipei: Zhongwen, 1990), 656–94; Mukōyama Hiroo 向山寬夫, *Riben tongzhi xia de Taiwan minzu yundong shi* [A history of the nationalist movement in Taiwan under Japanese rule], trans. Yang Hongru et al. (Taipei: Fulushou, 1999 [1987]); Wakabayashi Masahiro 若林正丈, *Taiwan kangri yundongshi yanjiu* [A study on the history of Taiwanese anti-Japanese movement] (Taipei: Xinziran zhuyi, 2007 [2001]); Chen Cuilian 陳翠蓮, *Taiwanren de dikang yu rentong, 1920–1950* [The resistance and identity of the Taiwanese, 1920–1950] (Taipei: Yuanliu, 2008); Thomas Fröhlich and Yishan Liu, eds., *Taiwans unvergänglicher Antikolonialismus: Jiang Weishui und der Widerstand gegen die japanische Kolonialherrschaft. Mit einer*

Übersetzung von Schriften Jiang Weishuis aus dem Chinesischen und Japanischen (Bielefeld, Ger.: Transcript Verlag, 2011).

3. For research on Jiang Weishui, see Fröhlich and Liu, *Taiwans unvergänglicher Antikolonialismus*. See also Mingcheng Lo, *Doctors Within Borders: Profession, Ethnicity, and Modernity in Colonial Taiwan* (Berkeley: University of California Press, 2002), 66, 70–71. For analyses of how the collective memory of Jiang Weishui has been constructed and reconstructed in postwar Taiwan, see Thomas Fröhlich, "Einführung," in *Taiwans unvergänglicher Antikolonialismus: Jiang Weishui und der Widerstand gegen die japanische Kolonialherrschaft. Mit einer Übersetzung von Schriften Jiang Weishuis aus dem Chinesischen und Japanischen*, ed. Thomas Fröhlich and Yishan Liu (Bielefeld. Ger.: Transcript Verlag, 2011), 13–39; Thomas Fröhlich, "Identität und Widerstand: Jiang Weishuis Antikolonialismus und seine Nachwirkungen," in *Taiwans unvergänglicher Antikolonialismus: Jiang Weishui und der Widerstand gegen die japanische Kolonialherrschaft. Mit einer Übersetzung von Schriften Jiang Weishuis aus dem Chinesischen und Japanischen*, ed. Thomas Fröhlich and Yishan Liu (Bielefeld, Ger.: Transcript Verlag, 2011), 43–92; and A-chin Hsiau, "Wer erinnert sich an Jiang Weishui? Kollektive Erinnerung an den japanischen Kolonialismus im Taiwan der Nachkriegszeit," in *Taiwans unvergänglicher Antikolonialismus: Jiang Weishui und der Widerstand gegen die japanische Kolonialherrschaft. Mit einer Übersetzung von Schriften Jiang Weishuis aus dem Chinesischen und Japanischen*, ed. Thomas Fröhlich and Yishan Liu (Bielefeld, Ger.: Transcript Verlag, 2011), 93–127.

4. Wu Naiteh 吳乃德, "Ren de jingshen linian zai lishi biange zhong de zuoyong" [The role of moral value in political change: Explaining democratic transition in Taiwan], *Taiwan zhengzhi xuekan* [Taiwanese political science review] 4 (2000): 93.

5. Li Xiaofeng 李筱峰, *Taiwan minzhu yundong sishinian* [Forty years of Taiwan's democratic movement] (Taipei: Zili wanbao, 1987), 89–90.

6. Huang Xinjie was born in Taipei City in 1928. Late in the colonial period he went to Japan to attend middle school. He graduated in 1951 from Taiwan Provincial College of Public Administration (Taiwan shengli xingzheng zhuanke xuexiao, the forerunner of the Law and Business College of National Chung Hsing University and National Taipei University). Huang helped out on Gao Yushu's non-KMT campaign for Taipei mayor in the late 1950s. Starting in 1961 he served two terms as Taipei city councilor. See Ye Boxiang 葉柏祥, *Huang Xinjie qianzhun: Minjindang de youngyuan dalao* [A biography of Huang Xinjie: A big hitter in the Democratic Progressive Party forever] (Taipei: Yuedan, 1994). Kang Ningxiang was born in what is now Wanhua, Taipei City, in 1938. He graduated from National Chung Hsing University. His first experience of politics was in 1969, when he was elected Taipei city councilor. Before this time he had worked as a private teacher, a salesman, and a gas jockey. See Kang Ningxiang 康寧祥, *Wenzheng sannian* [Three-year involvement with legislative interpellation]

(Taipei: Taiwan zhenglun zazhishe, 1975), 1, and the preface by Huang Xinjie 黃信介, "Huang xu," 6.

7. The book He Wenzhen referred to is Zhang Junhong 張俊宏 et al., *Taiwan she-huili de fenxi* [Analysis of Taiwan's social forces] (Taipei: Huanyu, 1972). This book, which Xu Xinliang wrote with Zhang Junhong, Bao Qingtian, and Zhang Shaowen, was originally published in article format: Bao Qingtian 包青天 (Bao Yihong 包奕洪) et al., "Taiwan shehuili de fenxi (shang)" [Analysis of Taiwan's social forces (part 1)], *Daxue zazhi* [The intellectual] 43 (1971): 32–35; Bao Qin-gtian (Bao Yihong) et al., "Taiwan shehuili de fenxi (zhong)" [Analysis of Tai-wan's social forces (part 2)], *Daxue zazhi* 44 (1971): 14–19; and Bao Qingtian (Bao Yihong) et al., "Taiwan shehuili de fenxi (xia)" [Analysis of Taiwan's social forces (part 3)], *Daxue zazhi* 45 (1971): 20–26. See also chapter 3.

8. He Wenzhen 何文振, "Zhuisui lixiang de xinqingnian" [New youths in pursut of their ideals], *Daxue zazhi* [The intellectual] 62 (1973): 39.

9. Jin Wenji 金文吉 (Zhang Jince 張金策), "Pochu huanxiang-miandui wenti" [Shed the illusions and tackle the problems], *Taiwan zhenglun* [Taiwan political review] 3 (1975): 13.

10. E.g., Zhang Junhong 張俊宏, "Women de hua" [Our words], *Zheyidai zazhi* [New generation] 1 (1977): 3; Huang Huangxiong 黃煌雄, *Guomindang wang hechu qu?* [Whither is the Chinese Nationalist Party going?] (Taipei: Changqiao, 1978), 9; Song Guocheng 宋國誠, "Lixing de piping, chengken de huyu—Song xu" [A rational criticism and sincere call—preface by Song], in *Xinshengdai de nahan* [The call of the new generation], ed. Song Guocheng and Huang Zongwen (Taipei: Self-published, 1978), 3.

11. The magazine *Minzhu chao* (Current democracy), founded in 1950, was the organ of the Chinese Youth Party (Zhongguo qingniandang), one of the only two polit-ical parties sanctioned by the KMT government (the other being the China Democratic Socialist Party [Zhongguo minzhu shehui dang]). Established in Paris in 1923 by a group of Chinese students, the Chinese Youth Party followed the KMT government to Taiwan in 1949.

12. He Wenzhen 何文振, *Gei Guomindang de zhengyan* [Advice to the Chinese Nation-alist Party] (Taipei: Chunfeng, 1978), 17–18.

13. He Wenzhen, *Gei Guomindang de zhengyan*, 21–22. Zhang Junhong was born in 1938 in Nantou. He got a Master's degree in Political Science from NTU. In the summer of 1968 he joined *The Intellectual*. Later he was employed at the KMT headquarters. In 1973 he left the KMT and joined the Dangwai. He campaigned for Taipei city councilor but lost. See Zhang Junhong 張俊宏, *Wo de chensi yu fendou—liangqian ge jianao de rizi* [My contemplation and struggle—two thousand tormenting days] (Taipei: Self-published, 1977), 65–126. In 1977 he was elected Taiwan provincial assemblyman.

14. In the election at the end of 1975 to expand the Legislative Yuan, university students like Lin Zhengjie, Wu Nairen, Wu Naiteh, Xiao Yuzhen, and Tian

Qiujin campaigned for Guo Yuxin. When Guo lost, he accused Lin Rongsan of vote buying, and two young lawyers who helped Guo in the lawsuit, Lin Yixiong and Yao Jiawen, later joined the Dangwai. In the five types of local government office elections at the end of 1977, students like Lin Zhengjie and others helped out on the campaign of Xu Xinliang, who had left the KMT to run for mayor of then Taoyuan County. Zhang Junhong and other Dangwai figures were elected to mayoral or provincial assembly positions. In the election at the end of 1978 to expand the ranks of national parliamentary representatives, many young intellectuals campaigned, including Lü Hsiulien, Yao Jiawen, Chen Guying, Chen Wanzhen, Wang Tuo, and Huang Huangxiong. See Li Xiaofeng, *Taiwan minzhu yundong sishinian*, 120–28; Chen Chu 陳菊, "Dizao wo mingyun de ren—huainian Guo Yuxin xiansheng" [The one who shaped my fate—cherishing the memory of Mr. Guo Yuxin], in *Guo Yuxin jinian wenji: Taiwan minzhu chuanjiaoshi* [A collection of essays in memory of Guo Yuxin: An evangelist of democracy in Taiwan], ed. Guo Huina and Lin Hengzhe (Taipei: Qianwei, 1988), 35.

15. Li Xiaofeng, *Taiwan minzhu yundong sishinian*, 122–33.

16. Bashi niandai bianjibu 八十年代編輯部, "Xu Xinliang zhuanfang" [Interview with Xu Xinliang], *Bashi niandai* [The eighties] 1, no. 3 (1979): 10.

17. Nanfang Shuo 南方朔 (Wang Xingqing 王杏慶), "Xu—bokai misi zhi wang" [Preface—unveil the web of myth], in *Qingnian husheng* [The call of youth], by Chen Guoxiang, (Taipei: Siji, 1979), 1.

18. Zhang Junhong 張俊宏, "Chaoliu de xunxi" [The message emerging from the trend], in *Yongzhe buju: wo weishenmo yao jingxuan lifa weiyuan?* [The brave fear nothing: Why do I want to run for legislator?], by Chen Wanzhen, (Taipei: Changqiao, 1978), 17.

19. Wu Jiabang 吳嘉邦, "Yougan liangci danren jingxuan zongganshi" [My thoughts about serving twice as a chief campaign strategist], *Zheyidai zazhi* [New generation] 13 (1978): 13. Wu Jiabang was born in 1942 in Changhua and graduated from Tamkang College of Arts and Sciences.

20. See also Huang Huangxiong 黃煌雄, "Jinnian wuxiang gongzhi xuanju de lishi yiyi" [The historical significance of this year's local elections for five types of local government offices], in *Dao minzhu zhi lu* [The way to democracy], by Huang Huangxiong (Taipei: Self-published, 1980 [1977]), 8; Zhang Junhong, *Wo de chensi yu fendou*, 6–10; Zhang Junhong, "Chaoliu de xunxi," 17; Zhuang Junqing 莊俊清, "Yige dangyuan han minxuan yiyuan de zhenxinhua—Xu Xinliang 'Fengyu zhisheng' shujie" [The sincere words of a KMT member and an elected provincial councilor—introducing Xu Xinliang's *The Sound of Wind and Rain*"], *Xiachao* [China tide] 2, no. 6 (1977): 60; Bashi niandai bianjibu, "Xu Xinliang zhuanfang," 7.

21. Chen Wanzhen 陳婉真, *Yongzhe buju: wo weishenmo yao jingxuan lifa weiyuan?* [The brave fear nothing: Why do I want to run for legislator?] (Taipei: Changqiao,

1978), 19. Chen Wanzhen was born in 1950 in Changhua City and graduated from the Department of Social Education at National Taiwan Normal University.

22. For the Election Assistance Team, see *Zheyidai zazhi* [New generation] 15 (November 1978): 31; and 16 (December 1978): 4–8.

23. Hungmao Tien, *The Great Transition: Political and Social Change in the Republic of China* (Stanford, Calif.: Hoover Institution Press, 1989), 95–97.

24. Li Xiaofeng, *Taiwan minzhu yundong sishinian*, 138; Tien, *The Great Transition*, 96.

25. Bashi niandai bianjibu, "Xu Xinliang zhuanfang," 7, 10–11.

26. Bao Siwen 包斯文 (Geng Rongshui 耿榮水), "Liangtiao luxian liangzhong celue— 'Meilidao' zazhi chuangkan zhihou" [Two lines, two strategies—after the foundation of *Formosa* magazine], in *Dangwai renshi hequ hecong?* [Whither are the Dangwai figures going?], ed. Bao Siwen (Taipei: Siji, 1980 [1979]), 81–85.

27. Li Xiaofeng, *Taiwan minzhu yundong sishinian*, 145; Tien, *The Great Transition*, 96.

28. Lin Zhengjie 林正杰, "Zhanhou xinshengdai de yangchengqi" [The cultivation period of the postwar new generation], in *Qiling niandai—lixiang jixu ranshao* [The 1970s: ideals continue to flame], ed. Yang Ze (Taipei: Shibao wenhua, 1994), 85.

29. Huang Xinjie 黃信介, "Fakan ci: Gongtong lai tuidong xinshengdai zhengzhi yundong" [Inaugural statement: Let's work together to push the political movement of the new generation], *Meilidao* [Formosa] 1, no. 1 (1979): inner flap–1. The motto on the contents page of the inaugural issue of *Formosa* was "Nourish the life of the new generation and establish a rational society." The article chosen for the leader of the first issue was headlined "Minzhu wansui" (Long live democracy). See Meilidao zazhishe 美麗島雜誌社, "Minzhu wansui" [Long live democracy], *Melidao* 1, no. 1 (1979): 4–9; Meilidao zazhishe, "Meiyou gaige jiu meiyou qiantu—shuangshi guoqing ganyan" [No reform, no future—comments at the Double Tenth National Day], *Melidao* 1, no. 3 (1979): 4, 5.

30. Meilidao zazhishe, "Minzhu wansui," 4.

31. Meilidao zazhishe, "Meiyou gaige jiu meiyou qiantu," 7.

32. Meilidao zazhishe, "Minzhu wansui," 4.

33. Huang Xinjie, "Fakan ci," 1.

34. Meilidao zazhishe, "Minzhu wansui," 7–9.

35. He Wenzhen 何文振, "Taiwan dadizhu" [Big landlord in Taiwan], *Taiwan zhenglun* [Taiwan political review] 3 (1975): 15.

36. Huang Huangxiong 黃煌雄, "Jinnian wuxiang gongzhi xuanju de lishi yiyi" [The historical significance of this year's local elections for five types of local government offices], *Zheyidai zazhi* [New generation] 6 (1977): 6.

37. Yao Jiawen 姚嘉文, "'Panguo' lun—guo buke pan, min buke ru" [On "treason"— the country cannot be rebelled against and the people cannot be humiliated], *Meilidao* [Formosa] 1, no. 1 (1979): 61, 65.

38. Yao Jiawen 姚嘉文, "Aiguo lun: you shengmin zhi guo, ziyou aiguo zhi min" [On patriotism: If there is a country which can help people improve their life,

naturally there will be a patriotic people], *Meilidao* [Formosa] 1, no. 3 (1979): 93–94.

39. Bashi niandai chubanshe bianjibu 八十年代出版社編輯部, " 'Ziyou Zhongguo' xuanji zongxu" [General preface to *Selections from "Free China"*], in *"Ziyou Zhongguo" xuanji* [Selections from *"Free China"*], ed. Bashi niandai chubanshe bianjibu (Taipei: Bashi niandai chubanshe bianjibu, 1979), 11.

40. Meilidao zazhishe, "Meiyou gaige jiu meiyou qiantu," 6, 7.

41. Zhang Junhong, *Wo de chensi yu fendou*, 157–58, 229–30, 245–46.

42. Lin Zhuoshui 林濁水, "Taiwan shi meilidao" [Taiwan is a beautiful island], *Bashi niandai* [The eighties] 1, no. 4 (1979): 20–21. Lin Zhuoshui was born in 1947 in Puli, Nantou, and graduated with a degree in political science from National Chengchi University.

43. Wang Fuchang 王甫昌, "Fandui yundong de gongshi dongyuan: yijiu qijiu-yijiu bajiu nian liangpo tiaozhan gaofeng de bijiao" [Consensus mobilization of the political opposition in Taiwan: Comparing two waves of challenges, 1979–1989], *Taiwan zhengzhi xuekan* [Taiwanese political science review] 1 (1996): 155–65.

44. Kang Ningxiang and Chen Zhengnong 康寧祥、陳政農, *Taiwan, dapin: Kang Ningxiang huiyilu* [Taiwan, work hard: Memoirs of Kang Ningxiang] (Taipei: Yunchen, 2014), 27–29, 38–43.

45. See "Jinian geming xianxian Jiang Weishui xiansheng shishi 46 zhounian zuotanhui" [Symposium commemorating the forty-sixth anniversary of the death of the revolutionary sage Mr. Jiang Weishui], *Zheyidai zazhi* [New generation] 2 (August 1977): 59.

46. "Jinian geming xianxian Jiang Weishui xiansheng shishi 46 zhounian zuotanhui," 60. In the symposium held in memory of Jiang Weishui in 1977, Kang Ningxiang also mentioned that the time he stumped for Huang Xinjie was his "proudest hustings."

47. Zheng Hongsheng 鄭鴻生, *Qingchun zhi ge: zhuiyi yijiu qiling niandai Taiwan zuoyi qingnian de yiduan ruhuo nianhua* [Song of youth: Recalling the wild years of leftist youth in 1970s Taiwan] (Taipei: Lianjing, 2001), 181.

48. Chen Shaoting 陳少廷, "Lin Xiantang xiansheng yu 'zuguo shijian'—jianlun Taiwan zhishi fenzi kangri yundong de lishi yiyi" [Mr. Lin Xiantang and the "Ancestral Land Incident"—also on the historical significance of the anti-Japanese movement of Taiwanese intellectuals], *Daxue zazhi* [The intellectual] 43 (1971): 4–8.

49. Chen Shaoting, "Lin Xiantang xiansheng yu 'zuguo shijian,'" 4. The July 7th Incident, a battle near what is now Beijing between the ROC Army and the Japanese Army in early July 1937, was generally regarded as the beginning of the Second Sino-Japanese War. It is commonly known as the "Marco Polo Bridge Incident."

50. Chen Shaoting, "Lin Xiantang xiansheng yu 'zuguo shijian,'" 4, 8.

51. See *Lifayuan gongbao* [Official gazette of the Legislative Yuan] 64 (16) (February 22, 1975): 6.

52. See *Lifayuan gongbao* [Official gazette of the Legislative Yuan] 64 (19) (March 5, 1975): 8.

53. See *Lifayuan gongbao* 64 (19): 9–14.

54. See *Lifayuan gongbao* 64 (19): 19.

55. Zhang Junhong, *Wo de chensi yu fendou*, 192–93.

56. See "Jinian geming xianxian Jiang Weishui xiansheng shishi 46 zhounian zuotanhui," 59–60.

57. "Jinian geming xianxian Jiang Weishui xiansheng shishi 46 zhounian zuotanhui," 59.

58. "Jinian geming xianxian Jiang Weishui xiansheng shishi 46 zhounian zuotanhui," 62.

59. Zhang Junhong, *Wo de chensi yu fendou*, 192–93. Also, He Wenzhen agreed with Zhang Junhong's high opinion of Kang Ningxiang. See He Wenzhen, *Gei Guomindang de zhengyan*, 26.

60. Ye Rongzhong 葉榮鐘, "Taiwan minzu yundong de puluren Cai Huiru" [Cai Huiru, the man who paved the way for the Taiwanese national movement], *Taiwan zhenglun* [Taiwan political review] 1 (1975): 56; Fan Fu 凡夫 (Ye Rongzhong), "Taiwan minzu shiren Lin Youchun" [Taiwan's national poet Lin Youchun], *Taiwan zhenglun* 3 (1975): 69; Fan Fu (Ye Rongzhong), "Gemingjia Jiang Weishui" [Revolutionary Jiang Weishui], *Taiwan zhenglun* 5 (1975): 77–78. See chapter 2 for Ye's daughter's remembrance of his father's historical writing in the 1960s.

61. Huang Hua 黃華, "Jianxingren de xinxin" [The confidence of one who received a commuted sentence], *Taiwan zhenglun* [Taiwan political review] 3 (1975): 40. Huang was born in 1939 in Keelung. Zhang Junhong stated that he saw Huang Hua as a saint, and that to Kang Ningxiang he was a leading icon in Dangwai politics. See Zhang Junhong, *Wo de chensi yu fendou*, 162–73.

62. Zhenghong 正宏, trans., "Ribenren yanzhong de Taiwan kangri yundong" [The Taiwanese anti-Japanese movement seen through Japanese eyes], *Taiwan zhenglun* [Taiwan political review] 4 (1975): 48.

63. Lin Zhengjie, "Zhanhou xinshengdai de yangchengqi," 88.

64. Lin Zhengjie, "Zhanhou xinshengdai de yangchengqi," 88–89.

65. Chen Fangming 陳芳明, "Jiliu luanyun" [Torrents of water and chaotic clouds], in *Qiling niandai—lixiang jixu ranshao* [The 1970s: Ideals continue to flame], ed. Yang Ze (Taipei: Shibao wenhua, 1994), 47–48.

66. *New Generation* was punished with a one-year ban in January 1979. *The Eighties* was banned in December 1979, after the Kaohsiung Incident.

67. Huang Huangxiong, *Guomindang wang hechu qu?*, 19–21; Huang Huangxiong 黃煌雄, "Yixiang zhuangyan de jianyi—jinian Jiang Weishui xiansheng shishi sishiqi zhounian" [A solemn proposal: In memory of the forty-seventh anniversary of Mr. Jiang Weishui's death], *Zheyidai zazhi* [New generation] 12 (1978): 20. See also "Taiwan jindai 'xianjuezhe' de jingshen yichan zuotanhui"

[Symposium on the spiritual legacy of modern Taiwanese "visionaries"], *Zheyidai zazhi* 3 (1977): 18.

68. Huang Huangxiong 黃煌雄, *Taibao kangri shihua* [A historical story of Taiwanese compatriots' anti-Japanese resistance] (Taipei: Self-published, 1977), 11.

69. Zheng Nanrong 鄭南榕, "'Zhen youli' de zhengzhi sixiangjia—Huang Huangxiong: fangwen Huang Huangxiong" [A "truly powerful" political thinker—Huang Huangxiong: Interview with Huang Huangxiong], *Zhengzhijia* [The statesman] 26 (1982): 7.

70. Huang Huangxiong, "Jinnian wuxiang gongzhi xuanju de lishi yiyi," 6.

71. Lin Zhengjie 林正杰, "Wo de zhengzhi jianjie: Huang Huangxiong fangwen ji" [My political views: Interview with Huang Huangxiong], *Zheyidai zazhi* [New generation] 15 (1978): 53.

72. Huang Huangxiong 黃煌雄, *Taiwan de xianzhi xianjuezhe—Jiang Weishi xiansheng* [Taiwan's visionary prophet—Mr. Jiang Weishui] (Taipei: Self-published, 1976); Huang Huangxiong, *Taibao kangri shihua* [A historical story of Taiwanese compatriots' anti-Japanese resistance) (Taipei: Self-published, 1977); and Huang Huangxiong, ed., *Beiyapozhe de nuhou—Jiang Weishui xiansheng xuanji* [The roar of the oppressed—a selection of Mr. Jiang Weishui's writings] (Taipei: Changqiao, 1978). The title of the second as listed on the cover was *Beiyapo de Taibao kangri shihua* (A historical story of the anti-Japanese resistance of suppressed Taiwanese compatriots), while the word *beiyabo* (suppressed) was not present in the title as listed on the copyright page or in Huang Huangxiong's later references. *Taiwan de xianzhi xianjuezhe—Jiang Weishi xiansheng* and *Taibao kangri shihua* were published again in 1978 with different titles by Changqiao: *Gemingjia—Jiang Weishui* [Revolutionary—Jiang Weishui] and *Feibaoli de douzheng* [Nonviolent struggle]. In the early 1990s Huang rewrote and republished both books, and the titles were changed again: Huang Huangxiong, *Jiang Weishui zhuan—Taiwan de xianzhi xianjue* [Biography of Jiang Weishui—Taiwan's visionary prophet] (Taipei: Qianwei, 1992); and Huang Huangxiong, *Taiwan kangri shihua* [A historical story of the anti-Japanese resistance in Taiwan] (Taipei: Qianwei, 1992). See the following discussion.

73. Huang Huangxiong, *Taibao kangri shihua*, 189; Huang Huangxiong, *Guomindang wang hechu qu?*, 186; Huang Huangxiong, "Cong Jiang Weishui jingshen tanqi: jianlun Taiwan de zuotian jintian yu mingtian—minguo liushiqi nian shiyi yue shiqi ri zai 'Jiang Weishui jiniange fabiaohui' shang zhuanti yanjiangci" [A discussion beginning with the Jiang Weishui spirit: Also on Taiwan's yesterday, today, and tomorrow—keynote speech at the "Launch of Tribute Song in Memory of Jiang Weishui" on November 17, the sixty-seventh year of the ROC calendar], *Zheyidai zazhi* [New generation] 16 (1978): 44–45.

74. "Taiwan jindai 'xianjuezhe' de jingshen yichan zuotanhui" [Symposium on the spiritual legacy of modern Taiwanese "visionaries"), *Zheyidai zazhi* [New generation] 3 (1977): 18. Also see Zhang Junhong's and Kang Ningxiang's similar opinions in this symposium (17, 21).

75. Huang Huangxiong, *Taibao kangri shihua*, 184–202.

76. Huang Huangxiong, *Gemingjia*, 24.

77. Huang Huangxiong 黃煌雄, "Yiduan chenfeng de shiji—fang Huang Huangxiong tan Taiwanshi" [A dust-covered trace of history—interview with Huang Huangxiong about Taiwanese history], in *Dao minzhu zhi lu* [The way to democracy], by Huang Huangxiong (Taipei: Self-published, 1980 [1979]): 175–76.

78. Huang Huangxiong, "Yixiang zhuangyan de jianyi," 21.

79. Huang Huangxiong, *Gemingjia*, 218–28, 261–82.

80. Huang Huangxiong, *Gemingjia*, 283.

81. Huang Huangxiong, *Guomindang wang hechu qu?*, 8–9, 22; Huang Huangxiong, "Yixiang zhuangyan de jianyi," 20; Huang Huangxiong, "Jingzhengzhe zhi lu—Guomindang yu dangwai de jianquanhua" [The roads for competitors—the Chinese Nationalist Party and the betterment of the Dangwai], *Bashi niandai* [The eighties] 1, no. 1 (1979): 8

82. Guo Yuxin lost out in the election to expand the Legislative Yuan at the end of 1975. Two years later he left for America. He died in the 1980s. The lawyer Lin Yixiong, who had entered the Dangwai by taking on the election litigation pressed after Guo Yuxin's loss, was elected to the provincial assembly representing Yilan at the end of 1977. He later went to prison in the Kaohsiung Incident. See also note 14 of this chapter.

83. See *Zhengzhijia* [The statesman] 26 (April 1982): 13, 14; Zheng Nanrong 鄭南榕, "Huang Huangxiong you xianjian zhi ming" [Huang Huangxiong has foresight], *Zhengzhijia* 26 (1982): 15.

84. Zhang Junhong 張俊宏, "*Guomindang wang hechu qu* xuwen: zhipei zhe yishi jingzheng zhe?" [Preface to *Whither Is the Chinese Nationalist Party Going?* dominator or rival], *Zheyidai zazhi* [New generation] 14 (1978): 51–52.

85. Zheng Nanrong, "'Zhen youli' de zhengzhi sixiangjia," 7–8; see also Huang Huangxiong 黃煌雄, *Taiwan de zhuanleidian: fangwen yanjiang pian* [A turning point for Taiwan: The visits and interviews volume] (Taipei: Self-published, 1983), 47–49.

86. Lü Hsiulien (Annette Lu) 呂秀蓮, *Xinnüxing zhuyi* [New feminism] (Taipei: Youshi yuekan she, 1974), 4, 36–41, 206.

87. Lü Hsiulien (Annette Lu) 呂秀蓮, *Xunzhao ling yishan chuang* [Searching for another window] (Taipei: Shuping shumu, 1974), i–ii (preface to the second edition). According to Yin Di, who had served as editor-in-chief of several literary magazines and established an important literary publisher in 1975, *Searching for Another Window*, a collection of Lü's newspaper columns, became a best seller. See Yin Di 隱地, "Fanzhuag de niandai: jiantan qiling niandai de wenyifeng" [An era of transformation: Also on the literary and artistic trends in the 1970s], in *Qiling niandai—lixiang jixu ranshao* [The 1970s: Ideals continue to flame], ed. Yang Ze (Taipei: Shibao wenhua, 1994), 33.

88. Lü Hsiulien (Annette Lu) 呂秀蓮, *Taiwan de guoqu yu weilai* [The past and the present of Taiwan] (Taipei: Tuohuang zhe, 1979), 63–64; Li Wen 李文, *Zongheng*

wushinian—Lü Hsiulien [Five decades of fights and struggles—a biography of Lü Hsiulien] (Taipei: Shibao wenhua, 1996), 98–99.

89. Su Beng (Shi Ming) 史明, *Taiwanren shibainian shi* [Four hundred years of Taiwanese history] (San Jose, Calif.: Paradise Culture Associates, 1980 [1962]); Ong Joktik 王育德, *Taiwan: kumen de lishi* [Taiwan: A depressing history] (Taipei: Zili wanbao, 1993 [1964]).

90. Lu Hsiulien (Lü Hsiulien, Annette Lu) and Ashley Esarey, *My Fight for a New Taiwan: One Woman's Journey from Prison to Power* (Seattle: University of Washington Press, 2014), 76. For further discussion, see A-chin Hsiau, *Contemporary Taiwanese Cultural Nationalism* (London: Routledge, 2000), 157–58.

91. Lü Hsiulien, *Taiwan de guoqu yu weilai*, 63.

92. Lü Hsiulien, *Taiwan de guoqu yu weilai*, 233. Further citations of this work are given in parentheses in the text.

93. Lü Hsiulien was actually a member of the KMT for most of the 1970s. She joined at the beginning of the 1970s. But after the election was called off in December 1978, her membership was revoked because she had "stirred up ideas of Taiwan independence" during the election. See *Bashi niandai* [The eighties] 1, no. 1 (1979): 68.

94. Lin Zhuoshui, "Taiwan shi meilidao," 20. By Heluo, the editor meant the region between the Yellow River and Luo River (Luoshui) on the Chinese mainland, that is, the Central Plains. In postwar Taiwan, the KMT Sinocentric historical narrative typically claimed that this region was the ancestral homeland of local Taiwanese as part of the Han nation.

95. E.g., Lin Zhuoshui 林濁水 et al., eds., *Wajie de diguo* [A collapsing empire] (Taipei: Boguan, 1984); Shi Minhui 施敏輝, ed., *Taiwan yishi lunzhan xuanji* [Selected articles from the debate on Taiwanese consciousness] (Taipei: Qianwei, 1988); see the discussion in Hsiau, *Contemporary Taiwanese Cultural Nationalism*, 158–74; and Hsiau A-chin 蕭阿勤, *Chonggou Taiwan: dangdai minzu zhuyi de wenhua zhengzhi* [Reconstructing Taiwan: The cultural politics of contemporary nationalism] (Taipei: Lianjing, 2012), 291–322.

96. From the early 1980s on, Lü's *guer* (orphaned sons) metaphor was echoed by a new discourse about Taiwanese literature articulated by anti-KMT local Taiwanese writers like Chen Fangming. Chen's conceptions, *guer yishi* (orphan consciousness) and *guer wenxue* (orphan literature), as mentioned in chapter 5, were intended to characterize the spirit and works of senior local Taiwanese writers in the 1950s and 1960s.

97. Jiang Xun 蔣勳, "Qiling—" [The 1970s—], in *Qiling niandai: chanqinglu* [The 1970s: A collection of confessions], ed. Yang Ze (Taipei: Shibao wenhua, 1994), 112–13.

98. On the dissemination of Taiwanese consciousness in the 1980s, as well the various means the KMT used to suppress the radical wing of the Dangwai, causing it to become even more radical, moving from the pursuit of "democratization" to the quest for Taiwanese nationalism, see Wang Fuchang, "Fandui yundong de gongshi dongyuan," 165–73. For the process by which local Taiwanese cultural

activists became Taiwanese nationalists after the Kaohsiung Incident, see Hsiau, *Contemporary Taiwanese Cultural Nationalism*.

99. Huang Huangxiong 黃煌雄, "Jiang Weishui qiren qishi" [Jiang Weishui: The man and his story], in *Jiang Weishui shishi liushi zhounian jinian ji Taiwanshi xueshu yantaohui lunwen jiyao* [Selected proceedings of the Conference Commemorating the Sixtieth Anniversary of Jiang Weishui's Death and on Taiwanese History], ed. Kaohsiung County Government (Kaohsiung: Kaohsiung County Government, 1991), 12–13, 16.

100. Zhang Yanxian 張炎憲, "Yijiu erling niandai de Jiang Weishui" [Jiang Weishui in the 1920s], in *Jiang Weishui shishi liushi zhounian jinian ji Taiwanshi xueshu yantaohui lunwen jiyao* [Selected proceedings of the Conference Commemorating the Sixtieth Anniversary of Jiang Weishui's Death and on Taiwanese History], ed. Kaohsiung County Government (Kaohsiung: Kaohsiung County Government, 1991), 17, 32–33. For the role played by scholars of Taiwanese history like Zhang Yanxian in the emergence of the pro-Taiwan historiographic perspective, see Hsiau, *Contemporary Taiwanese Cultural Nationalism*, 164–68.

101. Huang Huangxiong, *Jiang Weishui zhuan*; Huang Huangxiong, *Taiwan kangri shihua*. See also note 72 of this chapter.

102. Huang Huangxiong might have in mind works such as Cai Peihuo 蔡培火 et al., *Taiwan minzu yundong shi* (A history of Taiwanese national movement) (Taipei: Zili wanbao she wenhua chubanbu, 1971). Its five coauthors included elderly anti-colonial activists like Cai Peihuo, Wu Sanlian, and Ye Rongzhong.

103. Huang Huangxiong, *Jiang Weishui zhuan*, 10–11; Huang Huangxiong, *Taiwan kangri shihua*, 4–5.

104. Huang Huangxiong 黃煌雄, "Tongbao xu tuanjie, tuanjie zhenyouli" [We compatriots must unite, for in unity there is truly strength], in *Jiang Weishui shishi qishi zhounian jinian zhuankan* [Special volume commemorating the seventieth anniversary of Jiang Weishui's death], ed. Wang Yujing (Taipei: Taiwan yanjiu jijinhui, 2001), 5.

105. Also, the four characters of the gift calligraphy President Chen presented to the conference organizers were *Tai wan jing shen*, meaning "Taiwanese spirit." See Wang Yujing 王玉靜, ed., *Jiang Weishui shishi qishi zhounian jinian zhuankan* [Special volume commemorating the seventieth anniversary of Jiang Weishui's death] (Taipei: Taiwan yanjiu jijinhui, 2001), 84.

106. Hannah Arendt, *The Human Condition* (Chicago: University of Chicago Press, 1998 [1958]), 175–88, 199–207.

Conclusion

1. Ye Hongsheng 葉洪生, "Zheshi ge shemo shidai?" [What is the present era?], in *Niannian yijue piaohuameng* [Awaking from a twenty-year blossoming dream], by Ye Hongsheng (Taipei: Huangyu, 1972 [1971]), 68–69.

2. Wu Fengshan 吳豐山, *Wo neng wei guojia zuoxie shemo?* [What can I do for the country?] (Taipei: Yuanjing, 1978), 158. Wu Fengshan was born in 1945 in what was then Tainan County and graduated from National Chengchi University with a Master's degree in journalism. In 1972 he was elected as Tainan County representative to the National Assembly. In 1978 he was working as general editor at *Zili wanbao* (Independent evening post), which tended to support the Dangwai opposition movement.

3. Robert Wohl, *The Generation of 1914* (Cambridge, Mass.: Harvard University Press, 1979), 5.

4. Edward P. Thompson, *The Making of the English Working Class* (New York: Vintage Books, 1963), 9.

5. June Edmunds and Bryan S. Turner, "Introduction: Generational Consciousness, Narrative, and Politics," in *Generational Consciousness, Narrative, and Politics*, ed. Edmunds and Turner (Lanham, Md.: Rowman & Littlefield, 2002), 2.

6. Stevan Harrell and Huang Chünchieh argue that "as late as the 1970s, there was still a local rural culture in any Taiwan village, a local culture that both signaled its own low position by its parochial nature and proclaimed its uniqueness in the face of similar, but still not identical, cultural traditions in neighboring and more distant communities." See Stevan Harrell and Huang Chünchieh, "Introduction: Change and Contention in Taiwan's Cultural Scene," in *Cultural Change in Postwar Taiwan*, ed. Harrell and Huang (Boulder, Colo.: Westview Press, 1994), 3.

7. David C. Schak, *Civility and Its Development: The Experiences of China and Taiwan* (Hong Kong: Hong Kong University Press, 2018), 10, 112, 120.

8. Schak, *Civility and Its Development*, 120–35; see also Richard Madsen, *Democracy's Dharma: Religious Renaissance and Political Development in Taiwan* (Berkeley: University of California Press, 2007).

9. Lü Hsiulien (Annette Lu) 呂秀蓮, "Tuohuangzhe de gushi: cong 'xinnüxing' dao 'minzhuren' " [The story of a pioneer: From a "new woman" to a "democrat"], in *Qiling niandai—lixiang jixu ranshao* [The 1970s: Ideals continue to flame], ed. Yang Ze (Taipei: Shibao wenhua, 1994), 67, 72.

10. Nanfang Shuo 南方朔 (Wang Xingqing 王杏慶), "Nashi, Taiwan cai zhangda" [Only then did Taiwan grow up], in *Qiling niandai—lixiang jixu ranshao* [The 1970s: Ideals continue to flame], ed. Yang Ze (Taipei: Shibao wenhua, 1994), 117–18.

11. Yang Zhao 楊照, "Faxian 'Zhongguo': Taiwan de qiling niandai" [Discovering "China": the 1970s in Taiwan], in *Qiling niandai—lixiang jixu ranshao* [The 1970s: Ideals continue to flame], ed. Yang Ze (Taipei: Shibao wenhua, 1994), 132–33.

12. See A-chin Hsiau, *Contemporary Taiwanese Cultural Nationalism* (London: Routledge, 2000), 96–98; Hsiau A-chin 蕭阿勤, *Chonggou Taiwan: dangdai minzu zhuyi de wenhua zhengzhi* [Reconstructing Taiwan: The cultural politics of contemporary nationalism] (Taipei: Lianjing, 2012), 191–95.

13. See also Wu Naiteh 吳乃德, "Ren de jingshen linian zai lishi biange zhong de zuoyong" [The role of moral value in political change: Explaining democratic transition in Taiwan], *Taiwan zhengzhi xuekan* [Taiwanese political science review] 4 (2000): 85.

14. Su Beng (Shi Ming) 史明, *Taiwanren shibainian shi* [Four hundred years of Taiwanese history] (San Jose, Calif.: Paradise Culture Associates, 1980 [1962]).

15. This kind of criticism became very common in both Taiwan and the PRC since about 2001 and was mostly directed at President Chen Shuibian's DPP government. There were virulent attacks on "indigenization," "de-Sinification," "Taiwan independence in culture" (*wenhua Taidu*), "Taiwan independence in literature" (*wenxue Taidu*), and the like, especially by critics in the PRC. There was a veritable outpouring of such criticism into various media and forums on the internet. For example: Lin Jin 林勁, "Qianxi 'wenhua Taidu' de shizhi ji yingxiang" [A basic analysis of the essence and impact of "Taiwan independence in culture"], *Huaxia jingwei* [huaxia.com], 2001, http://big5.huaxia.com/zt/2001-19/32739.html; Chen Yingzhen 陳映真, "Lun 'wenxue Taidu'" [On "Taiwan independence in literature"], *Huaxia*, June 27, 2001, http://big5.huaxia.com/zt/2001-19/32790.html; Zhao Xiaqiu 趙遐秋, "Yao jingti 'wenxue Taidu' de exing fazhan" [Stay alert for the vicious development of "Taiwan independence in literature"], *Huaxia jingwei*, 2001, http://big5.huaxia.com/zt/2001-19/32775.html; Wang Jingqiong 王京瓊, "Jianxi 'wenhua Taidu'" [A brief analysis of "Taiwan independence in culture"], *Zhongguowang* [china.com.cn], 2002, http://www.china.com.cn/chinese/zhuanti/179287.htm; Li Xinyi 李新乙, "'Wenhua daitu' dangbuzhu Zhongguo tongyi jincheng" ["Taiwan independence in culture" cannot stop the process of China's unification], *Huaxia jingwei* [huaxia.com], May 9, 2002, http://www.huaxia.com/thpl/lbyl/bfyl/05/42141.html; Zhang Shijian 張詩劍, "Zhonghua wenhua zhi gen buke dongyao—bo 'wenhua Taidu'" [The root of Chinese culture cannot be shaken—refuting "Taiwan independence in culture"], *Zhongguowang*, 2002, http://big5.china.com.cn/chinese/TCC/haixia/112070.htm; Liao Yi 廖翊, "Yuri juzeng de buan—fang Taiwan daxue jiaoshou Huang Guangguo" [Increasing anxiety: Interview with Professor Huang Guangguo of National Taiwan University], *Renminwang* [people.cn], 2002, http://www.people.com.cn/BIG5/shizheng/18/20/20020806/793786.html; Jilin Laoxiu 吉林老朽, "Tai dangju, shudian wangzu, yugai mizhang" [The authorities of Taiwan recount history but forget their origins; the more they try to cover it up, the more it will be known], *Renminwang*, 2003, http://tw.people.com.cn/GB/21879/2108918.html; Li Daoxiang 李道湘, "'Wenhua Taidu' de shizhi han weihai" [The reality and danger of "Taiwan independence in culture"], *Renminwang*, 2004, http://tw.people.com.cn/BIG5/14811/14873/2482842.html; *Aomen ribao* 澳門日報, "Aomen ribao: bian dangju zhengzhi yu wenhua bingju tuijin 'Taidu'" [Macao daily news: Chen Shuibian's administration push forward "Taiwan independence" in both politics and culture], *Xinlang xinwen zhongxin* [news.sina

.com.cn], November 27, 2004, http://news.sina.com.cn/c/2004-11-27/20254366095s.shtml; Lu Yixin 盧一心, "'Wenhua Taidu' genben jiu bukan yiji" ["Taiwan independence in culture" no doubt doesn't hold water], *Xinlang xinwen zhongxin* [news.sina.com.cn], December 9, 2004, http://news.sina.com.cn/c/2004-12-09/16155172948.shtml; Chen Yunlin 陳雲林, "Jianjue fandui 'taidu' fenlie huodong nuli zhengqu zuguo heping tongyi guangming qianjing" [Resolutely opposing "Taiwan independence" separatist activities and struggling for bright prospects of peaceful reunification], *Qiushi zazhi* [Truth-seeking magazine] 4 (2005): 16–18; Xu Bodong and Lou Jie 徐博東、婁傑, "'Qu Jianghua' baocang 'Taidu' huoxin" ["De-Chiang Kaishek-ification" contains the evil plot of "Taiwan independence"], *Zhongguowang*, June 12, 2007, http://www.china.com.cn/review/txt/2007-06/12/content_8376865.htm. See also Guowuyuan Taiwan shiwu bangongshi xinwenju 國務院台灣事務辦公室新聞局, *Lü Hsiulien "Taidu" yanlun pipan* [A critique of Lü Hsiulien's discourse on "Taiwan independence"] (Beijing: Jiouzhou tushu, 2000); Zhao Xiaqiu and Zeng Qingrui 趙遐秋、曾慶瑞, *Wenxue Taidu mianmianguan* [On various aspects of Taiwan independence in literature] (Beijing: Jiouzhou, 2001); Liu Denghan 劉登翰, *Zhonghua wenhua yu Mintai shehui—Mintai wenhua guanxi lungang* [Chinese culture and Fujianese and Taiwanese societies—an outline study of the cultural relationship between Fujian and Taiwan] (Fuzhou: Fujian renmin chubanshe, 2002); Pan Chaoyang 潘朝陽, "Taidu Taiwanshi shi huangminhua sanjiaozi weishi" [The pro-Taiwan-independence Taiwanese history is Japanized collaborators' fake history], *Haixia pinlun* [Straits review monthly] 185 (2006): 58–60; and so forth. Also there have been countless similar criticisms targeted at President Tsai Ingwen's DPP administration on the internet since she was inaugurated in May 2016. E.g., Xu Zhengxuan 徐政璿, "Qu Zhongguohua! Caizhengfu cong lishi keben xiashou; Guomindang: shudian wangzu" [De-Sinification! The Tsai Ingwen administration starts with history textbooks; the KMT: Recount history but forget their origins], *ETtoday*, July 5, 2017, https://www.ettoday.net/news/20170705/959578.htm; Pan Weiting 潘維庭, "Tsai Ingwen han Taiwan shi guojia; Ding Shouzhong: wei latai xuanqing tiao liang'an duili" [Tsai Ingwen called Taiwan a country; Ding Shouzhong: In order to draw more votes, she provoked the cross-Taiwan Strait conflict], *Zhongshi xinwenwang* [China times], August 4, 2018, https://www.chinatimes.com/ realtime-news/ 20180804001248-260407; Wei Wei 魏煒, "Shudian wangzu renzei zuofu Tsai Ingwen de Taiwan jiazhi" [Recount history but forget her origins and take a thief as her father: Tsai Ingwen's Taiwan value], *US-China Forum*, February 24, 2018, http://www.us-chinaforum.com/ 27599369133554222727/4364124; Zhong Lihua 鍾麗華, "Guotaiban pi 'sangxin bingkuang'; luweihui huiji 'xiachong buke yubing'" ["Frenzied and perverse": China's Taiwan Affairs Office criticized; "An Insect that lives only one summer cannot be expected to know what ice is": Taiwan's Mainland Affairs Council counter-criticized], *Ziyou shibao* [Liberty Times net], June 13, 2018, https://news.ltn.com.tw/news/politics

/breakingnews/2457429; Sang Pingzai 桑品載, "Erling erling shi Taidu peizang-nian" [2020 is the year when Taiwan independence will be buried with the dead], *Zhongshi xinwenwang*, January 1, 2019, https://www.chinatimes.com/newspapers/20190111001603-260109.

16. For instrumentalist theories of nationalism, see Brendan O'Leary, "Instrumen-talist Theories of Nationalism," in *Encyclopaedia of Nationalism*, ed. Athena S. Leoussi (New Brunswick, N.J.: Transaction, 2001), 148–53.

17. C. Wright Mills, *The Sociological Imagination* (Oxford: Oxford University Press, 1959), 5–6.

Bibliography

Aomen ribao 澳門日報. "Aomen ribao: bian dangju zhengzhi yu wenhua bingju tuijin 'Taidu'" [Macao daily news: Chen Shuibian's administration push forward "Taiwan independence" in both politics and culture]. *Xinlang xinwen zhongxin* [news .sina.com.cn], November 27, 2004. http://news.sina.com.cn/c/2004-11-27/2025 4366095s.shtml.

Anderson, Benedict. *Imagined Communities: Reflections on the Origin and Spread of Nationalism.* Rev. and extended ed. London: Verso, 1991 (1983).

Andrews, Molly. "Generational Consciousness, Dialogue, and Political Engagement." In *Generational Consciousness, Narrative, and Politics*, ed. June Edmunds and Bryan S. Turner, 75–87. Lanham, Md.: Rowman & Littlefield, 2002.

Appleton, Sheldon. "Regime Support Among Taiwan High School Students." *Asian Survey* 13 (1973): 750–60.

——. "Taiwanese and Mainlanders on Taiwan: A Survey of Student Attitudes." *China Quarterly* 44 (1970): 38–65.

Arendt, Hannah. *The Human Condition.* Chicago: University of Chicago Press, 1998 (1958).

Bai Xianyong (Pai Hsienyung) 白先勇. "Liulang de Zhongguoren—Taiwan xiaoshuo de fangzhu zhuti" [The wandering Chinese—the exile theme of Taiwanese novels], trans. Zhou Zhaoxiang. *Mingbao yuekan* [Mingbao monthly] (January 1976): 152–55.

——. *Taibeiren* [Taipei people]. 12th ed. Taipei: Chenzhong, 1975 (1971).

Bao Qingtian 包青天 (Bao Yihong 包奕洪) et al. "Taiwan shehuili de fenxi (shang)" [Analysis of Taiwan's social forces (part 1)]. *Daxue zazhi* [The intellectual] 43 (1971): 32–35.

———. "Taiwan shehuili de fenxi (zhong)" [Analysis of Taiwan's social forces (part 2)]. *Daxue zazhi* [The intellectual] 44 (1971): 14–19.

———. "Taiwan shehuili de fenxi (xia)" [Analysis of Taiwan's social forces (part 3)]. *Daxue zazhi* [The intellectual] 45 (1971): 20–26.

Bao Siwen 包斯文 (Geng Rongshui 耿榮水). "Liangtiao luxian liangzhong celue—'Meilidao' zazhi chuangkan zhihou" [Two lines, two strategies—after the foundation of the *"Formosa"* Magazine]. In *Dangwai renshi hequ hecong?* [Whither are the Dangwai figures going?], ed. Bao Siwen, 77–85. Taipei: Siji, 1980 (1979).

Barker, Chris. *Cultural Studies: Theory and Practice*. London: Sage, 2000.

Barker, Chris, and Dariusz Galasiński. *Cultural Studies and Discourse Analysis: A Dialogue on Language and Identity*. London: Sage, 2001.

Barthes, Roland. "Introduction to the Structural Analysis of Narratives." In *Image, Music, Text*, ed. and trans. Stephen Heath, 79–124. New York: Hill and Wang, 1977 (1966).

Bashi niandai bianjibu 八十年代編輯部. "Xu Xinliang zhuanfang" [Interview with Xu Xinliang]. *Bashi niandai* [The eighties] 1, no. 3 (1979): 6–16.

Bashi niandai chubanshe bianjibu 八十年代出版社編輯部. "'*Ziyou Zhongguo' xuanji* zongxu" [General preface to *Selections from "Free China"*]. In *"Ziyou Zhongguo" xuanji* [Selections from *"Free China"*], ed. Bashi niandai chubanshe bianjibu, 3–12. Taipei: Bashi niandai chubanshe bianjibu, 1979.

Bennett, Andrew, and Nicholas Royle. *An Introduction to Literature, Criticism, and Theory*. 2nd ed. London: Prentice Hall Europe, 1999.

Braungart, Richard G. "Historical Generations and Generation Units: A Global Pattern of Youth Movements." *Journal of Political and Military Sociology* 12 (1984): 113–35.

Bruner, Edward M. "Ethnography as Narrative." In *Memory, Identity, Community: The Idea of Narrative in the Human Sciences*, ed. Lewis P. Hinchman and Sandra K. Hinchman, 264–80. Albany, N.Y.: State University of New York Press, 1997 (1986).

Bukh, Alexander. *These Islands Are Ours: The Social Construction of Territorial Disputes in Northeast Asia*. Stanford, Calif.: Stanford University Press, 2020.

Burner, David. *Making Peace with the 60s*. Princeton, N.J.: Princeton University Press, 1996.

Cai Mingyan 蔡明諺. *Ranshao de niandai—qiling niandai Taiwan wenxue lunzheng shilue* [A flaming era—an outline history of debates on Taiwanese literature in the 1970s]. Tainan: Guoli Taiwan wenxue guan, 2012.

Cai Peihuo 蔡培火 et al. *Taiwan minzu yundong shi* [A history of the Taiwanese national movement]. Taipei: Zili wanbao she wenhua chubanbu, 1971.

Cai Yuanhuang 蔡源煌. "Zuihou de langman zhuyi zhe" [The last romanticists]. In *Qiling niandai—lixiang jixu ranshao* [The 1970s: Ideals continue to flame], ed. Yang Ze, 179–86. Taipei: Shibao wenhua, 1994.

Caituan faren guojia wenhua yishu jijinhui 財團法人國家文化藝術基金會. *Disanjie guojia wenhua yishu jijinhui wenyijiang zhuanji* [Special report on the Third National

Awards for Arts from the National Culture and Arts Foundation]. Taipei: Caituan faren guojia wenhua yishu jijinhui, 1999.

Callahan, William A. "National Insecurities: Humiliation, Salvation, and Chinese Nationalism." *Alternatives* 29 (2004): 199–218.

Carr, David. "Getting the Story Straight: Narrative and Historical Knowledge." In *Historiography Between Modernism and Postmodernism: Contributions to the Methodology of the Historical Research*, ed. Jerzy Topolski, 119–33. Amsterdam: Rodopi, 1994.

Chang Maukuei and Hsiao Hsinhuang 張茂桂、蕭新煌. "Daxuesheng de 'Zhongguo jie' yu 'Taiwan jie'—ziwo rending yu tonghun guannian de fenxi" [The "China complex" and the "Taiwan complex" of university students—an analysis of self-identity and idea about intermarriage]. *Zhongguo luntan* [China tribune] 25, no. 1 (1987): 34–52.

Chang Maukuei and Wu Xinyi 張茂桂、吳忻怡. Guanyu minzuzhuyi lunshu zhong de rentong yu qingxu—zunzhong yu chengren de wenti [On identity and emotion in nationalist discourse—the issues about respect and recognition]. In *Minzuzhuyi yu liangan guanxi: hafo daxue dongxifang xuezhe de duihua* [Nationalism and the relations across the Taiwan Strait: A dialogue at Harvard University between scholars from the East and the West], ed. Lin Jialong and Zheng Yongnian, 140–80. Taipei: Xin ziran zhuyi, 2001.

Chang, Sung-sheng Yvonne. *Modernism and the Nativist Resistance: Contemporary Chinese Fiction from Taiwan*. Durham, N.C.: Duke University Press, 1993.

———. "Representing Taiwan: Shifting Geopolitical Frameworks." In *Writing Taiwan: A New Literary History*, ed. David Der-wei Wang and Carlos Rojas, 17–25. Durham, N.C.: Duke University Press, 2007.

Chen Chu 陳菊. "Dizao wo mingyun de ren—huainian Guo Yuxin xiansheng" [The one who shaped my fate—cherishing the memory of Mr. Guo Yuxin]. In *Guo Yuxin jinian wenji: Taiwan minzhu chuanjiaoshi* [A collection of essays in memory of Guo Yuxin: An evangelist of democracy in Taiwan], ed. Guo Huina and Lin Hengzhe, 33–36. Taipei: Qianwei, 1988.

Chen Chuanxing 陳傳興. "Hengtang de tongtianta" [A Babel tower lying down]. In *Qiling niandai: chanqinglu* [The 1970s: A collection of confessions], ed. Yang Ze, 31–35. Taipei: Shibao wenhua, 1994.

Chen Cuilian 陳翠蓮. "Quzhimin yu zaizhimin de duikang: yi yijiusiliu nian 'Tairen nuhua' lunzhan wei jiaodian" [The conflict between decolonization and recolonization: The debate on "the enslavement of the Taiwanese People" of 1946 in focus]. *Taiwanshi yanjiu* [Taiwan historical research] 9, no. 2 (2002): 145–201.

———. *Taiwanren de dikang yu rentong, 1920–1950* [The resistance and identity of the Taiwanese, 1920–1950]. Taipei: Yuanliu, 2008.

Chen, Edward I-te. "Formosan Political Movements Under Japanese Colonial Rule, 1914–37." *Journal of Asian Studies* 31, no. 3 (1972): 477–97.

Chen Fangming 陳芳明. "Jiaguo banshiji—Taiwan de zhengzhi yu wenxue" [My native country in the past century—politics and literature in Taiwan]. *Wenxue Taiwan* [Literary Taiwan] 2 (1992): 73–82.

——. "Jiliu luanyun" [Torrents of water and chaotic clouds]. In *Qiling niandai—lixiang jixu ranshao* [The 1970s: Ideals continue to flame], ed. Yang Ze, 39–49. Taipei: Shibao wenhua, 1994.

——. *Taiwan xinwenxue shi (shang)* [A history of modern Taiwanese literature (vol. 1)]. Taipei: Lianjing, 2011.

Chen Fangming and Peng Ruijin 陳芳明、彭瑞金. "Chen Fangming, Peng Ruijin duitan: liqing Taiwan wenxue de yixie wuyun anri" [A dialogue between Chen Fangming and Peng Ruijin: Get rid of the dark clouds in Taiwanese literature]. *Wenxuejie* [Literary Taiwan] 24 (1987): 17–46.

Chen Guoxiang 陳國祥. *Qingnian husheng* [The call of youth]. Taipei: Siji, 1979.

Chen Guying 陳鼓應. "Kaifang xuesheng yundong" [Lift the ban on student movements]. *Daxue zazhi* [The intellectual] 46 (1972): 64–68.

——. "Qishi niandai yilai Taiwan xinsheng yidai de gaige yundong (shang)" [The reform movement of the new generation in Taiwan since the 1970s (1)]. *Zhongbao yuekan* [Zhongbao monthly] 28 (1982): 27–35.

——. "Qishi niandai yilai Taiwan xinsheng yidai de gaige yundong (zhong)" [The meform movement of the new generation in Taiwan since the 1970s (2)]. *Zhongbao yuekan* [Zhongbao monthly] 29 (1982): 25–33.

——. "Qishi niandai yilai Taiwan xinsheng yidai de gaige yundong (xia)" [The reform movement of the new generation in Taiwan since the 1970s (3)]. *Zhongbao yuekan* [Zhongbao monthly] 30 (1982): 33–38.

——. "The Reform Movement Among Intellectuals in Taiwan Since 1970." *Bulletin of Concerned Asian Scholars* 14, no. 3 (1982): 32–47.

——. "Rongren yu liaojie" [Tolerance and understanding]. *Daxue zazhi* [The intellectual] 37 (1971): 6–7.

——. "Shuohua shi yizhong tianfu de quanli (xu)" [Preface: Speech is an inborn right]. In *Rongren yu liaojie* [Tolerance and understanding], by Chen Guying, 1–4. Taipei: Baijie, 1978 (1971).

——. "Zailun 'xuesheng yundong'" [Reexamining "student movements"]. *Daxue zazhi* [The intellectual] 53 (1972): 65–70.

Chen Luhuei 陳陸輝. "Taiwan xuanmin zhengdang rentong de chixu yu bianqian" [Change and continuity of party identification among the electorate in Taiwan]. *Xuanju yanjiu* [Journal of electoral studies] 7 (2000): 108–39.

Chen Mingzhe 陳明哲. "Women xuyao qi bian de jingshen" [We need the spirit of standing up for change]. In *Zhishiren de chulu* [A way out for intellectuals], ed. Hong Sanxiong, 73–75. Changhua: Xinsheng, 1973 (1972).

Chen Sanjing 陳三井. "Guomin keming yu Taiwan" [The Nationalist Revolution and Taiwan]. In *Taiwan shiji yuanliu* [The origin and change of historical relics in

Taiwan], ed. Taiwansheng wenxian weiyuanhui, 470–517. Taichung: Taiwansheng wenxian weiyuanhui, 1981.

Chen Shaoting 陳少廷. "Chen xu" [Preface by Chen]. In *Zhishiren de chulu* [A way out for intellectuals], ed. Hong Sanxiong, 1–2. Changhua: Xinsheng, 1973.

——. "Lin Xiantang xiansheng yu 'zuguo shijian'—jianlun Taiwan zhishi fenzi kangri yundong de lishi yiyi" [Mr. Lin Xiantang and the "Ancestral Land Incident"—also on the historical significance of the anti-Japanese movement of Taiwanese intellectuals]. *Daxue zazhi* [The intellectual] 43 (1971): 4–8.

——. "Lun zheyidai zhongguo zhishi fenzi de zhixiang (daixu)" [On the ambitions of the present generation of Chinese intellectuals (in lieu of preface)]. In *Zheyidai zhongguo zhishi fenzi de jianjie* [The views of the present generation of Chinese intellectuals], ed. Daxue congkan bianweihui, 1–10. Taipei: Huanyu, 1970.

——. *Taiwan xinwenxue yundong jianshi* [A basic history of the Taiwan New Literature movement]. Taipei: Lianjing, 1977.

——. "Wusi yu Taiwan xinwenxue yundong" [May Fourth and the New Literature movement in Taiwan]. *Daxue zazhi* [The intellectual] 53 (1972): 18–24.

——. "Zailun zhongyang minyi daibiao de gaixuan wenti" [Reexamining the issue about the reelection of national parliamentary representatives]. *Daxue zazhi* [The intellectual] 49 (1972): 93–98.

——. "Zheyidai zhongguo zhishi fenzi de zeren" [The duty of the present generation of Chinese intellectuals]. *Daxue zazhi* [The intellectual] 1 (1968): 4–5.

Chen Shuhong 陳樹鴻. "Taiwan yishi—dangwai minzhu yundong de jishi" [Taiwanese consciousness—the cornerstone of the Dangwai democratic movement]. In *Taiwan yishi lunzhan xuanji* [Selected articles from the debate on Taiwanese consciousness], ed. Shi Minhui, 191–205. Taipei: Qianwei, 1988 (1983).

Chen Wanzhen 陳婉真. *Yongzhe buju: wo weishenmo yao jingxuan lifa weiyuan?* [The brave fear nothing: Why do I want to run for legislator?]. Taipei: Changqiao, 1978.

Chen Wenjun 陳文俊. "Taiwan daxuesheng de shengji yishi yu guojia rentong" [Consciousness of provincial background and national identity among university students in Taiwan]. *Zhongshan shehui kexue xuebao* [Journal of Sunology: A social science quarterly] 8, no.2 (1994): 41–91.

——. "Taiwan diqu xuesheng de zhengzhi wenhua: zhong, daxuesheng de zhengzhi taidu yu Taiwan minzhuhua de qianjing" [Political culture among students in Taiwan: Political attitudes of high school and university students and the future of Taiwan's democratization]. *Guoli zhongshan daxue shehui kexue jikan* [National Sun Yatsen University social science quarterly] 1, no. 3 (1998): 23–60.

——. *Taiwan diqu zhongxuesheng de zhengzhi taidu ji qi xingcheng yinsu—qingshaonian de zhengzhi shehuihua* [Political attitudes of high school students in Taiwan and their formation factors—political socialization of teenagers]. Taipei: Zixun jiaoyu tuiguang zhongxin jijinhui, 1983.

——. *Zhengzhi shehuihua yu Taiwan de zhengzhi minzhuhua: da (zhuang) xuesheng de zhengzhi taidu yu jiazhi zhi yanjiu* [Political socialization and political democratization in Taiwan: A study of political attitudes and values of college students]. Kaohsiung: Zhongshan daxue zhengzhixue yanjiusuo, 1997.

Chen Xiaolin 陳曉林. "Fu xiaoxiao—tan nianqingren de wenti" [A reply to Xiaoxiao—on the problem of the youth]. *Zhongyang ribao* [Central daily news] January 17 and 18, 1968.

Chen Yangde 陳陽德. "Xian jieduan qingnian qingxiang zhi fenxi—dui shuqi guojia jianshe yanjiuyuan de fanying zhi diaocha ji fenxi" [An analysis of the inclination of youth at the present stage—a survey and analysis on the reaction of the researchers of the summer Workshop on National Construction]. *Daxue zazhi* [The intellectual] 46 (1971): 35–41.

Chen Yingzhen 陳映真. "Cong 'xihua wenxue' dao 'xiangtu wenxue'" [From "Westernized literature" to "Nativist literature"]. In *Zhongguo xiandai wenxue de huigu* [A review of modern Chinese literature], ed. Qiu Weijun and Chen Lianshun, 172–78. Taipei: Longtian, 1978.

——. *Diyijian chaishi* [My first case]. Taipei: Yuanjing, 1975.

——. "Guer de lishi-lishi de guer: shiping 'Yaxiya de guer'" [Orphan's history and history's orphan: A preliminary review of "Orphan of Asia"]. In *Guer de lishi-lishi de guer* [Orphan's history and history's orphan], by Chen Yingzhen, 83–95. Taipei: Yuanjing, 1984(?).

——. "Lun 'wenxue Taidu'" [On "Taiwan independence in literature"]. *Huaxia*, June 27, 2001. http://big5.huaxia.com/zt/2001-19/32790.html.

——. "Wenxue laizi shehui fanying shehui" [Literature arises out of the society and reflects the society]. *Xianrenzhang zazhi* [Cactus magazine] 1, no. 5 (1977): 65–78.

——. "Xiang neizhan, lengzhan yishixingtai tiaozhan—qiling niandai Taiwan wenxue lunzheng zai Taiwan wenyi sichao shi shang huashidai de yiyi" [Challenging the ideology of civil war and cold war—the epoch-making significance of the 1970s literary debates in the history of Taiwanese literary and artistic trends]. *Lianhe wenxue* [Unitas] 158 (1997): 57–76.

Chen Yiyan 陳義彥. "Butong zuqun zhengzhi wenhua de shidai fenxi" [A generational analysis of political culture of different ethnicities]. *Zhengzhi xuebao* [Chinese political science review] 27 (1996): 83–91.

——. *Taiwan diqu daxuesheng zhengzhi shehuihua zhi yanjiu* [A study of university students' political socialization in Taiwan]. Taipei: Jiaxin shuini gongsi wenhua jijinhui, 1978.

——. *Woguo daxuesheng zhengzhi shehuihua zhi yanjiu—shiwunian lai zhengzhi jiazhi yu taidu zhi bianqian* [A study of political socialization of university students in our country—the change in political values and attitudes in the past fifteen years]. Final report of research project granted by National Science Council. Taipei: Zhengzhi daxue xuanju yanjiu zhongxin, 1991.

Chen Yunlin 陳雲林. "Jianjue fandui 'taidu' fenlie huodong nuli zhengqu zuguo heping tongyi guangming qianjing" [Resolutely opposing "Taiwan independence" separatist activities and struggling for bright prospects of peaceful reunification]. *Qiushi zazhi* [Truth-seeking magazine] 4 (2005): 16–18.

Chen Zhangsheng 陳漳生. "Jinri zhishi qingnian zhi chujing" [The situation of intellectual youths today]. *Daxue zazhi* [The intellectual] 46 (1971): 32–34.

Chen Zhengti 陳正醍. "Taiwan de Xiangtu wenxue lunzhan (1977–1978)" [The Nativist literature debate in Taiwan (1977–1978)]. In *Taiwan xiangtu wenxue- huangmin wenxue de qingli yu pipan* [Nativist literature in Taiwan—clarifications and criticisms of the imperial-subject literature], ed. Zeng Jianmin, 129–81. Taipei: Renjian, 1998 (1981).

Cheng Daxue 程大學. "Taiwan de Xianxian xianlie" [Sages and martyrs in Taiwan]. In *Taiwan shiji yuanliu* [The origin and change of historical relics in Taiwan], ed. Taiwansheng wenxian weiyuanhui, 518–48. Taichung: Taiwansheng wenxian weiyuanhui, 1981.

Chuang Yachung. *Democracy on Trial: Social Movements and Cultural Politics in Postauthoritarian Taiwan.* Hong Kong: Chinese University Press, 2013.

Cioran, Emil Mihai. "Advantages of Exile." In *Altogether Elsewhere: Writers on Exile,* ed. Marc Robinson, 150–52. Boston: Faber and Faber, 1994 (1956).

Corcuff, Stéphane, "Introduction: Taiwan, A Laboratory of Identities." In *Memories of the Future: National Identity Issues and the Search for a New Taiwan,* ed. Stéphane Corcuff, xi–xxiv. Armonk, N.Y.: M. E. Sharpe, 2002.

——, ed. *Memories of the Future: National Identity Issues and the Search for a New Taiwan.* Armonk, N.Y.: M. E. Sharpe, 2002.

Daxue zazhishe 大學雜誌社. "'Riju shidai de Taiwan wenxue yu kangri yundong' zuotanhui—jinian Taiwan guangfu di ershijiu zhounian" [Symposium on "Taiwanese literature and the anti-Japanese resistance in the Japanese occupation period"—commemorating the twenty-ninth anniversary of the Retrocession of Taiwan]. *Daxue zazhi* [The intellectual] 79 (1974): 26–33.

DeGroot, Gerard J. *The Sixties Unplugged: A Kaleidoscopic History of a Disorderly Decade.* Cambridge, Mass.: Harvard University Press, 2008.

Dowd, James J. "The Reification of Age: Age Stratification Theory and the Passing of the Autonomous Subject." *Journal of Aging Studies* 1, no. 4 (1987): 317–35.

Du Guoqing 杜國清. "'Li' shishe yu Taiwan shitan" [The "Li" Poetry Society and Taiwanese poetry circles]. *Taiwan wenyi* [Taiwan literature] 118 (1987): 13–23.

Du Weiming 杜維明. "Zai xueshu wenhua shang jianli ziwo" [Establishing the self in the academic and cultural field]. *Daxue zazhi* [The intellectual] 3 (1968): 5–7.

Edmunds, June, and Bryan S. Turner. *Generations, Culture and Society.* Buckingham, UK: Open University Press, 2002.

——. "Introduction: Generational Consciousness, Narrative, and Politics." In *Generational Consciousness, Narrative, and Politics,* ed. June Edmunds and Bryan S. Turner, 1–12. Lanham, Md.: Rowman & Littlefield, 2002.

Elder, Glen H., Jr. *Children of the Great Depression: Social Change in Life Experience*. Chicago: University of Chicago Press, 1974.

Eyerman, Ron. "Intellectuals and the Construction of an African American Identity: Outline of a Generational Approach." In *Generational Consciousness, Narrative, and Politics*, ed. June Edmunds and Bryan S. Turner, 51–74. Lanham, Md.: Rowman & Littlefield, 2002.

Fan Fu 凡夫 (Ye Rongzhong 葉榮鐘). "Gemingjia Jiang Weishui" [Revolutionary Jiang Weishui]. *Taiwan zhenglun* [Taiwan political review] 5 (1975): 76–79.

——. "Taiwan minzu shiren Lin Youchun" [Taiwan's national poet Lin Youchun]. *Taiwan zhenglun* [Taiwan political review] 3 (1975): 66–69.

Fairclough, Norman. *Critical Discourse Analysis: The Critical Study of Language*. New York: Longman, 1995.

Fang Hao 方豪. *Taiwan minzu yundong xiaoshi* [A brief history of the Taiwanese nationalist movement]. Taipei: Zhengzhong, 1951.

Fröhlich, Thomas. "Einführung." In *Taiwans unvergänglicher Antikolonialismus: Jiang Weishui und der Widerstand gegen die japanische Kolonialherrschaft. Mit einer Übersetzung von Schriften Jiang Weishuis aus dem Chinesischen und Japanischen*, ed. Thomas Fröhlich and Yishan Liu, 13–39. Bielefeld, Ger.: Transcript Verlag, 2011.

——. "Identität und Widerstand: Jiang Weishuis Antikolonialismus und seine Nachwirkungen." In *Taiwans unvergänglicher Antikolonialismus: Jiang Weishui und der Widerstand gegen die japanische Kolonialherrschaft. Mit einer Übersetzung von Schriften Jiang Weishuis aus dem Chinesischen und Japanischen*, ed. Thomas Fröhlich and Yishan Liu, 43–92. Bielefeld, Ger.: Transcript Verlag, 2011.

Fröhlich, Thomas and Yishan Liu, eds. *Taiwans unvergänglicher Antikolonialismus: Jiang Weishui und der Widerstand gegen die japanische Kolonialherrschaft. Mit einer Übersetzung von Schriften Jiang Weishuis aus dem Chinesischen und Japanischen*. Bielefeld, Ger.: Transcript Verlag, 2011.

Fu Bo 傅博. "Riju shiqi Taiwan xinwenxue de pingjia wenti" [The problem of evaluating the Taiwan New Literature in the Japanese occupation period]. *Wenxing* [Apollo] 104 (1987): 107–14.

Fu Jianzhong 傅建中. "Meiguo xuechao ji qi fanji" [The trend of student movements in America and its counteraction]. *Minzhong ribao* [The commons daily], May 19, 1969.

Gao Shangqin 高上秦 (Gao Xinjiang 高信疆). "Tansuo yu huigu—xie zai 'Longzu pinglun zhuanhao' qianmian" [Exploration and review—a note prefacing the "*Poetry Journal of the Dragon Nation*'s special commentary issue"]. In *Wenxue xiuzou—xiandai wenxue de kaocha* [Literature, don't leave—an examination of modern literature], ed. Zhao Zhiti, 162–71. Taipei: Yuanxing, 1976 (1973).

Gao Zhun 高準. "Pinfu ji daigou maodun de jiejue zhi dao—xiangei suoyou zai Taiwan de guanxin guoshi de tongbao, lun Taiwan shehui de sizhong neibu maodun zhi san" [The rich/poor and generational-gap conflicts and the solutions to them—dedicated to all compatriots concerned about national affairs in Taiwan, on the third of the four internal conflicts in Taiwanese society]. *Mingbao yuekan* [Mingbao monthly] 10, no. 4 (1975): 29–34.

———. "Taiwan quanli maodun ji qi jiejue zhi dao—xiangei suoyou zai Taiwan de guanxin guoshi de tongbao, lun Taiwan shehui de sizhong neibu maodun zhi yi" [The power clashes in Taiwan and the solutions to them—dedicated to all compatriots concerned about national affairs in Taiwan, on the first of the four internal conflicts in Taiwanese Society]. *Mingbao yuekan* [Mingbao monthly] 10, no. 1 (1975): 78–83.

Giddens, Anthony. *Modernity and Self-Identity: Self and Society in the Late Modern Age*. Stanford, Calif.: Stanford University Press, 1991.

Giele, Janet Z., and Glen H. Elder Jr., eds. *Methods of Life Course Research: Qualitative and Quantitative Approaches*. Thousand Oaks, Calif.: Sage, 1998.

Gold, Thomas B. "Civil Society and Taiwan's Quest for Identity." In *Cultural Change in Postwar Taiwan*, ed. Stevan Harrell and Huang Chünchieh, 47–68. Boulder, Colo.: Westview Press, 1994.

———. *State and Society in the Taiwan Miracle*. Armonk, N.Y.: M. E. Sharpe, 1986.

———. "Taiwan's Quest for Identity in the Shadow of China." In *In the Shadow of China: Political Developments in Taiwan since 1949*, ed. Steve Tsang, 169–92. Honolulu: University of Hawai'i Press, 1993.

Guo Rongzhao 郭榮趙. "Yige lishi gongzuozhe dui shiju de fanxing" [A historical researcher's reflection on the current situation]. *Lianhe bao* [United daily], September 16, 1971.

Guo Tingyi 郭廷以. *Taiwan shishi gaishuo* [An outline of Taiwanese history]. Taipei: Zhengzhong, 1954.

Guowuyuan Taiwan shiwu bangongshi xinwenju 國務院台灣事務辦公室新聞局. *Lü Hsiulien "Taidu" yanlun pipan* [A critique of Lü Hsiulien's discourse on "Taiwan independence"]. Beijing: Jiouzhou tushu, 2000.

Guying 孤影. "Yige xiaoshimin de xinsheng" [The voice of an ordinary citizen]. In *Dui nianqingren de zhenxinhua* [My sincere words for young people], by Guying, 1–68. Taipei: Zhongyang ribao she, 1976 (1972).

Hanne, Michael, ed. *Creativity in Exile*. Amsterdam: Rodopi, 2004.

Hardy, Melissa A., and Linda Waite. "Doing Time: Reconciling Biography with History in the Study of Social Change." In *Studying Aging and Social Change: Conceptual and Methodological Issues*, ed. Melissa A. Hardy, 1–21. Thousand Oaks, Calif.: Sage, 1997.

Harrell, Stevan, and Huang Chünchieh. "Introduction: Change and Contention in Taiwan's Cultural Scene." In *Cultural Change in Postwar Taiwan*, ed. Stevan Harrell and Huang Chünchieh, 1–18. Boulder, Colo.: Westview Press, 1994.

Harrison, Mark. *Legitimacy, Meaning, and Knowledge in the Making of Taiwanese Identity*. New York: Palgrave Macmillan, 2006.

He Wenzhen 何文振. *Gei Guomindang de zhengyan* [Advice to the Chinese Nationalist Party]. Taipei: Chunfeng, 1978.

———. "Gei zhishi fenzi de yaoqingshu" [An invitation to intellectuals]. *Daxue zazhi* [The intellectual] 47 (1971): 25.

———. "Taiwan dadizhu" [Big landlord in Taiwan]. *Taiwan zhenglun* [Taiwan political review] 3 (1975): 15–9.

———. "Zhuisui lixiang de xinqingnian" [New youths in pursut of their ideals]. *Daxue zazhi* [The intellectual] 62 (1973): 39.

He Xin 何欣. "Baodao wenxue yu wenxue chuangzuo" [Reportage literature and literary creation]. In *Zhongguo xiandai xhiaoshuo de zhuchao* [The main trend of modern Chinese fiction], by He Xin, 177–96. Taipei: Yuanjing, 1979 (1978).

———. "Ouyang Zi shou le xie sheme" [What Ouyang Zi has expressed in words]. *Wenji* [Literary season] 1 (1973): 43–60.

———. "Zhongguo xiandai xiaoshuo de chuantong—yige shi de kaocha" [The tradition of modern Chinese fiction—a historical investigation]. In *Zhongguo xiandai xhiaoshuo de zhuchao* [The main trend of modern Chinese fiction], by He Xin, 1–42. Taipei: Yuanjing, 1979 (1977).

———. *Zhongguo xiandai xhiaoshuo de zhuchao* [The main trend of modern Chinese fiction]. Taipei: Yuanjing, 1979.

He Xiuhuang 何秀煌. "Zhengfeng, jiaoyu yu liuxuesheng" [Political quality, education, and students studying abroad]. *Daxue zazhi* [The intellectual] 25 (1970): 15–17.

Hinchman, Lewis P., and Sandra K. Hinchman. "Introduction." In *Memory, Identity, Community: The Idea of Narrative in the Human Sciences*, ed. Lewis P. Hinchman and Sandra K. Hinchman, xiii–xxxii. Albany, N.Y.: State University of New York Press, 1997.

Hirsch, Marianne. "Past Lives: Postmemories in Exile." In *Exile and Creativity: Signposts, Travelers, Outsiders, Backward Glances*, ed. Susan Rubin Suleiman, 418–46. Durham, N.C.: Duke University Press, 1998.

Hobsbawm, Eric, and Terence Ranger, eds. *The Invention of Tradition*. Cambridge: Cambridge University Press, 1983.

Hong Liande 洪鎌德. "Deguo dazhuan xuesheng saodong de fenxi" [An analysis of the unrest of college students in West Germany]. *Dongfang zazhi* [Eastern miscellany] 2, no. 6 (1968): 12–15.

Hong Sanxiong 洪三雄. "Dui xuexiao kaidao, xiang shehui jinjun" [Launch a critique against the school and mount an attack on the society]. In *Zhishiren de chulu* [A way out for intellectuals], ed. Hong Sanxiong, 135–36. Changhua: Xinsheng, 1973(1971).

———. *Fenghuo dujuancheng: qiling niandai Taida xuesheng yundong* [The signal fires in Azalea City: Student movements at National Taiwan University in the 1970s]. Taipei: Zili wanbao, 1993.

———. ed. *Zhishiren de chulu* [A way out for intellectuals]. Changhua: Xinsheng, 1973.

Hood, Steven J. *The Kuomintang and the Democratization of Taiwan*. Boulder, Colo.: Westview Press, 1997.

Hsia, Chihtsing. "Foreword." In *Chinese Stories from Taiwan: 1960–1970*, ed. Joseph S. M. Lau and Timothy A. Ross, ix–xxvii. New York: Columbia University Press, 1976.

Hsiao Hsinhuang 蕭新煌. "Dangdai zhishi fenzi de 'xiangtu yishi'—shehuixue de kaocha" [The "native-soil consciousness" of contemporary intellectuals—a sociological investigation]. *Zhongguo luntan* [China tribune] 265 (1986): 56–67.

Hsiau A-chin 蕭阿勤. *Chonggou Taiwan: dangdai minzu zhuyi de wenhua zhengzhi* [Reconstructing Taiwan: The cultural politics of contemporary nationalism]. Taipei: Lianjing, 2012.

———. *Contemporary Taiwanese Cultural Nationalism*. London: Routledge, 2000.

———. "Defending Diaoyutai Islands Movement and Pan-Chinese Nationalism (Taiwan)." In *The Wiley-Blackwell Encyclopedia of Social and Political Movements*, vol. 1: *A–E*, ed. David A. Snow et al. 2nd ed. Oxford: Wiley-Blackwell, forthcoming.

———. "The Indigenization of Taiwanese Literature: Historical Narrative, Strategic Essentialism, and State Violence." In *Cultural, Ethnic, and Political Nationalism in Contemporary Taiwan: Bentuhua*, ed. John Makeham and A-chin Hsiau, 125–55. New York: Palgrave Macmillan, 2005.

———. "Jizhu Diaoyutai: lingtu zhengduan, minzu zhuyi, zhishi fenzi yu huaijiu de shidai jiyi" [Remember Diaoyutai Islands: Territorial dispute, nationalism, and generational memory of nostalgic intellectuals in Taiwan]. *Taiwanshi yanjiu* [Taiwan historical research] 24, no. 3 (2017): 141–208.

———. "Language Ideology in Taiwan: the KMT's Language Policy, the Tai-yü Language Movement, and Ethnic Politics." *Journal of Multilingual and Multicultural Development* 18, no. 4 (1997): 302–15.

———. "Wer erinnert sich an Jiang Weishui? Kollektive Erinnerung an den japanischen Kolonialismus im Taiwan der Nachkriegszeit." In *Taiwans unvergänglicher Antikolonialismus: Jiang Weishui und der Widerstand gegen die japanische Kolonialherrschaft. Mit einer Übersetzung von Schriften Jiang Weishuis aus dem Chinesischen und Japanischen*, ed. Thomas Fröhlich and Yishan Liu, 93–127. Bielefeld, Ger.: Transcript Verlag, 2011.

———. "Yijiu baling niandai yilai Taiwan wenhua minzu zhuyi de fazhan: yi 'Taiwan (minzu) wenxue' weizhu de fenxi" [The development of Taiwanese cultural nationalism since the early 1980s: A study on Taiwanese (national) literature]. *Taiwan shehuixue yanjiu* [Taiwanese sociological review] 3 (1999): 1–51.

Hsung Raymay, Chang Fengbin, and Lin Yafeng 熊瑞梅、張峰彬、林亞鋒. "Jieyan hou minzhong shetuan canyu de bianqian: shiqi yu shidai de xiaoying yu yihan" [Changes of participation in voluntary associations after the lift of martial law: Effects and implications of period and cohort]. In *Taiwan de shehui bianqian 1985–2005: chuanbo yu zhengzhi xingwei* [Social change in Taiwan, 1985–2005: Mass communication and political behavior], ed. Chang Maukuei, Lo Venhwei, and Shyn Huoyan, 283–328. Taipei: Zhongyang yanjiuyuan shehuixue yanjiusuo, 2013.

Hu Qingyu 胡晴羽. "Zhengchu yitiao zhanxin de lu" [Struggling for a brand new way] In *Sheilai jingli Zhongguo* [Who will be in charge of China], ed. Lai Zhiming, 55–57. Taipei: Xiangcaoshan, 1977.

Hu Qiuyuan 胡秋原. "Hu xu—tan Yang Kui xiansheng ji qi zuopin" [Preface by Hu—on Mr. Yang Kui and his works]. In Yang Kui's *Yangtou ji* [Sheep's head collection], 3–12. Taipei: Huihuang, 1976.

Huang Chunming 黃春明. "Shayaonala-zaijian" [Sayōnara-goodbye]. *Wenji* [Literary season] 1 (1973): 97–131.

———. "Yige zuozhe de beibi xinling" [The despicable mind of an author]. *Xiachao* [China tide] 23 (1978): 57–62.

Huang Defu 黃德福. "Xuanju yu Taiwan diqu zhengzhi minzhuhua" [Elections and political democratization in Taiwan]. In *Minzhu zhengzhi de fazhan yu chengjiu* [The development and achievements of democratic politics], ed. Taiwan shengzhengfu xinwenchu, 1–33. Taichung: Taiwan shengzhengfu xinwenchu, 1995.

Huang Deshi 黃得時. "Huang xu" [Preface by Huang]. In *Taiwan xinwenxue yundong jianshi* [A basic history of the Taiwan New Literature movement], by Chen Shaoting, 1–4. Taipei: Lianjing, 1977.

———. "Taiwan guangfu qianhou de wenyi huodong yu minzuxing" [The literary and artistic activities and national character before and after the Retrocession of Taiwan]. *Xin wenyi* [New literature and arts] 190 (1972): 37–47.

———. "Taiwan xinwenxue yundong gaiguan (yi)" [Overview of the Taiwan New Literature movement (1)]. *Taibei wenwu* [Taipei historical documents quarterly] 3, no. 2 (1954): 2–12.

———. "Taiwan xinwenxue yundong gaiguan (er)" [Overview of the Taiwan New Literature movement (2)]. *Taibei wenwu* [Taipei historical documents quarterly] 3, no. 3 (1954): 18–22.

———. "Taiwan xinwenxue yundong gaiguan (san)" [Overview of the Taiwan New Literature movement (3)]. *Taibei wenwu* [Taipei historical documents quarterly] 4, no. 2 (1955): 104–20.

Huang Hua 黃華. *Biewu xuanze—geming zhengzha* [There is no alternative: A revolutionary struggle]. Taipei: Qianwei, 2008.

———. "Jianxingren de xinxin" [The confidence of one who received a commuted sentence]. *Taiwan zhenglun* [Taiwan political review] 3 (1975): 39–41.

———. "Huang Hua xiansheng fangtanlu" [Interview with Mr. Huang Hua]. In *Yijiu liuling niandai de duli yundong—quanguo qingnian tuanjie cujinhui shijian fangtanlu* [The Taiwan Independence movement in the 1960s—collected interviews about the Incident of Association for Promoting Nationwide Youth Solidarity], interviewed by Zeng Pincang and Xu Ruihao, transcribed by Zeng Pincang, 103–46. Taipei: Guoshiguan, 2004.

Huang Huangxiong 黃煌雄, ed. *Beiyapozhe de nuhou—Jiang Weishui xiansheng xuanji* [The roar of the oppressed—a selection of Mr. Jiang Weishui's writings]. Taipei: Changqiao, 1978.

———. "Cong Jiang Weishui jingshen tanqi: jianlun Taiwan de zuotian jintian yu mingtian—minguo liushiqi nian shiyi yue shiqi ri zai 'Jiang Weishui jiniange fabiaohui' shang zhuanti yanjiangci" [A discussion beginning with the Jiang Weishui spirit: Also on Taiwan's yesterday, today, and tomorrow—keynote speech at the "Launch of Tribute Song in Memory of Jiang Weishui" on November 17, sixty-seventh year of the ROC calendar]. *Zheyidai zazhi* [New generation] 16 (1978): 44–45.

———. *Feibaoli de douzheng* [Nonviolent struggle]. Taipei: Changqiao, 1978.

———. *Gemingjia—Jiang Weishui* [Revolutionary—Jiang Weishui]. Taipei: Changqiao, 1978.

———. *Guomindang wang hechu qu?* [Whither is the Chinese Nationalist Party going?]. Taipei: Changqiao, 1978.

———. "Jiang Weishui qiren qishi" [Jiang Weishui: The man and his story]. In *Jiang Weishui shishi liushi zhounian jinian ji Taiwanshi xueshu yantaohui lunwen jiyao* [Selected proceedings of the Conference Commemorating the Sixtieth Anniversary of Jiang Weishui's Death and on Taiwanese History], ed. Kaohsiung County Government, 5–16. Kaohsiung: Kaohsiung County Government, 1991.

———. *Jiang Weishui zhuan—Taiwan de xianzhi xianjue* [Biography of Jiang Weishui— Taiwan's visionary prophet]. Taipei: Qianwei, 1992.

———. "Jingzhengzhe zhi lu—Guomindang yu dangwai de jianquanhua" [The roads for competitors—the Chinese Nationalist Party and the betterment of the Dangwai]. *Bashi niandai* [The eighties] 1, no. 1 (1979): 6–8.

———. "Jinnian wuxiang gongzhi xuanju de lishi yiyi" [The historical significance of this year's local elections for five types of local government offices]. *Zheyidai zazhi* [New generation] 6 (1977): 6–7.

———. "Jinnian wuxiang gongzhi xuanju de lishi yiyi" [The historical significance of this year's local elections for five types of local government offices]. In *Dao minzhu zhi lu* [The way to democracy], by Huang Huangxiong, 7–13. Taipei: Self-published, 1980 (1977).

———. *Taibao kangri shihua* [A historical story of Taiwanese compatriots' anti-Japanese resistance]. Taipei: Self-published, 1977.

———. *Taiwan de xianzhi xianjuezhe—Jiang Weishi xiansheng* [Taiwan's visionary prophet—Mr. Jiang Weishui]. Taipei: Self-published, 1976.

———. *Taiwan de zhuanleidian: fangwen yanjiang pian* [A turning point for Taiwan: The visits and interviews volume]. Taipei: Self-published, 1983.

———. *Taiwan kangri shihua* [A historical story of the anti-Japanese resistance in Taiwan]. Taipei: Qianwei, 1992.

———. "Tongbao xu tuanjie, tuanjie zhenyouli" [We compatriots must unite, for in unity there is truly strength]. In *Jiang Weishui shishi qishi zhounian jinian zhuankan* [Special volume commemorating the seventieth anniversary of Jiang Weishui's death], ed. Wang Yujing, 4–5. Taipei: Taiwan Research Foundation, 2001.

———. "Yiduan chenfeng de shiji—fang Huang Huangxiong tan Taiwanshi" [A dust-covered trace of history—interview with Huang Huangxiong about Taiwanese history]. In *Dao minzhu zhi lu* [The way to democracy], by Huang Huangxiong, 175–87. Taipei: Self-published, 1980 (1979).

———. "Yixiang zhuangyan de jianyi—jinian Jiang Weishui xiansheng shishi sishiqi zhounian" [A solemn proposal: In memory of the forty-seventh anniversary of Mr. Jiang Weishui's death]. *Zheyidai zazhi* [New generation] 12 (1978): 19–21.

Huang, Mab (Huang Mo). *Intellectual Ferment for Political Reforms in Taiwan, 1971–1973*. Ann Arbor: Center for Chinese Studies, University of Michigan, 1976.

Huang Mo (Mab Huang) 黃默. "Cong jin jinianlai meiguo qingnian canjia shehui zhengzhi huodong kan minzhu zhengzhi" [Viewing democracy in terms of American young people's participation in social and political activities in recent years]. *Si yu yan* [Thought and words] 5, no. 3 (1967): 1–2, 7.

Huang Xinjie 黃信介. "Fakan ci: Gongtong lai tuidong xinshengdai zhengzhi yundong" [Inaugural statement: Let's work together to push the political movement of the new generation]. *Meilidao* [Formosa] 1 (1979): inner flap-1.

——. "Huang xu" [Preface by Huang]. In *Wenzheng sannian* [Three-year involvement with legislative interpellation], by Kang Ningxiang, 6. Taipei: Taiwan zhenglun zazhishe, 1975.

Huang Zongwen 黃宗文. "Yisheng hongliang de nahan—Huang xu" [A resounding call—preface by Huang]. In *Xinshengdai de nahan* [The call of the new generation], ed. Song Guocheng and Huang Zongwen, 5–8. Taipei: Self-published, 1978.

Hughes, Christopher. *Taiwan and Chinese Nationalism: National Identity and Status in International Society*. London: Routledge, 1997.

Israel, John. "Politics on Formosa." *China Quarterly* 15 (1963): 3–11.

Jacobs, J. Bruce. *Democratizing Taiwan*. Leiden: Brill, 2012.

——. "Taiwanese and the Chinese Nationalists, 1937–1945: The Origins of Taiwan's 'Half-Mountain People' (*Banshan Ren*)." *Modern China* 16, no. 1 (1990): 84–118.

——. "'Taiwanization' in Taiwan's Politics." In *Cultural, Ethnic, and Political Nationalism in Contemporary Taiwan: Bentuhua*, ed. John Makeham and A-chin Hsiau, 17–54. New York: Palgrave Macmillan, 2005.

Jacobs, J. Bruce and Peter Kang, eds. *Changing Taiwanese Identities*. London: Routledge, 2017.

Jaspers, Karl T. *The Origin and Goal of History*. New Haven, Conn.: Yale University Press, 1953 (1949).

Jiang Menlin 蔣夢麟. "Tan Zhongguo xinwenyi yundong—wei jinian wusi yu wenyijie er zuo" [On China's new literary and artistic movement—in memory of May Fourth and Culture and Arts Day]. In *Zhongguo wenyi fuxing yundong* [The movement of Chinese literary and artistic renaissance], ed. Zhongguo wenyi xiehui [The Chinese Literary Association], 41–66. Taipei: Zhongguo wenyi xiehui, 1961.

Jiang Xun 蔣勳. "Qiling —" [The 1970s —]. In *Qiling niandai: chanqinglu* [The 1970s: A collection of confessions], ed. Yang Ze, 109–14. Taipei: Shibao wenhua, 1994.

Jilin Laoxiu 吉林老朽. "Tai dangju, shudian wangzu, yugai mizhang" [The authorities of Taiwan recount history but forget their origins; the more they try to cover it up, the more it will be known]. *Renminwang* [people.cn], 2003. Accessed February 28, 2019. http://tw.people.com.cn/GB/21879/2108918.html (site discontinued).

Jin Wenji 金文吉 (Zhang Jince 張金策). "Pochu huanxiang-miandui wenti" [Shed the illusions and tackle the problems]. *Taiwan zhenglun* [Taiwan political review] 3 (1975): 12–14.

Johnson, Paul. *Modern Times: A History of the World from the 1920s to the Year 2000*. London: Phoenix Press, 1997.

Ka Er 卡爾. "Yishi gaizao—you Wang Xingqing de xuanze tandao dangqian lishi de juewu" [The remaking of consciousness—from Wang Xingqing's choice to the historical awakening at present]. In *Zhishiren de chulu* [A way out for intellectuals], ed. Hong Sanxiong, 47–49. Changhua: Xinsheng, 1973 (1971).

Kang Ningxiang 康寧祥. *Wenzheng sannian* [Three-year involvement with legislative interpellation]. Taipei: Taiwan zhenglun zazhishe, 1975.

Kang Ningxiang and Chen Zhengnong 康寧祥、陳政農. *Taiwan, dapin: Kang Ningxiang huiyilu* [Taiwan, work hard: Memoirs of Kang Ningxiang]. Taipei: Yunchen, 2014.

Kao, George. "Editor's Preface." In *Taipei People* (Chinese-English bilingual ed.), Chinese text by Pai Hsienyung, trans. Pai Hsienyung and Patia Yasin, ed. George Kao, xiv–xxv. Hong Kong: Chinese University of Hong Kong, 2000.

Kawahara Isao 河原功. "Yang Kui xiaoshuo pinglun yinde" [Index to reviews of Yang Kui's works of fiction], trans. Yang Jingting. In *Yang Kui ji* [Collected works of Yang Kui], ed. Zhang Henghao, 347–53. Taipei: Qianwei, 1991(?).

Kedourie, Elie. *Nationalism.* Oxford: Blackwell, 1993 (1960).

Kertzer, David I. "Generation as a Sociological Problem." *Annual Review of Sociology* 9 (1983): 125–49.

King, Ambrose Y. C. 金耀基. "Gudu de yiqun—tan zai meiguo de Zhongguo zhishi fenzi" [A lonely crowd—on Chinese intellectuals in America]. *Daxue zazhi* [The intellectual] 20 (1969): 5–6.

Kleeman, Faye Yuan. *Under an Imperial Sun: Japanese Colonial Literature of Taiwan and the South.* Honolulu: University of Hawai'i Press, 2003.

Kolakowski, Leszek. "In Praise of Exile." In *Altogether Elsewhere: Writers on Exile*, ed. Marc Robinson, 188–92. Boston: Faber and Faber, 1994 (1985).

Langxing 朗星. "Xingqu han tiancai de shuailuo" [The decline of taste and talent]. In *Taidaren de shizijia* [The cross that National Taiwan University people carry], by Taida xuesheng, 60–63. Taipei: Taida daxue xinwenshe, 1972.

Lau, Joseph S. M. "Echoes of the May Fourth Movement in *Hsiang-t'u* Fiction." In *Mainland China, Taiwan, and U.S. Policy*, ed. Huang-mao Tien, 135–50. Cambridge, Mass.: Oelgeschlager, Gunn & Hain, 1983.

——. " 'How Much Truth Can a Blade of Grass Carry'? Ch'en Ying-chen and the Emergence of Native Taiwanese Writers." *Journal of Asian Studies* 32, no. 4 (1973): 623–38.

Lau, Joseph S. M., and Timothy A. Ross, eds. *Chinese Stories from Taiwan: 1960–1970.* New York: Columbia University Press, 1976.

Laufer, Robert S. "Sources of Generational Conflict and Consciousness" In *The New Pilgrims: Youth Protest in Transition*, ed. Philip G. Altbach and Robert S. Laufer, 218–37. New York: David Mckay, 1972.

Laufer, Robert S., and Vern L. Bengtson. "Generations, Aging, and Social Stratification: On the Development of Generational Units." *Journal of Social Issues* 30, no. 3 (1974): 181–205.

Lee, Leo Oufan. "'Modernism' and 'Romanticism' in Taiwan Literature." In *Chinese Fiction from Taiwan: Critical Perspectives*, ed. Jeannette L. Faurot, 6–30. Bloomington: Indiana University Press, 1980.

Lemke, Jay L. *Textual Politics: Discourse and Social Dynamics*. London: Taylor & Francis, 1995.

Leroux, Alain. "Poetry Movements in Taiwan from the 1950s to the late 1970s: Breaks and Continuities." *China Perspectives* 68 (2006): 1–18.

Li Ang 李昂. *Qunxiang—Zhongguo dangdai yishujia fangwen* [Profiles—interviews with contemporary Chinese artists]. Taipei: Dahan, 1976.

——. "Xiyue de beimin—Yang Qingchu fangwen" [Joyful sorrow and compassion—interview with Yang Qingchu]. *Shuping shumu* [Book review and bibliography] 24 (1975): 74–87.

Li Ao 李敖. "Laonianren han bangzi" [The old man and the baton]. *Wenxing* [Apollo] 49 (1961): 5–9.

——. *Li Ao huiyilu* [Memoir of Li Ao]. Taipei: Shangye zhoukan, 1997.

——. "Shisan nian han shisan yue." [Thirteen years and thirteen months]. *Wenxing* [Apollo] 63 (1963): 7–12.

Li Daoxiang 李道湘. "'Wenhua Taidu' de shizhi han weihai" [The reality and danger of "Taiwan independence in culture"]. *Renminwang* [people.cn], 2004. Accessed February 28, 2019. http://tw. people.com.cn/BIG5/14811/14873/2482842.html (site discontinued).

Li Kuixian 李魁賢. "Li de licheng" [The journey of Li]. *Li shikan* [Li poetry magazine] 100 (1980): 36–53.

——. "Wu Yongfu shi zhong de zuguo yishih han ziyou yishi" [The consciousness of ancestral land and freedom in Wu Yongfu's poetry]. *Li shikan* [Li poetry magazine] 87 (1978): 2–7.

Li Nanheng 李南衡, ed. *Riju xia Taiwan xinwenxue, mingji* [Taiwan New Literature under the Japanese occupation, Ming volumes], 5 vols. Taipei: Mingtan, 1979.

Li Shaoyi and Chen Jing'an 李少儀、陳景安. "Xuesheng de quanli yu yiwu" [The rights and obligations of students]. *Daxue zazhi* [The intellectual] 53 (1972): 57–61, 70.

Li Wen 李文. *Zongheng wushinian—Lü Hsiulien* [Five decades of fights and struggles—a biography of Lü Hsiulien]. Taipei: Shibao wenhua, 1996.

Li Xiangmei 李祥枚. "Wu fei wu" [Mist, and yet not mist]. *Zhongyang ribao* [Central daily news], February 8, 1968.

Li Xiaofeng 李筱峰. *Taiwan minzhu yundong sishinian* [Forty years of Taiwan's democratic movement]. Taipei: Zili wanbao, 1987.

Li Xinyi 李新乙. "'Wenhua daitu' dangbuzhu Zhongguo tongyi jincheng" ["Taiwan independence in culture" cannot stop the process of China's unification]. *Huaxia jingwei* [huaxia.com], May 9, 2002. http://www.huaxia.com/thpl/lbyl/bfyl/05/42141. html.

Li Xuerui 李學叡. "Da jizhen qiangxinji" [Giving some injections of cardiotonic]. *Daxue zazhi* [The intellectual] 26 (1970): 1.

Li Yunhan 李雲漢. "Guomin geming yu Taiwan guangfu de lishi yuanyuan" [The historical relationship between the Nationalist Revolution and the Retrocession of Taiwan]. In *Taiwan shiji yuanliu* [The origin and change of historical relics in Taiwan], ed. Taiwansheng wenxian weiyuanhui, 396–469. Taichung: Taiwansheng wenxian weiyuanhui, 1981.

Liang Jingfeng 梁景峰. "Chunguang guanbuzhu—lun Yang Kui de xiaoshuo" [Spring sunshine can't be shut up—on Yang Kui's fiction]. In *Yang Kui de ren yu zuopin* [Yang Kui: The man and his works], ed. Yang Sujuan, 239–60. Taipei: Minzhong ribao she Taibei guanlichu, 1979(1976).

——. "Wenxue de qizi—yu Ye Shitao, Yang Qingchu changtan" [A literary banner—a free conversation with Ye Shitao and Yang Qingchu]. In *Xiangtu yu xiandai: Taiwan wenxue de pianduan* [Native land and modernity: fragments of Taiwanese literature], by Liang Jingfeng, 59–80. Taipei: Taibei xianli wenhua zhongxin, 1995 (1976).

Liao Yi 廖翊. "Yuri juzeng de buan—fang Taiwan daxue jiaoshou Huang Guangguo" [Increasing anxiety: Interview with Professor Huang Guangguo of National Taiwan University]. *Renminwang* [people.cn], 2002. Accessed February 28, 2019. http://www.people.com.cn/BIG5/shizheng/18/20/20020806/793786.html (site discontinued).

Lin Bian 林邊 (Lin Zaijue 林載爵). "Renkan cangsheng hanru—Lai He xiansheng de wenxue" [Cannot bear to sit by and watch the people suffering and being humiliated—Mr. Lai He's literary works]. In *Riju xia Taiwan xinwenxue, mingji 1: Lai He xiansheng quanji* [Taiwan New Literature under the Japanese occupation, Ming volume 1: The complete works of Mr. Lai He], ed. Li Nanheng, 455–87. Taipei: Mingtan, 1979.

Lin Fan 林梵 (Lin Ruiming 林瑞明). "Yang Kui huaxiang" [A portrait of Yang Kui]. *Xianrenzhang zazhi* [Cactus magazine] 1, no. 3 (1977): 235–65.

——. *Yang Kui huaxiang* [A portrait of Yang Kui]. Taipei: Bijiashan, 1978.

Lin Hengdao 林衡道, ed. *Taiwanshi* [A history of Taiwan]. Taichung: Taiwansheng wenxian weiyuanhui, 1977.

Lin Huaimin 林懷民. *Chan* [Cicada]. Taipei: Dadi, 1973.

——. "Chan" [Cicada]. In *Chan* [Cicada], by Lin Huaimin, 107–210. Taipei: Dadi, 1973 (1969).

——. "Chengzhang de suiyue" [My growing years]. In *Qiling niandai—lixiang jixu ranshao* [The 1970s: Ideals continue to flame], ed. Yang Ze, 61–66. Taipei: Shibao wenhua, 1994.

——. "Chuan hongchenshan de nanhai" [The boy in the red shirt]. In *Chan* [Cicada], by Lin Huaimin, 3–31. Taipei: Dadi, 1973 (1968).

——. "Cicada." In *Chinese Stories from Taiwan: 1960–1970*, ed. Joseph S. M. Lau and Timothy A. Ross, 242–319. New York: Columbia University Press, 1976 (1969).

——. *Gaochu yanliang: Lin Huaimin wudao suiyue gaobai* [Bright view from the heights: Lin Huaimin's confession about his dancing years]. Taipei: Yuanliu, 2010.

———. "Shizu yu qibu: menwai de gaobai" [Stumble and start: Confession outside]. In *Wo de diyibu (xia ce)* [My first step (vol. 2)], by Lin Huaimin et al., 1–18. Taipei: Shibao wenhua, 1979.

Lin Jin 林勁. "Qianxi 'wenhua Taidu' de shizhi ji yingxiang" [A basic analysis of the essence and impact of "Taiwan independence in culture"]. *Huaxia jingwei* [huaxia .com], 2001. Accessed February 28, 2019. http://big5.huaxia.com/zt/2001-19/32739 .html (site discontinued).

Lin Ruiming 林瑞明. "Xianjieduan Taiyu wenxue zhi fazhan ji qi yiyi" [The current development of local-Taiwanese-language literature and its significance]. *Wenxue Taiwan* [Literary Taiwan] 3 (1992): 12–31.

Lin Thunghong 林宗弘. "Zaitan Taiwan de shidai zhengzhi: jiaocha fenlei suiji xiaoying moxing de yingyong, 1995–2010" [Generational politics in Taiwan revisited: Application of a cross-classified random effects model, 1995–2010]. *Renwen ji shehui kexue jikan* [Journal of social sciences and philosophy] 27, no. 2 (2015): 395–436.

Lin Wengeng 林問耕 (Lin Zaijue 林載爵). "Lishi de gouhuo—'Yang Kui huaxiang' xu" [The historical bonfire—preface to "A Portrait of Yang Kui"]. In *Yang Kui huaxiang* [A portrait of Yang Kui], by Lin Fan, 1–3. Taipei: Bijiashan, 1978.

Lin Xingyue 林惺嶽. *Taiwan meishu fengyun sishinian* [Forty years of vicissitude of fine arts in Taiwan]. Taipei: Zili wanbao, 1987.

Lin Yinwen 林尹文. "Gengyunzhe Yang Kui" [Yang Kui the cultivator]. In *Yang Kui de ren yu zuopin* [Yang Kui: The man and his works], ed. Yang Sujuan, 127–31. Taipei: Minzhong ribao she Taibei guanlichu, 1979 (1974).

Lin Zaijue 林載爵. "Heichao xia de beige" [Elegy under the Kuroshio current: Yang Hua the poet]. *Xiachao* [China tide] 1, no. 8 (1976): 64–67.

———. "Hese de taiyang" [The black sun—Zhang Shenqie's journey]. *Xiachao* [China tide] 3, no. 3 (1977): 65–70.

———. "Riju shidai Taiwan wenxue de huigu" [A review of Taiwanese literature in the Japanese occupation period]. *Wenji* [Literary season] 3 (1974): 133–65.

———. "Taiwan wenxue de liangzhong jingshen—Yang Kui yu Zhong Lihe zhi bijiao" [The two types of spirits of Taiwanese literature—a comparison between Yang Kui and Zhong Lihe]. *Zhongwai wenxue* [Chung Wai literary quarterly] 2, no. 7 (1973): 4–20.

Lin Zhengjie 林正杰. "Wo de zhengzhi jianjie: Huang Huangxiong fangwen ji" [My political views: Interview with Huang Huangxiong]. *Zheyidai zazhi* [New generation] 15 (1978): 53–57.

———. "Zhanhou xinshengdai de yangchengqi" [The cultivation period of the postwar new generation]. In *Qiling niandai—lixiang jixu ranshao* [The 1970s: Ideals continue to flame], ed. Yang Ze, 85–91. Taipei: Shibao wenhua, 1994.

Lin Zhuoshui 林濁水. "Taiwan shi meilidao" [Taiwan is a beautiful island]. *Bashi niandai* [The eighties] 1, no. 4 (1979): 20–24.

Lin Zhuoshui 林濁水 et al., eds. *Wajie de diguo* [A collapsing empire]. Taipei: Boguan, 1984.

Ling Shuru 凌淑如. "Budong liulei de yidai" [A generation that doesn't understand tears]. In *Sheilai jingli Zhongguo* [Who will be in charge of China], ed. Lai Zhiming, 13–24. Taipei: Xiangcaoshan, 1977 (1975).

Liu Daren 劉大任. "Liuxuesheng de sixiang kuangjia" [The frame of thinking of students studying abroad]. *Daxue zazhi* [The intellectual] 25 (1970): 39–41.

Liu Denghan 劉登翰. *Zhonghua wenhua yu Mintai shehui—Mintai wenhua guanxi lungang* [Chinese culture and Fujianese and Taiwanese societies—an outline study of the cultural relationship between Fujian and Taiwan]. Fuzhou: Fujian renmin chubanshe, 2002.

Liu Ichou 劉義周. "Political Support and Voting Participation of Taiwan College Students." *Journal of National Chengchi University* 41 (1979): 37–44.

——. "Taiwan de zhengzhi shidai" [Political generations in Taiwan]. *Zhengzhi xuebao* [Chinese political science review] 21 (1993): 99–120.

——. "Taiwan xuanmin zhengdang xingxiang de shidai chayi" [Generational difference of party image among Taiwanese voters]. *Xuanju yanjiu* [Journal of electoral studies] 1, no. 1 (1994): 53–73.

Liu Ruojun 劉若君. "Zhong Lihe duanpian xiaoshuo duhou" [Reading report on Zhong Lihe's short stories]. *Wenji* [Literary season] 2 (1973): 77–81.

Liu Zaifu 劉載福. *Shate lun* [On Jean-Paul Sartre]. Taichung: Putian, 1968.

Liu Zhengshan 劉正山. "Shidai zhijian zhengzhi rentong chayi de tuxiang: yi duochong duiying fenxi jiehe xiguan lingyu shiye jinxing de tansuo" [Visualizing habitual domains differences across political generations: Exploring the patterns with multiple correspondence analysis]. *Xiguan lingyu qikan* [Journal of habitual domains] 7, no. 2 (2016): 27–50.

Lo, Mingcheng. *Doctors Within Borders: Profession, Ethnicity, and Modernity in Colonial Taiwan*. Berkeley: University of California Press, 2002.

Lōa, Hô (Lai He). *Scales of Injustice: The Complete Fiction of Lōa Hô*. Trans. Darryl Sterk. Handforth, UK: Honford Star, 2018.

Lu Hanxiu 路寒袖. "Qiling niandai wenhua shishi" [The ten major events in the cultural circles in the 1970s]. In *Qiling niandai—lixiang jixu ranshao* [The 1970s: Ideals continue to flame], ed. Yang Ze, 259–67. Taipei: Shibao wenhua, 1994.

Lü Hsiulien (Annette Lu) 呂秀蓮. *Taiwan de guoqu yu weilai* [The past and the present of Taiwan]. Taipei: Tuohuang zhe, 1979.

——. "Tuohuangzhe de gushi: cong 'xinnüxing' dao 'minzhuren'" [The story of a pioneer: from a "new woman" to a "democrat"]. In *Qiling niandai—lixiang jixu ranshao* [The 1970s: ideals continue to flame], ed. Yang Ze, 67–72. Taipei: Shibao wenhua, 1994.

——. *Xinnüxing zhuyi* [New feminism]. Taipei: Youshi yuekan she, 1974.

——. *Xunzhao ling yishan chuang* [Searching for another window]. Taipei: Shuping shumu, 1974.

Lu, Hsiulien (Lü Hsiulien, Annette Lu) and Ashley Esarey. *My Fight for a New Taiwan: One Woman's Journey from Prison to Power*. Seattle: University of Washington Press, 2014.

Lu Yixin 盧一心. "'Wenhua Taidu' genben jiu bukan yiji" ["Taiwan independence in culture" no doubt doesn't hold water]. *Xinlang xinwen zhongxin* [news.sina.com.cn], December 9, 2004. http://news.sina.com.cn/c/2004-12-09/16155172948.shtml.

Lü Zhenghui 呂正惠. "Riju shidai Taiwan xinwenxue yanjiu de huigu—qiling nian-dai yilai Taiwan diqu de yanjiu gaikuang" [A review of the research on Taiwan new literature in the Japanese occupation period—an overview of the research in Taiwan since the 1970s]. *Taiwan shehui yanjiu jikan* [Taiwan: A radical quarterly in social studies] 24 (1996): 143–70.

——. *Zhanhou Taiwan wenxue jingyan* [The postwar literary experience in Taiwan]. Taipei: Xindi, 1992.

Ma Yingjeou 馬英九. "Liuxuesheng de shizijia" [The cross students studying abroad carry]. In *Liu xuesheng de shizijia* [The cross students studying abroad carry], ed. Boshidun tongxun bianji weiyuanhui, 353–58. Taipei: Shibao, 1982 (1981).

MacIntyre, Alasdair. *After Virtue: A Study in Moral Theory*. Notre Dame, Ind.: University of Notre Dame Press, 1984.

Madsen, Richard. *Democracy's Dharma: Religious Renaissance and Political Development in Taiwan*. Berkeley: University of California Press, 2007.

Makeham, John, and A-chin Hsiau, eds. *Cultural, Ethnic, and Political Nationalism in Contemporary Taiwan: Bentuhua*. New York: Palgrave Macmillan, 2005.

Mannheim, Karl. "The Problem of Generations." In *Essays on the Sociology of Knowledge*, ed. Paul Kecskemeti, 276–320. London: Routledge & Kegan Paul, 1952 (1927).

Mao Han 茅漢 (Wang Xiaobo 王曉波). "Liuyiqi xuesheng shiwei jishi" [A true record of the student demonstration on June 17]. *Daxue zazhi* [The intellectual] 43 (1971): 24–7.

Matsunaga Masayoshi 松永正義. "Taiwan wenxue de lishi yu gexing" [The history and character of Taiwanese Literature], trans. Ye Shitao. In *Caifeng de xinyuan (Taiwan xiandai xiaoshuoxuan I)* [Caifeng's wish: a selection of modern Taiwanese stories], by Hong Xingfu et al., 117–49. Taipei: Mingliu, 1986(?).

——. "Taiwan xinwenxue yundong yanjiu de xinjieduan" [A new stage in the research on the Taiwan New Literature movement]. *Xindi wenxue* [New land literature] 1 (1990): 32–51.

Mattlin, Mikael. *Politicized Society: Taiwan's Struggle with Its One-Party Past*. Copenhagen: NIAS Press, 2018.

McWilliams, John C. *The 1960s Cultural Revolution*. Westport, Conn.: Greenwood Press, 2000.

Mei, Wenli. "The Intellectuals on Formosa." *China Quarterly* 15 (1963): 65–74.

Meilidao zazhishe 美麗島雜誌社. "Meiyou gaige jiu meiyou qiantu—shuangshi guoqing ganyan" [No reform, no future—comments at the Double Tenth National Day]. *Melidao* [Formosa] 1, no. 3 (1979): 6–7.

——. "Minzhu wansui" [Long live democracy]. *Melidao* [Formosa] 1, no. 1 (1979): 4–9.

Mencius. *Mencius*. Trans. Irene Bloom. New York: Columbia University Press, 2009.

Meyer, John. W. "Levels of Analysis: The Life Course as a Cultural Construction." In *Social Structures and Human Lives,* vol. 1: *Social Change and Life Course,* ed. Matilda White Riley, 49–62. Newbury Park, Calif.: Sage, 1988.

Miao Yenwei 苗延威. "Xiangchou siyun—Zhongguo xiandai minge yundong zhi shehuixue yanjiu" [Four stanzas on homesickness—a sociological study of the Chinese modern folk song movement]. M.A. thesis, National Taiwan University, Taipei, 1991.

Miller, Lucien. *Exiles at Home: Short Stories by Ch'en Ying-chen.* Ann Arbor: Center for Chinese Studies, University of Michigan, 1986.

Miller, Robert L. *Researching Life Stories and Family Histories.* London: Sage, 2000.

Mills, C. Wright. *The Sociological Imagination.* Oxford: Oxford University Press, 1959.

Ming Fengying 明鳳英, ed. "Zhongguo wenxue wang hechu qu? Zhongxi wenyi sichao zuotanhui" [Whither is Chinese literature going? Symposium on currents of literary and artistic thought in China and the West]. In *Minzu wenxue de zai chufa* [Restarting national literature], ed. Xianrenzhang zazhishe, 19–35. Taipei: Guxiang, 1979 (1977).

Minzu wanbao 民族晚報. "Meiguo qingnian fan yuezhan yundong de muhou" [The inside story of the anti-Vietnam War movement of American Youth]. *Minzu wanbo* [National evening news], October 18, 1965.

Mu Xiabiao 木下彪, ed. "Riben de xuechao" [The trend of student movements in Japan]. *Zhonghua zazhi* [China journal] 7 no. 2 (1969): 6–8.

Mukōyama Hiroo 向山寬夫. *Riben tongzhi xia de Taiwan minzu yundong shi* [A history of the nationalist movement in Taiwan under Japanese rule]. Trans. Yang Hongru et al. Taipei: Fulushou, 1999 (1987).

Nanfang Shuo 南方朔 (Wang Xingqing 王杏慶). "Nashi, Taiwan cai zhangda" [Only then did Taiwan grow up]. In *Qiling niandai—lixiang jixu ranshao* [The 1970s: Ideals continue to flame], ed. Yang Ze, 117–25. Taipei: Shibao wenhua, 1994.

——. "Xu—bokai misi zhi wang" [Preface—unveil the web of myth]. In *Qingnian husheng* [The call of youth], by Chen Guoxiang, 1–7. Taipei: Siji, 1979.

——. "Zhongguo ziyouzhuyi de zuihou baolei—Daxue zazhi jieduan de liang di fenxi (si)" [The last bastion of Chinese liberalism—a quantitative analysis of the phase of *The Intellectual* (part 4)]. *Xiachao* [China tide] 4, no. 6 (1978): 44–47.

O'Leary, Brendan. "Instrumentalist Theories of Nationalism." In *Encyclopaedia of Nationalism,* ed, Athena S. Leoussi, 148–53. New Brunswick, N.J.: Transaction, 2001.

Ong Joktik 王育德. *Taiwan: kumen de lishi* [Taiwan: A depressing history]. Taipei: Zili wanbao, 1993 (1964).

Ozaki Hotsuki 尾崎秀樹. "Zhanshi de Taiwan wenxue" [Taiwanese literature in the wartime period], trans. by Xiao Gong. In *Taiwan de zhimindi shanghen* [Colonial scars in Taiwan], ed. Wang Xiaobo, 185–238. Taipei: Pamier, 1985 (1971).

Pan Chaoyang 潘朝陽. "Taidu Taiwanshi shi huangminhua sanjiaozi weishi" [The pro-Taiwan-independence Taiwanese history is Japanized collaborators' fake history]. *Haixia pinlun* [Straits review monthly] 185 (2006): 58–60.

Pan Jingwei 潘敬尉, ed. *Xue nong yu shui* [Blood is thicker than water]. Taichung: Taiwansheng wenxian weiyuanhui, 1981.

Pan Weiting 潘維庭. "Tsai Ingwen han Taiwan shi guojia; Ding Shouzhong: wei latai xuanqing tiao liang'an duili" [Tsai Ingwen called Taiwan a country; Ding Shouzhong: In order to draw more votes, she provoked the cross-Taiwan Strait conflict]. *Zhongshi xinwenwang* [China times], August 4, 2018. https://www.chinatimes.com/realtimenews/ 20180804001248-260407.

Peng, Mingmin. *A Taste of Freedom: Memoirs of a Formosan Independence Leader.* New York: Holt, Rinehart, and Winston, 1972.

Peng Ruijin 彭瑞金. "Cong Xiangtu wenxue dao Sanmin zhuyi wenxue—fang Ye Shitao xiansheng tan Taiwan wenxue de lishi" [From Nativist literature to Three-Principles-of-the-People Literature—interview with Ye Shitao about the history of Taiwanese literature]. *Taiwan wenyi* [Taiwan literature] 62 (1979): 5–31.

——. "Dangqian Taiwan wenxue de bentuhua yu duoyuanhua—jianlun youguan Taiwan wenxue de yixie yishuo" [Current indigenization and pluralization of Taiwanese literature—also on some perverse views on Taiwanese literature]. *Wenxue Taiwan* [Literary Taiwan] 4 (1992): 11–36.

——. *Taiwan xinwenxue yundong sishi nian* [Forty years of Taiwan's New Literature movement]. Taipei: Zili wanbao, 1991.

——. "Xiangtu wenxue yu qiling niandai de Taiwan wenxue" [Nativist literature and Taiwanese literature in the 1970s]. In *Taiwan wenxue tansuo* [Exploring Taiwanese literature], by Peng Ruijin, 250–59. Taipei: Qianwei, 1995 (1991).

——. "Ye Shitao, Zhang Liangze duitan: bingzhu tan Lihe" [A conversation between Ye Shitao and Zhang Liangze: On Zhong Lihe by the light of a candle]. *Taiwan wenyi* [Taiwan literature] 54 (1977): 7–16.

——. "Yi wenxue wei shengming zuo jianzheng—Zhong Lihe ji xu" [Use literature to bear witness to life—preface to *The Zhong Lihe Collection*]. In *Zhong Lihe ji* [The Zhong Lihe collection], ed. Peng Ruijin, 9–12. Taipei: Qianwei, 1991.

Philips, Louise and Marianne W. Jørgensen. *Discourse Analysis as Theory and Method.* London: Sage, 2002.

Pilcher, Jane. "Mannheim's Sociology of Generations: An Undervalued Legacy." *British Journal of Sociology* 45, no. 3 (1994): 481–95.

Polkinghorne, Donald E. *Narrative Knowing and the Human Sciences.* Albany, N.Y.: State University of New York Press, 1988.

Qi Yishou 齊益壽. "Xiangtu wenxue zhi wojian" [My views on Nativist literature]. In *Xiangtu wenxue taolunji* [Collected discussions on Nativist literature], ed. Yu Tiancong, 587–95. Taipei: Yuanliu, 1978.

Qiu Weijun 丘為君 et al., eds. *Taiwan xuesheng yundong, 1949–1979 (zhong)* [Student movements in Taiwan, 1949–1979, vol. 2]. Taipei: Longtian, 1979.

Rigger, Shelley. *Taiwan's Rising Rationalism: Generations, Politics and "Taiwanese Nationalism."* Washington, D.C.: East West Center, 2006.

Ringmar, Erik. *Identity, Interest and Action: A Cultural Explanation of Sweden's Intervention in the Thirty Years War.* Cambridge: Cambridge University Press, 1996.

Rojas, Carlos. "Introduction." In *Writing Taiwan: A New Literary History*, ed. David Der-wei Wang and Carlos Rojas, 1–14. Durham, N.C.: Duke University Press, 2007.

Ryder, Norman B. "The Cohort as a Concept in the Study of Social Change." *American Sociological Review* 30 (1965): 843–61.

Said, Edward W. "Intellectual Exile: Expatriates and Marginals." In *Representations of the Intellectual*, by Edward W. Said, 47–64. New York: Pantheon Books, 1994.

Sang Pingzai 桑品載. "Erling erling shi Taidu peizangnian" [2020 is the year when Taiwan independence will be buried with the dead]. *Zhongshi xinwenwang* [China times], January 1, 2019. https://www.chinatimes.com/newspapers/20190111001603 -260109.

Schak, David C. *Civility and Its Development: The Experiences of China and Taiwan.* Hong Kong: Hong Kong University Press, 2018.

Scott, Jacqueline. "Is It a Different World to When You Were Growing Up? Generational Effects on Social Representations and Child-rearing Values." *British Journal of Sociology* 51, no. 2 (2000): 355–76.

Shahidian, Hammed. "Sociology and Exile: Banishment and Tensional Loyalties." *Current Sociology* 48, no. 2 (2000): 71–99.

Sheng Xingyuan 盛杏湲. "Tongdu yiti yu Taiwan xuanmin de toupiao xingwei: yijiu-jiuling niandai de fenxi" [The issue of Taiwan independence vs. unification with the mainland and voting behavior in Taiwan: An analysis in the 1990s]. *Xuanju yanjiu* [Journal of electoral studies] 9, no. 1 (2002): 41–80.

Shi Jiaju 石家駒 (Chen Yingzhen 陳映真). "Zai minzu wenxue de qizhi xia tuanjie qilai" [Unite under the banner of national literature]. In *Minzu wenxue de zai chufa* [Restarting national literature], ed. Xianrenzhang zazhishe, 223–38. Taipei: Guxiang, 1979 (1978).

Shi Junmei 史君美 (Tang Wenbiao 唐文標). "Lai xiai Zhong Lihe" [Come to love Zhong Lihe]. *Wenji* [Literary season] 2 (1973): 60–76.

Shi Minhui 施敏輝, ed. *Taiwan yishi lunzhan xuanji* [Selected articles from the debate on Taiwanese consciousness]. Taipei: Qianwei, 1988.

Shih Chiayin 石佳音. "Zhongguo guomindang de yishi xingtai yu zuzhi tezheng" [The ideology and organizational traits of the Chinese Nationalist Party]. Ph.D. dissertation, Department of Political Science, National Taiwan University, 2008.

Somers, Margaret R. and Gloria D. Gibson. "Reclaiming the Epistemological 'Other': Narrative and the Social Construction of Identity." In *Social Theory and the Politics of Identity*, ed. Craig Calhoun, 37–99. Oxford: Blackwell, 1994.

Song Dongyang 宋冬陽 (Chen Fangming 陳芳明). "Chaoxiang xuyuan zhong de liming: shilun Wu Zhuoliu zuopin zhong de 'Zhongguo jingyan'" [Toward the dawn we wished for: On the "Chinese experience" in Wu Zhuoliu's works]. *Wenxuejie* [Literary Taiwan] 10 (1984): 127–46.

———. "Xianjieduan Taiwan wenxue bentuhua de wenti" [The present problem of the indigenization of Taiwanese literature]. *Taiwan wenyi* [Taiwan literature] 86 (1984): 10–40.

Song Guocheng 宋國誠. "Lixing de piping, chengken de huyu—Song xu" [A rational criticism and sincere call—preface by Song]. In *Xinshengdai de nahan* [The call of the new generation], ed. Song Guocheng and Huang Zongwen, 1–4. Taipei: Self-published, 1978.

Sorensen, Diana. *A Turbulent Decade Remembered: Scenes from the Latin American Sixties.* Stanford, Calif.: Stanford University Press, 2007.

Su Beng (Shi Ming) 史明. *Taiwanren shibainian shi* [Four hundred years of Taiwanese history]. San Jose, Calif.: Paradise Culture Associates, 1980 (1962).

Su Junxiong 蘇俊雄. "Lun daxue de renwu yu zhengzhi gexin" [On the mission of universities and political reform]. *Daxue zazhi* [The intellectual] 37 (1971): 40–43.

Su Yuzhen 蘇玉珍. "Moxige xuechao qianhou" [The antecedents and consequences of the student movements in Mexico]. *Zhongyang ribao* [Central daily news], October 16, 1968.

Suleiman, Susan Rubin, ed. *Exile and Creativity: Signposts, Travelers, Outsiders, Backward Glances.* Durham, N.C.: Duke University Press, 1998.

Sun Zhen 孫震. "Wokan 'Yige xiaoshimin de xinsheng'" [My views on "The Voice of an Ordinary Citizen"]. In *Pian'an xintai yu zhongxing xintai—ping "Yige xiaoshimin de xinsheng"* [The mentality of false ease and the mentality of rejuvenation—on "The Voice of an Ordinary Citizen"], ed. Yang Guoshu et al., 38–41. Taipei: Huanyu, 1972.

Suri, Jeremi. *Power and Protest: Global Revolution and the Rise of Détente.* Cambridge, Mass.: Harvard University Press, 2003.

Taida daxue xinwenshe 台大大學新聞社. "'Gexin' cong 'gexin' zuoqi ["Reform" begins with "reform of heart"]. In *Taidaren de shizijia* [The cross that National Taiwan University people carry], ed. Taida daxue xinwenshe, 29–31. Taipei: Taida daxue xinwenshe, 1972(?).

———. "Liangxin de zijue" [The self-consciousness of conscience]. In *Taidaren de shizijia* [The cross that National Taiwan University people carry], ed. Taida daxue xinwenshe, 25–28. Taipei: Taida daxue xinwenshe, 1972(?).

———. "Ziyou yu zeren—tan xuexiao de shengao zhidu" [Freedom and responsibility—on the censorship system on campus]. In *Taidaren de shizijia* [The cross that National Taiwan University people carry], ed. Taida daxue xinwenshe, 21–22. Taipei: Taida daxue xinwenshe, 1972(?).

Taida fayan she 台大法言社. "Zhichi quanmian gaixuan de qingnian xinsheng" [Voices from the hearts of the young people who support a comprehensive reelection]. In *Taiwan xuesheng yundong 1949–1979 (xia)* [Student movements in Taiwan, 1949–1979 (vol. 3)], ed. Qiu Weijun et al., 714–17. Taipei: Longtian, 1979 (1971).

Taiwan ribao 台灣日報. "Meiguo ying su zhizhi xuesheng shiwei yundong" [America should stop student protests as soon as possible]. *Taiwan ribao* [Taiwan daily], May 13, 1970.

Taiwansheng wenxian weiyuanhui 台灣省文獻委員會. *Taiwan shihua* [A history of Taiwan]. Taichung: Taiwansheng wenxian weiyuanhui, 1974.

———, ed. *Taiwanshi* [A history of Taiwan]. Taipei: Zhongwen, 1990.

Tang Feng'e 湯鳳娥. "Quan wode zhangfu liuzai shufang" [Advising my husband to stay in his study]. In *Rongren yu liaojie* [Tolerance and understanding], by Chen Guying, 195–201. Taipei: Baijie, 1978.

Tang Wenbiao 唐文標. "Shi de moluo: Xianggang Taiwan xinshi de lishi pipan" [The decline of poetry: A historical criticism of new poetry in Hong Kong and Taiwan]. *Wenji* [Literary season] 1 (1973): 12–42.

Tang Zemin 唐澤民. "Riben xuesheng yundong de dongxiang" [The direction of student movements in Japan]. *Fanggong* [Counterattack magazine] 330 (1969): 27–9.

Tannenbaum, Edward R. *1900: The Generation Before the Great War*. Garden City, N.Y.: Anchor Press, 1976.

Taylor, Charles. *Sources of the Self: The Making of the Modern Identity*. Cambridge: Cambridge University Press, 1989.

Thompson, Edward P. *The Making of the English Working Class*. New York: Vintage Books, 1963.

Tien, Hungmao. *The Great Transition: Political and Social Change in the Republic of China*. Stanford, Calif.: Hoover Institution Press, 1989.

Tocqueville, Alexis de. *The Old Regime and the French Revolution*. Trans. Stuart Gilbert. New York: Anchor, 1955 (1856).

Turner, Bryan S. *Classical Sociology*. London: Sage, 1999.

———. "Outline of a Theory of Generations." *European Journal of Social Theory* 1, no. 1 (1998): 91–106.

———. "Strategic Generations: Historical Change, Literary Expression, and Generational Politics." In *Generational Consciousness, Narrative, and Politics*, ed. June Edmunds and Bryan S. Turner, 13–29. Lanham, Md.: Rowman & Littlefield, 2002.

United States Department of State, Bureau of Public Affairs. *American Foreign Policy, Current Documents, 1958*. Washington, D.C.: United States Government Printing Office, 1962.

Wachman, Alan M. *Taiwan: National Identity and Democratization*. Armonk, N.Y.: M. E. Sharpe, 1994.

Wakabayashi Masahiro 若林正丈. *Taiwan: fenlie guojia yu minzhuhua* [Taiwan: The divided nation and democratization]. Trans. Hong Jinzhu and Xu Peixian. Taipei: Yuedan, 1994.

———. *Taiwan kangri yundongshi yanjiu* [A study on the history of Taiwanese anti-Japanese movement]. Taipei: Xinziran zhuyi, 2007 (2001).

Wang, Chihming. *Transpacific Articulations: Student Migration and the Remaking of Asian America*. Honolulu: University of Hawai'i Press, 2013.

Wang Du 王渡. *Mayingjiu xianxiang* [Ma Yingjeou phenomena]. Taipei: Putian, 2002.

Wang Fuchang 王甫昌. "Fandui yundong de gongshi dongyuan: yijiu qijiu-yijiu bajiu nian liangpo tiaozhan gaofeng de bijiao" [Consensus mobilization of the political opposition in Taiwan: Comparing two waves of challenges, 1979–1989]. *Taiwan zhengzhi xuekan* [Taiwanese political science review] 1 (1996): 129–210.

——. "You 'Zhongguo shengji' dao 'Taiwan zuqun:' hukou pucha jibie leishu zhuanbian zhi fenxi" [From Chinese original domicile to Taiwanese ethnicity: An analysis of census category transformation in Taiwan]. *Taiwan shehuixue* [Taiwanese sociology] 9 (2005): 59–117.

Wang Fusu 王復蘇. "Wu yu" [Without words]. In *Fuzhong xia de chensi* [Deep thinking under the Fu Bell], by Wang Fusu, 63–64. Taipei: Maolian, 1990(?).

Wang Gao 王高. "Chuishou tingxun" [Listening to instructions obediently]. *Daxue zazhi* [The intellectual] 36 (1970): 1.

Wang Hongjiu 王紘久 (Wang Tuo 王拓). "Yixie youlu: tan Ouyang Zi de 'qiuye'" [Some worries: On Ouyang Zi's "Autumn Leaves"]. *Wenji* [Literary season] 1 (1973): 76–82.

Wang Hongjun 王洪鈞. "Jingshen shang de diqiya" [Low in spirits]. *Wenxing* [Apollo] 1, no. 1 (1957): 24.

——. "Butaoteng han dapao" [The grapevine and the cannon]. *Wenxing* [Apollo] 5, no. 1 (1959): 11.

——. "Ruhe shi qingnian jieshang zheyibang?" [How to get young people to take the baton?]. *Ziyou qingnian* [Free youth] 25, no. 7 (1961): 7.

Wang Jinjiang 王錦江 (Wang Shilang 王詩琅). "Riju shiqi de Taiwan xinwenxue" [Taiwan new literature in the Japanese occupation period]. *Taiwan wenyi* [Taiwan literature] 1, no. 3 (1964): 49–58.

Wang Jingqiong 王京瓊. "Jianxi 'wenhua Taidu'" [A brief analysis of "Taiwan independence in culture"]. *Zhongguowang* [china.com.cn], 2002. Accessed February 28, 2019. http://www. china.com.cn/chinese/zhuanti/179287.htm (site discontinued).

Wang Shangyi 王尚義. "Cong 'yixiangren' dao 'shiluo de yidai': Kamiu, Haimingwei yu women" [From "*The Stranger*" to "the Lost Generation": Camus, Hemingway, and Us]. In *Cong yixiangren dao shiluo de yidai* [From *The Stranger* to the Lost Generation], by Wang Shangyi, 35–56. Taipei: Wenxing, 1964(1962).

——. *Yegezi de huanghun* [Wild pigeons' dusk]. Taipei: Shuiniu, 1968.

Wang Shilang 王詩琅. "Riji xia Taiwan xinwenxue de shengcheng ji fazhan—daixu" [The emergence and development of Taiwan New Literature under the Japanese occupation—in lieu of preface]. In *Riju xia Taiwan xinwenxue, mingji 1: Lai He xiansheng quanji* [Taiwan New Literature under the Japanese occupation, Ming volume 1: The complete works of Mr. Lai He], ed. Li Nanheng, 1–12. Taipei: Mingtan, 1979.

Wang Tuo 王拓. "Nian shiji Taiwan wenxue fazhan de dongxiang" [The developmental trend of Taiwanese literature in the twentieth century]. In *Jiexiang gusheng* [Drum sounds from the streets], by Wang Tuo, 81–91. Taipei: Yuanjing, 1977.

——. "Shi 'xianshi zhuyi' wenxue, bushi 'xiangtu wenxue'" [It is "Realist" literature, rather than "Nativist literature"]. In *Xiangtu wenxue taolunji* [Collected discussions on Nativist literature], ed. Yu Tiancong, 100–119. Taipei: Yuanliu, 1978 (1977).

——. "Wenxue yu shehui zhengyi" [Literature and social justice]. In *Zhongguo xiandai wenxue de huigu* [A review of modern Chinese literature], ed. Qiu Weijun and Chen Lianshun, 240–58. Taipei: Longtian, 1978.

Wang Wenxing 王文興. "Wo dui 'Yige xiaoshimin de xinsheng' de kanfa" [My views on "The Voice of an Ordinary Citizen"]. In *Pian'an xintai yu zhongxing xintai—ping "Yige xiaoshimin de xinsheng"* [The mentality of false ease and the mentality of rejuvenation—on "The Voice of an Ordinary Citizen"], ed. Yang Guoshu et al., 119–26. Taipei: Huanyu, 1972.

Wang Xiaobo 王曉波. "Taiwan xinwenxue zhi fu—Lai He yu tade sixiang" [The father of the Taiwan New Literature—Lai He and his thoughts]. In *Bei diandao de Taiwan lishi* [Taiwan history turned upside down], by Wang Xiaobo, 129–52. Taipei: Pamier, 1986 (1979).

——. "Zeren yu xinxin—tan liuxue wenti" [Duty and confidence—on the issue of studying abroad]. *Daxue zazhi* [The intellectual] 20 (1969): 14–15.

Wang Xingqing 王杏慶. "Qianze han huyu" [Condemnation and appeal]. *Daxue zazhi* [The intellectual] 48 (1971): 58.

Wang Xingqing 王杏慶 et al. "Zhe shi juexing de shihou le!" [This is the time for awakening!]. *Daxue zazhi* [The intellectual] 47 (1971): 23.

Wang Yujing 王玉靜, ed. *Jiang Weishui shishi qishi zhounian jinian zhuankan* [Special volume commemorating the seventieth anniversary of Jiang Weishui's death]. Taipei: Taiwan yanjiu jijinhui, 2001.

Wang Zhenhuan 王振寰. "Taiwan de zhengzhi zhuanxing yu fandui yundong" [Political transformation and the opposition movement in Taiwan]. *Taiwan shehui yanjiu jikan* [Taiwan: A radical quarterly in social studies] 2, no. 1 (1989): 71–116.

Wei Wei 魏煒. "Shudian wangzu renzei zuofu Tsai Ingwen de Taiwan jiazhi" [Recount history but forget her origins and take a thief as her father: Tsai Ingwen's Taiwan value]. *US-China Forum*, February 24, 2018. http://www.us-chinaforum.com/27599369133554222727/4364124.

Weiss, Gilbert, and Ruth Wodak. "Introduction: Theory, Inerdisciplinarity and Critical Discourse Analysis." In *Critical Discourse Analysis: Theory and Inerdisciplinarity*, ed. Gilbert Weiss and Ruth Wodak, 1–32. New York: Palgrave Macmillan, 2003.

Wen Meiling 溫美玲. "Tiejian dan daoyi de Yang Kui" [Yang Kui, who carries moral burden on his iron shoulders]. In *Yang Kui de ren yu zuopin* [Yang Kui: The man and his works], ed. Yang Sujuan, 169–78. Taipei: Minzhong ribao she Taibei guanlichu, 1979 (1975).

Wen Rongguang 文榮光. "Wuxin you 'qiqi' yan—'xiaoshimin' xinsheng duhou" [There is "compassion" in my heart—my thoughts after reading "The Voice of an Ordinary Citizen"]. In *Taidaren de shizijia* [The cross that National Taiwan University people carry], by Taida xuesheng, 222–25. Taipei: Taida daxue xinwenshe, 1972.

Wen Shou 文壽. "Qingnian qizhi" [Youth temperament]. *Zhongyang ribao* [Central daily news], March 10, 1968.

Weng Jiayin 翁佳音. *Taiwan hanren wuzhuang kangrishi yanjiu (1895–1902)* [A study on the history of the armed anti-Japanese resistance of the Han Chinese in Taiwan, 1895–1902]. Taipei: Daoxiang, 2007 (1986).

Wenji zazhishe 文季雜誌社. "Fakanci: women de nuli han fangxiang" [Inaugural statement: Our efforts and direction]. *Wenji* [Literary season] 1 (1973): 1–2.

Wennerlund, Pelle. *Taiwan: In Search of the Nation.* Stockholm: Department of Chinese Studies, Stockholm University, 1997.

White, Hayden. "The Value of Narrative in the Representation of Reality." In *The Content of the Form: Narrative Discourse and Historical Representation,* by Hayden White, 1–25. Baltimore, Md.: Johns Hopkins University Press, 1987.

Whitebrook, Maureen. *Identity, Narrative and Politics.* London: Routledge, 2001.

Winckler, Edwin A. "Cultural Policy on Postwar Taiwan." In *Cultural Change in Postwar Taiwan,* ed. Stevan Harrell and Huang Chünchieh, 22–46. Boulder, Colo.: Westview Press, 1994.

Wohl, Robert. *The Generation of 1914.* Cambridge Mass.: Harvard University Press, 1979.

Wood, Linda A., and Rolf O. Kroger. *Doing Discourse Analysis: Methods for Studying Action in Talk and Text.* Thousand Oaks, Calif.: Sage, 2000.

Wright, Teresa. "Student Mobilization in Taiwan: Civil Society and Its Discontents." *Asian Survey* 39, no. 6 (1999): 986–1008.

Wu Fengshan 吳豐山. *Wo neng wei guojia zuoxie shemo?* [What can I do for the country?]. Taipei: Yuanjing, 1978.

Wu Guodong 吳國棟. "Wu ershi qingnian zijue yundong" [The May Twentieth Youth Self-Awakening movement]. In *Taiwan xuesheng yundong 1949–1979 (shang)* [Student movements in Taiwan, 1949–1979, vol. 1], ed. Qiu Weijun et al., 35–48. Taipei: Longtian, 1979(?).

Wu Jiabang 吳嘉邦. "Yougan liangci danren jingxuan zongganshi" [My thoughts about serving twice as a chief campaign strategist]. *Zheyidai zazhi* [New generation] 13 (1978): 11–3.

Wu Naiteh 吳乃德. "Jiating shehuihua han yishixingtai: Taiwan xuanmin zhengdang rentong de shidai chayi" [Family socialization and ideology: The differences of party-identification between generations among Taiwanese voters]. *Taiwan shehuixue yanjiu* [Taiwanese sociological review] 3 (1999): 53–85.

——. "The Politics of a Regime Patronage System: Mobilization and Control within an Authoritarian Regime." Ph.D. dissertation, University of Chicago, 1987.

——. "Ren de jingshen linian zai lishi biange zhong de zuoyong" [The role of moral value in political change: Explaining democratic transition in Taiwan]. *Taiwan zhengzhi xuekan* [Taiwanese political science review] 4 (2000): 57–103.

Wu Yingtao 吳瀛濤. "Gaishu guangfu qian de Taiwan wenxue (yi)" [An overview of Taiwanese literature before the Retrocession (1)]. *Youshi wenyi* [Youth literary] 216 (1971): 274–82.

——. "Gaishu guangfu qian de Taiwan wenxue (er)" [An overview of Taiwanese literature before the Retrocession (2)]. *Youshi wenyi* [Youth literary] 221 (1972): 54–60.

Wyatt, David. *Out of the Sixties: Storytelling and the Vietnam Generation*. New York: Cambridge University Press, 1993.

Xiao Yangji 蕭揚基. "Taiwan diqu gaozhong xuesheng guojia rentong ji qi xiangguan yinsu" [National identity of high school students in Taiwan and related factors]. *Gongmin xunyu xuebao* [Bulletin of civic and moral education] 11 (2002): 67–108.

Xu Bodong and Lou Jie 徐博東、婁傑. "'Qu Jianghua' baocang 'Taidu' huoxin" ["De-Chiang Kaishek-ification" contains the evil plot of "Taiwan independence"]. *Zhongguowang* [china.com.cn], June 12, 2007. http://www.china.com.cn/review/txt/2007-06/12/content_8376865.htm (site discontinued).

Xu Fuguan 徐復觀. "Youguan Taiwan de liuxue zhengce wenti" [Problems about Taiwan's policy on studying abroad]. In *Xu Fuguan wenlu (yi) wenhua* [Collected essays by Xu Fuguan, vol. 1: Culture], by Xu Fuguan, 182–5. Taipei: Huanyu, 1971(1968).

Xu Junya 許俊雅. "'Riju shiqi Taiwan wenxue' yanjiu gaikuang" [An overview of studies on "Taiwanese Literature in the Period of Japanese Occupation"]. In *Taiwan wenxue sanlun* [Essays on Taiwanese literature], 1–36. Taipei: Wenshizhe, 1994.

Xu Nancun 許南村 (Chen Yingzhen 陳映真). "'Xiangtu wenxue' de mangdian" [The blind spot of "Nativist literature"]. *Taiwan wenyi* [Taiwan literature] 55 (1977): 107–12.

Xu Shikai 許世楷. *Riben tongzhi xia de Taiwan* [Taiwan under Japanese rule]. Taipei: Yushanshe, 2006 (1972).

Xu Zhengxuan 徐政璿. "Qu Zhongguohua! Caizhengfu cong lishi keben xiashou; Guomindang: shudian wangzu" [De-Sinification! The Tsai Ingwen administration starts with history textbooks; the KMT: Recount history but forget their origins]. *ETtoday*, July 5, 2017. https://www.ettoday.net/news/20170705/959578.htm.

Yang Bichuan 楊碧川. *Riju shidai Taiwanren fankangshi* [A history of Taiwanese resistance in the period of Japanese occupation]. Taipei: Daoxiang, 1988.

Yang Guoshu 楊國樞. "Xinren yu zunzhong women de qingnian—yu youren tan 'Yige xiaoshimin de xinsheng' zhiyi" [Trust and respect our young people—discussing with my friend about "The Voice of an Ordinary Citizen," part 1] In *Pian'an xintai yu zhongxing xintai—ping "Yige xiaoshimin de xinsheng"* [The mentality of false ease and the mentality of rejuvenation—on "The Voice of an Ordinary Citizen"], ed. Yang Guoshu et al., 1–17. Taipei: Huanyu, 1972.

Yang Kui 楊逵. *Emama chujia* [Mother Goose gets married]. Taipei: Minzhong ribao she Taibei guanlichu, 1979 (1975).

——. "Houji" [Epilogue], in *Emama chujia* [Mother Goose gets married], by Yang Kui, 210-12. Taipei: Minzhong ribao she Taibei guanlichu, 1979 (1975).

——. "Mofancun" [Model village]. *Wenji* [Literary season] 2 (1973): 105–42.

Yang Qingchu 楊青矗. *Bisheng de huixiang* [The resounding of the pen]. Kaohsiung: Dunli, 1978.

——. "Shemo shi jiankang de wenxue?" [What is a wholesome literature?]. In *Xiangtu wenxue taolunji* [Collected discussions on Nativist literature], edited by Yu Tiancong, 297–99. Taipei: Yuanliu, 1978 (1977).

——. "Xianshi yu wenxue" [Reality and literature]. In *Zhongguo xiandai wenxue de huigu* [A review of modern Chinese literature], ed. Qiu Weijun and Chen Lianshun, 225–30. Taipei: Longtian, 1978.

Yang Sujuan 楊素絹, ed. *Yang Kui de ren yu zuopin* [Yang Kui: The man and his works]. Taipei: Minzhong ribao she Taibei guanlichu, 1979 (1976).

Yang Yongyi and Hong Sanxiong 楊庸一、洪三雄. "Minyi hezai?—Ping Zhongyang ribao de yipian wenzhang" [Where is the public opinion?—comment on an article in the *Central Daily News*]. In *Zhishiren de chulu* [A way out for intellectuals], ed. Hong Sanxiong, 63–66. Changhua: Xinsheng, 1972.

Yang Zhao 楊照. "Faxian 'Zhongguo:' Taiwan de qiling niandai" [Discovering "China": the 1970s in Taiwan]. In *Qiling niandai—lixiang jixu ranshao* [The 1970s: Ideals continue to flame], ed. Yang Ze, 127–34. Taipei: Shibao wenhua, 1994.

Yang Ziqiao and Chen Qianwu 羊子喬、陳千武, eds. *Guangfu qian Taiwan wenxue quanji* [Complete pre-Retrocession Taiwanese literature], vols. 9–12. Taipei: Yuanjing, 1982.

Yang Zujun 楊祖珺. *Meigui shengkai: Yang Zujun shiwunian laishilu* [The rose blossoms: The path Yang Zujun trod in the past fifteen years]. Taipei: Shibao wenhua, 1992.

Yanliang 彥良. "Yu you tan guoshi—yongren, dang timing yu zhengzhi gexin" [Discussing with my friend about national affairs—the promotion of talents, party nomination, and political reform]. *Daxue zazhi* [The intellectual] 47 (1971): 24.

Yao Jiawen 姚嘉文. "Aiguo lun: you shengmin zhi guo, ziyou aiguo zhi min" [On patriotism: If there is a country which can help people improve their life, naturally there will be a patriotic people]. *Meilidao* [Formosa] 1, no. 3 (1979): 93–97.

——. "'Panguo' lun—guo buke pan, min buke ru" [On "treason"—the country cannot be rebelled against and the people cannot be humiliated]. *Meilidao* [Formosa] 1, no.1 (1979): 61–65.

Ye Boxiang 葉柏祥. *Huang Xinjie qianzhun: Minjindang de youngyuan dalao* [A biography of Huang Xinjie: A big hitter in the Democratic Progressive Party forever]. Taipei: Yuedan, 1994.

Ye Guanghai 葉廣海. "Shouqi meiyougen de fennu" [Refraining from rootless anger]. *Zhongyang ribao* [Central daily news], February 23, 1968.

Ye Hongsheng 葉洪生. "Niannian yijue piaohuameng—cong yige nianqingren de shidai ganshou tanqi" [Awaking from a twenty-year blossoming dream: Speaking from a young person's feeling for the present era]. *Daxue zazhi* [The intellectual] 47 (1971): 34–43.

——. "Zheshi ge shemo shidai?" [What is the present era?]. In *Niannian yijue piaohuameng* [Awaking from a twenty-year blossoming dream], by Ye Hongsheng, 59–71. Taipei: Huangyu, 1972 (1971).

———. "Zheyidai de fangxiang—du 'Fu xiaoxiao' yougan" [The direction of this generation—my thoughts after reading "A Reply to Xiaoxiao"]. *Zhongyang ribao* [Central daily news], January 26, 1968.

———. "Zixu" [Preface by the author]. In *Zheyidai de fangxiang* [The direction of this generation], by Ye Hongsheng, 1–4. Taipei: Huangyu, 1976 (1972).

Ye Rongzhong 葉榮鐘. "Taiwan minzu yundong de puluren Cai Huiru" [Cai Huiru, the man who paved the way for the Taiwanese national movement]. *Taiwan zhenglun* [Taiwan political review] 1 (1975): 56–58.

Ye Shitao 葉石濤. *A History of Taiwan Literature*. Trans. Christopher Lupke. Amherst, N.Y.: Cambria Press, 2020.

———. "Jianjie Chen Shaoting xiansheng de 'Taiwan xinwenxue yundong jianshi'" [Introducing Mr. Chen Shaoting's *A Basic History of the Taiwan New Literature Movement*]. *Shuping shumu* [Book review and bibliography] 53 (1977): 34–37.

———. "Liangnian lai de shengji zuojia ji qi xiaoshuo" [The writers of this province and their works of fiction in the recent two years]. *Taiwan wenyi* [Taiwan literature] 19 (1968): 37–45.

———. "Liushi niandai de Taiwan xiangtu wenxue" [Nativist literature in 1960s Taiwan]. *Wenxun* [Wenhsun magazine] 13 (1984): 137–46.

———. "Taiwan de xiangtu wenxue" [Taiwan's Nativist literature]. *Wenxing* [Apollo] 97 (1965): 70–73.

———. *Taiwan wenxue rumen: Taiwan wenxue wushiqi wen* [Introduction to Taiwanese literature: Fifty-seven questions about Taiwanese literature]. Kaohsiung: Chunhui, 1997.

———. *Taiwan wenxue shigang* [An outline history of Taiwanese literature]. Kaohsiung: Wenxuejie, 1987.

———. "Wu Zhuoliu lun" [On Wu Zhuoliu]. *Taiwan wenyi* [Taiwan literature] 12 (1966): 25–30.

———. "Yang Kui de 'Emama chujia'" [Yang Kui's "Mother Goose Gets Married"]. *Daxue zazhi* [The intellectual] 87 (1975): 33–35.

———. "Zhuanxie Taiwan wenxueshi yingzou de fangxiang" [The direction writing the history of Taiwanese literature should take]. In *Taiwan wenxue de kunjing* [The dilemma of Taiwan literature], by Ye Shitao, 13–23. Kaohsiung: Paise wenhua, 1992(?).

———. "Zuojia de shidai" [The generational background of writers]. In *Taiwan xiangtu zuojia lunji* [Collected essays on Taiwan's Nativist writers], by Ye Shitao, 45–47. Taipei: Yuanjing, 1979(?).

Ye Shitao and Peng Ruijin 葉石濤 · 彭瑞金. "Ye Shitao, Peng Ruijin duitan: yinian lai de xiaoshuojie" [A conversation between Ye Shitao and Peng Ruijin: Fiction circles in the recent year]. *Taiwan wenyi* [Taiwan literature] 66 (1980): 180–97.

Ye Yunyun 葉芸芸. "Bianji baogao" [Editorial note]. In *Ye Rongzhong Quanji* [Complete works of Ye Rongzhong], ed. Yu Yunyun, 11–16. Taipei: Chenxing, 2000.

Yin Di 隱地. "Fanzhuag de niandai: jiantan qiling niandai de wenyifeng" [An era of transformation: Also on the literary and artistic trends in the 1970s]. In *Qiling niandai—lixiang jixu ranshao* [The 1970s: Ideals continue to flame], ed. Yang Ze, 31–38. Taipei: Shibao wenhua, 1994.

Yin Ying 殷穎. "You meiguo liuhua xuesheng suo dianran de Zhongguo qingnian zijue yundong" [The Self-Awakening movement of Chinese youth stimulated by an American student studying in China]. In *Taiwan xuesheng yundong 1949–1979 (zhong)* [Student movements in Taiwan, 1949–1979 (vol. 2)], ed. Qiu Weijun et al., 361–66. Taipei: Longtian, 1979(?).

You Shengguan 游勝冠. *Taiwan wenxue bentu lun de xingqi yu fazhan* [The rise and development of the indigenization discourse in Taiwanese literature]. Taipei: Qianwei, 1996.

Yu Guangzhong 余光中. *Baiyu kugua* [The white jade bitter gourd]. Taipei: Dadi, 1974.

——. "Four Stanzas on Homesickness." In *China: Adapting the Past, Confronting the Future*, ed. Thomas Buoye et al., 540. Ann Arbor: Center for Chinese Studies, University of Michigan, 2002 (1974).

Yu Lihua 於梨華. *Youjian zonglü, youjian zonglü* [Palms again]. Taipei: Tingyun, 2015 (1967).

Yu Tiancong 尉天驄. *Lu bushi yigeren zouchulai de* [A way cannot be tread out only by one person]. Taipei: Lianjing, 1976.

——. "Manmu yanshi bu liao wugou: dui xiandai zhuyi de kaocha, jianping Ouyang Zi de 'qiuye'" [Curtains can't hide the dirt: an examination of modernism, and a review of Ouyang Zi's "Autumn Leaves"]. *Wenji* [Literary season] 1 (1973): 61–75.

——. "Xihua de wenxue" [Westernized literature]. In *Zhongguo xiandai wenxue de huigu* [A review of modern Chinese literature], ed. Qiu Weijun and Chen Lianshun, 155–66. Taipei: Longtian, 1978.

——. "Xu" [Preface]. In *Diyijian chaishi* [My first case], by Chen Yingzhen, 1–16. Taipei: Yuanjing, 1975.

Yu Tiancong 尉天驄 et al. "Dangqian de Zhongguo wenxue wenti" [Current issues about Chinese literature]. In *Xiangtu wenxue taolun ji* [Collected discussions on Nativist literature], ed. Yu Tiancong, 761–85. Taipei: Yuanliu, 1978 (1977).

Zeng Pincang 曾品滄. "Yijiu liuling niandai zhishi qingnian de duli yundong—yi 'Quanguo qingnian tuanjie cujinhui shijian' weili" [The Taiwan Independence movement initiated by intellectual youths in the 1960s—the case of "the Incident of Association for Promoting Nationwide Youth Solidarity"]. In *Yijiu liuling niandai de duli yundong—quanguo qingnian tuanjie cujinhui shijian fangtanlu* [The Taiwan Independence movement in the 1960s—collected interviews about the Incident of Association for Promoting Nationwide Youth Solidarity], interviewed by Zeng Pincang and Xu Ruihao, transcribed by Zeng Pincang, 1–39. Taipei: Guoshiguan, 2004.

Zeng Xubai 曾虛白. "Cong Meiri xuechao tanqi" [A discussion beginning with student movements in America and Japan]. *Dongfang zazhi* [Eastern miscellany] 3, no. 6 (1969): 6–9.

Zhang Dongcai 張棟材. "Faguo de xuegongchao yu daxuan" [Student and labor movements and the general election in France]. *Wenti yu yanjiu* [Issues & studies] 7, no. 10 (1968): 1–4.

——. "Riben zuopai xuesheng zouxiang baolihua" [Japanese leftist students are moving toward violence]. *Wenti yu yanjiu* [Issues & studies] 7, no. 9 (1968): 15–9.

Zhang Guangzhi 張光直, ed. *Zhang Wojun wenji* [Zhang Wojun collection]. Taipei: Chunwenxue, 1975.

Zhang Henghao, Lin Fan (Lin Ruiming), and Yang Ziqiao 張恆豪、林梵 (林瑞明)、羊子喬. "Chuban zongzhi ji bianji tili" [Purpose of publication and principles of editing]. In *Guangfu qian Taiwan wenxue quanji* [Complete pre-Retrocession Taiwanese literature], ed. Zhong Zhaozheng and Ye Shitao, 1–6. Taipei: Yuanjing, 1979.

Zhang Hongyuan 張宏遠. "Shuo jiju neixin de hua" [Let me say some words from my heart]. *Daxue zazhi* [The intellectual] 47 (1971): 17–19.

Zhang Hua 張華. "Zhifu yu xiangyata de aiguoxin—shehui fuwu yundong" [The patriotism lying dormant in the ivory tower—the Social Service movement]. In *Taiwan xuesheng yundong 1949–1979 (shang)* [Student movements in Taiwan, 1949–1979, vol. 1], ed. Qiu Weijun et al., 173–89. Taipei: Longtian, 1979(?).

Zhang Jinghan 張景涵 (Zhang Junhong 張俊宏). "Daxuesheng diaocha baogao, taolun yu jianyi—daxuesheng dui xuexiao de taidu" [Report, discussion, and suggestion about an investigation of university students—university students' attitudes toward their universities]. *Daxue zazhi* [The intellectual] 24 (1969): 24–26.

Zhang Jinghan 張景涵 (Zhang Junhong 張俊宏) et al. "Guoshi zhengyan" [Advice about national affairs]. *Daxue zazhi* [The intellectual] 46 (1971): 1–10.

Zhang Junhong 張俊宏. "Chaoliu de xunxi" [The message emerging from the trend]. In *Yongzhe buju: wo weishenmo yao jingxuan lifa weiyuan?* [The brave fear nothing: Why do I want to run for legislator?], by Chen Wanzhen, 3–6. Taipei: Changqiao, 1978.

——. "*Guomindang wang hechu qu* xuwen: zhipei zhe yishi jingzheng zhe?" [Preface to *Whither Is the Chinese Nationalist Party Going? A dominator or rival*]. *Zheyidai zazhi* [New generation] 14 (1978): 51–52.

——. *Wo de chensi yu fendou—liangqian ge jianao de rizi* [My contemplation and struggle—two thousand tormenting days]. Taipei: Self-published, 1977.

——. "Women de hua" [Our words]. *Zheyidai zazhi* [New generation] 1 (1977): 3–5.

Zhang Junhong 張俊宏 et al. *Taiwan shehuili de fenxi* [Analysis of Taiwan's social forces]. Taipei: Huanyu, 1972.

Zhang Liangze 張良澤. "Buqu de wenxue hun—lun Yang Kui jiantan riju shidai de Taiwan wenyi" [Unyielding literary soul—on Yang Kui and Taiwanese literature and art in the Japanese occupation period]. In *Yang Kui de ren yu zuopin* [Yang Kui: The man and his works], ed. Yang Sujuan, 209–26. Taipei: Minzhong ribao she Taibei guanlichu, 1979 (1975).

——. "Buqu de wenxue hun—lun Yang Kui jiantan riju shidai de Taiwan wenyi (si zhi yi)" [Unyielding literary soul—on Yang Kui and Taiwanese literature and art in the Japanese occupation period (part 1 of 4)]. *Zhongyang ribao* [Central daily news], October 22, 1975.

——, ed. *Emama chujia* [Mother Goose gets married]. Tainan: Daxing, 1975.

——. "Wu Xinrong xiansheng zhuanlüe" [A brief biography of Mr. Wu Xinrong]. *Daxue zazhi* [The intellectual] 105 (1977): 20–21.

——. "Xulun" [Introduction]. In *Emama chujia* [Mother Goose gets married], by Yang Kui 1–5. Taipei: Minzhong ribao she Taibei guanlichu, 1979 (1975).

——. "Zhong Lihe de wenxue guan" [Zhong Lihe's views on literature]. *Wenji* [Literary season] 2 (1973): 48–59.

——. "Zhong Lihe zuopin zhong de riben jingyan yu zuguo jingyan" [The experiences of Japan and ancestral land in Zhong Lihe's works]. *Zhongwai wenxue* [Chung Wai literary quarterly] 2, no. 11 (1974): 32–57.

Zhang Shijian 張詩劍. "Zhonghua wenhua zhi gen buke dongyao—bo 'wenhua Taidu'" [The root of Chinese culture cannot be shaken—refuting "Taiwan independence in culture"]. *Zhongguowang* [china.com.cn], 2002. Accessed February 28, 2019. http://big5.china.com.cn/chinese/TCC/haixia/112070.htm (site discontinued).

Zhang Xiaofeng 張曉風. *Chouxiang shi* [Homesick stone]. Taipei: Chenzhong, 1971.

Zhang Xiguo 張系國. "Tan liuxuesheng" [On students studying abroad]. *Daxue zazhi* [The intellectual] 20 (1969): 11.

——. "Zhishi fenzi de gudu yu gudu de zhishi fenzi" [The solitude of intellectuals and the solitary intellectuals]. *Daxue zazhi* [The intellectual] 6 (1968): 14–15.

Zhang Yanxian 張炎憲. "Yijiu erling niandai de Jiang Weishui" [Jiang Weishui in the 1920s]. In *Jiang Weishui shishi liushi zhounian jinian ji Taiwanshi xueshu yantaohui lunwen jiyao* [Selected proceedings of the Conference Commemorating the Sixtieth Anniversary of Jiang Weishui's Death and on Taiwanese History], ed. Kaohsiung County Government, 17–34. Kaohsiung: Kaohsiung County Government, 1991.

Zhang Zhaowei 張釗維. *Shei zai nabian chang ziji de ge* [Who is singing their own songs over there]. Taipei: Shibao wenhua, 1994.

Zhao Xiaqiu 趙遐秋. "Yao jingti 'wenxue Taidu' de exing fazhan" [Stay alert for the vicious development of "Taiwan independence in literature"]. *Huaxia jingwei* [huaxia.com], 2001. http://big5.huaxia.com/zt/2001-19/32775.html.

Zhao Xiaqiu and Zeng Qingrui 趙遐秋、曾慶瑞. *Wenxue Taidu mianmianguan* [On various aspects of Taiwan independence in literature]. Beijing: Jiouzhou, 2001.

Zhao Xunda 趙勳達. *Kuangbiao shike—Rizhi shidai Taiwan xinwenxue de gaofengqi (1930–1937)* [A *Sturm und Drang* moment—the peak of Taiwan New Literature in the Japanese colonial period (1930–1937)]. Tainan: Guoli Taiwan wenxueguan, 2011.

Zhao Zhiti 趙知悌, ed. *Wenxue xiuzou—xiandai wenxue de kaocha* [Literature, don't leave—an examination of modern literature]. Taipei: Yuanxing, 1976.

——. "Xu" [Preface], in *Wenxue xiuzou—xiandai wenxue de kaocha* [Literature, don't leave—an examination of modern literature], ed. Zhao Zhiti, 1–13. Taipei: Yuanxing, 1976.

Zheng Hongsheng 鄭鴻生. *Qingchun zhi ge: zhuiyi yijiu qiling niandai Taiwan zuoyi qingnian de yiduan ruhuo nianhua* [Song of youth: Recalling the wild years of leftist youth in 1970s Taiwan]. Taipei: Lianjing, 2001.

Zheng Nanrong 鄭南榕. "Huang Huangxiong you xianjian zhi ming" [Huang Huangxiong has foresight]. *Zhengzhijia* [The statesman] 26 (1982): 15.

———. "'Zhen youli' de zhengzhi sixiangjia—Huang Huangxiong: fangwen Huang Huangxiong" [A "truly powerful" political thinker—Huang Huangxiong: Interview with Huang Huangxiong]. *Zhengzhijia* [The statesman] 26 (1982): 6–12.

Zhenghong 正宏, trans. "Ribenren yanzhong de Taiwan kangri yundong" [The Taiwanese anti-Japanese movement seen through Japanese eyes]. *Taiwan zhenglun* [Taiwan political review] 4 (1975): 48–52.

Zhong Lihe 鍾理和. "Pinjian fuqi" [A poor and lowly couple]. *Wenji* [Literary season] 2 (1973): 82–90.

Zhong Lihua 鍾麗華. "Guotaiban pi 'sangxin bingkuang'; luweihui huiji 'xiachong buke yubing'" ["Frenzied and perverse": China's Taiwan Affairs Office criticized; "An insect that lives only one summer cannot be expected to know what ice is": Taiwan's Mainland Affairs Council countercriticized]. *Ziyou shibao* [Liberty times net], June 13, 2018. https://news.ltn.com.tw/news/politics/breakingnews/2457429.

Zhong Zhaozheng 鍾肇政. "Jiankun guji de zuji—jianshu sishi niandai bensheng xiangtu wenxue" [Difficult and lonely footprints: A brief introduction to the Nativist Literature of this province in the 1950s]. *Wenxun* [Wenhsun magazine] 9 (1984): 122–34.

———. *Taiwan wenxue shijiang* [Ten lectures on Taiwanese literature], ed. Zhuang Zirong. Taipei: Qianwei, 2000.

———. "Taiwan wenxue zhi gui—Ye Shitao" [The spirit of Taiwanese literature—Ye Shitao]. *Taiwan chunqiu* [Taiwan veracity] 8 (1989): 314–37.

Zhong Zhaozheng and Ye Shitao 鍾肇政、葉石濤, eds. *Guangfu qian Taiwan wenxue quanji* [Complete pre-Retrocession Taiwanese literature]. 8 vols. Taipei: Yuanjing, 1979.

Zhongyang ribao 中央日報. "Meiguo xuechao yu feibang shentou" [Student movements in the United States and the communist gang's infiltration]. *Zhongyang ribao* [Central daily news], May 17, 1970.

Zhou Qier 周棄兒. "Waishengren de kumen" [The depression of Mainlanders]. *Taiwan zhenglun* [Taiwan political review] 5 (1975): 64–65.

Zhu Quanbin 朱全斌. "You nianling, zuqun deng bianxiang kan Taiwan minzhong de guojia ji wenhua rentong" [A positional analysis of Taiwanese people's national and cultural identities]. *Xinwenxue yanjiu* [Mass comunication research] 56 (1998): 35–63.

Zhu Xining 朱西寧. "Ye lao yuanding" [Paying a call on the old gardener]. *Zhongwai wenxue* [Chung Wai literary quarterly] 3, no. 8 (1975): 18–21.

Zhu Yunhan 朱雲漢. "Lishi, shiju yu guoyun" [History, world situation, and the destiny of our nation]. *Xianrenzhang zazhi* [Cactus magazine] 9 (1977): 181–89.

——. "Maixiang ershiyi shiji de yidai—zhishi qingnian yu Zhongguo weilai" [A generation moving toward the twenty-first century—intellectual youth and China's future]. In *Zhishi fenzi yu Zhongguo* [Intellectuals and China], ed. Zhou Yang-shan, 423–27. Taipei: Shibao, 1980 (1979).

Zhuang Junqing 莊俊清. "Yige dangyuan han minxuan yiyuan de zhenxinhua—Xu Xinliang '*Fengyu zhisheng*' shujie" [The sincere words of a KMT member and an elected provincial councilor—introducing Xu Xinliang's "*The Sound of Wind and Rain*"]. *Xiachao* [China tide] 2, no. 6 (1977): 59–62.

Ziyou Zhongguo bianji weiyuanhui 自由中國編輯委員會. "Jinri de wenti (er): Fang-gong dalu wenti" [Today's issues (part 2): The issue of launching a counterattack on the mainland]. *Ziyou Zhongguo* [Free China] 17, no. 3 (1957): 69–71.

Index

aboriginal literature: development of, *114*; tradition of, 112

actual generation, *16*, 20, *22*; definition of, 16–17; return-to-reality generation as, 10–11

age cohort, 15, 83, 138

American Indian ethnography, 199n55

amnesty, 140

"Analysis of Taiwan's Social Forces" (*Taiwan shehuili de fenxi*), 50, 53

ancestral land: in Dangwai historiography, Taiwanese anti-Japanese resistance and, 133–34; Ye Shitao on, 115–16

Andrews, Molly, 19–20; on conscientization, 8; Freire related to, 17; on generational consciousness and narrative, 18

anticommunist literature (*fangong wenxue*), 111

anti-Japanese resistance movement: *The Intellectual* on, 133; New Literature as, 64, 67, 68, 69, 75;

Wang Tuo on, 100; Yang Kui in, 77, 80; Ye Shitao on, 86

Apollo (Wenxin), 29, 43

Arendt, Hannah, 165

arrests: of Chen Guying, 60; of Lei Zhen, 30, 190n6; of Yu Dengfa, 128

baby boom generation, 26–27, 168

baihua (Mandarin), 62–63

Bai Xianyong, 33, 221n15

banshan ren (Half-Mountain People), 212n12

baodao wenxue (reportage literature), 95–96, 223n40

Baodiao movement, 14, 166; Chen Guying and, 42–43; nationalism from, 84; response to, 94; return-to-reality generation in, 48–49; significance of, 97; YeShitao on, 116

Bao Qingtian, 51

Barker, Chris, 19

Baron, Don (Di Renhua), 29

Barthes, Roland, 18

Basic History of the Taiwan New Literature Movement, A (Chen Shaoting), 85–86; Huang Deshi on, 85–86; Ye Shitao on, 86–87

Battleship Building for Revenge movement (*Jianjian fuchou yudong*), 28

benshengren. See local Taiwanese

Biography of Jiang Weishui—Taiwan's Visionary Prophet (Huang Huangxiong), 163

birth cohort, 15

"borrowed life, A" (*Duosang*) (film), 220n7

"Boy in the Red Shirt, The" (Lin Huaimin), 44

Braungart, Richard G., 17–18

Bruner, Edward M., 199n55

campaigning, 128

Camus, Albert, 42

candidates, 126–27

Chang, Sung-sheng Yvonne, 101

Chen Fangming (Chen Jianong, Song Dongyang), 237n96; on Chen Shaoting, 218n82; in *Taiwan Literature*, 111, 226n64

Chen Guying, 59; arrest of, 60; Baodiao movement and, 42–43; democracy and, 54; generation of, 53; on new generation, 14

Chen Jianong. *See* Chen Fangming

Chen Shaoting, 87; Chen Fangming on, 218n82; on colonial resistance activism, 132–34; and Huang Deshi, 85–86; May Fourth essay by, 67–69, 84, 85; on reelection, 58–59; on Taiwan New Literature, 67–69, 75–76, 218n82

Chen Shuibian (president), 165, 173, 240n15; election of, 118–19; opening address by, 164

Chen Wanzhen, 128, 231n14, 231n21

Chen Yingzhen, 33, 110–11; on national identity, 113, 115; on return-to-reality generation, 71–72; "Tang Qian's Comedy" by, 41; on the West, 96–97

Chen Yishan (fictional character), 35

Chiang Chingkuo (president), 28, 128, 134, 137, 208n13

Chiang Kaishek (president), 27–28, 208n13; amnesty after his death, 140; ideology of, 32; manifesto against, 30

China Quarterly, 31–32, 33–34

China Tribune (*Zhongguo luntan*), 90

China Youth Anti-Communist National Salvation Corps (CYC), 27–28

Chinese identity, 59, 68, 170, 172

Chinese language, 82, 91–94, 99, 217n72

Chinese Literary Association (*Zhongguo wenyi xiehui*), 220n8

Chinese Modern Folk Song movement, 21–22, 198n49, 205n50

Chinese modernity, 69

Chinese nationalism, 27–28, 120; Taiwan New Literature and, 64, 66

Chinese nationalist historical narrative, 7, 9–10, 21, 43–44

Chinese Nationalist Narrative Template of Taiwan's Nativist Literature, 107, *108*

Chinese Nationalist Party (KMT), 2, 202n24; against Association for Promoting Nationwide Youth Solidarity, 30; against Dangwai Movement legitimization, 141–42; DPP or, 23–24, 173; *Free China* against, 130; "Half-Mountain People" with, 212n12; Kang Ningxiang and, 136–37; Lü Hsiulien and, 157–58, 237n93; Nativist literature reception and, 99, 101;

NTU and, 49, 60; return-to-reality generation related to, 53–54, 166; against student movement, 59–60; young intellectuals and, 27

Chinese Nationalist Template of Historical Narrative, 7, 52, 68

Chineseness, 107–8; Gao Xinjiang on, 104; Huang Huangxiong and, 156; Kang Ningxiang and, 135–37; Li poets and, 95; of the return-to-reality generation, 71–72; of Taiwan New Literature, 88–89; Yang Qingchu on, 92–93

Chinese Youth Party (*Zhongguo qingniandang*), 230n11

Chouxiang shi (*Homesick Stone*) (Zhang Xiaofeng), 40

Chungli Incident, 126, 128, 130

"Cicada" (Lin Huaimin), 34, 37

civic nationalism, 168–69

civil rights activists, 125–26

class, 15–16, 167, 192n1; the return-to-reality generation and, 43–44, 55

class consciousness, 196n28

class membership, 196n28

Cloud Gate Dance Theater (Yunmen wuji), 21–22, 198n49

collective identity, 171–72

collective memory: Chinese nationalist, 6–7, 81; of the Holocaust, 40; of Japanese colonialism in Taiwan, 64; of Taiwanese anti-Japanese resistance, 66–67, 75–76; of Taiwan New Literature and Ye Shitao, 87

colonial resistance activism: Chen Shaoting on, 132–33; Kang Ningxiang on, 134–38

Communist Party of Taiwan, 141

Complete Pre-Retrocession Taiwanese Literature, 71, 87, 214n33

conscientization, 8, 17

consciousness, 26, 196n28; for generation, 18–20; in social change, 16; Taiwanese, 23, 59, 110–11, 159

constitution, 162–63

constitutional tradition (*fatong*), 56–57

criticism, 28, 33–34; against DPP, 240n15; of *Literary Season*, 116; from young intellectuals, 29–30, 35–36. *See also* literary modernism

cultural capital, 23

Current Democracy (*Minzhu chao*), 125, 230n11

CYC. *See* China Youth Anti-Communist National Salvation Corps

Dangwai: beginning of, 123; campaigning in, 123–24, 125–28, 155; candidates of, 126–27; Chinese consciousness of, 131–32; Chungli Incident and, 126, 128, 130; civil rights activists in, 125–26; experiences of, 124–25; *Formosa* in, 129–32, 232n29; generational politics in, 122; idealism in, 123–24, 126–27; independents in, 122–23; intentions in, 127–28; interview in, 128–29; as new generation, 14, 21, 124; retrospective in, 125; Taiwanese consciousness of, 23; term definition of, 11. *See also specific topics*

Dangwai historiography: Chinese patriotism in, 135–36; *The Eighties* and, 142, *143*, *148–50*, 234n66; *Formosa* and, 142, *144*, *151–52*; Kang Ningxiang and, 133, 134–39, 233n46, 233n49, 234n59; Lin Zhuoshui and, 160–61; Lü Hsiulien and, 158–61; *New Generation* on, 142, *142*, *145–47*, 234n66; nonviolent anticolonial activism in, 134; *Taiwan Political Review* on, 139–42, *140*; Zhang Junhong on, 138–39

Dangwai new generation (*Dangwai xinshengdai*), 14, 21, 124
Dangwai xinshengdai (Dangwai new generation), 124
Daxue zazhi. See *Intellectual, The*
de-exilic cultural politics, 7, 10, 21, 54, 144, 147, 162, 173
democracy, 125–26, 152; Chen Guying and, 54; in *Formosa*, 129–32, 232n29; for return-to-reality generation, 53–54
Democratic Progressive Party (DPP), 111, 118, 228n85; criticism against, 240n15; founding of, 123; KMT or, 23–24, 173
de-Sinification, 109, 110, 112, 240n15
Diaoyutai Incident, 46, 48; Nativist literature reception and, 97–98, 116–17; U.S. and, 2
Di Renhua (Baron, Don), 29
discourse analysis, 24–25
"discover China" (*faxian Zhongguo*), 170
"discover Taiwan" (*faxian Taiwan*), 170
Donghai Flower Garden, 78–79, 216n61
DPP. *See* Democratic Progressive Party
"Draft Constitution of Taiwan" (*Taiwan xianfa caoan*), 162–63
Dragon Nation Poetry Society (Longzu shishe), 102, 111, 223n40
Duosang ("A borrowed life") (film), 220n7

East Germany, 18
Edmunds, June, 14, 168, 196n28
Eighties, The, 142, *143*, *148–50*, 234n66; Lin Zhuoshui in, 160–61
elderly age strata, 23
election: of Chen Shuibian, 118–19; of Huang Huangxiong, 154–55; of Kang Ningxiang, 123; reelection of parliamentary representatives, 56–60

essentialism, 170–72
European nationalism, 197n44
exilic mentality, 5–7, 8, 31–32, 66, 103, 111, 209n27; criticisms of, 43, 54–55, 59; quasi–, 38–41, 45; semi-quasi–, 41, 45
existentialism, 43; Zhang Xiguo on, 41–42

Fanfu. *See* Ye Rongzhong
faxian Taiwan ("discover Taiwan"), 170
faxian Zhonggud ("discover China"), 170
feminism, 157, 158, 169; gender identity and, 192n2
Formosa (Meilidao): democracy in, 129–32, 232n29; and Kaohsiung Incident, 154; motto in, 232n29; on Taiwanese history, 142, *144*, *151–52*
Formosa Incident. See Kaohsiung Incident
Four Hundred Years of Taiwanese History (Su Beng), 157
"Four Stanzas on Homesickness" (Yang Xian), 39, 205n50
"Four Stanzas on Homesickness" (Yu Guangzhong), 39, 205n50
Free China (Ziyou Zhongguo), 30, 43, 130, 132
Freire, Paulo, 17
Fu Bo, 218n82

Gao Xinjiang, 102–4, 223n40
Gao Yushu, 229n6
Gao Zhun, 55
gender identity, 192n2
generation: actual, *16*, 16–18, 21; of Chen Guying, 53; consciousness for, 19; definitions of, 14–15, 167–68; location of, 16, *16*, 21; Mannheim on, 15–17, *16*

generational identity: gender identity related to, 192n2; Huang Huangxiong on, 152–53; narrativity on, 19–20; provincial background and, 13–14; of return-to-reality generation, 167–68; of young intellectuals, 29–30

generational politics, 122

generation for-itself, 17, 27, 167, 169

generation gap, 220n7; Chinese language in, 92–94; first-and second-generation of local Taiwanese writers in, 94–95; of local Taiwanese dissidents, 138; among Mainlanders, 95; national identity and, 93; third generation of local Taiwanese writers in, 94, 95; the West and, 94; Yang Qingchu on, 92–94

generation in-itself, 17, 27, 45, 169

generation location: Mannheim on, 16, *16*; of Taiwan, 21

Generation of 1914, The (Wohl), 167

generation theory, 15–18, 22–23, 83, 167–68

generation units, 16, *16*, 17, 21, 101

Giddens, Anthony, 19, 197n40

gongnongbing wenxue ("literature of workers, farmers, and soldiers"), 99

guangfu. See Retrocession

guchen (lone-minister) metaphor, 111, 226n63

guer (orphaned sons) metaphor, 111, 158, 237n96

Guo Rongzhao, 47–48, 56–57

Guo Yuxin, 230n14, 236n82

Half-Mountain People (*banshan ren*), 212n12

Han Kuoyu, 173

Han nation, 237n94; Ye Shitao on, 89

Han national identity, 164; Huang Huangxiong on, 163–64

Hardy, Melissa, 16

Harrell, Stevan, 239n6

Harrison, Mark, 3–4, 9–10

Heluo, 160, 237n94

Hemingway, Ernest, 42

He Wenzhen, 125, 131, *142*, 230n7; Xu Xinliang and, 123–24

He Xin, 103, 220n8, 221n15; on provincial background, 94; on reportage literature, 95–96

Hirsch, Marianne, 40–41

historical generation, 17–18, 167

historical identity, 80

Historical Story of the Anti-Japanese Resistance in Taiwan, A (Huang Huangxiong), 163

history, 115–16, 163, 238n102; in critique against literary modernism, 103–4; Huang Huangxiong on, 155–56; Kang Ningxiang on, 135–36, 137–38; Taiwanese, 142, *142–44*, 144, 147; of Taiwan New Literature, 62–63

Hoklo language (*Taiyu*). *See* language

Holocaust, 40

Homesick Stone (Chouxiang shi) (Zhang Xiaofeng), 40

Hong Kong, 102, 173

Hong Sanxiong, 14, 48, 55, 56

Hong Tong, 198n49

household registration and personal ID card system, 39, 205n50

Hsiao Hsinhuang, 59, 101

Huang, Mab (Huang Mo), 14

Huang Chünchieh, 239n6

Huang Chunming, 90, 91, 94; in Nativist literature reception, 98–99

Huang Deshi, 85–86

Huang Hua, 140–41, 234n61

Huang Huangxiong, 131, 144, *145–47*; assimilationism of, 156; constitution from, 162–63; election of, 154–55; on generational identity, 152–53; historical rewriting by, 163–64, 238n102; historiography and assimilation of, 147, 150, 152–56; on history, 155–56; on Jiang Weishui, 153–54, 162, 164–65; retrospective of, 150, 152; on Taiwanese visionaries, 153; writings by, 152–53, 235n72

Huang Xinjie, 123, 126, 128, 129, 133, 139, 141, 154, 229n6, 233n46

"Human Rights Day," 154

imperialization movement, 61

independents, 122–23

instrumentalism, 170–72

Intellectual, The (Daxue zazhi): on anti-Japanese resistance movement, 133; Chinese nationalist resistance in, 67–68; letter to editor of, 43–44; Mab Huang on, 14; on parliamentary representatives reelection, 57; for return-to-reality generation, 49–51, 123, 169; return-to-reality spirit in, 54–55

intergenerational apathy, 31–38

Jacobs, J. Bruce, 60

Japan: anticolonial resistance against, *108*; imperialization movement from, 61; older generation and, 50; PRC and, 46–47. *See also* anti-Japanese resistance movement

Japanese colonial period, 83–85, 87, 89, *140, 142*; *The Eighties* on, *148–50*; *Formosa* on, *151–52*; *New Generation* on, *145–47*; *Taiwan Political Review* on, 140

Japanese-educated generation, 89; age cohort definition of, 83; Mandarin Chinese in, 82, 217n72; before Nativist literature of the 1970s, 83–84; poets in, 83–84; postwar period for, 82–83; retrospective by, 84; return-to-reality generation and, 83; *Taiwan Literature* and, 84–85; Ye Shitao in, 82–83; Ye Shitao on, 86–87; Zhong Lihe as, 84–85

Japanese-educated generation reentry, 82–89

Japanese language, 50

Japanese literature, 62–63

Jewish survivors, 40–41

Jiang Menglin, 220n8

Jiang Weishui, 121–22, 137–38, *145*, 233n46; Huang Huangxiong on, 153–54, 162, 164–65; Zhang Yanxian on, 163

Jianjian fuchou yudong (Battleship Building for Revenge movement), 28

Ji Xian, 36

July 7th Incident (Marco Polo Bridge Incident), 133, 233n49

Kang Ningxiang, 124, 129, 229n6; in Dangwai historiography, resistance, 133, 134–39, 233n46, 234n59; election of, 123; on history, 135–36, 137–38; KMT and, 136–37; reforms from, 135; ROC and, 134–35; *Taiwan Political Review* and, 139–41, 234n61; Zhang Junhong on, 132, 137–38, 234n59

Kaohsiung Incident (*Formosa* Incident), 234n66, 236n82; setback from, 112; Shi Mingde and, 161–62; as suppression, 154

Kedourie, Elie, 20, 197n44

King, Ambrose Y. C. (Jin Yaoji), 45
Kissinger, Henry, 46
KMT. *See* Chinese Nationalist Party
Koxinga (Zheng Chenggong), 74, 135, 158

Lai He, 61, 63, 70; literary spirit from, 76, 88
languages: Chinese, 82, 91–94, 99, 217n72; of dissent, 27; Hoklo (*Taiyu*), 6, 62–63, 118; Japanese, 50; of mathematics and physics, 41; of May Fourth Movement, 62; of poetry, 102; Taiwanese, 62, 118, 159
Lau, Joseph, 92
Lee Tenghui, 202n21
Lei Zhen, 130; arrest of, 30, 190n6
Liang Shuming, 29
Li Ao, 28–29, 201n13
Li Kuixian, 94–95, 118–19, 224n56, 228n84
Li Nanheng, 87–88, 214n33, 218n87
Lin Fan (Lin Ruiming), 216n61, 216n63, 216n64
Lin Huaimin, 21–22; author's profile of, 37; "The Boy in the Red Shirt" by, 44; "Cicada" by, 34, 37
Lin Ruiming, 216n64; Yang Kui and, 78–81
Lin Xiantang, 37, 80, 133–34, 135, 139
Lin Xingyue, 223n40
Lin Yixiong, 230n14, 236n82
Lin Zaijue, 71, 77, 79–81, 211n1
Lin Zhengjie, 129, 141, 230n14
Lin Zhuoshui, 132, *143*, 233n42; in *The Eighties*, 160–61; "Taiwan Is a Beautiful Island" by, 160–61, 237n94
Li Poetry Society, *Li Poetry Magazine* (*Li shikan*) and Li poets, 70, 83–84, 94–95, 108–10, 111–13, 116, 118, 119–20, 224n56

Li Qiao, 119, 228n85
Li Shuangze, 21–22, 205n50
literary modernism: Chineseness and, 104; critique against, 74; history in, 103–4; influence of, 70, 101–4, 222n31; modernists in, 101; native soil in, 103; poetry in, 102–4
Literary Season, 79, 91, 102, 116, 214n35; in Taiwan New Literature canonization, 70–71, 73; Yang Kui in, 76–77
Literary Taiwan, 225n57, 226n66
"literature of workers, farmers, and soldiers" (*gongnongbing wenxue*), 99
Liu Daren, 44–45
Liu Yuxi, 221n15
local culture, 95, 106, 168–69, 239n6
local rural culture, 239n6
local Taiwanese, 2, 4, 6, 7, 8, 13, 21, 30, 36–38, 41, 49–51, 58–59, 69, 132, 159, 170
local Taiwanese writers: Chen Fangming on, 111; Chinese identity of, 99, 102; de-Sinification and, 109–10, 116–17; DPP and, 118–19; generational background of, 82–84, 94–95, 217n72; Li Poetry Society (*Li Poetry Magazine*) and, 83–84; Nativist literature and, 99, 101, 108–9, 116; return-to-native-soil trend and, 84–85, 94–95; Taiwanese identity of, 111–13, *114*, 117–18; Taiwanese Literature and, 84; Ye Shitao on, 87, 104–7, 116–17
lone-minister consciousness. *See guchen* (lone-minister) metaphor
Longzu shikan (*Poetry Journal of the Dragon Nation*). *See* Dragon Nation Poetry Society (Longzu shishe)
Lu, Annette. *See* Lü Hsiulien

Lü Hsiulien (Annette Lu), 144, 147, 173, 236n87; feminism of, 156, 157, 158, 169; gender identity of, 192n2; on immigration and colonization, 158–59; KMT and, 157–58, 237n93; national identity of, 156–57; orphaned sons metaphor of, 237n96; overseas historians and, 157; radicalism of, 159–60; on ROC independence, 160; on Taiwanese identity, 158–59; *Taiwan's Past and Future* by, 156, 157, 158, 160, 161, 162, 165; writings of, 156–58, 236n87

Lü Zhenghui, 219n89

Mainlanders, 31–32; Chinese nationalist narrative of, 21; literary writing on, 33–36; in return-to-reality generation, 51–52

Mandarin (*baihua*), 62–63

Mandarin Chinese, 6, 82, 87, 94, 217n72

Mannheim, Karl, 10–11, 101, 168; conscientization and, 17; on generation, 15–17, *16*; generational consciousness and, 18; 1970s Taiwan and, 21, *22*; on social change, 15–16; trauma and, 17, 196n28

Mao Zedong, 99

"Marco Polo Bridge Incident." *See* July 7th Incident

Marxists, 15, 196n28

Matsunaga Masayoshi, 36–37

"May Fourth and the New Literature Movement in Taiwan" (May Fourth essay) (Chen Shaoting), 67–69, 84, 85

May Fourth Movement, 67, 100, 102, 125; Chinese modernity from, 69; languages of, 62; Taiwan New Literature and, 68–69; Ye Shitao on, 86–87

May Fourth New Literature movement, 75

Ma Yingjeou (president), 48–49, 55, 173

Meilidao. See Formosa

Mencius, 226n63

military instructors, 30–31; removal of, 202n24

Mills, C. Wright, 172

Minzhu chao (Current Democracy), 125, 230n11

Modern Poetry (Xiandaishi) (Ji Xian), 36

Modern Poetry Debate (*Xiandaishi lunzhan*), 103, 115

Modern Poetry Society (*Xiandai shishe*), 36

mountain compatriots (*shandi tongbao*), 90

Mou Tianlei (fictional character), 34–35, 36, 204n43

Movement for the Establishment of a Taiwanese Parliament (*Taiwan yihui shezhi qingyuan yundong*), 121, 135

Mutual Defense Treaty Between the United States and the Republic of China, 128, 190n7

Nanfang Shuo (Wang Xingqing), 50, 55, 126, 169

narrative, 18–19, 196n32; action and, 18–19; generational, 19–20; identity and, 18–19; nationalism and, 20–21; public, 19–20

narrative identity theory, 18–19, 21, 24, 162, 165, 171–72

narrative turn, the, 18

national historical narrative, 23–24; generational identity and, 167; return-to-reality generation and, 25

national humiliation (*guochi*), 1, 7, 9–10

national identity: change of, 224n56; Chen Yingzhen on change of, 113,

115; generation gap in, 93, 220n7; Han related to, 164; of Lü Hsiulien, 156–57; in Nativist literature reception, 1980s, 108–13, 226n67

nationalism, 20; from Baodiao movement, 84; Chinese, 27–28, 120; civic, 168–69; European, 197n44; Taiwanese, 171, 173. *See also specific topics*

Nationalism (Kedourie), 20, 197n44

national narratives, 4, 20

National Taiwan University (NTU), 14, 35, 48; campus reform at, 50; KMT and, 49, 60; "Self-Awakening movement" from, 29

native soil (*xiangtu*), 8, 92, 103, 108, 221n22; consciousness of, 59; Dangwai and, 127, 153, 154, 159; Li Poetry Society and, 110; return to, 7, 8, 9, 21, 22, 43, 58, 69, 84, 88, 90, 95, 205n50, 223n40; *Taiwan Literature* and, 115; Ye Shitao on, 65–66, 106; Zhang Liangze on, 74

Nativism, 59, 91, 95, 99, 109, 120, 221n22

Nativist literature (*xiangtu wenxue*), 62, *114*; Peng Ruijin on, 109, 112, 115, 116, 118, 217n72, 218n82, 221n22, 226n67; recharacterization of, 109–18

Nativist literature Debate, 90–91, 110, 111–12, 116–17; Ye Shitao on, 117, 227n81

Nativist literature reception: critique against literary modernism in, 101–4, 223n40; Diaoyutai incident and, 97–98; generation gap and, 91–96, 220nn7–8, 221n15; Huang Chunming in, 98–99; KMT and, 99, 101; national identity in, 98; 1970s, 100, 113, *114*, 115; pre-1980s, Ye Shitao on, 104–7; writers and, 99–100

Nativist literature reception, 1980s, *114*, 115, 120; consciousness in, 111; developmental experience in, 112–13; national identity in, 108–9, 112–13, 226nn66–67; recharacterization in, 109–10, 225n57; *Roots (Shenggen)* in, 110–11

Nativist literature reception, 1990s, 120; exclusion in, *114*, 117–18; Peng Ruijin on, 116; Ye Shitao on, 115–17

nativist writers, 22

New Generation: on Japanese colonial period, 145–47; on Taiwanese history, 142, *142*, 145–47, 234n66

nianqing zhishi fenzi. *See* young intellectuals

1960s: baby boom generation in, 27; generational consciousness in, 26; higher education in, 27

1970s, 22, 169–70; cultural capital in, 23; Nativist literature reception in, *108*; return-to-reality generation in, 23

1980s, 170. *See also* Nativist Literature reception, 1980s; Ye Shitao

Nixon, Richard, 46–47

nonviolent anticolonial activism under the Japanese, 9, 135, 139, 153

NTU. *See* National Taiwan University

NTU Legal Logos (Taida fayan), 49, 54

NTU University News (Daxue xinwen), 54

nuhua (servitude), 8, 63

nuhua jiaoyu (slave's education), 50, 93

older generation: of local Taiwanese, 50–51, 63–66, 70, 82–88, 92–93; of Mainlanders, 29, 31–33, 49, 81

"Old Man and the Baton, The" (Li Ao), 28–29

Ong Joktik, 157

"Only Then Did Taiwan Grow Up"
(Nanfang Suo), 169
"On Wu Zhuoliu" (Ye Shitao), 65–66,
106–7
orphan consciousness. *See guer*
(orphaned sons) metaphor
orphaned sons (*guer*) metaphor. *See guer*
(orphaned sons) metaphor
Orphan of Asia (*Yaxiya de guer*) (Wu
Zhuoliu), 66, 76
Outline History of Taiwanese Literature, An
(Ye Shitao), 115–16
Ouyang Zi, 36, 102, 214n35
overseas studies: for Mou Tianlei
(fictional character), 34–35, 36;
national identity related to, 35,
141–42; Xu Fuguan against, 35–36;
Zhang Xiguo on, 36

Palms Again (Yu Lihua), 34–35, 204n43
Paperboy, The (*Songbaofu*), 80
parliamentary representatives reelection.
See election
patriotism, 90; in Dangwai
historiography, resistance, 135–36;
Yao Jiawen on, 131–32
Peng Mingmin, 30
Peng Ruijin, 85, 88; on Nativist
literature, 99, 109, 112, 115, 116, 118,
217n72, 218n82, 221n22, 226n67
People's Republic of China (PRC), 1,
190n7, 240n15; Japan and, 46–47; Ma
Yingjeou with, 173; Taiwan
compared to, 168–69; in UN, 10,
46–47; U.S. and, 128
personal ID card system, 39, 205n50
poetry, 102–4, 223n40. *See also specific*
works
Poetry Journal of the Dragon Nation
(*Longzu shikan*). *See* Dragon Nation
Poetry Society (Longzu shishe)

Portrait of Yang Kui, A (Lin Ruiming),
79–80
postmemory, 40–41
postwar politico-cultural change
literature: generational identity in,
14; provincial background
differences in, 13–14; quantitative
research on, 14
PRC. *See* People's Republic of China
"Problem of Generations, The"
(Mannheim), 15
pro-Taiwan view of history (*Taiwan*
shiguan), 163
provincial background: differences in,
13–14; exilic mentality and, 45;
generational background and, 21,
36–37, 167; Nativist literature Debate
and, 101; of Nativist writers and
readers, 94–95
public historical narrative, 19–20

Qian Mu, 29
Qi Yishou, 70, 99–100
quantitative research, 14
quasi-exile: as postmemory, 40–41;
trauma of, 40–41; of young
intellectuals, 38–40. *See also* exilic
mentality

reelection of parliamentary
representatives. *See* election
reflexive project of the self, 197n40
reportage literature (*baodao wenxue*),
95–96, 233n40
Republic of China (ROC), 1, 134–35,
160. *See also specific topics*
Retrocession (*guangfu*), 37, 63, 69, 84,
100, *108*, 167; Taiwan New Literature
and, 68, 75, 87
return-to-reality generation, 47, 66–67;
academic reform demanded by, 50,

56; as actual generation, 10–11, 21–22; "Analysis of Taiwan's Social Forces" and, 50; in Baodiao movement, 48–49; Chen Guying on, 53; Chen Yingzhen on, 71–72; in Cloud Gate Dance Theater, 21–22; critique against constitutional tradition, 56–57; critique against exilic mentality, 54–55; democracy and, 53–54; generational identity of, 50–53, 167–68; *The Intellectual* for, 49–51; KMT related to, 53–54, 166; Mainlanders in, 51–52; national historical narrative and, 25; older generation and, 50–51; parliamentary representatives reelection and, 56–60; pride of, 52–53; Taiwanese native-soil consciousness of, 59; in Taiwan New Literature canonization, 69–70, 72; Yang Kui and, 77–78, 81. *See also* Dangwai

Ringmar, Erik, 18–19
Roots (*Shenggen*), 110–11
Russell, Bertrand, 41–42

Said, Edward, 5, 39
Sartre, Jean-Paul, 41–42
Schak, David, 168–69
Searching for Another Window (Lü Hsiulien), 236n87
Second Sino-Japanese War, 62, 233n49
Second World War, 83, 199n55
Self-Awakening movement (*Zijue yundong*), 29, 31, 33
self-identity, 19, 197n40
semi-postmemory. *See* postmemory
semi-quasi-exilic mentality. *See* exilic mentality
servitude (*nuhua*), 63

Shehui fuwutuan ("Social Service Group"), 55
shengji (provincial origin), 2
shidai (generation), 14. *See also* generation
Shi Mingde, 161–62
Sinification, 71, 93
Sino-American Joint Commission on Rural Reconstruction, 220n8
social change, 15–16
"Social Service Group" (*Shehui fuwutuan*), 55
society for itself, 168–69
society in itself, 168–69
Sociological Imagination, The (Mills), 172
Songbaofu (*Paperboy, The*), 80
Song Dongyang. *See* Chen Fangming story, 196n32
strategic generation, 17–18
Su Beng (Shi Ming), 157, 171
Sun Yatsen, 153, 154, 159, 162, 164
Support Wuhan Student Anti-Communism movement (*Zhiyuan Wuhan qingnian xuesheng fangong kangbao yundong*), 28

Taida fayan (*NTU Legal Logos*), 49, 54, 58
Taipei People (*Taibeiren*) (Bai Xianyong), 33, 221n15
Taiwan: A Depressing History (Ong Joktik), 157
Taiwan Cultural Association (*Taiwan wenhua xiehui*), 121, 133, 135, 139
Taiwan difang zizhi lianmeng (Taiwan Local Self-Government League), 135
Taiwanese consciousness, 23, 59, 110–11, 159
Taiwanese history, 142, *142–44*, 144, 147
Taiwanese identity, 158–59
Taiwanese-language, 62, 118, 159

Taiwanese literature (*Taiwan wenxue*),
109–10, *114*, 117–18. *See also specific
topics*
Taiwanese nationalism, 23, 170–71;
criticism of, 171, 240n15. *See also
specific topics*
Taiwanese nationalist historical
narrative, 160–61
Taiwanese Nationalist Narrative
Template of "Taiwanese Literature,"
108–18, *114*
Taiwanese people (*Taiwanren*), 110
Taiwan folk sentiment, 93
Taiwan huawen (Taiwanese writing
system), 62
"Taiwan Is a Beautiful Island" (*Taiwan
shi meilidao*) (Lin Zhuoshui), 160–61,
237n94
Taiwanization, 119, 173; the 1970s and,
3, 10, 23; Nativist literature and, 120;
Taiwan New Literature and, 88
Taiwan Literary League, 76
Taiwan Literature (*Taiwan wenyi*), 84–85,
114, 118–20, 224n56; Chen Fangming
in, 111, 226n64; Nativist literature
and, 108–14; Taiwan Literary League
and, 76; Taiwan Pen Association and,
228n85; Ye Shitao in, 105–6; Zhong
Zhaozheng in, 84–85
Taiwan Local Self-Government League
(*Taiwan difang zizhi lianmeng*), 135,
139
Taiwan minbao (*Taiwan People's
Newspaper*), 62
Taiwan minzu yundong shi (A history of
Taiwanese national movement),
238n102
Taiwan New Literature, *22*; anti-
Japanese movement in, 67–68; Chen
Shaoting on, 67–69, 75–76, 85–87;
Chinese identity in, 68, 75–76;

Chinese modernity related to, 69;
history of, 62–63; Japanese-educated
generation reentry and, 82–89; May
Fourth Movement and, 67–69;
rediscovery of, 67, 88; Retrocession
and, 68, 75, 87; Yang Kui in, 76–82;
Ye Shitao on, 64–65, 85–87, 227n81;
Zhang Liangze on, 74–75
Taiwan New Literature, in ROC first
two decades: anti-Japanese
resistance in, 64; collective memory
of, 63–65; return-to-reality
generation and, 66–67; servitude
(*nuhua*) and, 63; *Taipei Historical
Documents Quarterly* and, 63–64; Ye
Shitao and, 64–66
Taiwan New Literature canonization,
75–76; Chinese nationalist narrative
in, 71–76; collections in, 71; *Literary
Season* in, 70–71, 73; Nativist
literature of the 1970s and, 72;
return-to-reality generation in,
69–72; *Zhang Wojun Collection* in,
73–74
*Taiwan New Literature Under the
Japanese Occupation, Ming Volumes*,
71, 87–88
"Taiwan New Poetry Retrospective"
(*Taiwan xinshi de huigu*), 84
Taiwan Pen Association, 119, 228n85
Taiwan People's Newspaper (*Taiwan
minbao*), 62
Taiwan Political Review, 139–42, *140*;
influence of, 141–42
Taiwan shiguan (pro-Taiwan view of
history), 163
Taiwan shi meilidao ("Taiwan Is a
Beautiful Island") (Lin Zhuoshui),
160–61, 237n94
"Taiwan's Nativist Literature" (Ye
Shitao), 64–65, 74, 82, 87, 105–6

Taiwan's Past and Future (Lü Hsiulien), 156, 157, 158, 160, 161, 162, 165

Taiwan turn, the, 3, 172–73

Taiwan wenhua xiehui (Taiwan Cultural Association), 121, 133, 135, 139

Taiwan wenxue (Taiwanese literature), 109–10, *114*, 117–18. *See also specific topics*

Taiwan xianfa caoan ("Draft Constitution of Taiwan"), 162–63

Taiwan yihui shezhi qingyuan yundong (Movement for the Establishment of a Taiwanese Parliament), 121, 135

Tanaka Kakuei, 46–47

Tang Qian (fictional character), 41

"Tang Qian's Comedy" (*Tang Qian de xiju*) (Chen Yingzhen), 41

Tang Wenbiao, 70, 102

Thompson, Edward P., 167

Tibet, 173

trauma, 17, 21, 40, 119

traumatic events, 17, 20, 40–41, 48, 83

Tsai Ingwen (president), 173, 240n15

Turner, Bryan S., 14, 168, 196n28

United Nations (UN), 2, 10, 48, 123, 154, 208n13; PRC in, 10, 46–47

United States (U.S.), 44, 46–48, 53; Diaoyutais Incident and, 2; higher education in, 27; PRC and, 128

Universal Declaration of Human Rights, 154

U.S. *See* United States

visionaries (*xianjuezhe*), 128, 141, 153

waishengren. *See* Mainlanders

Waite, Linda, 16

Wang Fusu, 39–40

Wang Hongjun, 32–33; "baton" article by, 28–29, 201n11

Wang Shangyi, 42

Wang Shilang, 64, 66, 68, 82, 133, *143*, 151

Wang Tuo, 83, 91, 94, 97–100, 154, 221n22

Wang Xiaobo, 48, 60

Wang Xingqing. *See* Nanfang Shuo

Wenxuejie (Literary Taiwan), 225n57, 226n66

Wenxue Taiwan (Literary Taiwan), 226n66

West, the, 168; baby boom generation in, 26; Chen Yingzhen on, 96–97; generation gap and, 37–38, 94; student activism in, 45

Wohl, Robert, 167

World Literature, 106, *108*, *114*

worldview, 24, 199n55

Wuchang Uprising, 132

Wu Fengshan, 166–67, 239n2

Wu Jiabang, 127–28, 231n19

Wu Naiteh, 23, 122

Wu Nianzhen, 220n7

Wu Yongfu, 62, 70, 76, 82, 84, 213n25

Wu Zhuoliu, 65–66, 84–85

Xiandaishi (*Modern Poetry*) (Ji Xian), 36

Xiandaishi lunzhan (Modern Poetry Debate), 103, 115

Xiandai shishe (Modern Poetry Society), 36

xiangtu. *See* native soil

xiangtu wenxue. *See* Nativist literature

xianjuezhe (visionaries), 153

Xinjiang, 173

Xu Fuguan, 29, 35

Xu Xinliang, 123–24, 128–29, 230n7, 230n14

Yang Kui: in anti-Japanese resistance movement, 77, 80; Lin Ruiming and, 78–81, 216n61; in *Literary Season*, 76–77; Mainlanders on, 81–82; pilgrimage to, 79–80; in the rediscovery of Taiwan New Literature, 71, 76–82, 214n31; return-to-reality generation and, 77–78, 81; Zhong Lihe compared to, 80–81

Yangnü (adopted daughters) metaphor, 158

Yang Qingchu, 83, 91, 99–101, 119, 154, 220n6, 228n85; in generation gap, 92–94

Yang Xian, 21–22, 39, 205n50

Yang Yunping, 61, 82, 88

Yang Zhao, 170

Yao Jiawen, 131–32

Yaxiya de guer (*Orphan of Asia*) (Wu Zhuoliu), 66, 76

Ye Hongsheng, 166

Ye Rongzhong (Fanfu), 37, 139, *140*

Ye Shitao, 112, 226n67; on anti-Japanese resistance movement, 86; on Baodiao movement, 116–17; change of national identity and literary perspective, 89, 115–17; on Chen Shaoting, 86–87; narrative template related to, 107, *108*; on Nativist Literature Debate, 116–17, 227n81; on Nativist literature in 1990s, 115–17; on "Nativist literature of this province," 105–6; Nativist literature reception before 1980s and, 104–7; "On Wu Zhuoliu" by, 65–66, 106–7; regionalism and, 105–6; on Taiwan New Literature, 85–87, 227n81; on third generation of local Taiwanese writers, 107; on writers'

generational background, 82–83; Zhong Zhaozheng and, 71, 87, 88, 89, 105

Ye Yunyun, 37–38

Yin Di, 236n87

young intellectuals (*nianqing zhishi fenzi*), 14; definition of, 22–23; alienation of, 36–38, 45; anti-KMT association of, 30; criticism from, 29–30, 35–36; CYC and, 27–28; exilic mentality of, 39–41, 205n50; harassment of, 30–31; KMT and, 27–28; overseas student movement criticism related to, 28; passivity of, 27, 34; postwar growth of, 26–27; preemption of, 27–28; quasi-exile of, 38–41

Yu Dengfa, 128

Yu Guangzhong, 39, 205n50

Yu Lihua, 34–35, 42, 204n43

Yu Tiancong, 33, 73–74, 91, 92, 98, 117

Zhang Ailing (Eileen Chang), 214n35

Zhang Junhong, 230n7, 230nn13–14; on generational background of dissidents, 138–39; on Huang Hua, 234n61; on Huang Huangxiong, 155; on Kang Ningxiang, 137–39, 233n46, 234n59; return-to-reality from, 54–55

Zhang Liangze, 214n39; on Nativist literature, 74–75; on Yang Kui, 75, 77; on Zhong Lihe, 73

Zhang Shenqie, 76

Zhang Wojun Collection, 73–74

Zhang Xiaofeng, 40

Zhang Xiguo, 36, 41–42

Zhang Yanxian, 163

Zhao Tianyi, 70, 95, 213n26, 221n11

Zhao Zhiti, 102

Zheng Chenggong (Koxinga), 74, 135, 158

Zhenghong, *140*, 141

Zheng Hongsheng, 77, 133, 216n64

Zheng Jiongming, 224n56, 225n57, 226n66

Zhiyuan Wuhan qingnian xuesheng fangong kangbao yundong (Support Wuhan Student Anti-Communism movement), 28

Zhongguo luntan (*China Tribune*), 90

Zhongguo qingniandang (Chinese Youth Party), 230n11

Zhong Lihe, 82, 217n72; articles on, 70–71; courage of, 73; Yang Kui compared to, 80–81

Zhong Zhaozheng, 105, 118, 119; national identity of, 224n56; in *Taiwan Literature*, 84–85; Ye Shitao and, 71, 82, 87, 88–89, 105

Zhu Ming, 198n49

Zhu Xining, 81–82

Zhu Yunhan, 38–39

Zijue yundong (Self-Awakening movement), 29, 31, 33